GNVQ Advanced Options

Living and working in Europe

Anne E. M. Fox

STANLEY
THORNES

First published in 1996 by:
Stanley Thornes (Publishers) Ltd
Ellenborough House
Wellington Street
CHELTENHAM
GL50 1YW
United Kingdom

96 97 98 99 00 / 10 9 8 7 6 5 4 3 2 1

A catalogue record for this book is available from the British Library.
ISBN 0 7487 2582 2

Typeset by Columns Design Ltd., Reading, Berks
Printed and bound in Great Britain by The Bath Press

Also published by Stanley Thornes (Publishers) Ltd:

Ann Harley, *Financial Services*
Roger Lewis and Roger Trevitt, *GNVQ Advanced Business Second Edition*
Rob Sibley, *Behaviour at Work*

To Tony and Gwen

Sådan klarer vi os sammen!

Contents

Preface

As a student you may want the answers to the following questions.

How should I use this book?

You should view this book as a base from which to start your studies. It presents the basic historical facts which do not change and also some general principles on how to approach certain problems. It contains many case studies to illustrate the general principles. There is also a great deal of statistical material. This you can use to make comparisons with similar data you obtain at the time you do your studies. For example, you will be able to see whether unemployment in the European Union (EU) has increased or decreased since this book was written and this can help you adjust any predictions made about the level of activity to be expected in specific markets. Finally, this book, and in particular Chapter 5, should help you locate appropriate sources of information and these tend not to change very quickly.

Does this book include everything I need to know?

No it doesn't. Although books can give you essential background and some ideas on how to carry out your work, it is not easy to keep them up to date. You have chosen to study a very interesting topic. One of the reasons that it is interesting is because the EU is still developing very quickly. The effects of the Single European Market are not yet fully clear and so as these developments and effects become apparent, you need to find out about them.

Another reason why you should not rely entirely on this book for your work is that you will be assessed on your ability to seek out, evaluate and use information sources as part of your GNVQ qualification. You therefore need to show that you are familiar with the main sources on this topic and can weigh up the value of each one.

So, where do I start?

There will, of course, be a programme of study outlined for you by your tutor. In addition it would be a good idea to run through the first three chapters that form Part 1 – The Basics. They will introduce you to the key ideas of what the EU is all about and why it is important to take it into account when drawing up business or career plans. Chapter 5 in particular will enable you to begin quickly any assignment or project work given to you by your tutor.

Many colleges and schools are running their GNVQ qualification on a modular basis which means that you will only have a few weeks of intensive study for this subject. The sooner you know where to go for the relevant information, the better your chance of collating evidence to contribute later to an overall Merit or Distinction grade.

Note to the lecturer

Matrix 1 illustrates how the performance criteria for the three syllabuses are covered within the book. At the start of each chapter these details are given again for that specific chapter.

I hope that the case studies will provide the necessary material for further activities which space did not permit me to suggest.

Matrix 2 shows how the outcomes for each of the three syllabuses could be met by using the assignments in this book.

RSA requirements can be met in five assignments; 1.1, 2.2, 4.1, 9.1 and one of 7.1, 7.2 and 8.1. The City & Guilds syllabus can be covered in five assignments; 2.1, 2.3, 3.1, 4.1, and 6.1. The BTEC option can be covered by completing assignments 3.1, 9.1, 10.1, 11.1, 12.1 and 12.2.

Assignments 2.1, 2.2, 3.1, 5.1 and 7.2 would be suitable work-based activities for employed students or the work placement element for full-time students. Assignments 1.1, 4.1 and 7.2 would be suitable small group activities.

Anne E M Fox

Acknowledgements

The author and publishers are grateful to the following companies and organisations for permission to reproduce photographs and other material: DTI/HMSO for the article on page 3; Reed Information Services Ltd for the Kompass numbering system on page 81; Kompass Denmark for the extract on page 83; Sue Forsyth Associates for the photograph on page 108; The New Scientist for the information on page 109; The Faculty of Economics and Social Science at the University of the West of England, Bristol for material from the Bristol Economic Bulletin in the case study on page 120; Bulletin in Group Corporate Communications (Sea Containers Services Limited) for the photograph on page 149; Pictor International for the cover photograph. Efforts have been made to contact copyright holders, and we apologise if any have been overlooked.

I have had help from many quarters in the production of this book and in particular I would like to thank Tony Fox for unfailing practical support and invaluable encouragement, and William Houfe for an inspired cuttings service. My former colleagues at Gloscat were instrumental in starting me on the road to Europe and I thank them all for their inspirational support, while former students helped me to hone some of the suggested activities. I am also grateful to the unknown reviewers who provided many useful suggestions.

The staff at Stanley Thornes, many of whom I know only from their disembodied telephone voices or fax messages, have provided continued support, especially when the syllabuses changed just as I had put the finishing touches to the first version of this text.

I made extensive use of the facilities at Århus Business School and the Danish National Library without whose comprehensive and free facilities little would have been possible.

Matrix I: Fulfilment of performance criteria by chapter

Units	BTEC: Living and working in Europe (Advanced): Unit I															RSA: Business and the European Union (Advanced): Unit 13																		C & G: The European Union and Business (Advanced): Unit 9												
Unit elements	16.1				16.2				16.3				16.4			13.1					13.2						13.3						9.1					9.2			9.3			
Performance criteria	1	2	3	4	1	2	3	4	1	2	3	4	1	2	3	1	2	3	4	5	1	2	3	4	5	6	1	2	3	4	5	6	1	2	3	4	5	1	2	3	1	2	3	4
Chapter 1																✓	✓																	✓										
Chapter 2																				✓															✓	✓	✓				✓	✓	✓	
Chapter 3							✓	✓								✓					✓												✓	✓										
Chapter 4										✓												✓												✓				✓			✓			
Chapter 5																		✓	✓			✓																✓	✓	✓				
Chapter 6																		✓	✓			✓																✓	✓	✓				
Chapter 7																					✓		✓		✓	✓																		
Chapter 8																					✓		✓		✓	✓																		
Chapter 9																					✓						✓	✓	✓	✓	✓	✓												
Chapter 10	✓	✓	✓			✓			✓	✓	✓														✓																			
Chapter 11	✓	✓	✓		✓																				✓	✓																		
Chapter 12	✓				✓	✓							✓	✓	✓										✓																			

Matrix 2: Assignment coverage of performance criteria

Assignment	Performance critera		
	BTEC	**RSA**	**C & G**
1.1 A single European market		1.2	1.3
2.1 The lobby plan			1.4, 1.5
2.2 Are we competitive?		1.4, 1.5	
2.3 Applying for funding to finance a study visit			3.1, 3.2, 3.3, 3.4
3.1 Compliance	2.2, 2.3, 2.4	1.1, 1.2, 2.1	1.1, 1.2, 1.3
4.1 Trade fair		1.3	1.3, 2.1, 3.1, 3.2, 3.3, 3.4
5.1 Setting up an information bank within a fixed budget		2.2	2.1, 2.3
6.1 Evaluation of Chamber of Commerce services			2.1, 2.2, 3.3
7.1 Radford		2.1, 2.2, 2.3, 2.4, 2.5, 2.6	
7.2 A live marketing exercise		2.1, 2.2, 2.3, 2.4, 2.5, 2.6	
8.1 Daloon		2.1, 2.2, 2.3, 2.4, 2.5, 2.6	
9.1 A distribution network	1.4	2.1, 3.1, 3.2, 3.3, 3.4, 3.5, 3.6	
10.1 Settling in	2.1, 3.1, 3.2, 3.3, 3.4, 4.1, 4.2, 4.3		
11.1 Career move	1.1, 1.2, 1.3, 1.4		
12.1 Careers exhibition	2.1, 3.1, 3.2, 3.4		
12.2 Career development	2.1, 3.3, 4.1, 4.2, 4.3		

The Member States of the European Union

1 Why Europe?

Use this chapter to find out:

- why businesses must think on a European scale;
- how trade barriers increase companies' costs;
- the difference between a customs union and an economic union;
- the effect of the Single Market on business.

This chapter covers the following performance criteria:
RSA   13.1.1, 13.1.2
City & Guilds   9.1.3

Introduction

Imagine your potential market is suddenly expanded sevenfold because you do not have to alter your product to satisfy local technical standards and all transactions can occur in one currency. Membership of the European Union (EU) affects all business and individual citizens. This chapter explains what the EU is and what these effects are.

Consider the impact of the EU on the business activities of:

- a medium-sized manufacturer renewing its various insurances;
- a multi-national with sales offices in nine EU Member States;
- an accounting partnership wishing to recruit an additional partner;
- a manufacturer of electric carving knives with a small part of the UK market.

All the above businesses are affected by the EU and the exact reasons for this are given in the conclusion to this chapter.

Why was the EU set up?

There were two major reasons for setting up the EU: one political, the other economic. The former stems from the period after the Second World War in 1945 when Germany had occupied or fought against many European countries. The idea was that economically interdependent European countries would be less likely to fight one another again. With no fighting between West European countries for 50 years, one could argue that this has worked.

The economic argument is that business costs are much reduced under a single set of commercial laws, and technical and safety standards, than with several different systems. A comparison is often made with the USA where prices are significantly lower in a large market with a single currency.

Origins

The present EU had its origins in an iron and steel agreement between Belgium, France, Germany, Italy, Luxembourg and the Netherlands, embodied in the European Coal and Steel Community (ECSC) of 1951. The ECSC sought to co-ordinate the mining of iron in France and coal in Germany when both basic materials were vital to economic success, especially in steel manufacturing. In 1956, the agreement was extended to a commitment to create a common market in all goods through an European Economic Community (EEC). The EEC was what the UK eventually joined in 1973 and which in turn became known as the European Community (EC) and then the European Union (EU). The common market is now known as the Single Market from the legislation which created it.

Current and future membership of the EU

In 1996, the 15 EU Member States are:
Austria, Belgium, Denmark, Finland, France, Germany, Greece, Ireland, Italy, Luxembourg, The Netherlands, Portugal, Spain, Sweden, and the United Kingdom.

Applications have also come from Cyprus, Malta and Turkey, although there are grave doubts about Turkey's eligibility because of its weak economy and poor human rights record.

Now East European countries are becoming more democratic, they also look to eventual EU membership. Applications have already been received from Poland and Hungary, two of the strongest East European economies.

The other industrialised countries of Europe – Iceland, Liechtenstein and Norway – are members of the European Economic Area (EEA) which was initially seen as a stepping stone to full EU membership (a step which Austria, Finland and Sweden have taken). Switzerland rejected EEA membership after a referendum and Norway is unlikely to seek to join the EU in the near future, having rejected the option in the 1995 referendum. The EEA agreement closely resembles the European Single Market without the free movement of labour.

Trade barriers

Anything restricting trade tends to increase prices of imported goods. Such restrictions are known as *trade barriers*. These may be natural barriers, such as differences in language which incur additional costs to translate promotional and technical material, or deliberate barriers set up by the importing country to restrict imports. An example of a trade barrier is shown in Figure 1.1.

The main deliberate barriers to trade are taxes on imports, called *tariffs*, and *quotas* which restrict the quantity of a particular product allowed into the country. This is frequently done in Europe to protect domestic industry and save jobs, for example, the voluntary quotas on Japanese car imports.

As international agreements, such as the General Agreement on Tariffs and Trade (GATT), reduce tariffs and quotas, so countries find more subtle ways of discouraging imports. Imposing technical standards on an exporter and making customs procedures slow and difficult are just two examples. The first increases costs by forcing exporters to make at least two different versions of their products. The second harms the exporter's reputation for speedy delivery and may increase costs by forcing exporters to carry

Sanctions against Serbia and Montenegro

United Nations Security Council Resolution 820 (1993) came into effect on Tuesday 27th April 1993, and includes a number of measures to tighten sanctions against the Federal Republic of Yugoslavia (Serbia and Montenegro). A significant new development is a prohibition on the provision of services, both financial and non-financial, to any person or body for purposes of any business carried on in the Federal Republic of Yugoslavia (Serbia and Montenegro), the only exceptions being telecommunications, postal services, certain legal services and, as approved on a case-by-case basis by the United Nations Sanctions Committee, services whose supply may be necessary for humanitarian or other exceptional purposes. The prohibition does not apply in respect of business carried on outside the Federal Republic of Yugoslavia (Serbia and Montenegro), although other sanctions may be relevant in such cases. It will be implemented by measures in UK and EC law. You are strongly advised to consult your legal advisers if you are in doubt as to whether the prohibition applies to your particular circumstances.

Further guidance is available from the:

Department of Trade and Industry Sanctions Unit,
Bay 654 Kingsgate House,
66–74 Victoria Street,
London SW1E 6SW
Tel: 0171-215 8512/8570
Fax: 0171-215 8386

While this extract serves as an example of a trade barrier, students should note that following the initialling of the Peace Agreement at Dayton on 22 November 1995 sanctions against Serbia and Montenegro were suspended. Further information regarding the remaining prohibition and the phased lifting of the arms embargo is available from the Sanctions Unit at the DTI as shown in the extract.

Source: The *Guardian*, 27 April 1994

Figure 1.1 Example of a trade barrier: DTI notice on Serbia and Montenegro

higher stock levels or simply by lengthening the delivery driver's journey.

Listed in Figure 1.2 (overleaf) are some factors making export to another country more difficult than trading in your own domestic market.

Language	Cost of translating labels and promotional material
Currency	Having to use a different currency – restrictions on moving currency across borders
Quotas	Restricting the amount which can be imported
Tariffs	Taxing imports
Import bans	For example, drugs, rare plants and animals, weapons
Export bans	For example, goods to Serbia
Documentation	Forms to be filled in for inspection by the customs authorities
Customs procedures	May be cumbersome and time-consuming
Culture	Differences must be considered when doing business and planning packaging and promotion
Units of measurements	May be different, thus requiring different sized packaging (e.g. kilograms and pounds)
Legal system	Will be different (e.g. law of contract, late payment)
Market	This is likely to differ significantly from the domestic market
Technical standards	Most countries have developed a long list of minimum standards which goods must meet (e.g. permitted or banned additives in food, minimum strength of materials used in various products). This either means making one version of the product to meet the highest standards (making it too expensive in some countries) or the expense of making several different versions of a product to meet different standards. For example, if car sales in the USA (where emission controls are high) slow down it is not easy to divert the cars to European markets instead because the higher specification makes them a more expensive product than Europeans are used to.

Figure 1.2 Trade barriers

Activity 1.1

Discuss the list in Figure 1.2 with a colleague and decide whether each barrier mentioned is natural or one deliberately established by the importing country to reduce imports. Can you add to the list? Are the deliberate barriers justified?

The cost of 'non-Europe'

In the eighties, the European Community (the EU's predecessor) aimed to reduce trade barriers as much as possible whilst recognising that some natural barriers, like language, cannot or should not be abolished. However, by the mid-eighties progress towards a Europe without barriers was very slow. The cost of the existing barriers (called the cost of non-Europe) was calculated in the Cecchini report of 1988. This listed the barriers to free trade within the EU (see Figure 1.3).

The barriers shown in Figure 1.3 added an estimated 174–258 billion ECU to prices paid by Europeans in 1988. If these removable barriers had not been operating, prices could have been, on average, 6 per cent lower across Europe that year.

At that time, Europe feared being left behind economically by the USA and Japan. The Cecchini report highlighted the benefits of a really effective single market and revitalised progress towards the original aims of the Treaty of Rome (see Chapter 3) through the Single Market Act. However, its prediction that the Single Market would add 4.5 per cent a year to economic growth has not happened. Since 1985, the effects of the Single Market have been estimated to add only about 0.4 per cent a year to Europe's economic

Products	Services	People and labour	Capital
Frontier controls and administrative barriers	National regulations	Frontier controls	Exchange controls
National standards and regulations	Restricted public sector purchasing	Residency requirements	Non-transfer-ability of securities
Differing rates of indirect taxation	Licensing and cross-border restrictions for banks and insurance	National qualifications and diplomas	
Restricted public sector purchasing	Quotas on road haulage		
State aids and subsidies	Price, market share, and access restrictions in air transport		
National patents			
Monopolistic practices	Restrictions on capital movements		

Source: based on the Cecchini Report

Figure 1.3 Barriers to trade in the EU

growth, although this may improve as Europe climbs out of the recession of the late eighties and early nineties.

Development of the EU

The evolution of the EU can be shown as a series of steps.

Step 1: Independent trade
Countries trade independently with a series of different tariffs on imported goods (to raise revenue or discourage certain imports). This means people pay more for imported goods than is necessary because of the imposition of tariffs.

Step 2: Formation of a free trade area
A group of countries agree to the free movement of goods within their areas but tariffs are retained on goods from countries outside the agreement, making goods traded within the free trade area cheaper.

Step 3: Formation of a customs union
Countries in the free trade area (FTA) agree to common tariffs so that there is no incentive for non-FTA exporters to send their products into the FTA through the cheapest tariff country. This is known as *setting a common external tariff* and results in a customs union.

Step 4: Formation of a common market
Free movement of finished products alone does not guarantee the lowest prices as there are still many trade barriers. The next step is to ensure free movement of the factors of

production (labour and capital) together with abolition of subtle trade barriers. For example, all EU Member States except Germany allowed additives in their beer, effectively barring the sale of non-German beer in Germany. This standard was not allowed to continue in the EU. (Note though that the Germans still overwhelmingly prefer the pure German product.)

Step 5: Formation of an economic union

A remaining barrier in a common or single market is the differing exchange rates of its members' currencies. To overcome the uncertainty in pricing which fluctuating exchange rates cause, together with the costs of currency exchange, the next logical step is a common currency throughout the common market. This is good for business, as long as the final exchange rates before the introduction of the common currency are a true reflection of each country's currency value. Politically, however, this is extremely controversial.

One of a government's main powers is that of raising revenue by taxation (covered in Mandatory Unit 1). A single currency, however, implies a common monetary policy giving individual countries less freedom to act in setting interest rates and taxation. This is a major loss of power for governments and is why moves to introduce a single European currency are so contentious. The EU is presently working towards the implementation of an economic union.

Step 6: Political union

If all countries in an economic union give up their power to set interest rates and taxation, a single governing body is required for these matters. In Europe this is planned to be the European Central Bank. It is a short step from this to complete political union, a major development which few European countries are willing to consider.

Technical standards

A major EU aim is to create a single (or common) market, which cannot occur while Member States require products to meet different standards. The case study below shows the benefits to one company of the harmonisation of standards.

Case study

Toys and Tonka

Public concern is easily provoked by highlighting the effect of dangerous imported toys on vulnerable young children. The conclusion is invariably that such items should not be allowed. The problem arises when other countries apply different safety standards.

Tonka, the makers of toy heavy vehicles, *Playdoh* and *Trivial Pursuits* is among the world's largest toy makers. In the mid-eighties it surveyed the different safety standards across its European markets and discovered that Germany banned PVC in small toys, Italy only permitted plastic bags with holes, and in Scandinavia the bags also had to carry health warnings.

Tonka tried to meet the highest standard on each point; for example, the German standard for materials, the Italian standard for bags, and so on. However, it still had to manufacture special German market versions which increased both product and stock-holding costs.

The Toy Safety Directive now ensures common standards across all Member States. (Directives state what should be achieved without specifying how they should be achieved. Each Member State then amends its legislation to meet the terms of the Directive. For more detail on how EU law operates see Chapter 3.) Compliance with the standards entitles the producers to use the CE logo (see Figure 1.4 below) as proof of this. Tonka influenced these standards by having an employee represent it on the EU standards committee, the CEN. Theoretically, it can now market one version of each toy across Europe and only worry about different standards in the rest of the world.

Standards, testing and certification of toys

The EU Toy Safety Directive (88/378/EEC) requires that only safe toys are supplied within the EU and covers the following aspects.

Physical and mechanical requirements

Toys and their parts must be strong enough to withstand stresses without breaking or distorting. If children play inside the toy (e.g. a Wendy house) an easy means of exit must exist. Toys for children younger than three years old must be large enough for them not to be swallowed.

Chemical requirements

There must be no risk of physical injury or poisoning through chewing, breathing or contact.

Flammability

Manufacturers must ensure flammable materials are slow burning and treated with flame retardant. Appropriate warnings must also be included on the toys.

Testing

The manufacturer is responsible for carrying out tests laid down in the Directive to show its products meet the required standards. Government bodies must also carry out random checks to ensure standards are met. If not, the product must immediately be withdrawn from sale.

Certification

The importer, distributor, wholesaler and purchaser can be confident that the toy meets European standards since no toy may be marketed within the EU without the CE logo (see Figure 1.4) which can only be displayed when the manufacturer proves that all the Directive's standards have been met.

Source: Department of Trade and Industry

Figure 1.4 The CE logo

Activity 1.2

Borrow a recently purchased toy from a young relative or acquaintance and identify how it meets the EU Toy Safety Directive. What evidence is there to support your identification?

Even companies trading locally within their own country will be affected by European legislation when producing items for which new common standards apply. At worst, a company's products become illegal overnight, even in the domestic market, if they do not meet the new standards. Although adapting the product may cause temporary difficulties, it saves money in the end because companies then know their products need no further modifications to meet requirements in other Member States. New standards have to be approved by the European Commission (EC) before implementation in the Member States.

Activity 1.3

Why must a new standard proposed by say, Spain, first be approved by the EU?

Standards directives state:
- the range (generally wide) of products covered;
- 'essential requirements' of the standard to be achieved but not how this is to be achieved;
- what counts as proof that the standard has been met (e.g. certification or testing).

The detail of the standard to be met is then worked out by one of the European standards bodies, composed of representatives from the national standards bodies (the British Standards Institute (BSI) in the case of the UK).

Further individual or 'daughter' directives may then deal with specific products or circumstances.

The effect of the Single Market on UK business

It is a little early to discern the effect of the Single Market on business although a major EU investigation into this is under way which should report in 1996. Preliminary results show that the Single Market is lowering prices, particularly in the banking and telecommunications equipment sectors. Figure 1.5 shows those industries expected to be significantly affected by the Single Market.

Small companies

Ninety per cent of all European companies are small or medium-sized enterprises (SMEs) with 200 or fewer staff. The business consultancy, PERA International, carried out a survey in 1993 of these SMEs in the UK and the rest of Europe to find out how the Single Market has affected them. PERA came to the following conclusions:
- SMEs believe that the Single Market presents opportunities only for exporters.
- SMEs face problems identifying new opportunities and there has been a low take-up rate of help available from government agencies (e.g. the Department of Trade and Industry (DTI)).

Type A   Those losing protection and expected to face greatly increased competition
- Financial services
- Pharmaceuticals
- Telecommunications

Type B   Those dependent upon public sector contracts
- Defence contractors
- Computer services

Type C   Those expected to benefit from economies of scale through the sale of homogenous goods
- Electronics
- White goods

Type D   Those changing from a fragmented and local market to a Europe-wide market
- Distribution
- Food processing

Type E   Those that experience a shift from non-EU imports to EU imports
- Electrical products
- Chemicals

Source: Bruce Jewell, *Business Education Today*

Figure 1.5 Industries expected to be particularly affected by the Single Market

- 70 per cent of survey respondents said the Single Market had brought no business benefits to UK SMEs.
- Over 70 per cent of SMEs in the UK expected to maintain their markets and do not expect to lose out to competitors based in continental Europe.
- Small companies already exporting thought most aspects, such as completing official paperwork, distribution and finding information on European markets, had become easier. However, in the area of technical standards, the failure of the rest of the EU to adopt universal European standards was causing greater difficulties than before.
- Many SMEs are including a Single Market perspective in their long-term business plans but few believe they need to do anything in the short term.

Source: *Opportunity or Threat – The Single Market Reality for SMEs*, PERA International

PERA International found the results of its survey worrying – it thought UK companies were too complacent. Just because a company does not plan to export does not mean that companies in other Member States are not planning to compete for its domestic business. PERA predicted that many UK SMEs will go out of business as competition intensifies. For example, off-licences in the South East of England were estimated to have lost £700 million worth of trade by the end of December 1993 due to increased personal import allowances brought in early that year. Thousands of Britons use this increased allowance by day-tripping to France to buy alcohol, hitting small off-licences, in partic-ular, very hard. The large supermarkets, such as Sainsbury and Tesco, have responded by opening branches in Calais.

Large companies

The Confederation of British Industry (CBI) carried out a similar survey amongst larger companies in 1993 which found:

- 68 per cent felt they were experiencing greater trading opportunities throughout Europe than five years ago.
- 78 per cent were actively seeking greater trading opportunities with the rest of the EU, most commonly in Germany, followed by France, the Netherlands and Spain.
- 51 per cent felt that they were facing more competition now from other Member States than five years ago.
- The remaining barriers in order of importance were felt to be: domestic loyalty; non-enforcement of EU legislation in other countries; language and cultural difficulties; and over-enthusiastic enforcement of EU legislation by the UK.
- 55 per cent felt that they had experienced no significant cost reductions from the Single Market.

Source: *Building on the Single Market – The Future Prosperity of Europe*, CBI, 1993

So although trading has increased, cost savings predicted by the Cecchini report have not yet happened. Specifically, companies complain of extra work since they were made responsible for the collection and remittance of value added tax (VAT) in 1993. This responsibility transferred to companies when customs formalities were eased. However, companies no longer need to fill in any export documentation when selling within the EU. Finally, a major area of complaint by businesses is the cost of complying with EU legislation.

Example

W G Eaton Ltd in the West Midlands says it will be forced to stop production of customised items by the Personal Protective Equipment Directive which requires costly testing and monitoring of the effectiveness of personal protective equipment such as safety goggles. This company specialises in very small orders and says the cost of testing each new product according to the rules makes the price uncompetitive since costs cannot be spread over a large production run.

The survey results summarised above should be set against the fact that not all the Single Market objectives have yet been achieved and in fact it may be more useful to ask such questions later when the Single Market will have had more time to succeed.

Furthermore, Europe has been in recession so the anticipated increase in demand has not yet occurred to offset additional costs. Perhaps the largest reduction in costs though would occur with a single currency but the prospect of this being in place by the end of the century looks increasingly remote. According to a 1995 CBI survey, business in general favours the UK joining a single currency.

Activity 1.4

Discuss the two sets of survey results above. Can you account for the differences between large companies and SMEs? Is there any evidence in your local area to support or refute the conclusions of the surveys? For example, scan the business section of the local press to find out news of recent closures, joint ventures or large EU orders.

Case study

The effect of the Single Market on insurance

The European insurance industry is one example where government controls are tight, especially in the life insurance sector where policies often supplement other pension arrangements. If any government allows an insurance company to fail then bad publicity follows, with all the ensuing media attention on the loss of life savings of elderly people. The EU Member States have evolved different regulatory systems making it very difficult for an insurance company to offer its services outside its national boundaries.

Four factors in particular make it attractive for successful insurance companies to offer their products across Europe.

- Although US and Asian companies are showing little interest in the European insurance market (compared with other industries), European insurers need to expand to remain competitive. This means companies need to cater for a larger market than is available in individual countries.

- The market for life insurance (including pension products) is likely to expand as the North European governments find state pensions increasingly difficult to fund because of the growing ratio between the retired population and those in employment. The UK has gone the furthest in encouraging private pension provision but France, Germany and Italy are likely to follow shortly as the contributions from the working population fail to meet the needs of the retired.

- Some areas of the EU are vastly under-insured compared to the EU average, so countries such as Greece and Portugal offer great potential for increased business as their populations become better off.

- The increasing sophistication of electronic systems means that it is now possible to operate efficiently over large geographical areas and still give customers the feeling of security which comes from being dealt with efficiently and quickly.

The UK has the largest insurance industry in the EU followed by France and Germany. The UK also has the most open and flexible industry and so should be well placed to offer innovative products in other Member States as markets open. However, the UK also has the most unprotected company structure in that it is relatively easy to take over a UK company by simply buying sufficient shares. Because other Member States place many obstacles to the takeover of companies in this way, UK insurers are as likely to find themselves the target of takeover bids from other countries as they are to expand overseas themselves.

What has the EU done to create a single market in insurance?
Insurance is a classic example where the EU tried to harmonise the rules across Europe but found it has had to settle for mutual acceptance. If an insurance company acts according to the law of its home base then it should be allowed to practise in all other Member States without having to meet additional requirements. This has been built up gradually by three sets of directives.

One example of how insurer's costs were increased before these directives came into force is that in many Member States companies were not allowed to offer insurance abroad without first establishing an additional group company in the new country of operation which could demonstrate that it had enough reserves to meet likely claims.

Although the directives were agreed by 1992, they were not due to come fully into force until mid-1994 and countries such as Spain, Portugal, Greece and Ireland have been granted until 1999 for full implementation.

Is there now a single market for insurance?
The insurance markets of the Member States are likely to remain very different even if they have now become a little more accessible. Different countries have different compulsory insurance. In the UK, it is illegal to drive without insurance and in France house insurance is compulsory. Major cultural obstacles must be overcome. For example, an unwillingness to insure possessions in Italy, a distrust of long-term life insurance in Greece (where inflation frequently reduced the value of the final pay-out to negligible levels) and, in the Netherlands, a strong preference for dealing with a well-known local company, are all obstacles to business.

How have some leading insurance companies reacted?
The major problems in marketing insurance are establishing an effective network for sales, the settlement of claims, and encouraging the trust of your customers. Many companies have, therefore, decided that the best way of expanding is to take over an existing local company in the target market, giving the parent company a network and an established brand image at the same time. Many insurance companies have acquired or merged with banks in order to secure an existing distribution network offered through bank branches. Some stop short of merger by establishing a joint venture which may be an agreement by both parties to market each other's products. An example is the arrangement between Royal Insurance (UK), AMB (Germany) and Fondiaria (Italy).

UAP is France's largest insurance company and the second largest in the EU. In 1991 it took over Sun Life, a UK company. UAP owns insurance companies in most of the Member States.

Aegon, one of the Netherlands biggest insurance companies, stated its European strategy as follows:

'Insurance continues to be essentially a local business, heavily influenced by the different tax, regulatory and socio-economic conditions prevailing in the various European states. In our view, this will remain true for many years to come. Our strategy is to build a number of successful autonomous national organisations in markets where we can achieve the necessary scale to compete effectively and profitably.'

Source: *Annual Report 1992,* Aegon

Conclusion
The strong North European insurers in the UK, France and Germany are likely to expand by taking over local companies in the growth markets of Spain, Portugal, Greece and Italy. Hence, the 4800 insurance companies which existed in Europe in 1988 are likely to greatly reduce in number within ten years of the opening of the Single Market. Increased efficiency and competition should lower premiums in most markets except in the UK where insurance companies already operate most efficiently.

Activity 1.5

1 Obtain recent company reports for several leading UK insurance companies to discover the answers to the following questions, for each company:
   a Where does it operate in Europe?
   b Is it owned by a foreign parent company and, if so, is the UK name retained? What are the reasons for this?
   c What are its future plans (including new product and geographical markets)?
2 Do your findings support those in the case study?

How should UK industry react?

Some people worry about the creation of a 'Fortress Europe' which, whilst making trade easier within the EU, may discourage trade between the EU and the rest of the world. The conclusion of the GATT talks, for example, included some concessions from the EU to make it easier for US and Japanese companies to have access to European markets.

It should be obvious from the above that doing nothing is not an option for UK businesses. Instead, UK businesses need to:

- take advantage of economies of scale by expansion, perhaps taking over EU competitors;
- ensure that they do not become overtaken by South East Asian or East European competitors either by relocation to those areas or by moving into another industrial sector;
- take full advantage of new EU privileges such as reduced export paperwork, cheaper distribution costs or permission to operate in other EU countries with the minimum of red tape;
- find out about the latest GATT agreement to ensure they will not be adversely affected. For example, if they use EU subsidised agricultural commodities in their products then these are likely to become dearer as the subsidies are removed. Conversely, GATT may expand some markets, such as textiles, where quotas will be lifted.

Conclusion

The main effect of the Single European Market on UK business is that it extends the domestic market from 57 million potential domestic consumers to a total of 370 million in the 15 Member States. However, the measures needed to create this domestic market are not yet fully operational and the major definition of a domestic market, operating with a single currency, seems unlikely in the near future within the present political climate.

More specifically, the companies described at the beginning of this chapter needed to take a European perspective for the following reasons:

- The manufacturer reviewing its insurance needs might find it cheaper to obtain the required cover outside the UK now that insurers are allowed to offer their products across national boundaries.

- The multi-national with nine sales offices might find it more efficient now to reduce its number as cross-border operations become easier.
- The accountancy partnership may attract applicants from other Member States whose qualifications would be valid in the UK.
- The manufacturer of electric carving knives may have to review the design of its product to ensure that it complies with the EU Directive on electro-magnetic compatibility. This is to ensure that the operation of electrical equipment does not cause interference to other machines operating in the vicinity (similar to the interference on your television when your neighbour uses the blender).

Summary

- The EU attempts to lower the costs of trading among the Member States by gradually abolishing as many barriers to trade as possible.
- A major objective is to harmonise technical standards across the EU.
- On balance, businesses are benefitting from the Single Market but there are also costs in complying with new European standards; in individual cases these can outweigh the benefits.
- Small businesses are in danger of losing customers to competitors from the rest of Europe even if they do not export.
- Large businesses need to grow, most likely by acquisition, if they are to compete against US and Asian companies.
- The UK insurance industry is one example of a UK industry greatly affected by the Single Market.

Information sources

- The *European* newspaper for current developments
- *European Integration – The Origins and growth of the European Union* by K Borchardt, Catalogue number CC-84–94–355-EN-C, 1995, European Commission
- *The Single Market*, Catalogue number CC-NX-95–001-EN-C, 1995, European Commission
- *The Single Market – Making it work for you*, 1994, DTI

Assignment 1.1
A single European market?

This assignment fulfils the following criteria:

RSA   13.1.2
City & Guilds   9.1.3

Your tasks

1 Use Figure 1.5 to compile a report on the effects of the Single Market for one of the five types of industries A to E. Try to focus your report on local companies in the relevant sector as this will enable you to obtain information from interviews with relevant personnel and reports from local newspapers. Key effects to monitor include:

- price and cost (of the finished product or key inputs);
- technical standards (are they now truly uniform across Europe?);
- market size (has it increased?);
- economies of scale (evidenced by merger or enlarged facilities);
- access to public sector contracts in other Member States.

The study period should date from approximately 1990 to the present.
Are the effects noted due to the successful implementation of the Single Market?

2 You should then compare your results with colleagues who have studied the other four industry types and between you prepare a summary overview of the effects of the Single Market on UK business. Has one sector benefitted or suffered proportionally more than the rest?

Additional sources

- Local newspaper archives
- Economic Development Unit of the local authority
- Chamber of Commerce
- Training and Enterprise Council
- Business Link
- European Information Centre
- Local export club

2 Structure, finance and funding

Introduction

The EU needs a means by which it can achieve its aims; to decide what needs to be done and how this will be achieved.

The institutions of the European Union (EU)

The three main EU institutions are the European Commission (EC), the Council of the European Union and the European Parliament (EP). The EC is equivalent to the EU civil service and is run by 20 senior civil servants known as *Commissioners* who are often drawn from the ranks of former politicians. Currently, larger Member States appoint two Commissioners each while the rest nominate one each. The EC suggests action and carries out decisions made by the Council and, increasingly, the EP. It is advised by the Economic and Social Committee (ECOSOC).

The EP has, until recently, been largely an advisory body to the other two institutions but is now acquiring more decision-making power. The Council is an opportunity for the ruling ministers in each Member State to make decisions on EC suggestions. Figure 2.1 shows how the four institutions are linked.

The European Commission (EC)

The composition of the EC is shown in Figure 2.2. In addition, the EC employs about 15,000 staff to carry out its responsibilities; over half of these are interpreters. The work of the EC is divided into 23 different departments known as Directorate-Generales (DGs) as shown in Figure 2.3 (on page 18).

The allocation of responsibilities is shown in Figure 2.4 (on page 18). One Commissioner is appointed as President and in 1995 Jacques Santer of Luxembourg began his five-year term as the new President of the Commission.

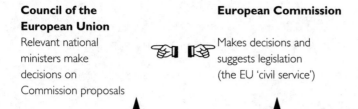

**Council of the
European Union**

Relevant national
ministers make
decisions on
Commission proposals

European Commission

 Makes decisions and
suggests legislation
(the EU 'civil service')

ECOSOC

Advises the
Commission

European Parliament

Gives opinions on proposals. Can veto budget
and Commission appointments. Since 1994, EP can
veto decisions in many policy areas.

Figure 2.1 The Institutions of the European Union (EU)

The European Commission

1 President
1 Vice-President
18 other members

The 20 members (or Commissioners)
are appointed by common accord of
the governments of the Member States
for a term of four years.

Members

Austria	1	Italy	2
Belgium	1	Luxembourg	1
Finland	1	Netherlands	1
Denmark	1	Portugal	1
France	2	Spain	2
Germany	2	Sweden	1
Greece	1	UK	2
Ireland	1		

Source: *The ABC of Community Law*, the European Commission

Figure 2.2 Composition of the European Commission

The European Parliament (EP)

In 1994, 567 Members of the EP (MEPs) were directly elected by the people of their own
countries. After the expansion of the EU to include Austria, Finland and Sweden, the
total number of MEPs is now 626. The EP expresses views on proposed legislation and
may suggest amendments to the EC. It can amend or reject a budget and express no
confidence in the EC which would then have to be reconstituted.

Additionally, since Maastricht (see Chapter 3), the EP now has the right to:

● veto decisions in 14 policy areas including transport, social policy, vocational training, research, environment and overseas development;

DG I	External Relations
DG II	Economic and Financial Affairs
DG III	Internal Market and Industrial Affairs
DG IV	Competition
DG V	Employment, Industrial Relations and Social Affairs
DG VI	Agriculture
DG VII	Transport
DG VIII	Development
DG IX	Personnel and Administration
DG X	Information, Communication and Culture
DG XI	Environment, Nuclear Safety and Consumer Protection
DG XII	Science, Research and Development
DG XIII	Telecommunications, Information Industries and Innovation
DG XIV	Fisheries
DG XV	Financial Institutions and Company Law
DG XVI	Regional Policies
DG XVII	Energy
DG XVIII	Credit and Investments
DG XIX	Budgets
DG XX	Financial Control
DG XXI	Customs Union and Indirect Taxation
DG XXII	Coordination of Structural Policies
DG XXIII	Enterprises Policy, Distributive Trades, Tourism and Social Economy

Source: the European Commission

Figure 2.3 The Directorates-Generales (DGs) of the European Commission

Commissioner	Country	Responsibility
Jaques Santer	Luxembourg	President
Martin Bangemann	Germany	Industry, IT, telecommunications
Leon Brittan	UK	Vice President, World trade, relations with developed countries
Ritt Bjerregaard	Denmark	Environment
Emma Bonino	Italy	Consumer policy, humanitarian aid, fisheries
Hans van den Broek	Netherlands	Central and eastern European relations
Edith Cresson	France	Science, research, training, education and youth
Joao de Deus Pinheiro	Portugal	Relations with developing countries
Franz Fischler	Austria	Agriculture and rural development
Padraig Flynn	Ireland	Employment and social policy
Anita Gradin	Sweden	Immigration, judicial affairs
Neil Kinnock	UK	Transport
Erkki Liikanen	Finland	Budget, personnel administration
Manuel Marin	Spain	Latin America, Middle East, Asia
Karel van Miert	Belgium	Competition
Mario Monti	Italy	Internal market, financial services, taxation
Marcelino Oreja	Spain	Institutional affairs, culture, media
Christos Papoutsis	Greece	Small firms, energy, tourism
Yves Thibault de Silguy	France	Economic and monetary affairs
Monika Wulf-Mathies	Germany	Regional aid

Source: the European Commission

Figure 2.4 Allocation of responsibilities to Commissioners

- approve the appointment of Commissioners;
- suggest new legislation;
- investigate maladministration or contravention of EU law or appoint an ombudsman to do this.

Role of MEPs

Since one of the major objectives of the EU is to improve European competitiveness, MEPs will assess proposed legislation before them in terms of whether it will aid business. MEPs cannot be experts in every area of business and it can be worthwhile lobbying your MEP if some legislation relevant to your industry is being considered so that the directive finally agreed helps rather than hinders. If your company feels that additional European legislation is needed to create a 'level playing field' then it could be proposed by the local MEP and the matter should be discussed with him or her.

As UK MEPs all have a geographical constituency they may be worth consulting about EU funding available within their area and they may be willing to help an application with a letter of support. It may also be worthwhile obtaining the support of MEPs who take a special interest in specific topics and are members of the related Parliamentary committees, in particular the following:

- agriculture, fisheries and rural development;
- external economic relations;
- transport and tourism;
- regional policy;
- environment, public health and consumer protection;
- social affairs, employment and the working environment;
- energy, research and technology;
- economic and monetary affairs, industrial policy.

The Council of the European Union

Formerly the Council of Ministers, the present Council of the EU consists of the relevant ministers of the Member States who meet to consider and approve (or otherwise) EC proposals. For example, the environment ministers would meet to discuss an anti-pollution proposal. Votes of Member States are weighted roughly in proportion to their populations. A threshold number of votes must be in favour to approve a measure. This system is called *qualified majority voting*. The weighting of votes and qualified majority are shown in Figure 2.5.

Each country takes it in turn to run the Council of the EU for six months at a time – known as *holding the Presidency*.

Matters of strategic national interest, such as environmental action, still require a

---

Each Member State's vote is weighted to reflect the size of its population as follows:

France	10	Belgium	5	Sweden	4
Germany	10	Greece	5	Denmark	3
Italy	10	The Netherlands	5	Finland	3
UK	10	Portugal	5	Ireland	3
Spain	8	Austria	4	Luxembourg	2

For a measure to be accepted by a qualified majority, it must gain at least 62 votes out of the 87 possible if all Member States are unanimously in favour.

Source: the European Commission

Figure 2.5 Voting in the Council of the European Union

unanimous vote before being agreed. To date, the votes in the Council of the EU have been secret, unlike votes in the EP, and there is pressure on EU governments to disclose how their ministers have voted.

Activity 2.1

1 Name the UK Minister who would attend Council of the EU meetings dealing with the following matters:
   a deciding on new fishing quotas;
   b a proposal to extend the health and safety responsibilities of employers;
   c a proposal to allocate funds to the creation of a Europe-wide Open University.
2 Assuming that the UK is keen to see agreement on a particular proposal, suggest three combinations of Member States which the UK could try to convince in order to ensure a qualified majority.

Figure 2.6 summarises the decision-making process across the EU institutions.

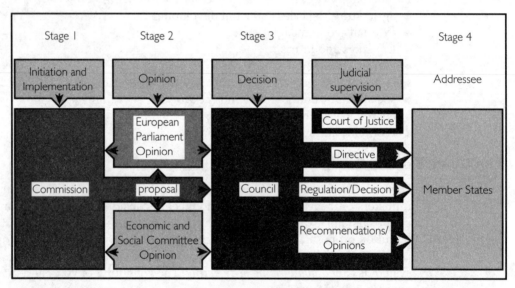

Source: *Who Decides What in the European Community?*, Commission of the European Communities, March 1993
Figure 2.6 Decision-making in the EU

Euro-summits

Euro-summits occur twice a year, attracting considerable publicity as the heads of member governments meet to agree the future direction of the EC's work. Euro-summits are chaired by the country currently holding the presidency.

The Economic and Social Committee (ECOSOC)

ECOSOC is composed of a panel of 189 experts drawn from business, trade unions, the self-employed and academics, that advises the EC on proposed legislation. Members are appointed by the Council of the EU. Since Maastricht, ECOSOC also includes the Committee of the Regions (see below).

The European Court of Justice (ECJ)

The ECJ ensures that EU legislation is applied. It deals with conflicts between Member States, between Member States and the EC, between individual organisations and their national governments, and between individual people and their national governments. The ECJ should not be confused with the European Court of Human Rights which is entirely separate from the EU.

Other EU bodies

There are several other institutions carrying out the work of the EU:

- The Court of Auditors examines the financial affairs of the EU to promote efficiency and detect fraud.
- The European Monetary Institute (EMI) began work on 1 January 1994 to plan how to achieve a single European currency by the Maastricht deadline of 1997–99, after which it will be replaced by yet another institution, the European Central Bank. The latter would then have responsibility for European monetary affairs.
- The Committee of the Regions (COR) was created by the Maastricht Treaty to advise the EC and the Council of the EU on aid to poorer regions, trans-European networks, public health, culture, and education and training. This is because about half the legislation adopted by the EU is ultimately implemented by regions and local authorities. COR has little power, as countries such as the UK want to exercise national as against European or regional control, and see it as another attempt to undermine national government.

Changes with enlargement

As three new Member States have been incorporated into the EU, bringing the total to 15, so the decision-making process is being reviewed. Many argue that there are too many Commissioners already and that the current 20 should be reduced to 10 or 12. This would mean that not all Member States would have a Commissioner. Since Commissioners are supposed to act in the best interests of Europe rather than the Member State from which they come, this should not matter. In addition, individual Member States's interests are represented in the Council of the EU.

Some people also argue that the rotating Presidency of the Council of the EU is inefficient. It may be that the six-month term is increased and groups of Member States get together to decide on a more long-term strategy, for example, over a five-year period, so that policy is more coherent. Already France and Germany agreed to a co-ordinated presidency over their combined term from July 1994 until June 1995. Some smaller countries have indicated that they have no wish to hold the Presidency. The number of votes needed to agree a decision has also been reviewed as new members join the EU. Finally, related more to Maastricht than to enlargement, we are likely to see the EP exercising much more power in the coming years. These and other matters are to be resolved at the Inter-Governmental Conference in 1996.

Activity 2.2

What are the main issues on the agenda of the 1996 Inter-Governmental Conference? These will have been extensively covered in the press immediately prior to and during the meeting.

Subsidiarity

Subsidiarity means that decisions should be taken at the lowest possible level. In this case, the EU should not make a decision at a European level that is more appropriately taken at a national level by an individual government. The move to subsidiarity is in response to the worries some governments have had that the EU is taking on too much power and interfering at a domestic level.

The principle of subsidiarity is now officially enshrined in the Maastricht Treaty. As a result, all new EU proposals must first be shown to need to be taken at European, rather than national level. Existing EU legislation can also now be challenged and if it does not satisfy the principle of subsidiarity, it will be repealed. This is likely in the case of water cleanliness standards where the UK and France argue that standards are too high and are too expensive to implement. In all, 25 per cent of EU legislation is likely to go but much of this would be 'tidying up' legislation which was brought in gradually step by step. Finally, there are worries that some countries will take this opportunity to dismantle the Single Market. The Department of Trade and Industry's (DTI's) deregulation unit is responsible for the UK's suggestions on what to devolve to national governments.

Consulting businesses

It may seem that businesses are subject to a barrage of Single Market measures with little say in the results. Yet one of the main messages from the DTI's 1992 campaign was that business opinions are important and are actively sought by the EC and the UK Government to help the voting decisions in the Council of the European Union.

There are five main methods by which businesses can try to influence EU decisions; these are as follows.

Lobbying MEPs

Just as individuals and organisations can lobby their Westminster MPs so they can lobby their European Members of Parliament (MEPs) about EU problems of concern to them.

Pressing for repeal under the subsidiarity rule
The new emphasis on subsidiarity means that organisations can suggest which directives should be repealed via the DTI, their local MEPs, or via a relevant EU institution.

Petitioning the European Parliament
Any individual or organisation may petition the EP regarding any problem with which the EU deals. This may relate to free movement of persons, goods, services and capital; equal treatment for men and women and between nationalities; tax; research and technology; the right to education, training and health services; and environmental protection. The EP has no power of judgement but may refer the appeal to the relevant authorities for action or may incorporate the concerns of the petition into new legislation.

Responding to UK Government consultation documents
The UK Government is also keen for its votes in the Council of the European Union to

be guided by the needs of businesses, so the DTI works hard to publicise decisions being discussed by the EC in order that the views of people in appropriate business sectors can be heard and taken into account before any decision is made.

Example

When the UK Government was preparing its response to the Third Life Insurance Directive (allowing companies in one Member State to offer life insurance in all other Member States) it sought views from insurance companies and any other interested parties on detailed aspects of the Directive.

The Directive proposed that the home state was responsible for warning other Member States of the financial instability of an insurance company, so that customers could be warned of the danger. The DTI said:

'We do not believe that this provision is strictly necessary, since we would expect such enquiries (into insurance companies' financial standing) to be made as a matter of course. We should, however, welcome other views on whether such a provision may cause difficulties.'

Lobbying ECOSOC

Most measures proposed by the EC affect businesses. The EC seeks business opinion through ECOSOC, so if measures are being discussed which directly affect a business, its representatives should make their views known to this Committee.

Case study

A day in the life of a Euro-lobbyist at the European Parliament

This morning I bump into a socialist group official who tells me an important report on food hygiene has been put on the agenda at the last minute. With three clients who will want to know, it's a dash to the phone to alert them.

I have five meetings with MEPs later today but their plans change so quickly I phone to remind them. Then it's a trip to collect all yesterday's documents – details of the votes, debate reports, press summaries, agendas for today and anything else vaguely interesting for any of our clients.

The next stop is a meeting of the Consumer Intergroup. *Intergroups* are informal groupings of MEPs from different parties and different Member States who want to raise interest in a particular issue. The Commissioner turned up and answered the question which the UK member agreed to put to him on behalf of our client.

Today I manage to meet four of my five contacts on VAT to check on their support for amendments about the classification of certain foods under the draft VAT regulations. I leave them all with a written brief reminding them of the issues at stake.

Then it's straight into the gallery to listen to the debate. I have a message for the Christian Democrat environment committee spokeswoman but she is not in her seat so I must call in at the Committee office. The food hygiene report gets through but VAT is postponed till next month. Then it's back to my hotel to write up an analysis of today's report on banking which the office wants by 8 a.m.

Activity 2.3

Suggest the names of companies which could be clients of the above Euro-lobbyist.

EU finances

Table 2.1 shows about one-third of the EU budget goes on price and income support for agriculture. Pressure from the rest of the world and more efficient agricultural nations, such as the UK, may further reduce this in future. Regional and social policy includes contributions to projects to help less well-off Member States. Under 5 per cent of the budget goes on administration.

Table 2.1 *How the budget was spent in 1989 and 1994*

Policy area	Percentage of EC budget	
	1989	**1994**
Agriculture and fisheries*	62	49
Regional policy	10	}32
Social policy	7	
Energy, research, industry, transport and environment	3	6
Development co-operation	1	6
Administration	5	5
Miscellaneous	12	2

* Two-thirds of which is price support

Source: *EP News*, London Office of the European Parliament

The European Currency Unit (ECU)

In 1979 the ECU (European Currency Unit) was created to provide a common EU unit of account. The European Monetary System (EMS) came into effect the same year with the long-term aim of creating a single currency.

The ECU was reset every five years based upon the average value of all Member States' currencies in proportion to relative strength. Table 2.2 shows the current contribution of each currency. This will not change again until the introduction of a single European currency, when the ECU will be renamed the *Euro*.

What is an ECU worth?

This depends on fluctuating European currency values on world markets but, because its value is a weighted average of several currencies, it tends to be relatively stable. Apart from a few commemorative coins, you will not see the ECU in everyday use, although it

Table 2.2   *Composition of the ECU*

	Percentage of ECU 1989
Deutsche Mark	30.1
French Franc	19.0
Pound Sterling	13.0
Italian Lira	10.1
Dutch Guilder	9.4
Belgian and Lux. Franc	7.9
Spanish Peseta	5.3
Danish Krone	2.5
Irish Punt	1.1
Portuguese Escudo	0.8
Greek Drachma	0.8

Source: European Commission

is widely used in international finance. On 16 April 1996 one ECU was worth 82p. Check the current rate in today's newspaper.

The effects of multiple currencies on business

One of the great uncertainties associated with exporting is fluctuating currencies.

Example

Say you received an order from Germany for ten items priced at £100. You fix the total price at £1050 (i.e. 10 × £100 plus £50 transport and insurance costs). How much is that in Deutsche Marks when £1 = 2DM?

The German buyer will have to convert (1050 × 2)DM which comes to 2100DM. You will have realised from earlier mandatory units that businesses tend to delay settling their bills. If the German buyer pays the bill two months after the price was agreed (allowing for delivery and invoice to be issued) when the exchange rate has altered to £1 = 2.5DM, how much must the German buyer then pay?

The bill is still £1050 but the price in Deutsche Marks is now 1050 × 2.5DM which is 2625DM; 525DM (or £210) more than originally agreed. The UK seller has lost nothing but the German buyer may not want to repeat the purchase fearing the same may happen again.

Buyers of goods generally bear the uncertainty of exchange rate fluctuations. Of course, the buyer in the example above could have benefited if the value of the Deutsche Mark had gone down instead of up. This uncertainty could be eliminated if there was a single currency. Similarly, the cost of transferring funds from one currency to another which, if you have been abroad you will know can be quite high, would also be eliminated.

The effects of a common currency on business

A single currency is not necessarily completely beneficial to businesses. Much depends on the level of exchange rates.

Example

To continue the example above, if a single currency had been fixed at £1 = 2DM, a UK business may have sold many goods to Germany but if the rate had been fixed at £1 = 2.5DM then many German buyers may have found the UK prices too high. So it is not hard to see why it will be difficult to agree on the final exchange rates between EU currencies before transfer to a single currency.

The European Monetary System (EMS) and the Exchange Rate Mechanism (ERM)

The European Monetary System (EMS) describes the way Member States set about establishing a stable monetary area. As a half-way step towards a single currency the Exchange Rate Mechanism (ERM) was set up in 1979. Member States wishing to participate in the ERM agreed to keep the value of their currencies within a very tight band of plus or minus 2.25 per cent between the highest and the lowest valued currencies. In 1979 the ERM included all the then 12 Member States except the UK, Greece and Portugal. When the UK joined the ERM in 1990, the pound was valued at £1 = 2.95DM. To allow for a settling and adjustment period, the pound was allowed to fluctuate within 6 per cent of this value which means that it could be valued between 3.13DM and 2.77DM – the pound soon reached the floor value of 2.77DM.

Mandatory Unit 1 showed you how an individual government influences the value of its currency. The ERM requires that, if a Member State's currency becomes too weak, that Member State should attempt to raise the value of the currency by purchasing it, thus increasing the demand for the currency on the international money markets. In addition, the Member State with the strongest European currency should at the same time help by selling its own currency, increasing its supply, whilst buying the weak currency.

The UK joined the ERM in 1990 but left in 1992 when the UK Government was unable to support the pound. Many felt the UK joined the ERM at too high a value of the pound and that this was why the Government finally ran out of reserves to support it. Italy has also left the ERM, unable to prevent a devaluation of its currency.

Case study

Pilkington

The pound's exit from the ERM and its subsequent fall in value provided Pilkington, the glass manufacturer, with a badly needed boost after three years of recession. The new price advantage meant the company was able to compete more effectively at home and since then it has recaptured more than 10 percentage points of market share so it once again controls more than half of the UK market. Its increased competitiveness meant it was able to raise glass prices 9 per cent in February 1993 and most of the increases have stuck, since continental manufacturers were unable to compete.

The lower pound has boosted production at Pilkington's UK plants to full capacity; a third of its output is being exported to Europe.

Activity 2.4

1 What were the effects on UK business of being in the ERM? Work this out by running through a similar example to that given earlier about the UK exporter and the German importer.
2 What sort of prices would be paid at £1 = 2.95DM compared with £1 = 2.77 DM and lower?
3 Can you show that prices of UK goods would have been relatively high but stable whilst the UK was within the ERM and relatively low but fluctuating once the UK had left the ERM?
4 Which situation posed in question 3 do you think UK businesses would have preferred and why? Would UK importers agree? Check your conclusions by interviewing managers from some local exporting and importing companies.

European Monetary Union (EMU)

A common currency implies a central monetary authority and hence the Maastricht treaty provided for the eventual creation of a European Central Bank. At this point, the issue of a common currency becomes a controversial political issue rather than just a convenience for business.

As EU economies converge they can then become part of the common currency area. Convergence means that inflation, unemployment and interest rates are broadly similar and healthy. If a Member State joined the common currency area with its economic indicators very different from those already in the single currency it would cause economic disruption as it adjusted. However, the leading European currency is the Deutsche Mark and many argue that the instability in the ERM was because the German authorities followed policies for the benefit of Germany rather than for the EU as a whole. Member States which do not want to be led by Germany are also wary of being led by a new EU central monetary authority as this would mean sacrificing a great deal of individual power regarding the setting of interest rates.

Effectiveness of EU monetary policy

The Maastricht Treaty provides for those Member States with healthy economies to create a single currency area in 1997 or possibly 1999, with other Member States joining as their economies become ready. However, the timetable was set during the relative boom years of the eighties and many Member States cannot foresee their economies being in good enough shape by 1997; even 1999 now looks unlikely. Quite apart from economic considerations, those with the idea of a common currency area seem to have underestimated the political controversy that it would give rise to. It is clear that whatever happens, no Member State can pursue its own monetary policy any longer without reference to what is happening in the rest of Europe.

EU funds and how to apply for them

Chapter 4 describes some of the major ways in which EU resources are redistributed in order to achieve specific aims such as the regeneration of old industrial areas and retraining of workers made redundant by structural changes in the economy.

Outside financial help can make the difference between profit and loss. Under Single Market rules, government incentives to business must be equally available to incoming businesses whatever their EU nationality. Thus a UK business can bid for funds to carry out work elsewhere in the EU, such as under the Cohesion Fund covering Greece, Ireland, Portugal and Spain. The following text describes how such money can be tapped.

Which EU schemes disburse funds?

Most EU resources go to the Common Agricultural Policy and so-called structural funds which include the Regional Development, Social and Cohesion funds. The EU supports infrastructure improvements under the Regional Development Fund to improve an area's attractiveness and contributes to training costs under the Social Fund.

European Coal and Steel Community schemes

Under the European Coal and Steel Community schemes, low-interest loans are available to industries which increase production, reduce costs, help the marketing or promote the consumption of coal and steel products. These loans are also available to schemes which create jobs in areas severely affected by decline in the coal and steel industries. Help with re-training and business start-up capital is also available directly to workers made redundant in these areas.

The European Investment Bank

The Bank grants low-cost loans for projects which will benefit the EU. Although mainly for large infrastructure schemes, applications for environmental protection projects and proposals for using advanced technology in the poorer regions stand a very good chance of being granted.

The European Agricultural Guidance and Guarantee Fund

This Fund will occasionally fund individual businesses in rural areas which help to improve the processing and marketing of agricultural and fisheries products.

Other EU funds include:

- RECHAR II helping the conversion of coal closure areas;
- RETEX promoting diversification of activities heavily dependent on textiles (a declining industry);
- KONVER helping areas affected by the run-down of defence industries;
- LEADER II developing the potential of rural areas, such as the promotion of rural tourism, aid to small firms and craft enterprises.

A 1994 survey by accountants Grant Thornton found that only 8 per cent of small or medium-sized enterprises had applied for EU money although a third considered they were short of resources to finance European expansion. It is apparent that the above schemes are not well known.

There are also many other funds providing EU money, such as the SOCRATES programme to promote the learning of EU languages. These may have contributed to EU exchanges in your college. Other funds promote research and development in key industries. This section will concentrate on the structural funds, the largest pot of money after the Common Agricultural Policy (CAP) (see Chapter 4).

Applying for Objective I funding

The EU has five major funding objectives (listed in Chapter 4). Most money is distributed under Objective I to help economically disadvantaged areas where the Gross Domestic Product (GDP) is 75 per cent or below of the European average and where unemployment is high. Certain UK areas qualify for funds from both the Regional Development and Social Funds. Objective I funding aims to improve an area's attractiveness to business by enhancing its physical infrastructure (roads, telecommunications etc) and human infrastructure (through training and retraining).

Who can apply?

Although authorised projects often require private sector companies to do the work, such as road improvements, it is public sector, voluntary or non-profit organisations which must organise and apply for the funds. Eligible applicants include local authorities, TECs, FE colleges, development corporations and charitable organisations such as the YMCA's training arm. Private companies may be eligible for such monies if they are carrying out work which is normally in the public sector in other countries, such as port authorities or airports.

What can the money be used for?

The following schemes all qualify:

- preparing sites for industrial development;
- building and refurbishing factories and offices;
- improving transport access to industrial, commercial and tourist developments;
- workforce training;
- training the long-term unemployed, young people and those at risk of being excluded from work;
- supporting research and development;
- promoting the cultural, arts and leisure industries of the region;
- supporting small and medium-sized companies;
- cleaning up the environment;
- helping the most disadvantaged communities.

What requirements must be met?

All projects must:

- be located in the designated region (e.g. Merseyside);
- deliver quantified outputs and set out attainable targets;
- have a sound funding package in place, including matching finance with necessary planning consents as required;
- demonstrate that project success relies upon European grant aid.

Priority criteria against which projects will be judged include:

- job creation;
- value for money (e.g. cost per job created);
- inclusion of private sector investment;
- market need;
- innovation;
- regional economic benefit;
- environmental improvement;
- building and strengthening of local partnerships.

How are projects selected?

In accordance with subsidiarity, projects are selected at a local level. Monitoring committees have been set up for each UK area eligible for Objective I funding. These include representatives from the local authorities, private sector, TECs, universities and FE colleges, development corporations, voluntary sector, environmental agencies and the appropriate Government office for the area (bringing together the DTI, Departments for Education and Employment, Environment, Transport and the Home Office).

Each monitoring committee will have a strategic plan for its area and will evaluate proposals against whether they contribute to the achievement of the overall targets. It is sensible to study the strategic plan before making an application to ensure that your proposal is in line with what is planned for the area.

All submitted proposals are scored against the appropriate priority criteria listed in the previous section. Those with the highest scores will get funding provided they fit in with the strategic plan, that there is no oversupply of similar projects in that area and that the funds are available (see Table 2.3).

Table 2.3   Objective I funds available for Merseyside 1994–99

	Mecu*	£m
1. Inward investment and corporate sector	186	143
2. Indigenous enterprise and local business development	149	114
3. Knowledge based industries	62	48
4. Cultural, media and leisure industries	54	41
5. People of Merseyside	361	278
6. Technical assistance	4	3
Total	816	627

* Millions of ECU.

Source: *A Guide to Objective I on Merseyside*, August 1994

How do you make a bid?

All projects require an official application form to be completed which will include:

- details of the proposal and area covered;
- estimated costs;
- details of amount and source of matching funding (no more than 50 per cent of the funds can come from EU sources);
- the results (outputs) to be achieved (e.g. the number of people being trained or the amount of land being cleaned up);
- who the partners are and what role they will play;
- how the proposal relates to the strategic plan for the area.

Forms are available from local authorities, Chambers of Commerce, TECs, colleges and voluntary sector networks. Since the project will be evaluated on the basis of the form it is extremely important to fill it in correctly and help is available for this from the above agencies.

What happens if a bid succeeds?

The money is paid via the local Government office and must be strictly accounted for. The progress of the project will be monitored to ensure that the promised outputs are being delivered and may have to be repaid if progress is unsatisfactory.

Case study

Quick collaborative route to counting heads

How many people are in the library, airport, station or shop? The partners in the PEDMON (PEDestrian MONitoring) project have equipment that can provide a continuous answer to that question. Led by MARI Computer Systems of Gateshead, they have devised a system based on a range of sensors operating in conjunction with a complex computer program. The information can assist public safety, security, energy conservation and management.

The idea for the project grew out of a system MARI developed in 1988 to monitor the number of people entering and leaving public buildings such as libraries. It used infra-red sensors processing the results on a PC. The logical next step was to reduce processing costs by replacing the PC with large-scale integration microelectronics: not a cheap technical step to make, and one that might interest a wide range of potential users. MARI put together a consortium of six partners from Italy and France, as well as the UK, that made a successful proposal for shared funding for the necessary technical development within the EU's ESPRIT programme. The consortium includes a well balanced group of organisations with expertise in special hardware and software networking, sensor development and software engineering. It also included the French national railway company SNCF, a typical user of the end product.

St Lazare station in Paris was the site chosen for surveillance by prototype monitoring systems. Such was the success of the trials that prototypes have already turned into products. Thanks to the experience gained with a wide range of sensors and new signal processing programs, MARI has already sold systems based on the new techniques and hopes to sell more in the near future.

Due to its success in securing EU funding MARI now acts as consultant to local authorities, small and medium-sized enterprises and other organisations on how to access European funding for research and development.

Without the benefits of collaboration with a number of partners it is unlikely that such an innovative product could have been developed and brought to market in such a short time.

Matching funds to organisations

It is always best to seek advice on whether an organisation is eligible for EU funding but certain key principles apply. Generally funding is available for:
- organisations based in designated disadvantaged areas;
- organisations in designated declining industrial sectors such as coal mining;
- carrying out or applying research in key growth industrial sectors such as telematics;
- promoting the learning of language, especially the less spoken languages such as Danish.

Summary

- The main institutions of the EU are the European Commission (EC), the European Parliament (EP), the Council of the European Union, ECOSOC and the European Court of Justice (ECJ).

- As the EU's remit widens under Maastricht so new institutions have been established to deal with this, notably the European Monetary Institute (EMI) and the Committee of the Regions (COR).
- As the EU has enlarged and developed, the decision-making process has had to be changed to speed it up and also to make it more democratic and open to appeal by governments, individuals and organisations.
- The pattern of EU spending is as described.
- The issues concerning a common currency and EU monetary policy are discussed.
- The procedure for applying for EU funds is explained.

Information sources

Who Decides What in the European Community, UK Office of the Commission, 1993
The European Commission 1995–2000, CC-86–94–973, 1995
Europe on the Move leaflets: *What is the EMS?*; *The ECU*; *Economic and Monetary Union*
Sources of European Community Funding, produced annually, available from the London Office of the European Commission
Fast-track guide to Successful Proposals (under the IT programme but the advice is generally applicable), DTI, Electronics and Engineering Division

Assignment 2.1
The lobby plan

This assignment fulfils the following criteria:
City & Guilds   9.1.4, 9.1.5

Your tasks

Scan recent newspapers for discussion of an EU proposal which would be of concern to one or more companies. What would the companies you have identified like the outcome to be? (For example, at the beginning of 1995, the weakening of the water quality directives is being considered; this would affect the water companies. They would support moves to reduce the cost of meeting higher water quality standards.)

Plan a lobbying campaign on behalf of one of the companies identified above. Which EU institutions would you seek to contact and how? This section of the plan should show that you understand the influence that each EU institution has and you should concentrate your efforts on those with the most power.

If writing letters, include drafts in your plan. Other issues to consider are whether to send personal representatives to meet with key contacts and whether to employ a public relations company.

Ensure that you balance the cost of your proposals against the expected benefit if you succeed.

Note: if this assignment is completed by covering all the content included in the following two chapters then this would fulfil the whole of element 9.1 in the City and

Guilds syllabus. This would entail showing, for example, in your draft letters, that you have a good understanding of the EU law involved, how this relates to relevant EU policy and current UK law.

Additional sources
- DTI
- Chamber of Commerce
- European Information Centre
- NatWest's Pharos database
- Business Link
- Relevant companies
- Trade press

Assignment 2.2
Are we competitive?

This assignment fulfils the following critria:
RSA   13.1.4, 13.1.5

A local company has been asked to give a talk to the local Chamber of Commerce entitled 'A Single European Currency: Good or Bad for — Ltd?' You have been asked to do the preparation.

Your tasks

Preliminary research
Choose a local manufacturing organisation and assume that it exports to the rest of the EU. Find out current retail prices of the goods in the UK and of similar competitors' goods in two other Member States. (Use your contacts or newspaper adverts.) Are the prices competitive once converted into one common currency? Remember to reduce the retail price by the appropriate VAT rate before making this comparison.

Assuming that current prices have not changed over the last 12 months, plot the price of the UK product in the two relevant currencies over the last year using old newspapers and taking figures fortnightly. (This means taking the value of the pound in the relevant currency and multiplying it by the price in pounds.)

By how much, in percentage terms, has the price of the UK product varied for the other two Member States? Who would have gained from these fluctuations?

Preparation for the talk
Use the results of the above research to prepare a talk with the given title. Points to consider include:
- Was the magnitude of the price fluctuation for the other two EU buyers worth worrying about?
- The effect on relations between buyer and seller of the price fluctuations – should

the UK company have absorbed the fluctuations in order to present a stable price to the EU buyers? Were the 'home-grown' alternatives becoming cheaper or dearer compared to the UK product?

- What would have been the effect if there had been a single currency in force? Consider the effect when the pound was at its lowest and its highest value over the last 12 months.
- Is the company in favour of a single European currency? Give reasons. Don't forget to consider the wider issues such as the likely effect on interest rates, the loss of the pound as a currency unit and the operation of a central European Bank.

Assignment 2.3
Applying for EU funding to finance a study visit

This assignment fulfils the following criteria:
City & Guilds   9.3.1 to 9.3.4

Your tasks

Explore the SOCRATES programme (Chapter III, Action 1e, formerly LINGUA Action IV) or LEONARDO (Strand 1, currently called PETRA) for the possibility of funding a joint educational visit to enhance your group's skills in one of the EU languages. Obtain relevant application forms and information from the Central Bureau for Educational Visits and Exchanges (10 Spring Gardens, London SW1A 2BN). Devise a project which meets the criteria and plan how the forms should be completed.

An actual exchange takes a minimum of six months to plan and complete so this exercise could be viewed as a training exercise prior to the undertaking of a live exchange. Interview staff in the college who have already secured such funding and get their hints and tips on running a successful project (from the point of view of satisfying EU rules). Discussion of what the EU is trying to achieve by such funding and comparisons with other local EU funding projects in the business community may help to clarify your approach to this application.

3 European Union law

Use this chapter to find out:

- the major EU treaties and acts;
- how EU law transfers into national law;
- the difference between directives, regulations and other EU decisions;
- how EU law affects UK businesses and individuals.

This chapter covers the following performance criteria:

BTEC	16.2.2, 16.2.3, 16.2.4
RSA	13.1.1, 13.1.2, 13.2.1
City & Guilds	9.1.1, 9.1.2

Where does the EU's legal power come from and how are decisions made?

Members signing the Treaty of Rome agree to be bound by a European system of law. In the UK, the Treaty of Rome was given legal effect with the European Communities Act 1972 requiring that European law takes precedence when in conflict with UK law.

Example

The Merchant Shipping Act 1988 and Spanish fisheries

The 1988 Act was passed by the UK Government to ensure that the EU fishing quotas allocated to the UK could only be used by UK-owned fishing fleets. It was brought in as a defence against Spanish companies registering their ships as UK ships and thus entitling them to UK fishing quotas.

The Spanish challenged the Act in the European Court. Although there were other legal points of interest in the case, the major outcome was that the UK was not allowed to reserve fishing in this way and the Merchant Shipping Act 1988 was repealed.

The legal framework is contained in the major treaties and acts whereas specific actions which must be taken to bring about the Single Market are contained in directives, regulations, decisions, recommendations and opinions, decided mainly by the Council of the EU.

The major treaties and acts

The Treaty of Rome

This is the original treaty which the founding members of the EU signed in 1957. It provided for the gradual creation of a Customs Union (see Chapter 1). All additional members since 1957 have signed this treaty which created for the first time a system of European law which takes precedence over national law in any Member State where the two are in conflict. The Treaty set out strictly defined areas in which European law could be enacted. These can be summarised as actions to secure the four freedoms needed to establish the Common Market.

The four freedoms

The four freedoms are:
- the free movement of goods – no tariffs or quotas, the reduction of paperwork and agreement on Europe-wide standards;
- the free movement of persons – for the purposes of work or running a business;
- the freedom to set up in business and offer services;
- the free movement of capital – no restrictions on the amount of money which can be transferred between the countries of the Common Market.

The Treaty of Rome also set out the areas in which a common European policy should be achieved.

The Single European Act 1987 (SEA)

By the mid-eighties it was obvious that very slow progress towards a truly single market was largely due to the unanimous voting system in the Council of the EU which, although not compulsory under the Treaty of Rome, had become the norm. In addition, the EU was attempting to set European standards in all aspects of trade.

The voting system

As membership increased, so unanimous decisions became more difficult until more decisions were blocked than passed. The SEA changed the voting system to enable most decisions to be made using the qualified majority voting system (see Chapter 2).

Common standards

The problem with setting European standards is that so many exist that it would have taken decades to wade through them all. The SEA stipulated that a product meeting the standard of one Member State could not be refused entry by another, saving the need to negotiate one common standard for every different type of product.

The SEA listed 282 legal measures needed to ensure a truly single market, setting the objective that these legal measures should be passed by the end of 1992.

The SEA recognised the need to assess the environmental impact of EU actions, an issue not mentioned in the Treaty of Rome. Whilst this has enabled the EU to protect some areas, there are other areas where EU money is accused of helping to destroy the environment, for example, in the EU's financial support for road improvements.

The SEA speeded up progress towards a functioning single market after many people doubted that it would ever happen, nearly 20 years after the Treaty of Rome was signed.

Maastricht and the Social Chapter 1991

The Treaty of Rome talked of creating an 'ever closer union' and in 1972 the Member States agreed to work towards economic and monetary union. The Maastricht Treaty set out a timetable for its achievement and added new political dimensions. Taking the old Economic Community as the original 'pillar', the Maastricht Treaty included economic and monetary union within this and added two new pillars: a common internal EU policy and a common external EU policy (see Figure 3.1 overleaf).

The Treaty also amended the decision-making process, reducing the EC's power while extending that of the European Parliament (EP). It defined more strictly what should be carried out at European level and at national level, based on subsidiarity. It also extended its activities to promote education, culture, public health, trans-European networks and the environment, partly through financial support via the Cohesion Fund to help Portugal, Greece, Ireland and Spain (the poorest Member States). Finally, the Treaty formalised what was formerly called the Social Charter, now known as the Social Chapter.

The Social Chapter

This is not strictly part of the main Maastricht Treaty because the UK negotiated to opt out of it at least until 1996. Any European law arising out of the Social Chapter will not apply to the UK.

The Social Chapter attempts to create a single market for labour, as has been done for goods and services, by ensuring that no Member State can take advantage of another's stricter employment laws. With open frontiers, a company might move to Member States where employment costs are cheaper – known as 'social dumping', because it leaves the dearer Member States with the cost of supporting the unemployed created by such moves. It also tries to extend the higher standards enjoyed by employees in richer Member States to the others, so that the benefits of the Single Market are not felt only by employers and shareholders.

The UK opted out of the Social Chapter because it receives a great deal of inward investment from non-EU companies wanting an EU base, especially US and Japanese companies. The UK feels that its low wage costs and relatively flexible employment laws is a major attraction for these companies. It also feels that employment law should be decided by national governments.

The Social Chapter aims to enhance workers' rights by ensuring:
- freedom of movement and equal treatment for men and women;
- equal treatment for part-time, temporary and contract workers as compared to full-time workers;
- the right to a weekly rest period and annual paid leave;
- the freedom to join or not join a trade union;
- the right to strike (except for the police, armed forces and civil servants);
- the right to collective bargaining;
- access to vocational training throughout working life;
- information, consultation and participation for workers in decisions by employers;
- no employment below the age of 15 and no night work employment below the age of 18;
- measures to provide jobs for the disabled;
- minimum health and safety standards at work.

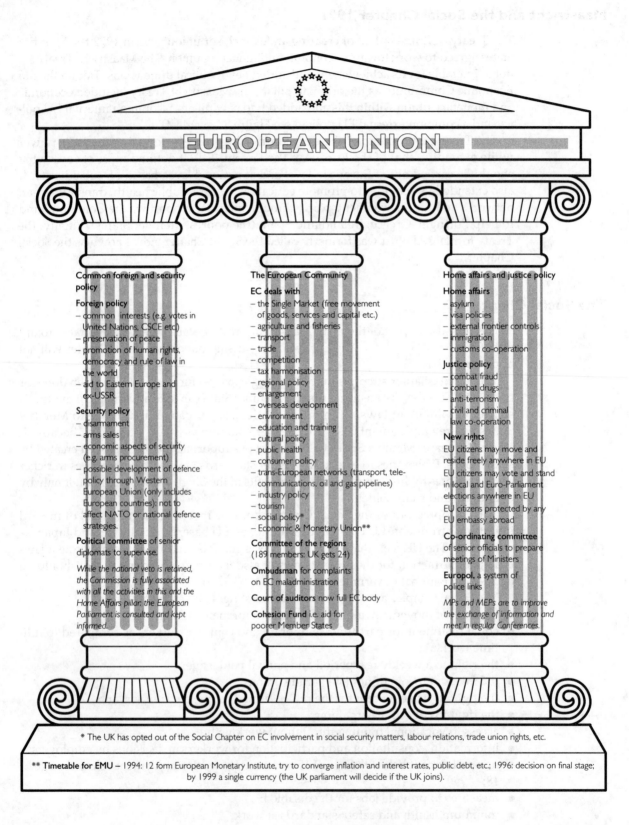

EUROPEAN UNION

Common foreign and security policy

Foreign policy
- common interests (e.g. votes in United Nations, CSCE etc)
- preservation of peace
- promotion of human rights, democracy and rule of law in the world
- aid to Eastern Europe and ex-USSR

Security policy
- disarmament
- arms sales
- economic aspects of security (e.g. arms procurement)
- possible development of defence policy through Western European Union (only includes European countries): not to affect NATO or national defence strategies.

Political committee of senior diplomats to supervise.

While the national veto is retained, the Commission is fully associated with all the activities in this and the Home Affairs pillar: the European Parliament is consulted and kept informed.

The European Community

EC deals with
- the Single Market (free movement of goods, services and capital etc.)
- agriculture and fisheries
- transport
- trade
- competition
- tax harmonisation
- regional policy
- enlargement
- overseas development
- environment
- education and training
- cultural policy
- public health
- consumer policy
- trans-European networks (transport, tele-communications, oil and gas pipelines)
- industry policy
- tourism
- social policy*
- Economic & Monetary Union**

Committee of the regions (189 members: UK gets 24)

Ombudsman for complaints on EC maladministration

Court of auditors now full EC body

Cohesion Fund i.e. aid for poorer Member States

Home affairs and justice policy

Home affairs
- asylum
- visa policies
- external frontier controls
- immigration
- customs co-operation

Justice policy
- combat fraud
- combat drugs
- anti-terrorism
- civil and criminal law co-operation

New rights
EU citizens may move and reside freely anywhere in EU
EU citizens may vote and stand in local and Euro-Parliament elections anywhere in EU
EU citizens protected by any EU embassy abroad

Co-ordinating committee of senior officials to prepare meetings of Ministers

Europol, a system of police links

MPs and MEPs are to improve the exchange of information and meet in regular Conferences.

* The UK has opted out of the Social Chapter on EC involvement in social security matters, labour relations, trade union rights, etc.

** **Timetable for EMU** – 1994: 12 form European Monetary Institute, try to converge inflation and interest rates, public debt, etc.; 1996: decision on final stage; by 1999 a single currency (the UK parliament will decide if the UK joins).

Figure 3.1 The three pillars of the European Union created by the Maastricht Treaty

Source: the Conservative Party

The UK's decision to opt out of the Social Chapter does not mean that UK workers have none of the above rights, as most of these are already covered by UK legislation. Where there is no legislation relating to a particular right it is because the UK Government believes that the cost to UK industry would be too great. In fact, out of all the Member States it is the UK which has transposed the most of the social measures into law even though it is not obliged to by virtue of its opt out.

Example

The maximum 48-hour week

One of the proposals which caused the most discussion was that of a maximum 48-hour working week. This limited night-shift work to 7 hours in every 24, plus the right to transfer to a day shift after a qualifying period. In industries running continuous processes 24 hours a day, such as chemicals, steel making, textiles and, increasingly, the car industry, it is common for night shifts to be longer than 7 hours. The Rover Longbridge plant, for example, has 12-hour shifts at the weekend. The Vauxhall car company claimed that it would cause great difficulties if night workers were given the right to 'bump out people on days.'

Activity 3.1

Compile a three- or four-line summary of the UK law under each of the Social Chapter headings and note where none exists. To help you, refer back to the work you did for Mandatory Unit 4 'Human Resources' and supplement this with an interview with a human resources professional, such as a personnel director.

The Maastricht Treaty clarified, with definite timescales, what were once generally worded goals in the Treaty of Rome. It has also strengthened the commitment to the environment which was included in the Single European Act and made explicit how the benefits of the EU are to be spread to all Member States who have signed the Social Chapter. Its new features are the political pillars of Figure 3.1.

Directives, regulations, decisions, recommendations and opinions

Although advised by the EP and the Economic and Social Committee (ECOSOC), it is the Council of the European Union and the EC which decide most of the practical measures which countries, organisations and individuals must take to bring about the Single Market. This is done in several ways.

Directives

Most rulings come in the form of directives which state what should be achieved without specifying how. Each Member State then amends its legislation to carry out the directive. Directives usually specify time limits within which all Member States must ensure implementation through national legislation. Some countries are very slow in adopting the directives. Table 3.1 shows how the Member States progressed at different rates to implement the 200 plus directives needed to complete the Single Market programme.

Table 3.1   Progress on the adoption of Single Market directives (per cent implemented)

Country	As at November 1994	As at November 1995	
Denmark	95.9	99.1	(highest)
Netherlands	94.9	96.4	
France	94.0	95.0	
Luxembourg	91.2	96.4	
UK	90.8	93.7	
Portugal	88.5	95.0	
Finland	–	95.0	
Italy	88.5	91.4	
Ireland	88.0	91.0	
Belgium	87.6	91.0	
Spain	87.1	92.8	
Sweden	–	93.2	
Germany	83.4	88.2	
Greece	77.9	88.2	
Austria	–	84.6	(lowest)

Source: DGXV, European Commission

Directives are given a reference number; the first two numbers identify the year of agreement. For example, the directive requiring minimum standards for drinking water, reference number 80/778, was passed in 1980.

There are four types of directives:

- maximum – limiting the highest standards which Member States can apply;
- minimum – setting the lowest acceptable standard which Member States must meet, for example, water quality directives;
- horizontal – applying to wide ranges of products and services, such as the 1979 Food Labelling Directive;
- vertical – applying to narrow areas such as the Jam Directive.

Lately the EU has found it more practical to adopt horizontal rather than vertical measures.

Most directives concern issues already covered by UK laws so new Acts of Parliament are rarely needed. Most are incorporated into UK law using existing Acts through regulations and orders referred to as statutory instruments (SIs).

An example which caused a great deal of comment because it was considered typical of the EC's concern with trivia, was Directive 88/180 entitled 'Permissible sound power level of lawn mowers' which sought to limit domestic lawn mower noise. After many sarcastic newspaper articles, it was incorporated into UK law through The Lawnmowers (Harmonization of Noise Emission Standards) Regulations 1992 (SI 1992 No. 168).

Some directives however, are incorporated into UK law through Acts of Parliament. For example, Directive 89/397 'Official Control of Foodstuffs (food inspection)' was implemented in the UK through the Food Safety Act 1990, and Directive 89/552, concerning the pursuit of television broadcasting activities, through the Broadcasting Act 1990.

Case study

The life history of a directive – The General Packaging Directive

Aim of the Packaging Directive
To reduce the environmental impact of packaging waste and to encourage lower consumption of raw materials and energy.

Which part of the Treaty of Rome does it support?
The Directive is proposed on the basis of Article 100a of the Treaty of Rome which refers to the free movement of goods rather than Article 130r about the need to safeguard the environment.

Why was it suggested?
Denmark was taken to the European Court for its laws which require that drinks be sold in recyclable containers. This outlawed canned drinks and forced shops to take back drink containers for which customers received a returnable deposit. Exporters to Denmark viewed this as a trade barrier since it meant they had to package drinks differently for the Danish market. However, because the purpose behind the legislation was to minimise waste, the European Court in 1988 upheld this Danish law. The EC then decided to issue a directive to encourage other Member States to promote recycling of drinks containers.

After preliminary discussions, it was decided that the Directive should deal with all packaging, partly in response to forthcoming German legislation which would place responsibility for waste packaging on manufacturers. The EC was perhaps worried that a similar challenge would be made in the European Court against the German legislation as had been made against the Danes and it therefore sought to create a 'level playing field' on this issue.

What does the General Packaging Directive require?
When it was first proposed in July 1991 the General Packaging Directive stipulated that the overall amount of packaging waste per capita should not exceed 1990 levels – the 'stand still' option. Maximum levels of toxic materials were specified and certain substances were to be phased out altogether. A 5 per cent tax on packaging material was included unless the item could be returned for a deposit. Non-recyclable packaging would be banned by the year 2000.

The Directive was then amended to require that ten years after its adoption:
- 90 per cent by weight of packaging waste should be recovered;
- 60 per cent by weight of each type of packaging waste material must be recyclable;
- a maximum of 10 per cent by weight may be put into landfill.

In addition, the use of toxic materials are to be minimised, packaging must be clearly labelled to enable its recycling and there was no longer a target for reducing the use of packaging.

In October 1993, environment ministers proposed that the target should be 60 per cent of all packaging recovered after five years, after which time the targets would be reviewed. Ireland, Portugal and Greece would not have to comply for five years.

In 1994, the Directive went back to the EP which wanted to increase these targets closer to the original 90 per cent rate. Germany, Denmark and the Netherlands were particularly keen to return to the higher recovery levels.

Interested parties
- EUROPEN (The European Organisation for Packaging and the Environment) was appalled at the German legislation, arguing that overall waste reduction should be the target instead of just focusing on packaging.
- Euronature (European Natural Heritage Fund) objected to the proposal in the Directive that burning the waste packaging to produce heat should be allowed to count as recycling.
- Retailers do not want to handle empty, dirty returned bottles and cans because of hygiene and space implications.
- Friends of the Earth (FOE) felt that the Directive should encourage waste reduction at source and the use of reusable containers. It also thought that the Directive's should allow Member States to set standards as high as they wished, whereas the proposal sets maximum limits and its minimum limits are lower than most existing national legislation, i.e. the Directive will not achieve much improvement if most Member States already meet its low standards anyway.

Conclusion
The General Packaging Directive has been one of the most controversial directives as industry and environmental requirements are in conflict. Hence it took a long time to be agreed, finally being adopted only at the end of 1994.

Source: From various information sources collated by Friends of the Earth

Activity 3.2

Scan recent newspapers for news of a directive currently under consideration. Summarise:
- what is proposed;
- which type of organisation it would affect;
- what the arguments are against it (usually concerning implementation costs);
- what the arguments are in favour of it (usually overcoming trade restrictions).

Regulations

Regulations must be directly implemented by Member States with no discretion about how the result is achieved and no need to amend national legislation. For example, one regulation concerns the requirement to accept social security contributions paid in other Member States for the purposes of calculating pension entitlement in the UK. Once this regulation had been agreed by the EU, each Member State simply abided by its requirements; no new legislation was necessary.

Activity 3.3

Use the DTI's *Euro Manual, Progress on Commission White Paper,* or *The Single Market – The Facts,* to select six different regulations. For each regulation suggest a local or

well-known organisation directly affected by the regulation and what that effect would be. Describe any actions or procedures the organisation would have to implement to comply with the regulation.

Decisions

Decisions, like regulations, require direct implementation but usually apply to only one or a few Member States, individuals or organisations. For example, Decisions 91/396 and 92/264 require all telephone companies to implement 112 as the common emergency number by 1996 and 00 as the common international access code by 1998. Before 16 April 1995 (BT's 'Phoneday'), dialling abroad from the UK was 010.

Recommendations and opinions

These illustrate what the EU thinks ought to happen but are not binding. In practice, publication of recommendations and opinions places a great moral pressure on governments, individuals or organisations to comply with them.

One example, Recommendation 87/176, concerns testing prior to the marketing of proprietary (i.e. over the counter) medicinal products. The DTI states that the UK already meets this recommendation and that the authority which licenses medicines in the UK encourages companies applying to have their new medicines approved to follow the guidelines contained in Recommendation 87/176.

Enactment of European law

Member States do not always interpret European law as intended. In these cases, affected individuals, organisations or the European Commission itself can apply for a ruling from the European Court of Justice (ECJ).

Examples

Example 1 – Transfer of undertakings
Directive 77/187 requires Member States to legislate to make the transferee of an undertaking liable for existing contracts of employment. The intention is that employees should not have their conditions of employment worsened by a transfer of ownership, say, after a takeover. In the UK this was implemented through the Transfer of Undertakings (Protection of Employment) Regulations SI 1981 No 1794 which defined undertakings as 'commercial ventures'. Workers affected by privatisation schemes were not covered and complained that they could have their conditions worsened, typically by having their pay cut, even though the original Directive had not restricted protection to 'commercial ventures' as the UK law did.

An ECJ judgement *Wren v Eastbourne Borough Council* 1993 ruled that public sector workers who are subsequently privatised should be covered by the Directive and so the UK amended its legislation in section 33 of the Trade Union Reform and Employment Rights Act 1993 to accommodate the ruling.

Example 2 – Pubblico Ministero v Ratti 1980
In this Italian case, a business using chemicals labelled its solvents in accordance with EU law even though this had not yet been transposed into Italian law. When it was

taken to national court for infringement of Italian labelling laws, the case was referred by the Italian court to the ECJ. Since the period for implementation of the directive had expired, the ECJ ruled in favour of the business.

Implementation of the Treaty of Rome

Figure 3.2 shows some of the ways in which the four freedoms, identified in the Treaty of Rome as necessary for the Single Market, have been built up through EU legislation.

Free movement of goods
- Regulation 4060/89 – eliminates controls at road and inland waterway frontiers
- Directive 92/116/EEC – standardises health rules for production and placing on the market of fresh poultry meat
- Directive 86/362/3 – fixes maximum levels of allowable pesticide residues in cereals and on food of animal origin
- Directive 89/107/EEC – lists additives authorised for use in foodstuffs intended for human consumption

Free movement of labour
- Directive 85/433/EEC – provides for the mutual acceptance of qualifications in pharmacy
- Directive 75/362/EEC – allows doctors to practise anywhere within the EU
- Directive 78/1026/EEC – allows veterinary surgeons to practise anywhere within the EU
- Directive 85/384/EEC – allows architects to practise anywhere within the EU
- Directive 89/48/EEC – allows anyone whose profession requires a minimum of three years' full-time university or equivalent education to practise anywhere within the EU; the first so-called General Directive

Free movement of capital
- Directive 88/361/EEC – ensures that money can be transferred freely across EU borders

Freedom of establishment
- Directive 89/646/EEC – allows banks to set up across the EU
- Directive 90/618/EEC – allows motor insurance to be offered across the EU

Figure 3.2 Examples of the legislation establishing the Four Freedoms

EU law and business

Businesses should be aware of EU requirements in the following areas.

Environment

Packaging – a new directive requires that 50–65 per cent of the packaging should be recyclable. Packaging will have to be labelled identifying the type of material used.

Companies in certain industries may have to carry out, and make public, regular environmental audits (i.e. an investigation to find out if the company's activities are harming the environment).

Transport

Transport companies will be allowed to work freely across the EU allowing them to make more efficient use of their fleets, thus reducing transport prices by up to 5 per cent.

Abolition of border controls should reduce travel times by up to 30 per cent. In addition, abolition of customs procedures saves time and should avoid hold-ups of consignments because of incorrectly completed customs forms.

Manufacturing

Directives concerning machinery safety, weighing instruments, electronic and electrical equipment, mobile machinery, lifting equipment and personal protective equipment all have to be considered.

Products

Directives in this area cover subjects such as food hygiene, additives, labelling and packaging.

Finance

Companies can now obtain all necessary financial services and insurance from other Member States (but remember from Chapter 1 that at present the most efficient, cheapest insurance in the EU is to be found in the UK).

After 1993, companies had to change their VAT records when responsibility for collecting VAT across European borders transferred from Customs and Excise to businesses themselves.

Marketing

Companies can protect distinctive trademarks across the EU by registering them as a Community Trade Mark, rather than having to register anew for each additional EU market.

Case study

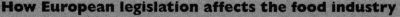

How European legislation affects the food industry

Food is one high profile area where the EC has enacted several directives. You may have heard of the curved cucumber controversy, which prevented bent cucumbers being allocated a Class I quality designation which commands a higher price.

European law tried to agree standard definitions, for example, of chocolate and jam, which would have taken years to cover every different foodstuff. This 'vertical' approach has now been replaced by 'horizontal' framework directives covering the following.

Labelling
- Information must be in a language the customer is likely to understand. This means multi-lingual packaging or, at the least, sticky labels placed over the original packaging.
- Drained weight must be shown.
- Most foods must show a 'consume by' date.
- Most foods must list ingredients in descending order of volume using standardised descriptions, for example, the E number classification for additives and flavourings.
- Alcoholic strength must be shown if over 1.2 per cent by volume.

- Restricted use of the word 'natural' in the name, label or ingredients list.

Additives and flavourings
- Lists permitted additives and flavourings.
- Lists which foods they may be used in.
- Sets acceptable purity levels.
- Labelling requirements are set out.

Contact materials (packaging)
- Ensures that packaging does not transfer unhealthy substances to wrapped food.
- Packaging approved for food use must be labelled clearly.
- Testing methods to prove safety are specified.
- Follow-up directives will eventually cover the range of possible packaging materials such as plastics, metal, glass, wood and paper.

Special dietary foods
- Prevents misleading claims being made by regulating labelling of foods designed for people with special needs such as babies, dieters, diabetics or those seeking low-fat or gluten-free foods.

However, manufacturers still try to get round the regulations by, for example, using several different types of sugar which can then be listed separately, low down on the ingredients list, to mislead people into thinking the product is low in sugar.

Food inspection
- Sets out essential standards to be met for food to be fit for sale.
- Requires that food tested in one Member State need not be retested if exported to another Member State.
- Sets out the testing procedures to be used.

Mutual recognition is the general principle; food items acceptable for sale in one Member State should automatically be acceptable in all the others. Germany prevented the import of Cassis de Dijon, a blackcurrant liqueur (strength 15–20 per cent), because it did not conform to German alcohol content requirements (a minimum of 25 per cent). Since the ban involved the definition of 'liqueur' rather than a threat to public health, the European Court ruled that because Cassis de Dijon was legally marketed in France, there was nothing to stop its legal sale in Germany. This mutual recognition leads to the free movement of goods.

Activity 3.4

1 Obtain detailed information on food labelling requirements from the Ministry of Agriculture, Fisheries and Food (MAFF), the DTI, Croner's *Europe* or a relevant trade organisation.
2 Examine four to six labels from packaged foodstuffs from the UK, the rest of the EU, and elsewhere. Identify all the items of information on each label which are included to comply with European law. In very isolated cases you may come across labels which do not comply.

Note that this activity could be presented as a diagram displaying the foodstuff label with arrows to relevant information at the edge of the page detailing the directive reference and title, plus a brief explanation of how it has been incorporated into UK law.

EU law and workers

Freedom of movement

This freedom was recognised as necessary for the Single Market by the original Treaty of Rome but it does not apply to everybody. It is necessary for workers, who are also allowed to bring their dependent relatives with them, and for those wishing to set up in business elsewhere in the EU. Others having a right to unrestricted travel within the EU are receivers of services (e.g. tourists), and providers of services (e.g. business people). Anyone not falling into any of these categories has to show that they have the financial means to support themselves (which could include a student grant or pension). The primary objective is to avoid EU citizens gravitating to those Member States where welfare payments are the highest, simply to register as unemployed under the best conditions.

The Schengen Agreement

The Schengen Agreement committed its signatories to waiving passport checks from 1994 for EU travellers moving within the participating countries; this means fewer formalities. It was signed by nine of the then 12 Member States. Denmark, Ireland and the UK refused to participate. Austria joined the Schengen area in 1995 whereas Finland and Sweden have opted out whilst they consider the implications. UK citizens do not benefit from the Schengen Agreement since the UK has opted out so this means that British passports are still checked for travel within the EU.

Comparability of qualifications

The freedom to work anywhere in the EU is not sufficient by itself to remove barriers to labour mobility. Many jobs require specific qualifications and each EU country has its own qualification system (see Chapter 12). Therefore the EU is working to promote the acceptance of appropriate qualifications to prevent the waste which occurs if a worker has to re-qualify simply in order to do the job which he or she is qualified to do anyway. There is an understandable wariness of 'foreign' qualifications which is due to unfamiliarity with every other Member State's education and qualification system together with the suspicion that other qualifications may not be as good or rigorous. What was needed was some way of assessing the standing of all EU qualifications.

Recognising this problem, the EU at first tried the vertical approach, looking at a series of professions in turn and defining which qualifications were equivalent. So-called *sectoral directives* were devised in relation to architects, doctors and mid-wives for example. But it was soon evident that this approach would take years and a more efficient method of mutual recognition was needed.

The first general directive on mutual recognition of qualifications covered regulated professional jobs requiring three years or more of university level education. A second directive deals with professional jobs requiring less than three years of post-secondary education. For other jobs which require simply the completion of secondary education no directive has been proposed. Instead the EU tried to compile an easily understandable table for each of several such jobs such as porter in hotel and catering, maintenance electrician or aircraft mechanic. The intention was that a Greek employer, for example, could easily look up what the equivalent qualifications would be for, say, an aircraft mechanic in the UK by using these tables. However, many jobs were covered and it became a very large task to compile, in addition to which the information quickly dated as qualifications in the different countries changed. No agreement has yet been reached on how to make the task of comparing such jobs easier.

Certificates of Experience and/or tests

Where qualifications are clearly not equivalent, or there is a substantial difference in practice between Member States (as there might be, for example, in law) then a migrating professional can have previous employment experience documented with a Certificate of Experience which is issued by the DTI in the UK. Depending on circumstances, it can also be appropriate to require a person to undertake a test or exam to prove competence or else to undergo a period of supervised work (no more than three years), after which they are deemed to be equivalently qualified.

All of the above of course, is subject to the proviso that the qualified worker has a working knowledge of the language of the country in which he or she intends to work. Even so, migration of people for work purposes is not occurring to any great degree for two major reasons. First, people tend to want to stay put and lack of language proficiency is a powerful disincentive for many, especially the British, who have a poor record of language learning. Secondly, many EU states still make it very difficult for nationals of other countries to have their qualifications recognised in spite of the EU's best efforts to facilitate and legislate for equal standing of qualifications.

Example

A UK building company tried to set up a branch in Germany and found that it needed to register with the local Chamber of Commerce according to German law. Once a member of the appropriate Chamber of Commerce, the company was required to employ only accredited master tradesmen who command high wages, where it had been its intention to employ UK qualified employees. These high wages meant that the UK business lost its price advantage operating in Germany.

Working conditions

The Workplace Directive requires adequate ventilation, emergency lighting for exit routes, rest rooms, facilities for pregnant women and nursing mothers, and facilities for handicapped staff, by the end of 1995. There are also additional requirements for safety signs warning of unavoidable hazards.

By 1996, workers using VDUs must have appropriate desks and chairs, and the employer must provide and pay for regular eye tests and any required treatment for these workers.

Another directive requires companies to purchase appropriate machinery and reorganise tasks and work areas to reduce the risk of injury from carrying heavy loads.

Since 1992, health and safety protection must be as good for temporary and part-time employees as for full-time employees; this may require additional training.

Part-time and temporary employees should be given the same terms of employment (pro rata) as full-time employees; this may incur additional costs to employers. The great variation in the importance of part-time work across the EU is partly due to cultural differences in attitudes to women in paid work but is also very dependent on whether employment legislation encourages employers to offer part-time work.

Example

GrandMet, which includes Burger King, Pizza Land, Berni, Peter Dominic, Pastificio and Chef & Brewer, employs 50,000 people in seven of the Member States. The proportion of part-timers the company employs varies from 80 per cent in the UK to under 20 per cent in Germany. Although fewer women work in Germany, this difference is mainly due to the legal climate since the work to be done in both countries remains the same. The EU's recent move to give added protection to part-timers is expected to shift employer demand from part-time to contracted-out staff.

Contracts of employment

All employees working over eight hours a week should be issued with a written statement of the main terms and conditions of their employment within two months of starting work. The statement should cover:

- pay and method of payment;
- hours of work;
- amount of paid holidays;
- place of work and start date;
- finishing date if the work is temporary;
- notice periods;
- indication of the job and category of employment;
- any relevant collective agreements.

This has been applied in the UK by means of the Trade Union Reform and Employment Rights Act 1993 and replaces previous UK provisions that were less comprehensive.

Equal opportunities

This is an area in which UK employers have had many well publicised judgments against them in the European Court of Justice, usually because the UK legislation has been too narrowly defined. To date, the EU has only been concerned with equality of opportunity as between the sexes but there are signs that it may turn its attention to the problem of racism, in and out of the workplace, in the near future.

Effect of the Social Chapter

Although the UK has opted out and is excluded from the decision-making process of issues relating to its achievement, employers are still affected by its provisions. For example, large companies (over 1000 workers) with branches in more than one Member State are required to set up works councils to include employees in decision making. Therefore UK organisations with operations elsewhere in the EU must do this even though the UK has opted out. Many well-known UK companies, including ICI and Pilkington, have set up these councils ahead of schedule.

The cost of compliance

In forming opinions about proposed directives, the UK Government applies a compliance cost assessment (CCA) test to every measure, working out the potential costs to affected industries of each new law. If predicted costs are too high, UK ministers will suggest amendments to reduce business compliance costs, for example, if a directive required many companies to buy costly new equipment or involved organisations in much extra paperwork. This work is done by the DTI's Deregulation Unit.

A similar assessment procedure is also carried out at European level by DG XXIII, the Directorate-Generale concerned with small and medium-sized enterprises. The DG produces fiches d'impact assessing each EC proposal for the extent of its impact. Individual businesses can contribute information to these since a list of future fiches d'impact is available from DG XXIII.

Case study

Additional safeguards for package tour customers

Proposal
The DTI carried out a CCA of a directive which would provide additional safeguards to package tour customers. This would provide customers with additional information, guarantee the quality and standards of the holiday and ensure they are provided with the costs of returning home if the tour company fails while they are on holiday. (This protection already existed for holidaymakers whose packages involve flights.)

Businesses affected
These include tour operators, travel agents, hotels which offer more than accommodation (e.g. Isle of Wight hotels often offer packages that include a ferry crossing), other establishments, such as schools and caravan parks, and volunteer groups.

Costs
CCAs usually quote a total cost to the industry, but here the list of organisations affected (see above) was so wide that estimates of total costs were impossible. Instead the DTI estimated – at 1989 prices – that this measure would cost between £5 and £15 per customer for insurance against liability for death and personal injury, and 1 per cent of turnover for insurance against providers going out of business and covering the costs of returning customers home. The DTI expected that these costs would be passed on to the customer.

Industry worries
These concerned the costs of including additional brochure information and dealing with passenger complaints.

Competitive position
The DTI thought this directive would not disadvantage UK companies compared to other EU companies, especially since the UK travel industry already offers substantial customer protection through self-regulatory schemes.

Non-compliance and remedies

Although most of the EU directives needed to complete the Single Market have been enacted, some Member States have been slow to implement them into national law, so companies still find barriers hindering their business throughout the EU. If the time limit for implementation of the directive has elapsed there are two ways a company can deal with the problem:

- The official method is to complain to the EU which sets in motion legal action forcing the offending country to implement the directive. The European Court of Justice can require the directive to be implemented immediately but the case can take months or years to be heard.
- The second method is to alert the DTI's Single Market Compliance Unit (SMCU) to make representations on the company's behalf. This may persuade the offending country to act more quickly.

Non-compliance should, however, only be a short to medium-term problem for UK businesses.

Summary

- EU law was set up originally by the Treaty of Rome and amended by later Treaties and Acts, including the Single Market Act and the Maastricht Treaty.
- Where EU law conflicts with national law, EU law takes precedence.
- The Treaty of Rome was intended to create a common market; the Single Market Act was intended to speed up that process; and the Maastricht Treaty extends the European Community (as the EU was then) into foreign and European political areas.
- The Social Chapter seeks to improve conditions for workers but is optional for the UK which wanted it excluded from the Maastricht Treaty.
- EU law is presented as directives, regulations, decisions, opinions and recommendations.
- EU law ensures freedom of movement for people in a number of ways although this is enforced unevenly across the EU.
- Special care is taken to ensure that compliance costs are not a burden.

Information sources

- The *European* newspaper for current developments.
- *The ABC of Community Law* and *The European Community 1992 and Beyond*, the European Commission.
- *Europe in Figures*, 1995 edition, Eurostat.
- *The Single Market – Making it work for you*, Department of Trade and Industry.

Assignment 3.1
Compliance

This assignment fulfils the following criteria:

BTEC 16.2.2, 16.2.3, 16.2.4
RSA 13.1.1, 13.1.2, 13.2.1
City & Guilds 9.1.1, 9.1.2, 9.1.3

Your tasks

Choose a company with which you are familiar and find out which directives, regulations and decisions it must comply with. Ensure you distinguish between directives already incorporated into UK law and those likely to affect the company in the future. Think in terms of:

- functional areas such as personnel (e.g. hours, health and safety, maternity rights)
- the product, and
- the process.

Present your results in an advisory report to the company identifying the costs and benefits of compliance. Identify some specific examples where the four freedoms have been enhanced for your company. Make some general observations on what EU law has done to the company's competitive position. To find relevant information use software such as Natwest's PHAROS, or publications like the DTI's *Euro Manual* or the DTI's *Progress on Commission White Paper*. Consider also interviews with relevant personnel.

Compile a list of action points for the company which it will need to attend to in order to ensure compliance with existing and proposed European legislation. Which points require urgent action and which can be allocated a lower priority?

Note: BTEC students need only consider the effect of EU legislation and social policy on personnel and working practices, as they relate to the following two freedoms:

- freedom of movement for people
- freedom of establishment (of a business).

4 European Union policies

Use this chapter to find out:

- the aims and effectiveness of the EU's main policies.

This chapter covers the following performance criteria:

BTEC	16.2.4
RSA	13.1.2, 13.1.3
City & Guilds	9.1.3, 9.2.1, 9.3.2

Introduction

Since the Treaty of Rome, the EU has set out some of its aims in the form of policies which can be achieved through a combination of European law and special funding. Some of the major policies are described below with effects on businesses highlighted with the symbol ☺ for opportunity or benefit and ☹ for threats.

The Common Agricultural Policy (CAP)

The CAP was almost the only policy derived directly from the Treaty of Rome. When Europe was still recovering from the devastation and shortages of war this policy aimed to:

- increase agricultural productivity;
- ensure a fair standard of living for the agricultural community;
- stabilise markets;
- provide certainty of supplies;
- ensure supplies to consumers at reasonable prices.

Farming is one basic primary industry declining in importance in employment terms as efficiency improves. The CAP was designed to ease people out of farming gently, preferably through retirement rather than redundancy or bankruptcy. Farming maintains the rural landscape and way of life, so supporting farmers helps slow the depopulation of rural areas and preserves the rural environment. Hence the CAP is a social security system for farmers with the added advantage of securing food supplies.

Under CAP the EU has become self-sufficient in almost all the major agricultural commodities including cereals, wheat, sugar, butter, cheese and beef. Different payment methods exist depending on product: for some, a guaranteed price is paid while for others, payment is in proportion to the area of land planted. Whatever the method, payments obviously encouraged farmers to produce the subsidised products leading to the infamous butter and beef mountains which cost the EU so much to maintain and dispose of. Butter, for example, was sold cheaply to the former Soviet Union, given free to pensioners and sold cheaply as cooking butter. These surpluses have now almost disappeared but there are still problems with overproduction of crops from the Mediterranean area including wine, fruit and vegetables.

☺ Agricultural suppliers should keep informed about which crops and livestock are attracting EU support under the CAP so that they can be prepared with appropriate products and services.

For non-EU countries wishing to export their agricultural produce into the EU, the EU imposes a levy which prices non-EU goods up to the set price paid to EU farmers. This ensures a market for what EU farmers produce but it also means higher than necessary food prices. It also hampers the progress of farming exports from the developing countries whose main competitive advantage should be their low prices.

The CAP is the most costly item in the EU budget accounting for about half of expenditure and has proved difficult to control. There are many pressures on the EU to lower this figure, for example:

● the biggest contributors to EU finances often have the smallest and most efficient agricultural sectors and so resent supporting inefficient agriculture elsewhere;
● the recent General Agreement on Tariffs and Trade (GATT) settlement requires reduction of EU agricultural subsidies;
● the future competitive position of the EU in the world will not lie in agriculture but other industries, especially high-tech sectors such as electronics and biotechnology, so these areas may be more worthy of financial support.

Case study

How farmers are reacting to CAP reform

Farmers are clearly altering their business planning to fit in with the new CAP and future effects of the GATT agreement. Uppermost in their minds is the need to cut costs and diversify as well as manage their set-aside land (see below). The aid payment reduction has led some farmers to set up ancillary businesses on their land to increase profits.

One farmer is stepping up his sales of straw to nearby racing stables and mushroom growers. Another has joined with Southern Electric to build a 20 mega watt straw-burning plant near his farm. He has also contacted Cargill, the agri-business company, for an agreement to take oilseed rape grown on his land for the company's biodiesel production plant.

A French farmer told of his efforts to reduce costs from £319 to £187 a hectare by reducing agro-chemical and fertiliser use. 'In the past we were influenced by the drive for intensive cultivation, but we were using too many inputs – since we cut them, our yields have not changed', he said.

Activity 4.1

Find out from local farmers how they have amended their activities, if at all, to take advantage of the help available under the CAP and what problems they experience working in an industry which is so tightly controlled by the EU.

The CAP was too successful, necessitating other schemes to reduce the surpluses. So guaranteed prices were tied to strict quotas which farmers must not exceed in order to ensure payment. More recently, 'set aside' was introduced. This encouraged farmers not to farm 15 per cent of their land for five years. This scheme, too, has problems since it has not led to hoped for falls in output, partly because small farmers producing less than 92 tonnes of cereal a year are exempt. Table 4.1 gives some examples of payments made to farmers under the CAP.

Table 4.1 Examples of CAP payments (per annum)

	£
For planting one hectare broad-leaved trees	1575
Per hectare of hemp	590
Per hectare of flax	585
Per hectare of linseed	478
Per hectare of oilseed rape	400
For creating wildlife habitats on former arable land	360
Per hectare of proteins (peas and beans)	355
Per hectare of set-aside	311
Extra annual payment for broad-leaved woodland	250
Per hectare of cereals	191
For converting a hectare to set-aside	90
For converting a hectare to organic farming	70

Source: The *Observer*, 10 July 1994

Common Fisheries Policy (CFP)

The need for a fisheries policy has arisen from the problems of reduced catches due to overfishing – a world-wide problem – but the EU's fisheries policy is also designed to ensure an adequate standard of living for producers, and stable markets. Fishing is particularly important to the UK, Denmark, France, Spain and Portugal. In contrast to the CAP, the CFP accounts for less than 1 per cent of the EU budget.

There has been a fisheries policy only since 1983 which covers:

- **Access to fishing waters** Waters up to 200 miles from the coast are open to fishing by all in the EU with the exception of certain inshore waters, the first 12 miles of which are restricted to locals. Total overall access is limited by a system of total allowable catches which are fixed each year in the light of estimates of the size of fish populations. These quotas are then divided up between Member States – a process which causes much argument about fairness. A minimum mesh size for the nets is set to ensure that young fish are not caught, thus helping the potential increase of fish populations. There are also penalties for landing fish in excess of the quotas (which results in reports of fishing vessels throwing fish back into the sea). Surveillance aircraft are used to police the fisheries.

- **Increased market efficiency** Modernisation of the fishing fleet is being encouraged by various financial incentives even though there is a contradiction in increasing the capability for fishing whilst at the same time reducing the quotas available. There is also a system of guide prices set annually for fish which, if the market price goes below the guides, triggers a price support system so that fishermen are not subject to wildly fluctuating incomes. This may happen, for example, if there were a sudden influx of cheap fish from outside the EU.

The EU's fisheries policy has not been greatly successful since fish stocks continue to reduce. There have been some widely publicised disagreements over fishing rights between France and the UK in British waters, between Spain and France and the UK in Spanish waters, and between Spain and Morocco. There is an argument for creating property rights in the fisheries as a more efficient way of conserving stocks since this seems to have worked in New Zealand.

Structural policies – The Regional, Social and Cohesion Funds

Structural funds are the second largest item of expenditure in the EU budget after agriculture (over 30 per cent in 1994). From the beginning of the Treaty of Rome, the uneven distribution of wealth was recognised and mechanisms were put into place to try and redress the balance. The European Social Fund (ESF) was set up in 1958, the European Agricultural Guidance and Guarantee Fund in 1964, the European Regional Development Fund (ERDF) in 1975, and finally the Maastricht Treaty created the Cohesion Fund to help the four poorest Member States (Greece, Ireland, Portugal and Spain) to develop economically.

The EU helps poorer regions differently from national governments. You will have learned in Mandatory Unit 1 that the UK targets aid to poorer areas through offering a portion of the costs of start-up, consultancy or innovation research, low-interest loans, or reductions in red tape. The EU tends not to support individual companies, but invites suggestions from central and local governments on desirable infrastructure projects which would not otherwise be funded. Once approved, projects go to tender.

These schemes aim to achieve six objectives:

1 promote the development of underdeveloped regions;
2 redevelop regions dependent on declining industries such as coal, steel and ship building;
3 combat long-term unemployment;
4 ease unemployment amongst young people, women and other disadvantaged groups;
5 modernise agriculture and fishing and promote rural development;
6 overcome the disadvantages (mainly high transport costs) experienced in the sparsely populated areas of Sweden and Finland.

Funding under objectives 1,2,5 and 6 is geographically limited whereas all areas can obtain funding under objectives 3, 4 and those sections of objective 5 related to agriculture and fishing. The main principle behind EU funding in these areas is that it should never replace national government funding. Governments cannot reduce their responsibilities, expecting the EU to pick up the bill instead. In most cases, national governments are expected to fund the EU-assisted projects on an equal basis, although this has been relaxed for the four poorest Member States. As the emphasis on agriculture declines, the EU is allocating more funds to regional and social policies.

The Maastricht Treaty greatly increased these structural funds with the new Cohesion Fund and some net contributor countries, such as Germany, are beginning to protest at the size of their contributions. However, projects such as the Athens Metro in Greece show that the flow is not all one way. Almost everything apart from the cranes and the labour is being supplied by non-Greek companies. The German Siemens company, for example, is supplying the rolling stock, signals and communications systems. Hence governments pay into the funds from taxation but their countries' businesses benefit from the resultant contracts awarded through the funds.

The European Regional Development Fund (ERDF)

Areas entitled to help from the ERDF are those with GDP per head of 75 per cent or less of the EU average, as shown in Figure 4.1 below). In the UK this includes Northern Ireland, Merseyside, South Yorkshire and the Scottish Highlands. In Germany this includes the whole of former East Germany.

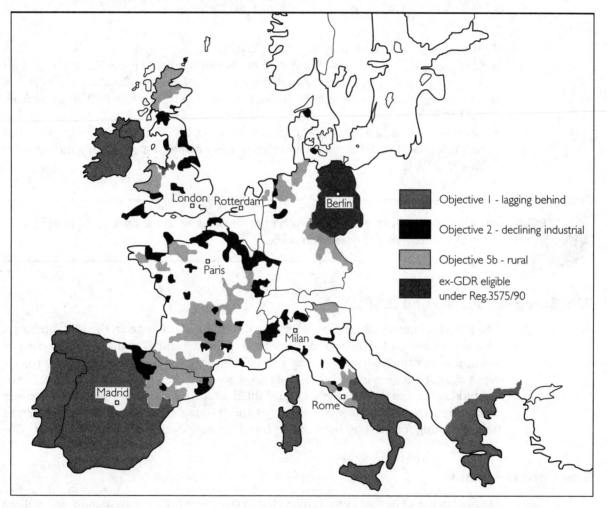

Source: European Commission

Figure 4.1   Regions qualifying for ERDF support

Funds are to be used mainly to improve infrastructure by modernising transport and communications links, improving energy and water supplies, encouraging research and development, providing training and helping small businesses.

Case study

Ireland

Since the Regional Development Fund started in 1975, Ireland has always qualified for aid under this programme. In the 1994–99 round it is expecting Ir£6 billion from the various structural funds. However economic growth for 1994 and 1995 is expected to be high, at about 5 per cent a year, and this may mean that when eligibility is next decided in 1999, Ireland will no longer qualify for aid as its GDP per head will exceed 75 per cent of the EU average. This will be due to a very few strong-performing export industries with unemployment expected to remain high and investment low. Ireland would not be completely cut off from EU funds but would fail to qualify for regional funding which accounts for 46 per cent of its EU support.

Examples of structural funding in the UK include:

- £24.8 million over 12 years awarded to the North Scotland Hydro Electric Board for a variety of projects to supply electricity to the Highlands and Islands;
- improvements to Northern Ireland's railway system from a £1.6 million grant from the ERDF;
- after the steel industry collapsed in Sheffield, the ERDF financed reclamation and redevelopment of derelict land and the expansion of new and existing industries at East End Park.

Activity 4.2

For each of the above examples explain how businesses in the area could benefit once the improvements have been made.

The European Social Fund (ESF)

The ESF concentrates on improving the quality of the workforce. In the UK, funding is available to designated areas under objectives 1,2 and 5 and to all areas under objective 3 whereas no funds are claimed by the UK under objective 4. Examples of projects receiving ESF funding in the UK include taxi-driving training courses for women, desktop publishing and design courses for disabled adults, courses for women from refugee communities to start their own businesses and training for jobs in commerce, catering and gardening for the long-term unemployed who are over 25 and have a learning disability.

The Cohesion Fund

Help from the Cohesion Fund is allocated to countries rather than regions and will go to Ireland, Greece, Portugal and Spain. These are the four poorest Member States with 90 per cent or less GDP per head than the EU average.

Effect on business

The EU claims that during 1975–89, the ERDF created or saved a million jobs through the funding of 40,000 projects. Whilst most businesses cannot expect direct funding under these schemes, the effect should be to improve the business environment in designated areas such as Merseyside which was granted objective 1 status in 1994. Opportunities exist for businesses to gain orders from funding in other EU areas, as the case study below demonstrates.

Case study

EU funds Portugal's growth

Portugal is the UK's 18th largest export market but will leap up the league table as UK companies take advantage of a £26 billion investment in the Portuguese economy over the next six years.

Former EU Commissioner Bruce Millan and the Portuguese Prime Minister, Cavaco Silva, signed the Community Support Framework Agreement for Portugal 1994–99. This releases £13 billion from the EU's Structural and Cohesion Funds matched by contributions from the Portuguese public and private sector up to £26 billion.

Trade Minister, Richard Needham said:

'The Regional Development Plan offers British industry a major opportunity to win orders for products and services. Many British companies are already established in Portugal and they should be well placed to benefit from this large EU funding programme. It should also act as an encouragement for more British companies to enter the market.

'We hope that British companies can provide effective partnership to Portuguese industry for both major investments and the smaller ventures.

'This investment will form a crucial element of the Portuguese economy with an expected growth of 1 per cent a year above the EU average over the next six years.'

Apart from infrastructure projects in communications, environment and power, the plan provides for significant investments in education, training and the development of the industrial base. Portuguese core industries are textiles, motor components (supported by the new Ford/Volkswagen plant), and tourism.

☺ As the case study above illustrates, structural funds present opportunities for UK companies in other Member States, so it is important companies keep well informed about projects under consideration by the EU.

Activity 4.3

Use a local business directory or the *Yellow Pages* to identify five companies able to provide the services described in the above case study on Portugal. In the role of export advisor to your Chamber of Commerce, draft a letter to advise them of the opportunities.

Environmental policy

Environmental damage crosses national boundaries. For example, mercury spilled into the Rhine at Basle, Switzerland, in 1986 affected Germany and the Netherlands too. The

EU can, and is expected to, act as a regulatory body in such areas but despite this it had no explicit environmental policy until the Single European Act 1987.

The 1987 Act's objectives are to:

- preserve, protect and improve the quality of the environment;
- contribute towards protecting human health;
- ensure a prudent and rational utilisation of natural resources.

Environmental action programmes

The EU focuses its activities by agreeing on the emphasis necessary in a series of programmes. The period 1993–2000 spans the fifth environmental action programme when the EU will focus its attention on:

- persuading industry to accept its responsibilities;
- curbing demand for energy;
- curbing demand for transport;
- improving soil and water quality in agriculture;
- reducing the effects of mass tourism;
- reducing the risk of environmental accidents (such as the sinking of the Braer off Shetland in 1993).

To promote the above aims the EU has several schemes to finance environmental projects. The Maastricht Treaty allowed for part of the new Cohesion Fund to be allocated to innovative environmental schemes.

☺ Although the UK is not covered by the Cohesion Fund there is no reason why a UK company should not apply to undertake work in the target countries of Spain, Portugal, Greece and Ireland.

The Eco-label scheme

To promote environmentally friendly production and prevent the proliferation of many different nationally based schemes, the EU has devised the Eco-label. This label (a flower made from the 12 EU stars) will be awarded to the most environmentally friendly products in 23 non-food areas as follows:

Washing machines	Hair sprays
Dishwashers	Solar heating systems
Light bulbs	Laundry detergents
Soil improvers	Insulation materials
Kitchen rolls	Paints
Toilet rolls	Batteries
Writing paper	Deodorants
Cat litter	Shoes
Packaging	Freezers
Photocopying paper	T-shirts
Bed linen	Glassware
Porcelain	

Companies will be able to compete for permission to use the label by submitting details of how they produce their products. Those judged to be the most environmentally friendly in their product group will be allowed to use the eco-label for a period of three years before needing to re-apply to assess whether they are still the most environmentally friendly companies or if others have overtaken them.

Pollution control

The EU has also shown a great deal of concern about pollution, both in reducing current levels and in trying to reduce future emissions. The EU operates the 'polluter pays' principle, transferring costs of emissions from the general public (payable in bad health, days off work, etc.) to the polluter, thus minimising pollution at the point of production. Therefore, a range of directives set common emission standards for specific industries and products including cars, lorries, detergents, paints, petrol and chemicals affecting the ozone layer.

Over 350 EU legal measures have been approved which seek to limit and control:

- water pollution;
- air pollution;
- noise levels;
- damage from chemical products;
- damage to the ozone layer;
- problems arising from the disposal of waste.

All these require companies to show more care in their operations but in many cases add to their costs.

☹ Companies with poor emission standards will find that their operations and also possibly their products are no longer legal. For example, National Power is having to install expensive desulphurisation equipment at its coal burning power stations.

☺ The new Copenhagen-based European Environment Agency (EEA) will create a demand for environmental monitoring technology and techniques to provide information on the state of the environment across the EU.

☺ The 'polluter pays' principle means that companies selling cleaner technologies will have many opportunities in countries such as Spain and Portugal where there is further to go to meet EU standards.

Example

The French water company Lyonnaise des Eaux-Dumez has a large waste management subsidiary, the Sita group, which in 1992 grew by 19 per cent. Local authorities and industrial companies increasingly need its services to treat their waste by re-use, recycling and sophisticated disposal, as European legislation makes it increasingly difficult to simply dump waste.

Activity 4.4

Table 4.2 (overleaf) shows the market size for environmental protection products and services. Which European markets for other products are of similar size?

However, environmental directives have been implemented slowly and inconsistently by many Member States. For example, the bathing water standards apply to places where 'large numbers' of people habitually bathe. This phrase is open to interpretation as it is not clearly specified. Hence, France defined 3000 beaches as needing to meet the standards whereas in the UK the number was 27 and in Germany a mere 14.

Table 4.2   Environmental protection markets 1988

	Percentage share				ECU Million
	Air	Noise	Waste	Water	
Belgium	n/a	n/a	n/a	n/a	1,300
Denmark	18.0	3.0	23.0	56.0	900
France	11.3	4.2	32.0	52.5	7,700
Germany*	29.8	2.7	21.0	46.5	14,600
Greece	17.0	1.0	32.0	50.0	200
Ireland	4.0	3.0	23.0	70.0	200
Italy	17.0	2.0	35.0	46.0	4,700
Luxembourg	n/a	n/a	n/a	n/a	100
Netherlands	20.0	3.4	28.7	47.9	2,000
Portugal	n/a	n/a	n/a	n/a	200
Spain	14.0	2.0	30.0	54.0	1,200
UK	22.0	4.0	28.0	46.0	6,900
Total EU	21.4	3.3	27.0	48.3	40,000

*West Germany   **Source:** *Europe in the Year 2000*, Euromonitor, 1990

Merger and competition policies

Controlling the activities of large companies is always a difficult problem. On the one hand, the Single Market aimed to create conditions within which European companies could compete effectively with the largest world companies – these tend to be US and Japanese. On the other hand, large companies can take advantage of their dominant positions to the disadvantage of suppliers and customers (covered in Mandatory Unit 1). EU policy tries to strike a balance between the two.

At the European level, the EU attempts to ensure companies do not enjoy unfair advantages from government financial subsidies. So, for example, British Aerospace had to pay an additional sum to the UK Government because the EU ruled that the price it originally paid in 1988 for the privatised car company, Rover, was artificially low. Other government actions restrict competition such as the state sanctioned monopolies often allowed in telecommunications and air transport. There are therefore EU deadlines by which time these state controlled enterprises must be opened up to competition. For example, for telecommunications this is 1997 when companies such as the Swedish Telia will be able to offer their services against the partially state-owned Danish telephone company, Tele-Danmark.

The Treaty of Rome forbids price fixing and market sharing agreements (on the lines of 'you take Germany and we'll take France and Spain'), predatory pricing, limiting production and refusal to supply. Companies found guilty may have to pay substantial fines. For example, 16 European steel firms, including British Steel, were fined a total of 104 million ECU in 1994 for price-fixing, market-sharing and restricting the exchange of commercially sensitive information amongst themselves. British Steel's fine was the largest at 32 million ECU. In the same year, however, the German company BMW's takeover of the UK car company Rover was allowed to go ahead, as was the Mirror newspaper group's joint takeover with Italian and Spanish companies of the *Independent* newspaper.

Since 1990 the EU has applied the following criteria to decide which mergers or takeovers should be referred:

- when the combined world turnover of the proposed merged company is more than 5 billion ECU, and
- the combined EU turnover of two of the companies is more than 250 million ECU.

Hence only very large companies may be referred to the EU. Non-EU companies could find themselves subject to EU competition law if their combined sales in the EU exceed 250 million ECU. In 1991 over 60 mergers were investigated of which one was rejected.

The EU also tries to promote competition by supporting research and development in high-tech industries which should be the emerging markets of the near future. For example, the fourth framework programme for European Community research and technological development running for four years from 1994 includes a large range of grants to help business co-operate in research and apply the results of others' research into their products.

Public procurement

One area previously tightly controlled was public procurement, i.e. purchases by governments and other public sector bodies. For example, central and local governments build and equip schools, hospitals, libraries and armies. An order to supply the entire French army with field rations for a year would be worth thousands of pounds.

Many countries restricted public sector purchasing exclusively to companies from their own countries. Since public purchasing accounts for a very large percentage of total business, from 11.6 per cent in Germany to 24.8 per cent in Denmark in 1991 this meant a great deal of trade (e.g. 148 billion ECU in Germany) to which most companies had no access (refer to Table 4.3). The EU has, therefore, stipulated that public purchasing must now be open to any EU company to bid for. This should make available to all EU companies about two-thirds of the amounts shown in Table 4.3.

Table 4.3 Percentage and value of public sector spending, 1991

	GDP (1000m ECU)	Public sector spending (1000m ECU)	Public sector as a % of total GDP
Austria	133	24.1	18.1
Belgium	159	23.4	14.7
Denmark	105	26.0	24.8
Finland	100	24.1	24.1
France	970	177.5	18.3
Germany	1274	147.8	11.6
Greece	57	11.2	19.6
Ireland	35	5.7	16.3
Italy	931	163.0	17.5
Luxembourg	8	1.4	17.1
Netherlands	235	33.6	14.3
Portugal	56	10.1	18.1
Spain	427	67.0	15.7
Sweden	192	51.3	26.7
UK	817	174.0	21.3

Source: *Basic Statistics of the Community*, 30th edition, Eurostat, 1993

As many governments privatised a great part of the public sector which tended to be some of the largest companies in a country, the EU has also legislated to open up contracts for what are called the *utilities*. These cover those basic industries on which other businesses depend such as water, energy, communications and transport.

The Utilities Directive, one of the procurement directives, requires contracts for supplies exceeding £299,456 (400,000 ECU) and works costing more than £3,743,203 (5,000,000 ECU) to be advertised across the EU to enable companies from other Member States to bid for the contracts. The same applies to public sector supplies although the amounts triggering the open purchase procedures are lower (see Table 4.4). There are strict definitions of what constitutes a 'contract' so that organisations cannot bypass the Directive by splitting large contracts into several smaller ones.

Table 4.4 Minimum value per contract of public sector and utilities purchases which trigger compulsory EU-wide tendering

Contractor	Contract	Threshold ECU	£
Central Government	Supplies	200,000	149,728
and other public	Works	5,000,000	3,743,203
bodies	Services	200,000	149,728
Utilities	Supplies	400,000	299,456
	Works	5,000,000	3,743,203
	Services	400,000	299,456

Source: adapted from HM Treasury

Tenders are advertised in the *Official Journal of the EC* and reproduced on the Tenders Electronic Daily (TED), an on-line data service available at local European Information Centres (see Figure 4.2). About 500 contracts are advertised weekly and this is likely to go up as the number of directives passed increases.

```
UK - Belfast: hospital
Language - English
Contract type: Public works contract
Awarding Authority: The Royal Group of Hospitals and Dental Hospital
HSS Trust
a) Site: Belfast, Northern Ireland
b) Works: Reference EB0994
New block containing main entrance, accident and emergency, medical
records, outpatients, operating theatres and intensive care.
Overall estimated value: £6m
Deadline for receipt of applications: 26.7.94
Award criteria (other than price): Economically most advantageous ten-
der in terms of price, period for completion and technical merit.

UK - Nottingham: wind turbine electricity generating station
Language - English
Contract type: Public works contract
Contracting authority: East Midlands Electricity plc
a) Site: Lincolnshire
b) Works: The procurement, supply, installation and commissioning of a
wind turbine electricity generating station.
Time limits for delivery or completion: 31.10.94
Award criteria: economically most advantageous offer based on price,
quality, performance and profitability.
```

Figure 4.2 Extract from Tenders Electronic Daily   **Source:** Tenders Electronic Daily

☹ If a company has relied heavily for many years on local authority or central government contracts for work, it may find itself having to compete against other European companies for the work, with the possibility of losing the contract.

☺ In 1991 the *Official Journal of the EC* contained 1218 invitations to tender for contracts to construct bridges, tunnels and shafts; there were 484 invitations for gas fitting and plumbing – 471 of them outside the UK.

These procurement directives have forced the public sector organisations and utilities companies to plan ahead much more. For example, they have to anticipate their purchases for the coming year so that they can calculate whether they need to advertise the contracts. It is also making these organisations choose their suppliers very carefully since the directives only allow choices to be made using unbiased standards. For example, a company is not allowed to say that it wishes to purchase 200 Rover Metros but can state a preference for a 1100 cc hatchback of the Rover Metro type or its equivalent, opening up the contract to Ford with Fiestas and Fiat with Puntos.

The Utilities Directive came into force on 1 January 1993 so the utilities at first experienced the disadvantages of setting up the paperwork for what has now become a very complicated procedure. British Energy, for example, only attracted three non-UK companies to tender within the first year of setting up the system.

☺ The procurement directives offer opportunities mainly in industrial markets and, by definition, to large companies.

Social policy

Since its inception the EU has sought to ensure that the economic benefits of the Single Market are felt by all citizens. More recently, in the Single European Act and the Maastricht Treaty, this distribution of benefits has been given more attention and has become very important because of the high levels of unemployment currently being experienced all over the EU. Some argue that social policy makes unemployment worse by adding to employer costs whilst others argue that it is precisely during periods of economic recession that the more vulnerable members of the EU should be given support.

Although it is true that some industry has migrated to the Mediterranean countries where costs are lower, including wages and health and safety requirements, most EU companies seeking lower costs look outside the EU to the Far East. To reduce pressures to decrease wages and worker protection in the rest of the EU, the EU is trying to raise standards for all workers.

Therefore whether working in the UK or elsewhere in the EU, you can expect the following:
- free movement of labour (see also Chapter 3) including recognition of your qualifications;
- equal pay for men and women – the EU intends to address the issue of racism in the future;
- access to social security for migrant workers as long as the contribution criteria have been fulfilled;
- public health programmes with priority being given to cancer, smoking, drugs, AIDS and alcohol abuse by co-ordinating research and information campaigns.

An example of the application of the EU's social policy is the setting up of the EURES (European Employment Services) network. This computer network, available in employment offices across the EU, has been financed out of EU funds and allows job seekers to find out about opportunities elsewhere in the EU as well as to obtain information on living and working conditions in other Member States. Use of the service is free and it should facilitate the free movement of labour within the EU.

The EU's social policy also includes measures to:

- alleviate poverty
- help the disabled and elderly
- provide employment and vocational training
- ensure minimum working conditions and minimum health and safety standards.

Health and safety policy

This is a policy area which was more explicitly stated in the Social Action section of the Single European Act and there has been a series of health and safety directives since the mid-eighties. Many aspects of health and safety were already covered in UK legislation by the Health and Safety at Work Act 1974 (refer to Mandatory Unit 2, Business Systems). Health and safety is not part of the Social Chapter (from which the UK has opted out) so any legislation arising under this heading is binding upon the UK.

In 1989, the Framework Directive for health and safety set out the responsibilities of employers and employees, how to make an assessment of risks, introduced preventative measures, detailed the use of health and safety advice, and provided for information and safety training, and consultation with workers' representatives.

Since then 'daughter' directives have been approved or proposed relating to exposure to cancer-inducing substances, asbestos, temporary workers, pregnant women, and fairground machinery, to name just a few. Directives also cover workplaces, work equipment, personal protective equipment (such as ear muffs and goggles), work with visual display units, handling of heavy loads, temporary or mobile work sites (mainly building sites), and agriculture and fisheries. The range of directives setting up technical standards in products also adds to the increased safety of workers and consumers.

Equal opportunities policy

EU directives in this area apply principally to equality of pay and benefits between the sexes. Although the UK was one of the first European countries to enact equal opportunity legislation, it has been this area which the UK has most often been forced to act on by the European Court of Justice. EU funds, especially the ESF, attempt to address the wider issues of equality of access to the employment market by earmarking finance for the training of women, the disabled and the young unemployed. The issue of equality of opportunity between the races has only recently been addressed with more action promised in the future.

Effect on business

The EU's social policy tends to add to employer costs in the short term. For example, the requirement to provide employees working at computer terminals with ergonomic seating requires money. However, these measures should make companies less liable to compensation claims from their employees in the future, whilst some of the measures will improve the quality of the workforce generally.

Consumer policy

An EU survey carried out on the completion of the Single Market asked consumers how they felt about cross-border transactions. The results showed that generally people felt these were more risky than doing business in their own country for four main reasons:

- difficulties with after-sales service (mentioned by 53 per cent);
- language problems (39 per cent);
- difficulties in settling disputes (29 per cent);
- difficulties in obtaining information and advice (27 per cent).

A single market for goods should result in more choice and lower prices. However a market's efficiency also increases when all parties have access to clear and relevant information about the choices open to them. The EU therefore seeks to increase the quality of information available to consumers and also to ensure that consumers maintain confidence in the products and services offered to them by ensuring safety standards, accurate labelling and simplifying the resolution of trans-border payment disputes for small amounts of money.

Areas giving rise to most complaints in the EU include cosmetics, package holidays and consumer credit. So these were targeted as priority areas for the second of the EU's three-year action plans running from 1993–95 as well as increasing consumer information (such as a product's impact on the environment) and including consumer organisations in the consultation process for future EU legislation. The third three-year plan for 1996–98 will concentrate on financial services, public utilities and foodstuffs.

There will also be action to promote sustainable development and to ensure EU citizens benefit from the developing information society of improved electronic communication. Information to consumers is still important and the Commission prepared a series of radio broadcasts for transmission at the end of 1995 as well as a new leaflet to explain consumer rights.

EU action in this area has been mainly in the form of directives although it is only since the Maastricht Treaty that consumer policy has been designated a major EU policy area. Previous chapters have already mentioned food labelling and package holiday directives. By 1993, 42 directives on consumer issues had been agreed.

The EU has considerable difficulty in improving access to justice in trans-border disputes because this involves amending national judicial procedures which most Member States are reluctant to do. Yet arguably this is one of the most important actions needed to give consumers absolute confidence in purchasing from other Member States.

☹ Of particular importance is a directive on product liability which means the producer (or the importer in the case of goods not manufactured in the EU) bears strict liability for defective goods irrespective of fault. Consumers no longer have to prove that a manufacturer was negligent. All they need do is prove that damage occurred due to the product being defective. This means care needs to be taken in the instructions for use supplied with products and that enough, and appropriate, testing was done on the product before its release on general sale.

☺ In most cases, EU action on consumer issues tends to add to suppliers' costs, for example, by specifying labelling requirements or providing for a seven-day 'cooling off' period for anything sold by a door-to-door salesforce. However companies should recognise that the more confidence consumers have that they will not be cheated or misled, the more inclined they will be to spend their money. Hence EU action in this area should benefit all businesses generally rather than specific companies only.

Activity 4.5

Of growing importance to the EU's consumer policy has been information to Europeans about their consumer rights. Obtain copies of the Commission publications listed at the end of this chapter and undertake a survey to find out how much the general public knows about the consumer rights they have as members of the EU. Use the survey results to highlight which areas consumers need more information on and suggest ways in which the Commission could communicate this information more effectively.

Other policies

There are many other areas in which the EU has a policy, for example, transport, aid to developing countries, research, energy and foreign relations; many of these may provide business opportunities.

Activity 4.6

Find out a little about the other EU policies mentioned in the previous paragraph and identify some of the business opportunities these present to specific UK companies or industrial sectors.

Conclusion

It is important to realise that many aspects of EU policies conflict. For example, moves to increase industrial competitiveness may result in lower levels of employee protection. The CAP in particular comes in for much criticism with consumer groups arguing that it means higher food prices (£10 a week for the average family of four) and it has been accused of helping to degrade the environment. Both the CAP and the structural funds are likely to be re-examined very carefully as Eastern European countries, such as Poland and Hungary, seek to join the EU since they would create huge demands on both funds until their economies improve.

Summary

- EU policy on agriculture, fisheries, the regions, the environment, competition, health and safety, consumer rights and money is discussed in this chapter.

Information sources

- Relevant UK Government departments for individual policies such as:
  - the DTI for competition
  - the DOE for environmental action
  - the MAFF for agriculture.
- The European Commission provides many free booklets including:

- *Environmental Policy in the European Community*
- *Our Farming Future*
- *Working for the Regions*
- *A Region of the European Union*, a series of booklets published by the European Commission office in the UK for each of the standard regions.
- Consumer Rights in the Single Market
- Consumer Guide

Assignment 4.1
Trade fair

This assignment fulfils the following criteria:
RSA   13.1.3
City & Guilds   9.1.3, 9.2.1, 9.3.1 to 9.3.4

This assignment can be completed to varying degrees of complexity, either comprehensively with work being apportioned to different members of a group, or with less detail as an individual assignment.

Your task

Plan a trade fair for the local business community on the theme of the opportunities offered by the EU's environmental policy. The assignment should be presented as a portfolio which may contain:

- a list of potential local exhibitors (including environmental technology firms and consultancies);
- a list of potential local visitors (including organisations with polluting processes, local authorities with waste disposal responsibilities etc);
- the preparation of a press release to generate interest in the event which could outline EU environmental policy and its implications for local business;
- the planning of several talks to be given during the trade fair covering specific sectors such as the environmental responsibilities of agriculture, environmental aspects of the structural funds, forthcoming waste disposal directives (of interest to local authorities), carrying out environmental impact assessments when applying for planning permission for large projects and the implications of the recently agreed General Packaging Directive.

Additional sources
- *Yellow Pages*
- Local business directories
- European Commission Office in London
- European Information Centre

5 Sources of information

Use this chapter to find out about:

- sources of information on many EU aspects.

This chapter covers the following performance criteria:
RSA   13.1.3, 13.2.2
City & Guilds   9.2.1, 9.2.2, 9.2.3

Introduction

There is a great deal of information that is relevant to organisations concerning the EU, both to ensure that European law is being adhered to and to find out about trading and funding opportunities. This chapter outlines the major sources of information which will also help you as a student in your research. However, beware that not all sources are appropriate for student use. The following symbols are used to guide you.

!!   Warning against possible bias or other unreliability

    Timesaver

Major sources of information

Libraries

You should make full use of all libraries available to you with their associated facilities.

College libraries
Many students know where to find the books they need for a specific topic but are not so familiar with the reference sections of their college libraries. Is your college on several sites? If so, that may mean there is more than one library and it may be worth exploring the libraries on other sites as they do not all necessarily keep the same stock.

Public libraries
As well as exploring your local public library each county now has a designated business library. Its reference section will have useful directories and market research reports which your college or town library cannot afford to buy.

Inter-library loans

This service allows you to borrow any title, even if your library does not stock it. However, it may take a few weeks for your book to arrive as it will be sent from the nearest library which has it in stock.

Other collections of published material

It may be possible for you to have access to books and other materials held by your local Chamber of Commerce or European Information Centre.

Books

The major disadvantage of using books is how quickly they date. On the plus side, however, since the EU and its effects on business has been such a live topic for at least five years, there has been an explosion in the number of books available on the subject. This has coincided with the huge growth in business publishing generally. Almost every relevant aspect is covered in at least one book, from legal implications to highly technical manuals on the new environmental standards. Some of these books can seem off-putting as they are often addressed to the senior managers of companies.

Locating relevant books

Another problem with finding books on Europe is that most libraries use the Dewy system of classification in which the topic 'European business' is not listed separately. This means that if you want to find something on business culture in Spain, for example, you may have to look under 'Spain', 'travel' or 'culture', but you will not find it under Europe.

When to use books

Use books for historical facts, for general principles, for case studies, for in-depth detail and for analysis.

!! Be wary of using any book which is more than five years old; a five-year-old book on business culture is probably still largely relevant whilst a five-year-old book on European law is probably very out of date in some parts. How would you know which parts could still be relied upon?

Some specific publications

- Croner's *Europe* is a continuously updated guide to all aspects of the EU including the law, the Treaties, marketing and the expected effect of the Single Market on businesses.
- Your college may subscribe to Europe 2000 which is a collection of booklets on all aspects of the EU including its structure, finance, individual countries, EU policies and individual industries.

Newspapers

Broadsheets

The greatest advantage of newspapers is that they are up-to-date; the greatest disadvantage is that they can be inaccurate. Reliable information about business in Europe can be found in the broadsheets, *The Times*, the *Daily Telegraph*, the *Guardian*, the *Independent* and the *Financial Times* with their associated Sunday editions.

Back issues

Relevant back issues of these papers over the last six to 12 months can be found in the indexes. You may also have access to a CD-ROM in which you can search back copies of *The Times* and the *Guardian* using key words. If, for example, you wanted to know more about the textile industry in Europe, you might try 'textile, Europe' as the key words and the CD-ROM system would then give you a list of all articles which contain those words either in the headline or in the text of the article itself. You can then choose to see any listed article on screen and print out any you think may be relevant.

Special surveys

A special survey is a series of articles about the same topic usually printed in the centre pages or as a separate part of the newspaper so that you can easily retain them for future reference. This area is one of the great strengths of the *Financial Times* (FT); it publishes several relevant surveys each month. The other broadsheets also publish them although less often.

FT surveys are usually about a specific country or industry and the Member States are often surveyed. There are also special surveys of UK towns or counties and some regions in other parts of the world. Find out from a librarian what is done with the special surveys as they are often filed apart and kept for longer than the main part of the newspaper. The following lists some relevant FT special surveys:

Date	Subject
24 October 1995	Business Locations, Luxembourg
6 November 1995	Copenhagen
8 November 1995	Portugal
8 November 1995	Southern France
27 November 1995	Mobile Communications
12 December 1995	Austria
15 December 1995	Sweden
14 February 1996	European Postal Systems
25 March 1996	Pharmaceuticals
26 March 1996	Portuguese banking

You can often obtain a list of forthcoming surveys from newspapers such as the FT or may find that the library has a copy of this list.

Other newspapers

Mention ought to be made of the *European* newspaper which often has feature articles comparing some aspect, for example, employment law, pay or advertising spend, across the Member States. Its perspective is of a wide Europe with a great deal of information on East Europe as well as the Member States and the European Free Trade Association (EFTA) members.

You should also try consulting any foreign newspapers to which your library may subscribe. This will help you to see matters from a different perspective and may give you information about German and French companies to complement what you have already learned about UK ones.

Periodicals

Periodicals are fairly 'serious' magazines. *The Economist*, which appears weekly, like the *Financial Times*, regularly publishes special industry and country surveys which are very informative.

Use the index to identify relevant articles instead of leafing through each individual issue.

The Economist also publishes a wide variety of market reports (£100 upwards) and there may be a library in your area which subscribes to a few of these. It might be worth finding out if they have something on a market which you are investigating.

Trade magazines will often carry relevant articles about how their industries are doing in Europe and any relevant EU legislation which will affect UK companies and their competitors. There are magazines covering functional areas such as law, personnel, marketing (see Figure 5.1) and accountancy, as well as specific markets such as retailing, insurance, banking, hotel and catering, farming, engineering, computing and leisure management.

HENLEY CENTRE

Planning a European ad budget

Marketing decisions are increasingly being taken at a Europe-wide level. For market sectors like household cleaners and soft drinks, countries in the EC should no longer be considered individually when being allocated promotional budgets by multinational advertisers. For other sectors, such as food, or financial services, this may be inappropriate).

Any yet, even now, the evaluation of advertising media strategies across European frontiers is generally dismissed as impossible, or inappropriate – like comparing apples and pears.

Total advertising costs vary tremendously between European countries and within countries the relative costs of advertising media differ greatly. A consequence of this is that advertising to sales ratios for the same products, and proportions of budgets spend in each media are different in every country. So can one compare advertising effectiveness between countries?

Source: *Marketing*, 13 February 1992

Figure 5.1 A 'European' story from a trade magazine

Do not forget relevant trade magazines from the Member State you are investigating which you may be able to obtain from any European contacts you may have.

Finally, *European Business* is a monthly magazine which your library may subscribe to and which is specifically about Europe.

Official information

The European Commission (EC)

The EC publishes a vast amount of material ranging from the very technical to the popular. Most of the popular material is free of charge. Write to the UK EC Information Office for a catalogue and order form. The three most useful types of information are:

- European documentation: a series of free booklets, on average 50 pages long, on a variety of topics, examples include:
  - *The European Community's Budget*
  - *The ABC of Community Law*
  - *EEC Competition Policy in the Single Market*
  - *The European Economic Area*;
- Weekly press releases (see Figure 5.2 overleaf) and occasional special reports: very useful to find out what is going on in the EU. The service is free of charge.

WE/3/96

THE WEEK IN EUROPE   25 January 1996

The single currency takes shape. The single currency will be good for growth and employment, Commission President Jacques Santer told participants at the single currency roundtable this week. Speaking at the close of the three-day meeting on Wednesday, he said discussions had confirmed the need for an information campaign to ensure that the financial sector and consumers were properly informed about the Euro. Stopping the clock would not halt the arrival of the 21st century, Santer said, and Europe had to be ready. An opinion poll showed almost 90% of EU citizens support having a publicity campaign before the single currency is introduced, he said, and 80% want more information. Reflecting the President's wish for the campaign to be undertaken on a decentralised basis, Geoffrey Martin, the Head of the Commission's Representation in the UK, emphasised the need to make a clear distinction between propaganda backed by advertising, which would not be used in the UK, and the provision of information to the public and national organisations wishing to inform their members.

Ban on veal crates. The Commission has proposed a ban on veal crates, with new welfare standards for housing calves. It would ban "individual pens" in the EU for calves more than eight weeks old, from 1 January 1998 for new or renovated holdings, and all others within a further ten years. Based on the opinion of the Scientific Veterinary Committee, the measure puts forward minimum standards to ensure that calves have adequate room to move and lie down. The proposal represents a good balance between animal welfare objectives and profitable veal production, Commissioner Franz Fischler said. It will now go to the Council and European Parliament.

Source: European Commission Office, London

Figure 5.2 Sample EC press release

- Eurostat: the EU's statistical service whose publications are charged for. As statistics need to be as up-to-date as possible it is more likely that your designated county business library has the best collection. If looking for statistics across several Member States it would be much more effective to obtain them from Eurostat if possible since this will avoid problems of comparability. Eurostat publications include:
  - *Basic Statistics of the Community* (a portable collection of EU statistics)
  - *Europe in Figures* (fourth edition, 1995, a very readable summary and analysis)
  - *Portrait of the Regions* (three volumes, useful for regional comparisons)
  - *Eurostat Yearbook '95*: a statistical eye on Europe 1983–93.

The Official Journal

This is the official source of much EU information. It is not very readable, since it is a definitive source which could be used in a court of law as evidence to support the interpretation of European law. It is available in European Documentation Centres and many other specialist libraries.

The *Official Journal* (OJ) is published daily; the L (legal) series contains the official version of Community legislation while the C (communication) series contains draft legislation, official announcements, written questions to the European Parliament, formal judgments by the European Court and a variety of other documents including job vacancies in the Commission. The S (supplement) series contains invitations to tender for large and public sector contracts all over the EU.

COM documents are working documents including reports on the implementation of, and proposals for, policy. For example COM (92) 345 FINAL was a proposal to amend Directive 71/305/EEC (about the co-ordination of procedures for the award of public works contracts) and was published in the *Official Journal* (OJ C225 1.9.92 p.13).

The European Parliament (EP)

The EP has an office in London which publishes *EP News*, a readable monthly magazine summarising recent events in the European Parliament and often giving very useful background information on diverse topics including policy, finances and organisational developments. This is distributed free with the European newspaper.

The Department of Trade and Industry (DTI)

This is the UK Government department responsible, among other things, for ensuring that UK business is fully informed about the implications of the Single European Market. It publishes a great deal of well-presented information which is easy to understand and often free of charge. However this is a service to business and not to students.

!! Do not ask for material direct from the DTI. It should not be difficult to persuade your library to request it and the DTI usually responds very quickly.

The DTI's list of publications and services keeps changing as material is updated but currently the most useful are as follows (with a description of contents in brackets where this is not obvious from the title):
- *The Single Market – Progress on Commission White Paper* (UK legal changes)
- *European Economic Area*
- *Spearhead* (describes DTI database)
- *Guide to Public Purchasing*
- *Business in Europe* (DTI services to help exporters to the EU).
- *Trading Within Europe*
- *The Single Market – making it work for you.*

Source: DTI, Europe Division

Other UK Government departments

Other ministries publish material relevant to their areas, for example, the Ministry of Agriculture, Fisheries and Food (MAFF) publishes information on the Common Agricultural Policy and the Department of the Environment publish information on environmental standards. Customs and Excise, for example, publishes *VAT: The Single Market* – Notice 175 and *VAT: Place of supply of services* – Notice 741.

Local government

Your local council may have set up an information or advisory section to enable local businesses to make the best of opportunities with the rest of Europe. This is more likely with the larger county councils. There is no standard provision so facilities may differ considerably from area to area. At the minimum you can expect a collection of published information, possibly access to information databases and, if you are lucky, expert advice.

European Information Centres (EICs)

There are 22 of these in the UK. Again they are designed to support small businesses. These centres are usually very small and hard-pressed for staff but they do contain a great deal of published material on companies and markets in Europe. They are likely to have up-to-date copies of business directories, for example. You should be able to find the location of your nearest EIC in the telephone directory but note that they are often housed within the local Chamber of Commerce.

What sort of questions do small businesses ask EICs?
- Is prior authorisation needed to export food to Germany?
- Can the words 'Made in the European Union' be displayed on products made in the EU?
- If my company has its registered office in Belgium but with sales premises and business in the Netherlands then in which country should the company be taxed on income earned in the Netherlands?

European Documentation Centres (EDCs)

If you live close to a university you might try finding out whether it is a European Documentation Centre as this would mean that it holds copies of all EU legislation, consultation documents and reports from the European Commission, European Parliament and Economic and Social Committee.

Chambers of Commerce

In the UK these are private organisations but elsewhere in Europe Chambers of Commerce are legally required by law, hence their coverage in this section. In the UK, Chambers of Commerce vary greatly from small local organisations based on one small town area, acting largely as a social focus for local business, to large, well-known ones whose services extend to the supervision of vocational qualifications like the London Chamber of Commerce Office and Administrative exams.

The larger Chambers of Commerce will have well-stocked libraries geared specifically to business. Again, access to these will be restricted, largely to the paid-up members, but requests for specific information may be successful if done on behalf of the group and preferably with your tutor's help.

Other Member States will have a national Chamber of Commerce, usually located in London, and these may also be worth contacting.

Foreign embassies

It may seem a good idea to try and find out about business opportunities in Spain by writing to the Spanish embassy in London and you will find out more about the services foreign embassies offer to businesses in Chapter 6. However, a general point to be made here is that countries usually prefer to promote exports from their own countries rather than encourage imports. Therefore, it would be more effective to get in touch with the British embassy in the target country.

Sometimes, however, information is available from the Economic or Trade Ministry of the country in which you are interested. The Belgian Ministry of Economic Affairs publishes *Your Investment Guide to Belgium* which contains a great deal of background information in English. Similarly, the Danish Ministry of Foreign Affairs has published a booklet, *Investment in Denmark*, again in English, which tells you much about Danish business conditions. These types of publications are advertised in the business press.

!! Be careful in your use of all official literature since it tends to be very uncritical. The Belgian Ministry of Economic Affairs, for example, is unlikely to tell you about the disadvantages of locating in Belgium.

National tourist boards

These tend to have London offices and may be useful for background information particularly for cultural differences as their literature may describe important habits and customs which could have a business application or be useful if you are considering moving to another Member State to live and work.

Companies

Anyone can request the latest company report for any public limited company (plc) in the UK. Individuals do so if, for example, they are considering the purchase of shares. Simply express an interest in the company; there is no need to go into great detail about the project you are undertaking. The information that you get in return is very much a matter of luck. Some companies simply present the financial information required by law – not very helpful to you – whereas others may contain a detailed analysis of the current state of the market with information on market share, competitors and a great deal more. Most companies publish something midway between these two extremes.

Other information that you can extract from a company's report is the extent and nationality of subsidiaries. However, note that a large group company with many subsidiaries will only list a selection so look carefully to see whether you have a complete list. The report will show you the range of activities the company is involved in.

You can obtain reports from other Member States by looking for the club symbol (as in the card suit) in the *Financial Times* share information on the company as it may be possible to send for the report via the FT. To make it even easier, the FT runs a service each June when readers are invited to send for the annual reports of a great range of non-UK companies. These can, however, take several weeks to arrive.

!! Company literature, like official publications, is unlikely to be critical. For example, you will not find a company admitting that its European strategy was wrong.

It is much more difficult to obtain published information about smaller private companies. Contacts may be a more productive way of finding out about these.

Other sources of published information

Banks

Most of the major high street banks publish free relevant material. The examples below give you an idea of what is provided but this will vary. Do not forget the main banks of the other Member States, many of whom will have a London office which you can write to.
- Barclays Bank has published a series of booklets on each of the Member States containing advice on business practices and employment law.

- The NatWest publishes a monthly 'lonely hearts' *International Trade Bulletin* where exporters and importers from all over the world looking for business advertise their requirements.
- The French Banque National de Paris (BNP) publishes, in English, a regular economic newsletter covering the whole of the world but with a bias towards the EU.
- The Algemene Bank Nederland (ABN), a Dutch bank, has published *The Netherlands, Country Report*, a 72-page booklet giving a great deal of useful information on the Netherlands.

Accountants and management consultants

The larger accountants and management consultants publish free information in the same way as the banks. These booklets may be advertised in the business press. Some examples (all English language) are given below for Denmark; most of these organisations will have a London office:

- HLB International – *Doing Business in Denmark* as well as a range covering other Member States;
- Price Waterhouse – *Setting up in Denmark – Cost Levels*;
- Coopers and Lybrand – *Foreign Nationals Working in Denmark – Tax and other Matters* (other countries are also covered).

Marketing organisations

Euromonitor is the main organisation to mention as it publishes an annual report of statistics (*European Marketing Data and Statistics*) which shows consumption and spending levels for many different types of products over the wider Europe (ie including non-EU countries). At the start of the report there is often an assessment of general market trends both in the immediate past and the short-term future.

The Economist Intelligence Unit (connected to *The Economist* magazine) publish reports on selected markets across Europe and for selected European countries.

Electronic sources

Software

The CD-ROM *Europe in the Round* (published by Vocational Technologies Ltd) gives background statistical information which you may find useful. You may also have access to Pharos, from the NatWest bank to find out the effect of EU law on a specific company.

Databases

European Information Centres may have the DTI's Spearhead database to find out which public sector contracts are available for tender to EU companies.

The EU itself also has much of its information on database including statistics, law, *Tenders Electronic Daily* (which advertises large public sector contracts) and *Info 92* (which covers the state of the implementation of the Single Market). Many of these databases are available on CD-ROM and increasingly also through the Internet (see below).

CORDIS is a centralised information service (nine databases in all) on all EU research and technological development activities. It can also provide services needed to help participants in EU research from finding partners, to successful project submission and market innovation. An organisation may be interested in applying the results of previous research or may be seeking EU financial support for its own planned research programme.

Electronic mail

If your college is set up for this you may be able to obtain information from fellow students or other organisations across Europe very quickly and cheaply. It is even possible to arrange an electronic conference whereby you could be in contact with several different countries at once to discuss a particular topic. This may be useful for finding out about cultural differences and consumer preferences. Although English is the most widely-used language of business in Europe, you might consider communicating in your fellow student's language.

ECHO

Hosts in electronic systems are gateways through which you can have access to various databases. The European Commission Host Organisation (ECHO) is a non-commercial host offering free of charge access to more than 20 on-line databases published by the EU in all community languages. Note 'echo' in one of the Internet addresses below.

The Internet

The Internet facilitates access to information from all over the world through your computer linked via the telecommunications system with a modem to other computers. To use the Internet you need the 'addresses' of the areas you are interested in and a few are given below. Otherwise, without the equivalent of a telephone directory to the Internet, you must use a browsing system into which you insert key words relating to the topic in which you are interested. 'Europe' plus the topic you are searching for is likely to yield the most useful addresses. For example, you could try:

- Europe, transport;
- Europe, law;
- Europe, technical standards.

If you are interested in a specific Member State then you should use its name as one of the key words. Since the Internet changes and grows all the time, it is worth browsing now and then to see what is new. Once you have accessed a relevant page, you will often find that this links you to other useful locations which it will then be easy for you to access.

It is quicker (and cheaper!) to use known addresses than to roam the Internet at random.

Some relevant Internet locations

Provided by the EU
EUROPA   http://www.cec.lu:8080/en/comm/opoce/wel.html
EUROPA is the main EU gateway for official EU information. Some specific locations include:

Telematics	http://www.echo.lu
Information Society	
Project Office (ISPO)	http://www.ispo.cec.be

The ISPO webserver contains more than 200 documents and allows you to follow a logical train of thought through them by providing over 1000 internal and external links.

Documents include general, short explanations of what the Information Society is about, tables showing the current status of the Information Society, green papers and legislative texts.

CORDIS
http://www.cordis.lu/
Documents available through this service include calls for proposals, work programmes, information packages and related programme information. Organisations can submit expressions of interest electronically through the CORDIS World Wide Web service.

ESPRIT programme
http://www.cordis.lu/home.html
The ESPRIT homepage has been designed to provide the user with a comprehensive overview of the programme, as well as guided access to information on programme implementation, including the following:
- call for proposals;
- general information about the ESPRIT programme;
- contact points for the ESPRIT information desk and within the Member States.

Information Market Europe (I-M Europe)
http://www.echo.lu/home.html
This service is to update users on the implementation of the Single Market.

General information
http://nearnet.gnn.com/gnn/wic/govt.toc.html#polact

Provided by others
http://www.helsinki.fi/~aunesluo/eueng.html
This covers a wide range of general information about the EU compiled by a worker at Helsinki University.

http://www.belgium-emb.org/usa/
This is a page compiled by the Belgian embassy in America with information for travellers and business people.

http://www.csc.fi/tiko/finland.html
This is Finland's home page; other countries provide similar information.

Business directories

These are lists of businesses ordered by geographical area and type of business. They are compiled for the benefit of other businesses which may need to find out, for example, from whom they might obtain stationery supplies.

!! Generally, every organisation listed in a directory pays for an entry or advertisement and so you should not rely on them as complete lists. However, when you know nothing about an area, it can help to see what types of businesses advertise to get an idea of the industrial structure.

The most well-known business directory is the *Yellow Pages*. Most European countries have a similar system and some even call them 'the Yellow Pages'. However, these do not tell you much about the businesses. For more information you should consult the Kompass directory for the country in which you are interested. Each directory is written in the language of the country to which it refers but a standard system of symbols means that you should be able to read off the entries quite easily once you have looked them up in the UK Kompass. These directories will only be found in main and business libraries.

Each Kompass directory has two volumes. Volume 1 lists companies according to the products with which they deal. The yellow pages at the front help you to find the reference number by which Kompass refers to the product you are interested in. By looking up the relevant number you will find a list of companies involved with that product, set out in tabular form. The symbols used are shown in Figure 5.3.

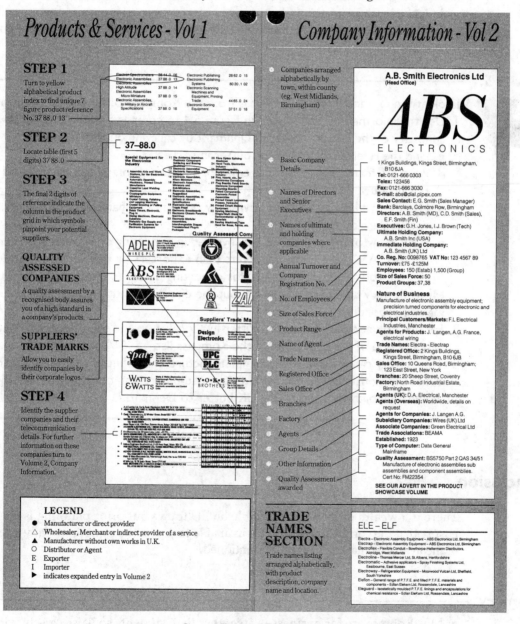

Source: *Kompass UK Products and Services 1993/94*, Reed Information Services Ltd

Figure 5.3 Kompass standard numbering system and symbols explained

Volume 2 contains details of the companies involved in the production of the goods you may have looked up in Volume 1.

Other media

It may be worth browsing through your college's video collection. The BBC have produced a number of series to explain the European Single Market and how it will affect businesses and individuals.

European matters will also be covered occasionally in business programmes both on Radio 4 and on television. On radio listen to 'Analysis', 'File on 4' and 'Business Matters'. On television keep an eye on 'The Money Programme', 'Business Breakfast' and 'Business Club' (in scrambled form).

The EU has over 240 videos available for purchase or loan and it may be that your college or local library has some of these.

Activity 5.1

Look at the extract in Figure 5.4 – it is from the Kompass Directory for Denmark.

1 Use the information reproduced in Figure 5.4 to compile a short, one-paragraph summary of the butter market in Denmark by carrying out the following:
- Find the reference number for butter in packets.
- Read off, from the appropriate column, how many companies are involved with this product.
- Use the symbols to find out how many of these companies are producers, wholesalers or agents.
- How many of the companies are involved in exporting or importing butter in packets? Are there more importers than exporters or vice versa? What does this tell you about the potential for exporting butter to Denmark?

   Hint: be very careful to be clear about the direction of trade described as exporting and importing.

2 Have a look at a pack of *Lurpak* butter in a local shop and see if you can identify the name of one of the companies in the Kompass list.

3 This activity cannot give you a complete picture of the butter market in Denmark. What additional information would you need before you could decide whether it would be worthwhile exporting UK butter to Denmark?

Conclusion

There is a wealth of material available on EU topics but prior planning is needed to ensure that the correct information is available to you at the right time. Only a selection of the available material has been mentioned.

Summary

- Most sources are for business users rather than students so liaise closely with your tutor in your use of these.
- Major information sources have been listed.

20-100

Dairy products, eggs

Code	Product
01	Cream and Milk, deep-frozen
02	Cream, not specialy treated
03	Milk, not specially treated
04	Milk, homogenized and sterilized, canned
05	Cream, homogenized and sterilized, canned
06	Milk, condensed, sweetened, canned
07	Milk, condensed, sweetened, canned
08	Milk, condensed, not canned
09	Skim milk powder
10	Milk powder
11	Cream powder
12	Butter in Bulk
13	Butter in packets
14	Tinned butter
15	Cheese, hard paste
16	Soft cheese, Danish blue cheese
17	Other soft cheese
18	Cream cheese, processed cheese
19	Cheese powder
20	Fresh hen's eggs

← **Read off product code here**

to know which column to read here

Fed skrift = Yderligere produktinformation i bind 2   E = Eksport   I = Import
Bold face = Further product information in volume 2   E = Export   I = Import

20-100

Company	Location	E	I	X	1	2	3	4	5	6	7	8	9	10	11	12	13	14	15	16	17	18	19	20
Andelssmør Am.b.A.*Postboks 2470* Tel 86287099	8260 Viby J	E		4													△	△						
Arctic Import*Postboks 143* Tel 98171422	9400 Nørresundby	E		2 0											○				○	○	○	○		○
BFJ/Food/A/S*Rosenkœret 11C* Tel 31565644	2860 København-Søborg	E		1												△	△							△
Bornholms Andelsmejeri* Tel 56966200	3782 Klemensker			4		●											●		●	●	●	●		
Dagrofa a/s* Gammelager 13* Tel 42451414	2605 Brøndby			6	△	△	△	△	△	△	△	△	△	△	△	△	△	△	△	△	△	△	△	△
Danish Crest Food A/S* Valbygaardsvej 62 B* Tel 36440700	2500 København Valby	E		1													▲	▲	▲	▲	▲	▲	▲	
Danish Dairy Farms K/S Postboks 414* Tel 39930293	1504 København V	E		3	●	●	●	●	●	●	●						●	●	●	●	●	●	●	
Edeka Danmark A/S* Mars Allé 32* Tel 79272727	8700 Horsens	E		3	△	△	△					△	△	△					△	△	△	△		△
Emborg Foods*Postboks 75* Tel 98131233	9100 Aalborg		I	5	●	●	●												△					△
Enigheden Produktion A/S* Lygten 39-41* Tel 31817001	2400 København NV	E		4					▲			▲	▲	▲		▲	▲		▲	▲	▲	▲		
Goodfood Export Denmark A/S*Postboks 433* Tel 98163377	9100 Aalborg	E		1												△	△		△		△			
Hansen A/S.J.*Postboks 127* Tel 86121022	8100 Arhus C	E	I	2	△	△	△	△	△	△	△	△	△	△	△				△	△	△	△		
Hedegaard & Christensens Eftf. A/S*Postboks 70* Tel 98171755	9400 Nørresundby	E		5		△						△	△	△					△	△	△	△		△
Hoffmann Denmark A/S* Postboks 33* Tel 98139266	9100 Aalborg	E		1												△	△		△		△	△		
K.K. Specialiteter I/S* Industrivej 8* Tel 97920788	7700 Thisted	E		3								△				△	△		△	△				
Kløver Mœelk A.m.b.a.* Postboks 66* Tel 75924988	7000 Fredericia	E		8								●	●			●	●	●	●	●		●	●	
Kraft General Foods A/S* Smedeland 36* Tel 43969622	2600 Glostrup	E	I	5							△								△	△	△	△		
MD Foods amba* Postboks 2400* Tel 86281000	8260 Viby J	E		8	●	●		●				●	●			●	●		●	●	●	●	●	●
Mejerigaarden A/S*Sennelsvej 1* Tel 97923500	7700 Thisted	E		5	●	●	●					●	●			●	●		△	△	△	●		
Milco International amba* Christian IX's Gade 1* Tel 33113702	1111 København K	E		3	●	●						●	●	●										
Møller & Melgaard AS* Halmtorvet 15* Tel 31313636	1700 København V			4												△			△		△			
N.A.F. International*Vester Farimagsgade 1* Tel 33151533	1606 København V	E	I	4				○	○	○			○	○		○	○	○		○	○	○		
Nordex Food A/S* Blytoekkervej 6* Tel 98843400	9330 Dronninglund	E		2					△							●	●		△	△	△	△		
Nowaco International A/S* Postboks 40* Tel 98134133	9100 Aalborg	E		3	△	△	△	△				△	△	△	△				△	△	△			
PiR Trading ApS*Restrup Kœrvej 35, St. Restrup* Tel 99834111	9240 Nibe	E	I	1				△	△								△		△	△	△	△	△	
Randers & Viborg Mejeriselskab* Mariagervej 49* Tel 86411111	8900 Randers	E		5	●	●	●	●	●							●	●		●					
Scandinavian Meat Company A/S* Postboks 9* Tel 53633435	4180 Sorø	E		1											○	○			○	○	○	○		○
Uhrenholt A/S.F.* Odensevej 11* Tel 64414041	5500 Middelfart	E	I	4	△		△	△	△	△	△	△	△	△	△	△	△		△	△	△	△	△	△
Wrist & Co. LTD. A/S. Over*Postboks 515* Tel 98137277	9100 Aalborg			4	△				△		△	△					△	△	△	△	△	△	△	△
Aalborg Skibshandel A/S* Postboks 8010* Tel 98152411	9220 Aalborg Øst		I		△				△		△	△					△	△	△	△	△	△	△	△

Source: *Kompass Denmark*, Volume I, A/S Forlaget Kompass Danmark, Denmark

Figure 5.4 Extract from Kompass, Volume I, for Denmark showing information on dairy products and eggs

Information sources

Advice on this is contained within the chapter.

Useful addresses

- Commission of the European Communities Information Office, Jean Monnet House, 8 Storey's Gate, London SW1P 3AT.
- Europe 2000, 7a Westminster Street, Yeovil, Somerset, BA20 1AF. This is an information subscription service specially tailored for teachers and students covering all aspects of Europe.

Assignment 5.1
Setting up an information bank within a fixed budget

This assignment fulfils the following criteria:

RSA 13.2.2
City & Guilds 9.2.1, 9.2.3

You work in the export section of a stationery company and have just received the following memo.

> ### Memorandum
>
> ```
> From: Marketing Director
> To:   Export section
> ```
> With substantial sales in Italy and the prospect of setting up a joint venture with a Dutch company, we must ensure that our access to relevant information is set up on a more systematic footing than hitherto.
>
> Would you draw up an annotated list of the sources you think we should have to hand within the company and of those which are easily available locally. Initially, we can allocate a budget of £500 to setting up this information bank.
>
> Assume that we will need information on the following:
> (a) EU legislation, especially relating to technical standards;
> (b) public sector contracts and how to go about being considered for them;
> (c) stationery markets in the Netherlands and Italy.
>
> ### Have I missed anything out?
>
> Please also highlight any likely problems with the information sources you recommend.

Your task

Act on this memo by assessing as many of the sources listed in this chapter as you think are relevant, as well as any others to which you may have ready access. Your recommendations should be costed to come within the specified budget.

6 Supporting services

Use this chapter to find out:

- why support services are offered by various agencies;
- the type of services needed by exporters;
- who offers support services;
- details of case studies regarding services offered;
- how trade fairs and missions can help an exporter.

This chapter covers the following performance criteria:
RSA   13.2.2
City & Guilds   9.2.1, 9.2.2, 9.2.3

Introduction

When a company decides to extend its market to other Member States it can involve a whole range of support agencies. These will be of two types:
- essential commercial services (e.g. foreign currency transactions from its bank and legal services in drawing up an agency agreement);
- advisory and information services mainly from the public sector (e.g. the DTI and local TECs) or from private non-profit making bodies (e.g. Chambers of Commerce or trade associations).

Fees for commercial services are at full cost whereas the advisory services are often offered at subsidised prices; the latter may be free, especially for small and inexperienced exporters.

Research suggests companies often start exporting as a result of an unsolicited order. Staff, therefore, usually have little experience and need outside help, especially in small companies. Large companies tend to use commercial services whilst smaller ones rely more on subsidised public sector services.

Activity 6.1

1 Consider a business plan which you have helped to produce or a local company with which you are familiar whose product or service could be exported and discuss the following:
  a What issues would you need to consider to incorporate exporting in an updated business plan? (Hint: consider the market, finance, distribution and promotion, etc.)
  b How would you obtain the information you need to finalise your plans?
  c What would be the cost of obtaining the above information?

2 Use the results of this activity to compile a 'shopping list' of the type of help which you would need as a first time exporter.

Who helps exporters and why?

Advisory export services are offered to UK businesses mainly by:
- European Union (EU) agencies;
- Central and Local Government;
- British and foreign embassies;
- Chambers of Commerce and other trade organisations;
- industry and employer organisations;
- private financial institutions such as the high street banks.

EU agencies

The EU has a vested interest in ensuring that the Single Market it has promoted works as well as possible.

Central government

In Mandatory Unit 1 you learned about the importance of the balance of payments and the weakness of the UK in that area. In the UK, there is a tendency for imports to out-weigh exports, where ideally the two should balance. In an open economy, such as the UK's, it is difficult to reduce imports so it is just as important to encourage exports. Incidentally, this means that businesses can expect little help on the importing side.

Local government

If local businesses thrive, more people with good incomes contribute their council tax to pay for local services. Aid to exporters may help to smooth out variations in the local market.

British and foreign embassies

The foreign embassies help UK companies to import products into the UK for the same reasons that the British embassies and the UK Government will help UK exporters.

Chambers of Commerce and other trade organisations

The Edinburgh Chamber of Commerce states its objectives as follows:
'To provide members with the best available advice and service, be the leading voice of business in Edinburgh and the Lothians and play a leading role in creating a busi-ness, economic and cohesive environment in the City and Region, on which members can prosper and compete effectively in world markets.'
This effectively sums up the reasons why the chambers of commerce offer help to exporters. Other trade organisations are also keen to see their members prosper and compete effectively abroad but the services they offer their members varies considerably depending on size and the industry concerned.

Industry and employer organisations

These organisations (e.g. the Institute of Directors and the Confederation of British

Industry) realise that by encouraging the export drive of their members greater UK employment and prosperity will result. They are also keen to see that members are aware of overseas opportunities.

Finance companies

If business customers diversify into foreign markets, this spreads the risk over several markets lessening the effect of domestic market decline. There is also the lure of much greater demand for financial services if business customers move into the more complicated foreign markets.

When is help needed?

Figure 6.1 shows the type of help needed at different stages of a business's plan to export.

Stage	Need	Facility/scheme	Source
1. Preparation for export	Market research	▶ Export Marketing Research Scheme ▶ Export Data Services ▶ Market Information Enquiry Service ▶ Country Desks (all EU members)	DTI
	Assessment of whether company is capable of exporting, e.g. is production capacity or cashflow sufficient?	▶ Free Business Review Subsidised consultancy 5–15 days if <500 employees ▶ Export Development Advisors ▶ Cash flow advice	DTI Chambers of Commerce Banks
	Information about licences, regulations and standards, plus EU legislation	▶ Technical Help to Exporters ▶ Information	DTI Chamber of Commerce Industry organisations
2. Finding and serving customers	Finding customers directly a. Public relations b. Meeting potential customers	▶ New Products From Britain ▶ Inward Trade Missions ▶ Outward Trade Missions ▶ Trade Fairs (financial help, free advice) ▶ Shop window for UK products ▶ Seminar support	DTI and British Embassies DTI TECs Employer/ Industry organisations Chambers of Commerce, Banks
	Finding an agent	▶ Export Representative Service ▶ Overseas Status Report Service	DTI and British Embassies
	Teaming up with local companies in a target market	▶ European Economic Interest Groupings ▶ Exporter/importer matching	EU e.g. NatWest and London Chamber of Commerce
	Translation	▶ Finding a translator	Chambers of Commerce
	Organising direct mail operation	▶ Help and advice with selling by direct mail methods	Royal Mail International
3. Administration and finance	Credit insurance	▶ Insurance against not getting paid	Export Credit Guarantee Department
	Transport	▶ Delivery and clearance through customs	Freight forwarders
	Financial services	▶ Currency transactions/transfers	Banks
	Meeting different VAT rules for EU transactions	▶ Information and advice	Customs and Excise
	Documentation	▶ Ensuring goods do not get held up at borders because of incorrectly filled in forms ▶ Free telephone advice	Simplification of Trade Procedures Board (SITPRO) DTI

Figure 6.1 Support offered at different stages of the exporting strategy

Who offers what?

The European Union

The whole Single Market programme is meant to encourage trade across frontiers within the EU but there are also more specific ways in which the EU tries to help businesses.

BC-NET (Business Co-operation Network) and BRE (Business Co-operation Centres)

These are computerised networks acting as a 'dating agency' bringing small and medium-sized businesses together from across the EU. A company can register its requirements or check details of featured companies for a fee. BC-NET covers sales outlets, suppliers and companies seeking technological partners and should be available through most chambers of commerce.

Case study

BC-NET in action

The French company Meridionale des Plastiques wanted an Italian partner in the production of irrigation systems. Its details ran in the BC-NET and a month later it met Berselli, an Italian company. Each company presented its products, compared aims and came to an agreement. Three months later they signed an international dealership contract.

European Information Centres (EICs)

The EU has set up a network of these local centres again targeted at small and medium-sized companies. Their activities are described in Chapter 5.

Europartenariat

These meetings are organised twice a year all over the EU and further afield to provide an opportunity for small companies to meet and develop business in the EU's less developed regions. Meeting were held in June 1993 (Lille, France), in December 1993 (Glasgow, UK) and June 1994 (Gdansk, Poland). Such meetings provide opportunities even for companies not in the designated areas.

Case study

Taking advantage of Europartenariat

For the Glasgow Europartenariat, 11 companies travelled up from Gloucestershire. One of them, AST, refurbishes tanks, aircraft and other equipment using special machinery. As a result of the meeting, the company obtained contracts in Lithuania and Egypt, found a distributor in Denmark and got involved in a technology transfer deal with a company in Scotland. Its representative Graham Dawson said 'The only way that you could have done the amount of business that our company did in two days would have been if we had visited each country in turn, which would have taken us five years.'

European Economic Interest Groupings (EEIGs)

This is not a scheme but an opportunity created by European law for small and medium-sized companies (defined as employing less than 500) to form a joint venture to undertake a specific non-profit making project which is distinct from their core businesses.

Thus a UK company may join with a Dutch company to collaborate in research, or a German company might join with an Italian company to set up a joint marketing operation for their products across Europe.

Activity 6.2

1 Find local case studies of companies which have used the above EU services. You could do this by consulting the local newspaper or contacting the European Information Centre, Chamber of Commerce, TEC or Export Club direct.
2 Do local businesses think these services are worthwhile?

UK Central Government

Since 1991, the work of the Department of Trade and Industry (DTI), the Foreign and Commonwealth Office (which is responsible for British embassies world-wide) and the relevant sections of the Welsh, Scottish and Northern Ireland Offices, has been co-ordinated under the title of Overseas Trade Services. The most visible of these is the DTI and its services are described below.

Main Department of Trade and Industry (DTI) services

The DTI's Enterprise Initiative offers a free business review to companies advising on a strategy for export. If the company employs fewer than 500 people, the DTI may award up to 50 per cent of the cost of devising an export marketing strategy taking five to 15 days to complete.

Export Data Services has an Export Market Information Centre (EMIC) in London giving access to a range of overseas economic statistics, trade and telephone directories, market reports and commercial databases. It operates a matching service linking overseas demands to potential sellers in the UK. In addition, the EMIC publishes four series of booklets:

- Hints to Exporters (in specific countries), £6 each;
- Setting up in Business in … , from £30 each;
- Country Profiles, £15 each;
- Sector Reports (for specific industries), from £30 each.

The Business in Europe Branch serves businesses wanting help specifically on the Single Market and selling to the European Free Trade Association (EFTA) and the European Economic Area (EEA). It services include:

- Country Desks – offering the most help through the nine desks which exporters can ring for advice on markets, national regulations (some still exist) and trading practices;
- Task Forces – these expert groups identify markets representing opportunities for UK businesses, inform relevant companies and help them to supply these markets. Previous task forces have helped UK companies market software to the Netherlands, giftware in Italy and career and workwear in France.

Other DTI services

Trade fairs

These are one to five day events usually dedicated to one product area such as computer software, environmental technology, toys or food. Companies attend either as exhibitors, hoping to generate interest and orders, or as visitors to assess the competition or arrange purchases. Well-established fairs (e.g. the Nuremburg Toy Fair) charge high fees to exhibitors since the presence of many, high-volume buyers from all over the world is guaranteed whereas a new trade fair with a short or no trading history will be cheaper to attend.

The DTI publicises forthcoming trade fairs and gives financial assistance to potential exhibitors as well as advice on making the most of the events.

Inward missions
Groups of influential buyers are invited to the UK to learn more about the UK companies which would be of interest to them as future suppliers. The DTI will support the cost of these missions if they are sponsored by a trade association or other approved non-profit making body, such as a chamber of commerce.

Seminar support
The DTI supports trade associations or other approved bodies in organising overseas presentations about UK products by giving up to 45 per cent of the costs and its advice. These events are suitable for more technical products.

Store promotions
Financial support to large shops overseas enables them to hold promotional events highlighting UK goods. The shop must make additional purchases of at least £75,000 worth of stock to qualify for support. This is obviously suitable for consumer goods.

British Embassies (Commercial Sections)
The Market Information Enquiry Service
This helps a company establish the potential for specific products or services, how to sell in that market and who to approach. Costs range between £30 and £350.

The Export Representative Service (ERS) and Overseas Status Report Service (OSRS)
The ERS helps companies wishing to find an overseas representative, such as an agent or distributor, for their products or services. Costs range from £355 to £1065.

UK companies with a potential overseas representative already in mind for their products or services can use OSRS to assess the suitability of that person or organisation, although financial stability is not assessed. Costs range from £70 to £355.

The New Products from Britain Service
This helps exporters to promote interesting UK products, processes and services which are new to specific foreign markets by providing a professionally written article which will be of interest to the media in those countries. The job of disseminating the article is undertaken by the relevant British embassy. The service includes translation into the relevant language. Costs are £60 for the first market and £30 for every additional one. Figure 6.2 shows an article that was disseminated by the embassy in Denmark.

A major objective of embassies all over the world is to encourage trade with the companies they represent. Day-to-day work involves assembling market information and arranging contacts between potential business partners but occasionally special events are arranged, as the following case study shows.

NEW PRODUCTS FROM BRITAIN

Grips Prevent Castor Marks on Carpets and Floors

Protective devices developed by a British company prevent damage or marking to carpets or floor surfaces, yet allow furniture to be re-sited easily.

Castor Grips snap-on shoes, from Castor Grip, accommodate both ball and wheeled castors to protect carpeted floors and hard surfaces, while permitting furniture to be retained firmly in position or moved freely when required.

The snap-on shoes remain on the ball or wheeled castors at all times. Plastic spikes on the underside of the *Castor Grips* for carpeted floors prevent the furniture moving and causing damage to wall decor by collision. The Grips are said to be popular with the elderly or the not-so-agile who have difficulty getting in and out of a chair without it shooting backwards at the wrong moment.

Source: British Embassy, Copenhagen

Figure 6.2 New products from Britain

Case study

The British Home for Europe

The British Embassy in Belgium organised a novel way of demonstrating UK products by inviting the house building company Custom Homes International to design one of its houses, together with a garden. This was then built in a popular suburb of Antwerp and was decorated and furnished entirely with UK products. The house was open for two months to the press, trade and public and then the major sponsors were each allocated a day when they could use it as they wished for promotional purposes. This project was advertised in Belgium, the Netherlands, France and Germany.

The Simplification of Trade Procedures (SITPRO) Board

Although trade within the EU requires much less paperwork than trade with the rest of the world, there is still a need to complete the required documents accurately to avoid delays. SITPRO has devised standard forms and software for use across the world and is pioneering electronic data interchange (EDI) allowing trade documents to be transmitted electronically by computer, company to company, instead of on paper.

Industry and employer organisations

Industry and trade organisations thrive on the success of their members and will, therefore, help them to export. Organisations such as the Confederation of British Industry (CBI) and the Institute of Directors (IoD) are umbrella organisations representing the majority of UK business employers but also offer services related to international trade.

Two examples of trade organisations are given below.

Examples

The Glass and Glazing Federation (GGF) represents the glass and glazing industry. It keeps an eye on the progress of relevant directives, such as the Distance Selling Directive, which have implications for double glazing sales techniques. The GGF keeps up-to-date with new standards and passes on this information to its members. It also tries to influence the final standards agreed by having representatives on the relevant European committees. Back in the UK the GGF organises information seminars for members on the developments and effects of the new standards on the industry.

'Food from Britain' is a jointly funded UK Government and industry body which aims to help the UK food and drink industry reduce this sector's trade gap of £5.5 billion by promoting better marketing of UK food at home and abroad. It offers consultancy and trade introduction services to exporters and organises UK food promotions in the retail and catering sectors.

Activity 6.3

Find out if there is a relevant trade organisation for the industry in which you are interested by scanning trade magazines or consulting the DTI's guide to sources of business information.

Other service providers

Many other businesses involved in providing services to exporters and importers can offer advice as well as basic services.

Example

Royal Mail International (RMI) is trying to boost its business by encouraging the growth of trans-border direct mailing. For certain products and services this is a serious alternative selling method to the more traditional appointment of an agent or selling direct through an established chain store. RMI has published a booklet on international direct mailing, *Marketing Without Frontiers*, together with its International Business Guide which has a great deal of information on business etiquette and cultural differences. Both these publications are free of charge to businesses.

RMI's International Direct Marketing Unit helps businesses find the right mailing lists and assists with direct mailing campaigns. Specifically, RMI will assist inexperienced small businesses.

Local services

Business Link

Local public sector and voluntary advisory services to business are being brought together under the heading of Business Link to reduce the number of contacts needed to obtain help. These include TECs, Chambers of Commerce, local DTI offices and other enterprise agencies.

Training and Enterprise Councils (TECs)

The network of TECs (Local Enterprise Companies (LECs) in Scotland) ensures that relevant employment training is provided within their areas. This should include courses for businesses wanting to take advantage of the Single Market.

Case study

Gloucestershire TEC

As part of its services to small companies, Gloucestershire TEC offers what it calls its Eurotrade Service which:

'co-ordinates regular marketing tours which travel to different European countries showcasing local products and services and establishing the local demands. In addition, the Eurotrade Service can advise on and oversee specific sales visits to Europe, providing support and guidance to secure profitable new trading relationships between your company and new European clients' (see figure 6.3).

Local Firms Unique Mobile Exhibition

Local businesses gathered together at Gloucestershire Training and Enterprise Council (TEC) recently to find out how their companies performed during a mobile exhibition in Holland.

The Business Link Caravan, sponsored by the Gloucestershire TEC, the Gloucestershire County Council and 12 companies toured the area around Rotterdam for five days, introducing the products of companies. Over 95 sales leads were generated during the trip.

Anthony Lunch, managing director of Business Link, said: 'Gloucestershire TEC is unique in running a number of highly successful visits to Europe for local businesses. This visit proved ideal for the inexperienced exporter and has given many businesses a foothold in Europe.'

Companies such as BSJ Systems Ltd, Calidair Manufacturing Ltd, Cannop Foundry, Cirencester Plastics, Duraflex BG Wendland Ltd, John Milman Ltd, Paterson Ltd, Phoenix Walking Stick

Company, Plastex International Ltd, R. J. Horlick and Redler Ltd all benefitted from the enquiries in Holland and will be following them up to turn them into sales. Doug Garland, enterprise manager at Gloucester TEC, said, 'We are delighted with the trip's success and will certainly try and help companies follow up these leads.

Source: Gloucestershire TEC

Figure 6.3 Publicity for a Gloucestershire TEC sponsored tour to Holland

Chambers of commerce

These vary in size and scope. Obviously, larger ones offer more comprehensive services to their members. These may include legal advice, market information and help with translation. Chambers may organise special events, such as outward missions which are trips to specific markets, for their member companies. These are similar to the Dutch trip organised by Gloucestershire TEC described in Figure 6.3.

Many services are offered in partnership with other agencies. For example, the Active Exporting Scheme (devised by the DTI) subsidises a Chamber to employ an Export Development Adviser to hunt out small and medium-sized companies in the local area that are currently not exporting or exporting only very little but which have the potential to do more overseas businesses. These companies are then helped to expand their exports. A Chamber will also work closely with its local TEC, the local authority and the local European Information Centre, often to mount joint events.

Example

Birmingham Chamber of Commerce's services include:
- monitoring new UK legislation implementing EU legislation to ensure its effects on local businesses are not harmful. (It lobbies both the UK Government and Brussels if it thinks changes are needed.)
- offering training courses, including many on aspects of trading with Europe;
- carrying out market research for members wishing to enter or expand EU markets, identifying competitors, customers and suppliers;
- researching more complicated Single Market issues, such as legal aspects, with the help of five computerised databases accessed directly from Brussels;
- offering a translation service – demand for this has grown rapidly;
- valuable links with chambers in other Member States;
- organising trade missions and exploratory business visits to help companies new to exporting;
- acting as an intermediary for the BC-NET computerised business matching service;
- publishing guides to what is going on in specific industries including construction, hospitality and tourism, printing, clothing, electrical engineering and electronics. (These give information on compliance with EU legislation as well as advice on how to meet the increased competition in a particular industry.)

National chamber organisations also exist such as the Association of British Chambers of Commerce which publishes the weekly magazine *Business Briefing* (replacing one formerly published by the DTI) and chambers promoting trade between specific countries such as the Netherlands-British Chamber of Commerce (NBCC). The NBCC provides a comprehensive enquiry service for UK exporters, produces market reports and organises seminars.

Export Clubs

These are informal meetings between people with responsibility for exports to encourage and assist the Club's members by sharing experiences. There are over 70 Export Clubs within the UK. These may be organised by the local Member of European Parliament (MEP) who may also lead trade missions.

High street banks

Most businesses starting to trade abroad will need to liaise with their bank if only to arrange for the receipt of money in other currencies. Banks offer a range of additional services such as arranging payment and factoring (collecting your debts). Many also offer market information services and publish newsletters and magazines on topics of interest to their exporting and importing clients.

Attending trade fairs and missions

Exhibitors attending trade fairs will demonstrate their products to the fair's visitors. Therefore, they need to have an eye-catching stand using posters, models, video film of the product in action and other point-of-sale material. The best trade fairs are those attracting major visitors – those with large budgets to spend. This means as few members of the general public as possible are allowed to attend, so often students are excluded.

A company exhibits in order to:

- make sales (to existing and new customers, agents, distributors or wholesalers);
- make new contacts with potential buyers;
- gauge reaction to new products;
- obtain feedback on existing products (basic market research);
- find out what competitors are offering.

A company will visit a trade fair in order to:

- make purchases;
- find out what is new on the market;
- make contacts with potential suppliers.

Attendance at a trade fair costs money, especially to one outside the UK. Companies need a clear set of objectives against which to measure the value of attendance. An exhibitor could put this in terms of sales targets and number of leads generated.

Since the number of trade fairs relevant to a company's products keeps increasing it must choose which are the best ones to attend. If a company is interested in making overseas contacts then the number of expected foreign visitors will be important. A good sign is if the leading companies in an industry are also booked to exhibit at the trade fair under consideration.

Some major trade fairs are shown in Figure 6.4.

Activity 6.5

Consult a relevant trade magazine around the time of a related trade fair (e.g. *The Grocer* for news of a food fair). What new products and services caught the attention of the press?

Outward trade missions are sometimes organised around a trade fair with the organisers setting up meetings with exhibitors for the mission's participants. Being part of a trade mission enables all participants to gain from the experience of the rest of the group and the organisers may even help out with negotiations with foreign buyers. For a company, therefore, this is often a more effective method than making a solo visit to a foreign market.

Month	Place	Name of fair	Theme
January	Stockholm	Afftiviaden	Sports equipment
January	Dublin	Showcase	Jewellery and giftware
January	Berlin	Fruit Logistica	Fruit and vegetables
January	Rimini	Sigep	Ice cream
January	Paris	Mode Enfantine	Children's wear
February	Nuremburg	Toy Fair	Toys and games
February	Dusseldorf	Euroshop	Display and shop equipment
February	Atlanta	Supershow	Sports equipment
February	Boston	Networks Expo	Computers, office machinery and telecoms
February	Milan	In Cosmetics	Cosmetics
April	Helsinki	Finnbuild	Building/ construction equipment and services
May	Berlin	ILA	Aircraft and aerospace
May	Santiago	Chile	Mining
May	Milan	Grafitalia	Books and publishing
May	Nice	Super Yacht	Ships and boats
October	Lyon	Pollutec	Water and air treatment
November	Munich	Electronica	Electrical/ electronic engineering
November	Brisbane	Interbuild	Building/ construction equipment and services

Source: The *Financial Times*

Figure 6.4 Selection of international trade fairs, 1996

Activity 6.6

Try to attend a local trade fair in order to find out how businesses use these events. Note the ways in which the different exhibitors try to attract attention. Which are the best positions in the exhibition area? How have the exhibition organisers tried to collect information on the number and type of visitors? Can you see any evidence of the methods used by individual exhibitors to keep track of the visitors to their stands? What additional facilities would the trade fair organisers and individual exhibitors have to offer for foreign visitors?

Conclusion: How helpful are these services?

At the level of the individual business, the value of the services described in this chapter could be assessed by comparing their costs against the expected profit to be gained from the exporting (or importing) activity. However, since establishing abroad takes a while, it is better to compare costs against export profits over the next five years. The costs of these services should also be balanced against expected profits if no exporting is done. Since the Single European Market enables other EU competitors easier access to the UK market, it could be that a business which does not export will find its domestic market shrinking so profits may be expected to fall.

Another aspect to evaluate is the quality of the information gained. Free or cheap market research data is of little value if it does not help a business succeed. Specifically, market information should be reliable, up-to-date and detailed enough for business use.

The DTI has been criticised in the past for providing services with no real appreciation of business needs. However, the newest schemes involve advisers seconded from industry so standards should improve. The Government's Overseas Trade Services is independently monitored monthly and reports a high level of customer satisfaction: 90 per cent of respondents regularly say that they will use the services again.

Summary

- Both public and private sector organisations have an interest in providing advice, information and other help to exporters.
- Public sector help tends to be free or subsidised but importers can expect little support.
- Public and private sector partnerships (such as chambers of commerce running DTI schemes) are increasingly common and have been formalised under the Business Link heading.
- The main types of support given are information about markets, legal advice, financial advice, distribution, necessary product adaptation and finding potential customers.
- Trade fairs and missions are organised and subsidised by a number of organisations.
- Evaluation of the value of export services should balance costs against expected profits over a reasonable time period.

Information sources

- Business in Europe pack from the DTI.
- *Guide to Sources of Advice*, DTI.
- Public relations materials from your local Chamber of Commerce and TEC.
- Free materials from the high street banks

Assignment 6.1
Evaluation of Chamber of Commerce services

This assignment fulfils the following criteria:
City & Guilds   9.2.1, 9.2.2, 9.3.3

Your tasks

1 Invite a representative from your local Chamber of Commerce to come and discuss with your group the services it gives members wishing to expand into Europe. Find out specific examples of companies which have been helped by the Chamber. Find out also the extent of its links with other advisory organisations such as the DTI and whether it is part of the Business Link network.

2 Obtain the views of some member companies (either by interview or by inviting them to speak on the same day) on how effective they think the Chamber is in helping them on European issues.

3 Depending on the depth of your analysis, the results of your investigation can be written up either:

  a as a press release targeted at the local newspapers (brief investigation), or

  b as a consultancy report for the Chamber of Commerce on its effectiveness in helping members with European problems (an in-depth investigation using structured interviews and/or questionnaires).

7 Trading opportunities

Use this chapter to enable you to:

- devise a rationale for expanding into the rest of the European Union (EU);
- apply general market research principles to the European context;
- examine some key issues, such as branding, in the European context;
- identify major European product markets.

This chapter covers the following performance criteria:
RSA   13.2.1, 13.2.3, 13.2.5, 13.2.6

Introduction

European marketing is more complex and covers a wider diversity of consumers than marketing solely within the UK. However, rules applying at the national level still apply at the international level. This chapter does not cover basic marketing principles but concentrates on highlighting specific European aspects of marketing. Since the greatest differences occur in consumer rather than industrial markets, most emphasis will be given to the former. Important basic information relating to European markets can also be found in Chapters 11 and 12.

Why expand into the rest of Europe?

Although many small companies begin European exports by chance, often prompted by enquiries from potential customers, it is more efficient to plan a strategy actively. Reasons for expanding beyond the national market include:

(a) **Saturation of the home market** – this does not happen in practice. Rather companies come to a point when it is more difficult to chase remaining potential domestic customers than it is to serve a larger number of foreign clients. For example, a survey of small (70–80 employees) Danish companies revealed that although they only supplied about 30 per cent of the sales potential within their own part of Denmark they typically exported to 10–12 other countries. Such companies merely skim each market for the easiest customers.

(b) **Growth** – this is closely linked to saturation of the home market but a growth strategy may be adopted before the domestic market is exhausted.

(c) **Reducing unit costs by expanding to reap economies of scale** – this is a major benefit of a single market but is particularly relevant to companies already dominant in their domestic market and wishing to expand overseas.

(d) **A depressed home market** – this only works if the new markets are at a different stage of the economic cycle. The UK's cycle is slightly ahead of that of the other Member States but all of Europe has experienced recession at the same time hence European companies look outside Europe, especially to Asia, for expansion.

(e) **To counter increased competition from the rest of the EU** – UK companies may find their traditional customer base under attack from other EU companies as a result of more accessible markets made possible by the various Single Market measures. Survival may require expansion of the market to other parts of the EU, which should be easier than exporting to other parts of the world precisely because the UK is part of a single market.

(f) **To enter the product life cycle at an earlier stage in a new market** – if a market is mature in the UK, it may be that the product's life can be extended by entering new markets where it will be at the launch or take-off stage.

(g) **As part of a strategy of diversification** – this may be either diversifying into additional products or into new markets in order to minimise the effect of a downturn in the domestic market.

Activity 7.1

Consider several small to medium-sized local companies with which you are familiar through previous coursework and which have activities in the rest of the EU. Can you attribute the reasons for their foreign involvement under the headings (a to g) given above? (Large public limited companies (plcs) are likely to have made their expansion on a world-wide scale and too long ago for the reasons to be clear.)

How to expand into the rest of Europe?

Several choices can be put into order of commitment to the idea of doing business in the rest of Europe. The list excludes the passive option of responding to one-off enquiries from potential customers.

Stage 1: agents and distributors

A European agent finds customers for a product in return for commission whereas a distributor actually buys a company's products thereby taking on the risk of not selling the goods. Since both the agent and the distributor will know the market better than the UK company, they can suggest product changes needed for European markets.

Stage 2: export

As the UK company gains confidence and experience, it may become active in exporting, setting up its own department, formulating its own export strategy and retaining as profit what was formerly paid as commission.

Stage 3: franchising/licensing

Licensing reduces the expense of setting up additional production facilities from scratch and is often used for low-value, high-bulk products, such as beer and soft drinks, where the main weight comes from water. The licensee is allowed to sell the product using the valued brand name, such as *Carlsberg* or *Coca-Cola*, in return for agreeing to manufacture and sell the product according to the strict instructions of the licensor.

Franchising is the low-cost option when providing a service or setting up a retail network; it is used by companies such as the Bodyshop and Benetton. In 1994, a survey by the British Franchise Association found that 54 per cent of UK franchisers anticipate operating units in mainland Europe by 1998 with 22 per cent already there. The latter include Prontaprint, Tie Rack and Sketchley.

Case study

Mr Clutch

In 1993, 'Mr Clutch' operated nearly 50 franchised outlets in the UK offering a clutch replacement service for cars. Seventeen more UK franchise outlets were planned for 1994 and 30 for 1995; the saturation point in the UK is estimated to be about 300 outlets. It is now planning expansion into the rest of the EU. Germany and Belgium are likely to be the first points of entry, with a pilot scheme in 1994 in Belgium because it is such a compact market.

Activity 7.2

Find out the extent of European involvement for several UK franchises. Is there a common pattern in the way in which they expand into the EU? Can you explain this?

Stage 4: joint ventures and European Economic Interest Groupings (EEIGs)

A joint venture is a formal agreement to collaborate with another company in some aspect of business. It can be for a limited period or indefinitely, and usually involves joint production, research and development, distribution or marketing. Many Japanese companies have entered into joint ventures with EU companies to establish their presence in the Single Market. An example is the link since 1979 between Honda and Rover which continued until Rover was taken over by BMW in 1994.

There are also many examples of joint ventures between EU companies, such as that linking aerospace companies British Aerospace (UK), Deutsche Aerospace (Germany), Construciones Aeronatics (Spain) and Aerospatialle (France), to produce the new European fighter plane. Here the objective is to benefit from economies of scale and pooling of technical knowledge and financial resources to produce profitably one specific product. The companies remain separate and independent in their production of all other types of aircraft.

A proposed EU Regulation would allow the creation of a European company, with the generic name Societas Europeae (SE), for large businesses with activities across at least two Member States. This would be equivalent to a plc in the UK.

European Economic Interest Groupings (EEIGs) are a new legal entity permitted by the EU and targeted at smaller companies to enable mutually beneficial collaboration but not for direct profit. At least two of the companies involved must come from different Member States. An EEIG may be set up to pool information, operate a joint marketing strategy or collaborate in research.

Stage 5: additional production facilities and/or relocation

Where proximity to markets is important it may be worthwhile to set up additional factories close to the new European markets. If the focus of your main markets were to change dramatically from the UK to Europe, it may be worthwhile relocating closer to the European centre, within the so-called 'Golden Triangle' created by joining Liverpool, Cologne and Paris on a European map, where the most numerous and well-off European consumers are located. Apart from building on a greenfield site, a less risky option may be to take over an existing EU company in the target location.

Activity 7.3

Find examples of UK companies which have expanded into Europe in the ways explained above. Which seems to be the most common approach? Can you relate specific company features to the way in which they become involved in Europe (e.g. size, product area or market)?

Market research

The usual procedure of carrying out desk and field research is still appropriate. Sources of information were discussed in Part Two.

Comparability

This is one of the major problems in the information you obtain for each market. For example, one initial problem an exporter meets is the different socio-economic categories used in other Member States.

Market sectors

Identify market sectors either on a geographical basis, country by country, or region by region (e.g. Benelux, Iberian Peninsula, etc.). For larger Member States, it may be useful to examine data at the level of the standard region. Figure 7.1 shows the population by standard region in Germany.

Unfortunately, the standard region used for official statistical purposes does not always correspond to marketing regions. In the UK these follow the ITV regional television boundaries whereas in Germany, at least, the marketing regions are groupings of the standard regions. Euromonitor gives information on consumption on a country-by-country basis and examples of ownership of consumer durables is given in Table 8.8.

Alternatively, attempts can be made to identify different types of consumers (see, for example, Euro lifestyles described in Chapter 10). However, these are expensive and time-consuming to carry out and it is not reasonable to expect to be able to access this type of data for student coursework.

Competitors

The usual information needs to be collected regarding:
- strengths;
- weaknesses

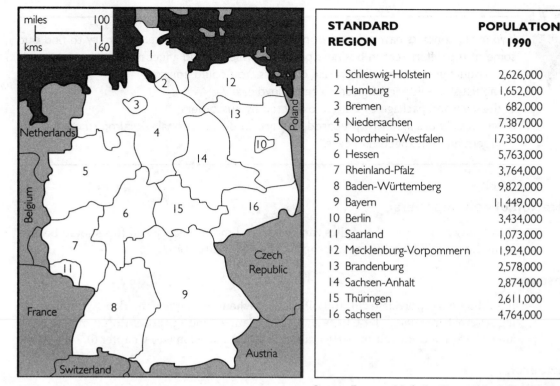

STANDARD REGION	POPULATION 1990
1 Schleswig-Holstein	2,626,000
2 Hamburg	1,652,000
3 Bremen	682,000
4 Niedersachsen	7,387,000
5 Nordrhein-Westfalen	17,350,000
6 Hessen	5,763,000
7 Rheinland-Pfalz	3,764,000
8 Baden-Württemberg	9,822,000
9 Bayern	11,449,000
10 Berlin	3,434,000
11 Saarland	1,073,000
12 Mecklenburg-Vorpommern	1,924,000
13 Brandenburg	2,578,000
14 Sachsen-Anhalt	2,874,000
15 Thüringen	2,611,000
16 Sachsen	4,764,000

Source: *European Marketing Data and Statistics 1994*, Euromonitor

Figure 7.1 Population in the standard regions of Germany

- prices; and
- advertising tactics;

using the sources described in Chapter 5 (e.g. business directories, local business magazines and newspapers). Competitor weakness is the most valuable information as it points to potential business opportunities for a newcomer to the market.

Activity 7.4

Carry out a competitor survey – collecting the information itemised in the paragraph above – as though you were planning to start one of the following businesses:
- a pizzeria near where one of your EU contacts lives;
- a new savoury biscuit to be sold in Italy.

Availability of business support services

Business directories and guides published by local chambers of commerce give some idea of locally available support services such as packaging, distribution, legal and financial services. The full range of support services, including the extensive facilities provided by the DTI, are discussed in Chapter 6.

Local business practice

Whatever the method of European expansion it will be very important to be aware of local business practices. This includes cultural differences, such as attitudes to punctuality when attending meetings, and legal differences which may affect the way in which business is transacted.

Activity 7.5

If your EU contacts have jobs or work experience in the private sector try to find out some of the differences in business practices which would affect marketing strategy in the product areas covered by those contacts. You could consider:

- the usual credit period given to settle invoices;
- the level and package of service expected by customers;
- business hours and how prepared staff are to do occasional overtime to complete urgent and unexpected orders.

Identification of new suppliers

Prices may be lowered if supplies can be sourced more cheaply and this should be easier in the Single Market using appropriate business directories.

Field research

It is difficult to appreciate cultural differences when serving new markets without making several trips there. These trips should be planned and purposeful, and may include attendance at a trade fair or participation in a trade mission (see Chapter 6).

Desk research

Market size

Various Eurostat publications, such as *Europe in Figures,* and Euromonitor provide consumption and production figures for the major product categories. If consumption exceeds production then the difference is obviously made up of imports and may indicate an opportunity for a UK company to supply some of the required shortfall in domestic production. Take the example of Italy in 1992: the production and consumption figures for three items are as follows:

	Production (units 000s)	Retail sales (units 000s)	Difference (units 000s)
Washing machines	5,165	1,450	3,715
Dishwashers	905	385	520
Tumble dryers	484	10	474

Sources: Economist Intelligence Unit and Euromonitor

In all three items Italy produces more than it sells and this suggests that there is not much of an export opportunity in Italy for these products unless a brand had a very special selling point. In fact in the up-market niches for these three items, Italians prefer German brands, such as Miele.

Segmenting the market

You should try and divide the market into its component segments exactly as you would in preparation for a UK marketing strategy. For example, dividing cars into hatchback, saloon, luxury and off-road. However, when doing this for European markets you should make sure that no profitable segment has been inadvertently forgotten just because it does not exist in the UK. So, for example, electric cars, although still uncommon, are genuine market segments in France and Denmark.

Demographic factors

Chapter 11 shows that the EU population is growing only slowly but with a changing age structure which influences the pattern of demand for a whole range of products in, for example, the leisure, health and clothing sector.

Consumer characteristics

Sociological

Depending on the product it may be relevant to determine marriage and divorce rates and attitudes to these. For example, now divorce is to be legalised in Ireland, you may expect to see a rise in the number of households as happened after the legalisation of divorce in Spain and Italy. Also relevant may be educational levels, living standards, average income and income distribution, noting in particular any differences in these between the UK and the target EU market.

Attitudes

Both hard facts and consumer opinion are relevant to construct an accurate picture of the Euro-consumer. Official statistics tell you that Denmark has the fourth largest per capita GDP (gross domestic product) in Europe but an attitude survey by Gallup tells you that 20 per cent of Danes feel they have difficulty managing on their income despite a narrow gap between rich and poor in that country. The evidence is, therefore, that while Danes could buy luxury items many probably will not because they do not feel well off. A successful marketing strategy in this case could involve offering credit but again attitudes to credit and hire purchase arrangements may have to be surveyed.

The same Gallup survey showed that 27 per cent of Germans were not proud to be German. This suggests promotions highlighting the German aspects of your product may be unsuccessful in Germany whilst such aspects were a prominent feature of the (German) AEG adverts in the UK for washing machines ('AEG – Advanced Engineering from Germany'). The survey also showed that the UK and Denmark are not keen EU members whereas a promotional approach emphasising the Euro-angle would probably be well received in France, Germany, the Netherlands, Italy and Belgium, which are all much more enthusiastic.

Individualism

People no longer act predictably according to their socio-economic groups. Earlier, marketing simply identified the various groups and targeted mass-produced products accordingly; *The Times* would boast to advertisers about its percentage of A and B class readers. Now it is much more difficult to predict behaviour on the basis of income alone and instead of studying groups, marketing departments need to look at behaviour at the individual level. This creates potentially large data collection problems.

Databases

Efficient and cheap database systems enable the cost-effective collection of large amounts of information on individuals' purchasing behaviour so they can be targeted with information (i.e. advertising) about products they are most likely to be interested in based on past purchases. The ACORN system in the UK works on this principle, enabling companies to reduce the amount of 'junk mail' sent out. For example, the system will identify whether the address being targeted is a flat or a house enabling companies to send enticing gardening product literature only to people with gardens.

With the distances and costs involved in operating across Europe, marketing databases are potentially very efficient at identifying very specific potential customers scattered all over Europe. However, many people are unhappy about their personal information being kept on these databases and as a result the EU has formulated a directive to protect individual privacy. In countries where such data protection laws exist (as in Germany) households receive mountains of junk mail because companies apply a shotgun approach and send the information to everyone in the absence of precise knowledge about the addressee. Table 7.1 below shows the wide differences across Europe in the use of direct mail as a result of these and other factors.

Table 7.1   Number of direct mail items received per year in selected European countries

Country received	No. of items per head in 1991
Austria	n/a
Belgium	80
Denmark	48
Finland	46
France	54
Germany	68
Greece	n/a
Ireland	14
Italy	n/a
Luxembourg	n/a
Netherlands	60
Portugal	5
Spain	23
Sweden	75
UK	38

Source: Euromonitor

All the evidence suggests direct mail techniques are one of the major marketing strategies of the future on a pan-European scale.

Technological developments

The growth industries of the future are heavily dependent on research and development (R&D) in a range of new technologies in the fields of:
- computer services;
- data processing;
- software;
- telecommunications;
- environmental protection services;
- new materials;

- computer integrated manufacturing (CIM);
- computer aided design (CAD).

These new technologies provide the potential for huge increases in productivity (up to 250 per cent) so that EU companies failing to apply them to their product range are likely to fail. The USA and Japan are the main rivals in the development of these technologies and if Europe fails to participate, European companies will have to pay a premium to use the results of US and Japanese research. The lack of competitiveness of European industry is of major concern. High labour costs are cited compared to the emerging economies in South East Asia but equally important is the development and application of new technologies.

As well as creating new products, technological developments affect production processes or the raw materials from which products are made, hence, new materials and processes represent as much of a threat or opportunity as a totally new product. New techniques could be profitably exploited but could also make current products obsolete. Companies unaware of new developments face falling demand and have no newly developed products ready to take their place.

Activity 7.6

1 Find out more about CAD and CIM from BTEC Science students or a representative from a relevant local company. How can these techniques be applied? What difference do they make to costs and procedures? Where do these technologies (as used by companies in the local area) come from currently?

2 Use your EU contacts to find out the use and application of new technologies in other Member States.

Case study

Diamond film

Diamond is amongst the hardest known substances. New technology enables the application of a thin film of diamond to other materials allowing them to be subjected to much higher temperatures than was previously possible. It may also make faster computers, and diamond filament light bulbs which could literally last a lifetime. One potential use of this technology is shown in Figure 7.2.

This development may force computer manufacturers to adopt the new technique, enable computer users to run more jobs on faster computers and force bulb manufacturers such as Philips to decide whether to make the new light bulbs or risk another company doing so, and stealing its market.

A serious problem is that European businesses seem unwilling to commit large sums of money to translate discoveries into commercial applications. Although the diamond film is being developed at Bristol University, the R&D costs have so far been paid by US firms such as Gillette and Rank Xerox.

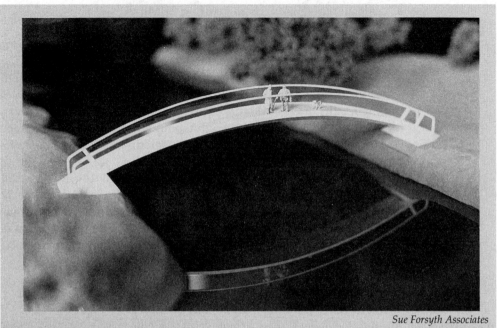

Sue Forsyth Associates

Figure 7.2 A diamond film coated bridge

Activity 7.7

Look through back copies of *New Scientist* and/or watch the BBC TV programme 'Tomorrow's World'.

1 Note one development which you think has widespread business potential, i.e. it is likely to be a mass market product or likely to have wide application in a number of industries.

2 Find out the names of companies which would be specifically affected (you could use the UK edition of the Kompass Directories) and explain what these effects would be.

3 If you have access to Kompass Directories for other EU Member States you could also find out how many other companies may be affected.

Figure 7.3 gives a summary of the changes in jobs expected as a result of technological advances.

Activity 7.8

There are many ways of using Figure 7.3 (apart from the career advice it contains!). For questions 2 to 4 it may be wise to focus on just one or two areas.

1 How far do you agree with the predictions? Discuss this with your colleagues.

2 Name local and well-known companies which would be affected by the predictions.

3 Collate evidence to show that these trends have already begun from the business press, company reports and other sources.

4 Compare your answers to the above questions with your EU contacts. Does any of their evidence constitute a threat or an opportunity to any of your local companies?

Shrinking trades	Replaced by
Air couriers	High-speed data networks
Answering machines	Computers
Insurance claims assessors	Neural networks
Bailiffs	Electronic credit freezes
Checkout staff	Image recognition software
Cash register suppliers	Computers
Coal and solid fuel merchants	Electricity
Company registration agents	Networks
Dictation and secretarial services	Voice recognition software
Layout artists	Computer templates
Duplicating equipment	Computers
Factory cleaning	Intelligent robots
Film processors	Digital chemical-free film
Hotel booking agents	Software
Industrial relations arbitrators	Employment deregulation
Notaries and Commissioners of Oaths	Video recording
Draughting equipment makers	Computer-aided design
Typewriter manufacturers	Computers
Window cleaners	Intelligent robots
Airlines	Rising fuel prices
Middle managers	Networks

Growth areas	Reason
Advertising	New media
Alarms and security equipment	Rising crime due to unemployment
Corporate entertainment	Keep staff and customers happy
Sports equipment	More leisure time
Hi-fi and computer dealers	Convergence of technologies
Cellular radio dealers	More networks
Cable manufacturers	More networks
Environmental systems	Tighter law
Recycling	Tighter laws, higher material costs
Computer programmers	Need for better interfaces
Designers	Producing and choosing computer templates
Telemarketing	Wider access to public
Career consultants	Increased redundancies
Trauma consultants	Rise in random criminal acts
Personal matchmakers	Less time for workers to socialise
Escort services	Importance of appearing sociable in public
Cruise companies	For leisurely business trips

New trades	Work done
Internet plumbers	To repair breakdowns in home computer network (e.g. automatic security lights)
Workgroup synthesisers	Bringing together ideas from staff on different projects in remote locations
System hosts	The DJs and talk-show hosts of the Internet, who will be famous for the discussions they provoke each day

Change from physical to electronic
Market research
Novelty goods
Lawyers
Doctors
Surveyors
Cinema
Detective agencies
Estate agents
Journalists
Writers

Source: *New Scientist*, 16 April 1994

Figure 7.3 Jobs expected to disappear and emerge as a result of technological changes

Specific European issues to consider

Pan-European approach

Within any product marketing strategy there are many points at which a decision can be taken to adopt a common approach or to cater individually for different markets (see Figure 7.4).

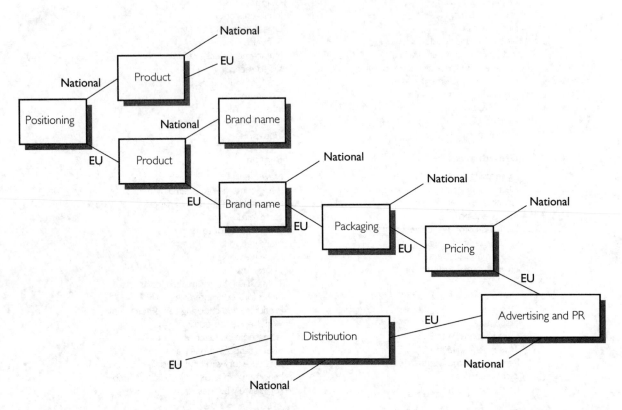

Source: 'The Myth of Globalisation', Y Wind, in the *Journal of Consumer Marketing*, Vol. 3, No. 2, Spring 1986

Figure 7.4 Key points at which to decide on a national or pan-European approach

First it must be decided whether the product will be the same across all markets. For example, a standard UK car is typically better equipped than its counterpart in Belgium, and ingredients, flavourings and textures of foods may have to be varied to suit different tastes.

If a well-established brand in the UK is entering Europe for the first time, UK advertising is unlikely to translate although it may be possible at a later date to move towards a common campaign.

Markets should also be prioritised in terms of their importance and stage of the product life cycle. Germany is commonly the most important continental market and would therefore require a higher level of support than some of the smaller markets. Key markets should be clustered and prioritised with smaller secondary markets dealt with later and within a smaller budget.

Branding

The fragmented consumer markets identified earlier are best served by the trend towards a recognisably similar product available across Europe. These so-called Eurobrands are found particularly in the car market, car hire, consumer electronics, high fashion couture, soft drinks, tobacco products, sports goods, watches, some jewellery, perfumes, wines and pharmaceuticals. Europe's 'Top Ten' brands are shown in Figure 7.5.

Franchises attribute their success to heavily branded products and are predicted to grow rapidly in the 1990s.

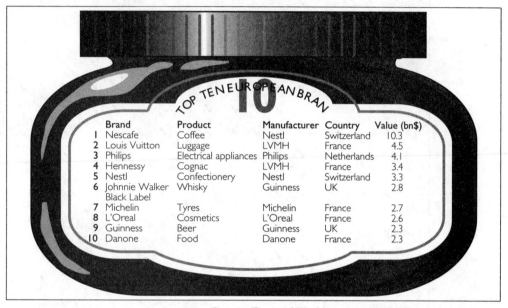

	Brand	Product	Manufacturer	Country	Value (bn$)
1	Nescafe	Coffee	Nestl	Switzerland	10.3
2	Louis Vuitton	Luggage	LVMH	France	4.5
3	Philips	Electrical appliances	Philips	Netherlands	4.1
4	Hennessy	Cognac	LVMH	France	3.4
5	Nestl	Confectionery	Nestl	Switzerland	3.3
6	Johnnie Walker Black Label	Whisky	Guinness	UK	2.8
7	Michelin	Tyres	Michelin	France	2.7
8	L'Oreal	Cosmetics	L'Oreal	France	2.6
9	Guinness	Beer	Guinness	UK	2.3
10	Danone	Food	Danone	France	2.3

Source: 'Financial World', reported in the *European*, 28 July 1995

Figure 7.5 Europe's 'Top Ten' brands, 1995

One type of brand which is having the most success is the brand of the retailer itself (such as Sainsbury in the UK) and so a parallel development has been the spectacular growth all over Europe of the so-called 'own label', 'own brand' or 'private label'. In these cases the retailer uses its own name instead of the brand name chosen by the manufacturer.

Sales promotion

The law differs greatly from country to country, so sales promotion activities still have to be carefully tailored to each nationality. Figure 7.6 (overleaf) gives some guidance as to the legal restrictions in some European countries.

Case study

The *European* newspaper competition

The *European* is available on news stands throughout the EU and beyond. In July 1994 it ran a competition with a limited edition Lotus Elan car as prize but anticipated problems in awarding the prize if the winner came from certain countries.

In Germany, high-value prizes are illegal as they are seen as an undue inducement to the consumer to buy the product (in this case the newspaper). In Italy,

	UK	Irish Republic	Spain	Germany	France	Denmark	Belgium	Netherlands	Portugal	Italy	Greece	Luxembourg	Austria	Finland	Sweden
On-pack reductions	✓	✓	✓	✓	✓	✓		✓	✓	✓		✓	✓	✓	✓
Banded offers	✓	✓	✓	?	✓	?	✗	✓	✓	✓	✓	✗	?	?	?
In-pack premiums	✓	✓	✓	?	?	?	✓	?	✓	✓	✓	✗	?	✓	?
Multiple-purchase offers	✓	✓	✓	?	✓	?	?	✓	✓	✓	✓	✗	?	?	?
Extra-product	✓	✓	✓	?	✓	✓	?	?	✓	?	✓	✓	?	✓	?
Free product	✓	✓	✓	✓	✓	✓	?	✓	✓	✓	✓	✓	✓	✓	✓
Re-usable/alternative	✓	✓	✓	✓	✓	✓	✓	✓	✓	✓	✓	✓	?	✓	✓
Free mail-ins	✓	✓	✓	✗	✓	?	✓	✓	✓	✓	✓	?	✗	✓	✗
With-purchase premiums	✓	✓	✓	?	✓	?	?	?	✓	✓	✓	✗	?	✓	?
Cross-product offers	✓	✓	✓	✗	✓	?	✗	?	✓	✓	✓	✗	?	?	?
Collector devices	✓	✓	✓	✗	?	?	?	?	✓	✓	✓	✗	✗	?	✗
Competitions	✓	✓	✓	?	?	?	✓	?	✓	✓	✓	?	?	✓	✓
Self-liquidating premiums	✓	✓	✓	✓	✓	✓	✓	?	✓	✓	✓	✗	✓	✓	✓
Free draws	✓	✓	✓	✗	✓	✗	✗	✗	✓	✓	✓	✗	✗	✓	✗
Share-outs	✓	✓	✓	✗	?	✗	✗	✗	✓	?	✓	✗	✗	?	✗
Sweepstake/lottery	✓*	?	?	?	?	✗	?	?	?	?	?	✗	?	✓	✗
Money-off vouchers	✓	✓	✓	✗	✓	?	✓	✓	✓	?	✓	?	?	?	?
Money-off next purchase	✓	✓	✓	✗	✓	✗	✓	✓	✓	?	✓	✗	✗	?	✗
Cash backs	✓	✓	✓	?	✓	✓	✓	✓	✓	✗	✓	✗	?	?	✓
In-store demos	✓	✓	✓	✓	✓	✓	✓	✓	✓	✓	✓	✓	✓	✓	✓

Table reproduced by kind permission of IMP. ✓ Permitted   ✗ Not permitted   ? May be permitted
*In 1995

Source: *Marketing Without Frontiers – The RMI Guide to International Direct Marketing*, Royal Mail International

Figure 7.6 Legality of sales promotion techniques across Europe

permission for awarding the prize would have to be sought from the Finance Ministry and entries are supposed to be sent to an Italian address. In the Netherlands, the value of the car exceeds the legal limit for prizes there. This illustrates the difficulty of operating a pan-European promotion. As it turned out the winner lived in the UK and so there was no problem.

Activity 7.9

Find examples of current promotions in the UK and use Figure 7.6 to identify in which European countries these promotions could run without making changes.

The *European* newspaper case study above does not mean that a pan-European sales promotion is not possible but it does suggest that minor adaptations may have to be made to ensure that sales promotions comply with the laws in each country. Indeed there are a sufficient number of common interests and events across Europe which make such a Europe-wide promotion possible, as Figure 7.7 illustrates.

Sporting events
- European Cup and World Cup
- Olympic Games
- Wimbledon
- Grand Prix Motor Racing

Music
- leading pop groups
- Eurovision Song Contest
- festivals in Salzburg and Bayreuth

Travel and transport
- holidays in other European countries
- Concorde
- New York, San Francisco and Hollywood
- Luxury cars like Mercedes, BMW and Jaguars
- Avis, Hertz and other car rentals

Television
- Baywatch
- Beverly Hills 90210
- LA Law

Children's interest
- space travel
- dinosaurs
- animals
- dolls
- pirates and buried treasure
- LEGO toys
- Disney

Fashion
- Levis
- Benetton
- Gucci

Financial services
- American Express, Visa, Mastercard
- Europ Assistance

Social concern
- Red Cross
- World Wide Fund for Nature
- the environment
- starvation relief
- drug abuse

Source: *European Sales Promotion*, Alan Toop, 1992, Kogan Page

Figure 7.7 Common European interests which could be used as the basis for a pan-European sales promotion

One example was the use made of the Olympics by the Scotch video tape brand which offered a free book about the Olympics. The book was printed in 12 different languages and the offer applied all over Europe.

Media

National media markets vary enormously across Europe. Print media, for example, are much more important in northern than in southern Europe, where television dominates. The UK has very little cable television whereas it is almost universal in the Netherlands. Posters account for 5 per cent of media spend in the UK but 15 per cent in France. Pan-European media is growing but is still limited in scope and includes the music channel MTV and publications such as *Newsweek*, *Time* and the *European* which appeal to narrow sections of consumers, the young and business people.

An important issue on mainland Europe is that of media overspill, when promotion and advertising in one country spills over into its neighbours. Belgium households, for example, have easy access to the Dutch, French, Luxembourg and German media, and you might want to ensure that the message about your product is not contradicted in these five markets.

Distribution

There are major differences in the way in which consumer products reach customers in the rest of the EU and it is important to be aware of these when formulating your marketing strategy (see Chapter 8 for more detail). Figure 7.8 shows the proportion of retail sales accounted for by the different types of outlet.

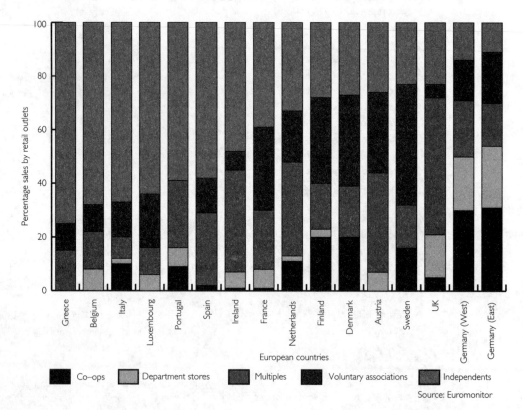

Figure 7.8 Percentage sales by type of retail outlet, 1990

The biggest difference between the UK and other European countries is the importance of the independent shop. Multiples account for an increasing share of sales all over Europe while co-operatives (except in Scandinavia) and department stores are declining.

Mail order is popular in France, Germany and the UK while tele-shopping is gaining in popularity in Italy and Germany (and has recently been launched in the UK).

Activity 7.10

Use Figure 7.8 to discuss how you would arrange for the distribution of a new shampoo in Spain and Germany.

Pricing

Although VAT rates are meant to converge as part of the Single Market, this is unlikely in the foreseeable future so account needs to be taken of the differing rates (see Table 7.2) and how they will affect the price the final consumer has to pay.

Table 7.2   VAT rates across the EU

	Reduced rate (%)	Standard rate (%)	Luxury rate (%)
Austria	10	20	25–34 (cars)
Belgium	6 and 12	19.5	–
Denmark	–	25	–
Finland	12 (food, from 1998)	22	–
France	2.1 and 5.5	20.6	–
Germany	7	15	–
Greece	4 and 8	18	36
Ireland	0, 2.7 and 10	12.5 and 16	21
Italy	4, 9 and 12	19	38
Luxembourg	3 and 6	15	–
Netherlands	6	18.5	–
Portugal	8	17	30
Spain	6	17	33 (cars)
Sweden	21	25	–
UK	0	17.5	–

Problems may occur if you position your product differently in separate markets. In the UK, both the Belgian *Stella Artois* and French *Kronenbourg* beers are sold as up-market products whereas in their respective home countries they are relatively cheap mass-market products. As it has become easier for UK consumers to import their own supplies, these two companies may find that they cannot sustain the relatively high prices of their products in the UK.

Companies trying to control the price of their products through a tight distributor network may find their efforts being undermined by independent operators who obtain the products through wholesalers and are then able to undercut the prices of the official distribution network, known as *parallel importing*. In the Single Market this is perfectly legal and therefore companies may find it easier to try and charge more or less the same price across the EU.

Servicing

A company will have to make decisions about the level of servicing to offer mainland European customers and whether to offer a Europe-wide guarantee. Therefore, attention will have to be paid to setting up an efficient servicing and repair service.

Mapping the market

The results of your market research, added to information about the wider environment of social and economic conditions (as described in Chapter 11), should enable you to produce PEST and SWOT analyses for any specific marketing proposal. To remind you:

P	Political		S	Strengths
E	Economic		W	Weaknesses
S	Social		O	Opportunities
T	Technological		T	Threats

Mapping the market means presenting all the information learned about a particular market in a structured way. This can then be used to identify specific opportunities for your product. Figure 7.9 shows all the headings which should be included and can be used as a blueprint for a market research report.

Overview of European markets

Future trends are often predicted by assuming past trends will continue. This may not be reliable but is often used. Below is a summary of recent trends.

The fastest growth sectors during 1986–91 have been consumer goods and some sectors of the food and drink industry which are treated in greater depth in the next chapter.

The capital goods sector has performed less well except for high-tech telecommunications equipment, office and data processing equipment, pharmaceutical products and plastics processing. 'Lower tech' sectors such as soft drinks manufacturing, textile finishing and the manufacture of pulp, paper and board (for packaging as a result of increased consumer demand) have grown well.

World conditions have been responsible for difficulties in the iron and steel, computer and defence industries. Slow growth or decline was experienced by textile-related industries, such as the manufacture of textile machinery, cotton, wool and leather tanning. The greatest decline was in agricultural machinery and articles of asbestos.

Activity 7.11

Obtain company reports for goods which are identified above as high-growth and slow-growth sectors. Use the Chairman's report and your own knowledge to identify the reasons for the high or slow growth.

The fastest growing industries also tend to be the ones attracting most competition from the rest of the world which means that EU companies will have to work hard not to lose out to foreign competitors in the following areas:
- office and electronic data processing (EDP) equipment;
- cycles and motorcycles;
- medical and surgical equipment;
- household textiles;
- motor vehicle parts and accessories;
- toys and sports goods;

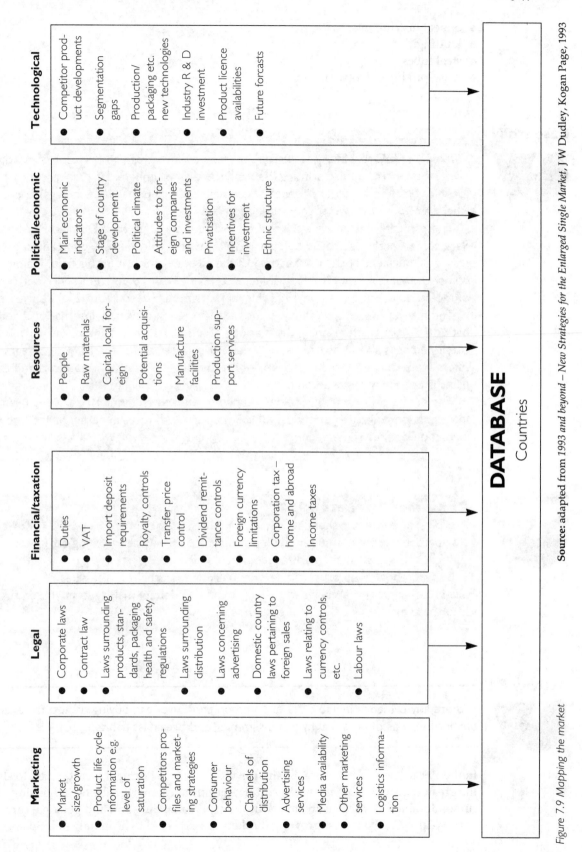

Marketing	Legal	Financial/taxation	Resources	Political/economic	Technological
• Market size/growth	• Corporate laws	• Duties	• People	• Main economic indicators	• Competitor product developments
• Product life cycle information e.g. level of saturation	• Contract law	• VAT	• Raw materials	• Stage of country development	• Segmentation gaps
• Competitors profiles and marketing strategies	• Laws surrounding products, standards, packaging health and safety regulations	• Import deposit requirements	• Capital, local, foreign	• Political climate	• Production/ packaging etc. new technologies
• Consumer behaviour	• Laws surrounding distribution	• Royalty controls	• Potential acquisitions	• Attitudes to foreign companies and investments	• Industry R & D investment
• Channels of distribution	• Laws concerning advertising	• Transfer price control	• Manufacture facilities	• Privatisation	• Product licence availabilities
• Advertising services	• Domestic country laws pertaining to foreign sales	• Dividend remittance controls	• Production support services	• Incentives for investment	• Future forcasts
• Media availability	• Laws relating to currency controls, etc.	• Foreign currency limitations		• Ethnic structure	
• Other marketing services	• Labour laws	• Corporation tax – home and abroad			
• Logistics information		• Income taxes			

DATABASE

Countries

Source: adapted from *1993 and beyond – New Strategies for the Enlarged Single Market*, J W Dudley, Kogan Page, 1993

Figure 7.9 Mapping the market

- optical instruments;
- knitting;
- steel tubes;
- mass-produced footwear.

Case study

An industrial market

Videojet, a GEC subsidiary, is currently foremost in the high-tech sector of continuous or industrial ink-jet printing. Its products print numbers, letters, barcodes and graphics on almost anything (delicately enough even to print on fresh eggs) and label items on ultra high-speed production lines.

The company has nearly a third of the world market, as does Domino Printing Services, a Cambridge based company, which, with two other UK companies, each having 10 per cent of the market, makes the UK pre-eminent in this field. Major competitors are a French and a Japanese company with 16 per cent and 7 per cent of the market respectively. In 1993 this market amounted to about 20,000 printers.

The market has grown rapidly in the past few years, driven by international and national legislation demanding the marking of foods, beverages and drugs with batch numbers and sell-by dates. New legislation planned for the labelling of eggs offers more opportunity for growth, whilst the labelling of pharmaceuticals and car parts is becoming more common.

The ink-jet printer market seems certain to expand at about 10 per cent a year from now on compared to the 25–30 per cent growth rates in earlier years when legislation created the demand.

Case study

Consumer markets 1994

A survey of consumer spending patterns in the first three months of 1994 showed that personal grooming and hygiene products are the fastest-growing categories in the five largest European markets (see Table 7.3).

Some trends relate to specific events unlikely to recur (e.g. the sales of painkillers and cold remedies in the UK in a flu epidemic) making it unwise to rush into these markets on the basis of figures alone.

Activity 7.12

Is there any evidence in Table 7.3 of common pan-European buying trends, for example, in the areas of personal hygiene, slimming and breakfast habits?

In the 1990s, Germany, Greece, Spain, Ireland, Italy and Portugal are expected to show the greatest growth in consumer spending; the strongest markets being in housing, consumer durables, health, leisure and education, personal transport and personal care. Up to the year 2000, the fastest-growing markets are expected to be in Italy and Spain.

Table 7.3　Fastest-growing markets, 1994

Country	Product	% increase
Spain	Sugar substitutes	174.1
	Pre-packaged sliced meat	115.4
	Dry dog food	45.0
	Non-processed cheese	41.1
	Cola drinks	33.6
	Mayonnaise/salad dressing	32.4
	Deodorants	29.1
	Ice-cream	26.7
	Frozen prepared meals	21.9
	Furniture polish/cleaner	21.9
France	Bath/shower additives	9.5
	Plastic foil/wraps	9.4
	Toothbrushes	8.9
	Cereals/muesli	6.9
	Cola drinks	5.6
	Toothpaste	4.1
	Hair conditioners	3.1
	Instant coffee (premium)	2.8
	Chewing gum	1.7
	Infant milk	1.4
UK	Oral analgesics	38.6
	Antacids	33.3
	Dishwater detergents	24.3
	Cough/cold medicine (child)	23.1
	Skin creams/lotions	18.1
	Hot sauces	18.0
	Cough/cold medicine (adult)	17.7
	Infant milk	17.7
	Slimming aids	16.2
	Chewing gum	16.0
Italy	Non-disposable razors	72.7
	Non-carbonated soft drinks	31.2
	Ice-cream	28.4
	Cereals/muesli	22.2
	Port/sherry/madeira	20.0
	Razor blades	19.6
	Frozen pizza	18.9
	Dry dog food	18.8
	Crackers	18.1
	Baby food	16.7
Germany	Dehydrated soup	36.4
	Air fresheners	30.0
	Panty liners	21.8
	Nuts	19.6
	Dishwater detergent	18.1
	Instant coffee (premium)	17.7
	Tampons	16.4
	Instant coffee	16.2
	Lipsticks	14.9
	Cereals/muesli	14.5

Source: Nielsen

Summary

- There are seven main reasons why a UK company may consider expanding into the rest of the EU.
- There are five main ways in which to expand into the rest of the EU which represent different levels of commitment and confidence.
- Market research should follow the same basic principles learned in your core modules but take care not to forget some specific European differences; for example, make sure that all market niches are identified.
- Issues requiring specific attention include whether to adopt a pan-European strategy, branding, distribution, sales promotion and use of the European media.
- Market research should be collated into a market map which can be used to identify opportunities.

Information sources

- Parts 2, 3 and 4 of this book.
- *Doing Business in the European Union: A Country by Country Guide to Marketing Opportunities, Consumer Behaviour, Business Etiquette and More* by Paul Gibbs, Kogan Page, 1994.
- *Marketing Without Frontiers*, Royal Mail International.
- *1993 and Beyond – New Strategies for the Enlarged Single Market* by J W Dudley, Kogan Page, 1993.

Assignment 7.1
Radford

This assignment fulfils the following criteria:
RSA   13.2.1 to 13.2.6

Radford of Bristol Ltd has, through innovation and development, built up a range of products in the production, installation and maintenance of refrigerated display cabinets and other equipment for supermarkets. It has become one of a number of UK manufacturers of similar size and products, employing 360 people in four divisions and five plants across the UK.

Division	Function
1	Retail Systems manufactures refrigerated display cabinets and supermarket shelving.
2	Radford Checkouts produces supermarket checkouts.
3	RMS Controls manufactures microprocessor units for monitoring and controlling refrigeration cabinets.
4	Radford Maintenance provides a range of services to retailers from depots in Bristol and Leeds.

As supermarkets expanded their market share in the post-war years Radford grew with them, supplying refrigerated display cabinets to a number of major customers including Sainsbury. In the 1980s it added microprocessor-based units, to monitor and control refrigeration systems, and supermarket shelving to its product range. More recently, it acquired a leading manufacturer of supermarket checkouts.

Radford faced an exceptionally strong demand for its products in 1990 and 1991 as supermarkets had to re-equip to meet the higher standards for food storage and display laid down in the Food Hygiene Act 1990. Capacity at its Chew Stoke factory, south of Bristol, was almost doubled.

The company has an active product development programme. In the past its products have been tailored to the needs and specifications of major customers. It has also launched standard equipment in all divisions which should prove attractive to other, smaller groups, such as the retail co-operatives, and enhance exports.

Radford's fortunes are closely linked with those of its customers, the food retailers, whose market in the UK is changing. The rate of new store development cannot be maintained indefinitely and the big supermarket groups will have to compete more on price, quality and service to gain market share.

The 'no frills' discount stores, such as Kwik Save and Germany's Aldi, are increasing in popularity so investment funds for new capital equipment, such as refrigerated cabinets and checkouts, may be reduced and the main UK groups may alter their traditional 'Buy British' policies. The rapid growth in convenience stores ('the corner shop'), expected to rise in number from the present 8000 to nearly 20,000 by the year 2000, also threatens the main UK supermarket groups.

Radford's integrated group approach provides a one-stop shop for all the mainstream equipment that a supermarket needs.

In 1990, Radford first exhibited in Germany and found that the UK was ahead in the use of microprocessors to control refrigeration plants. It has recently completed its first installation in the Netherlands, is currently working in Belgium and France, and obtaining distributors throughout the EU.

A strength of Radford's could be that, as food hygiene regulations are harmonised and standards raised to the levels in the UK, the company will benefit from already having refrigerated display cabinets and systems that can deliver those higher standards.

Your tasks

1 Produce a SWOT and a PEST analysis for the company (i.e. map the market). How do you think Radford should react to its weaknesses and any threats you have identified?

2 Might a more systematic approach to exporting to the rest of the EU be more efficient than simply responding to one-off requests from the Netherlands, France and Belgium? What systematic approaches might be considered?

Assignment 7.2
A live marketing exercise

This assignment fulfils the following criteria:
RSA   13.2.1 to 13.2.6

This assignment involves your group in finding a product or service to market in one of the other Member States and will necessitate at least one sales trip to the chosen market. However, if time and funds are limited, the assignment can be restricted to the preliminary market research stage.

(This exercise was undertaken in Belgium by the author and a group of Gloucestershire students in 1993 supported by EU funds under the SOCRATES (formerly LINGUA) scheme as well as by local sponsorship. Whether or not a foreign trip is possible, it is vital to collaborate with contacts in the target market.)

Your tasks

1 Brainstorm ideas for possible products or services to market in your target location. Depending on the size of your group try to identify three to five of the best ideas for further investigation.
2 Carry out market research on the chosen ideas. This will be mainly desk research but potential consumer reaction can be tested by using your EU contacts. Questionnaires can be administered, samples or photographs sent and information on local competition and conditions sought.

    Although your EU contacts will probably welcome the opportunity to practise their English, great care will have to be taken with questionnaires as they will have to be translated and you will have to be prepared to use the language skills available in your group. At this stage you should be aware of who your suppliers would be and their conditions (e.g. minimum order level, unit price etc.).
3 Once your market research has enabled you to choose the best product, you should then produce a marketing strategy which covers the following:
    ● pricing;
    ● sales promotion and advertising;
    ● sales targets;
    ● transport and distribution;
    ● after-sales service (e.g. policy on return of defective goods).
    Then, if you are making the sales trip, the following tasks should also be completed.
4 Obtain and export the goods.
5 Make the sales trip and try to achieve your objectives.
6 Compile an evaluation of the marketing exercise with recommendations for improvements and likely future markets.

8 Food and consumer durables markets

Use this chapter to:

- examine in more detail the food and consumer durables markets in the European Union (EU).

This chapter covers the following performance criteria:
RSA   13.2.1, 13.2.3, 13.2.4, 13.2.5, 13.2.6

Introduction

This chapter examines two markets in particular, food and consumer durables. Both cover a wide range of products and both are very important economically to most of the Member States in terms of market size and industrial output. They are also highly-visible consumer markets.

Food

This market includes:
- unbranded fresh fruit, vegetables, meat, fish and eggs;
- branded groceries including biscuits, pasta and breakfast cereals;
- preserved fruit, vegetables, meat and fish whether tinned, frozen or ready-prepared;
- ready-prepared meals.

Chapter 10 shows that there are many cultural differences in food so the best selling grocery brands across Europe are those foods least affected by cultural differences (see Table 8.1).

Table 8.1   Europe's top grocery brands, 1993

Brand	Manufacturer	Total sales $m
1 Coca-Cola	Coca-Cola	3,845
2 Jacobs coffee	Jacobs Suchard	1,255
3 Danone yoghurt	Gervais-Danone	1,240
4 Nescafe instant coffee	Nestle	1,190
5 Whiskas cat food	Pedigree Petfoods (Mars)	925
6 Danone fromage frais	Gervais-Danone	920
7 Fanta	Coca-Cola	860
8 Langnese ice cream	Unilever	845

Source: Nielsen

The following case study shows one company's adaptation of its product portfolio to include pan-European brands.

Case study

> ### Pernod-Ricard
> The original products of this French company, aniseed-flavoured *Pastis*, is typically French and little drunk outside of France. In order to expand, the company has bought several whisky brands including Irish *Jameson's*. However, recession and spirit taxes restrict the product range so the company also acquired the soft drink *Orangina* in 1984 and this has proved a truly international product.

Activity 8.1

What makes a successful pan-European food brand? Is it more or less difficult to sell a food product across the EU compared to other product areas? Suggest other food brands which may travel well. If possible, seek also the opinions of your EU contacts regarding these questions.

The pattern of demand for food

Food accounts for a falling percentage of consumers' spending as their real income increases. The poorer Member States – Greece, Ireland, Portugal and Spain – all spend a higher proportion on food than the EU average which has been decreasing as follows:

1979	20.9%
1984	19.5%
1989	17.6%

Source: Economist Intelligence Unit and Business International

Activity 8.2

Obtain figures for total EU gross domestic product (GDP) for the years 1979, 1984 and 1989, and calculate the total size of the food market using the given percentages. Has a falling percentage spent on food meant a shrinking food market?

Identifiable trends include a declining consumption of meat (especially red meat), fat, sugar and stimulants (tea and coffee), and increasing consumption of fish, whole grains, fruit and vegetables. There is also growing demand for organic and naturally produced products and increasing wariness of additives. These trends are particularly evident in northern Europe.

There are, of course, variations in these trends, with meat consumption still high in Germany and Denmark. Growth in the food market also varies across countries (see Tables 8.2 and 8.3) with UK growth very low and high growth in Germany, Ireland and Luxembourg. Spain and Portugal are predicted to show the highest future rates of growth.

Table 8.2   EU growth rates in spending on food (%), 1989–94

	1989	1990	1991	1992	1993	1994
Austria	1.07	1.07	1.06	1.12	na	na
Belgium	1.05	1.50	1.50	1.50	1.50	1.50
Denmark	−0.50	1.50	1.30	1.50	1.00	0.90
Finland	1.06	1.04	1.05	1.05	na	na
France	1.50	1.40	1.20	1.30	1.20	1.10
W Germany*	1.66	3.10	2.75	2.31	2.00	1.95
Greece	1.90	1.60	0.90	1.60	1.50	1.10
Ireland	3.70	2.50	1.90	1.90	2.00	2.00
Italy	1.70	1.40	1.20	1.40	1.50	1.20
Luxembourg	1.75	1.50	1.50	1.50	2.00	2.00
Netherlands	2.00	1.40	1.40	1.60	1.70	1.70
Portugal	1.12	1.14	1.13	1.14	na	na
Spain	2.00	2.00	2.00	1.75	1.75	1.75
Sweden	1.08	1.06	1.06	1.05	na	na
UK	0.59	0.93	1.09	0.86	0.63	0.41

*includes drinks and spending in bars and restaurants   **Source:** Economist Intelligence Unit

Table 8.3   EU per capita spending on food, 1989–94 (ECU 000s: current prices)

	1989	1990	1991	1992	1993	1994
Austria	1.43	1.55	1.65	1.87	na	na
Belgium	1.50	1.62	1.70	1.76	1.82	1.90
Denmark	1.44	1.47	1.48	1.50	1.52	1.52
Finland	1.83	1.84	1.87	1.68	na	na
France	1.48	1.56	1.61	1.69	1.76	1.83
W Germany*	1.84	1.97	2.11	2.24	2.35	2.47
Greece	1.10	1.20	1.29	1.35	1.42	1.48
Ireland	1.09	1.18	1.26	1.34	1.42	1.52
Italy	1.62	1.72	1.78	1.88	2.00	2.10
Luxembourg	1.34	1.41	1.48	1.54	1.62	1.69
Netherlands	1.14	1.19	1.25	1.30	1.36	1.43
Portugal	0.86	0.94	1.03	1.13	1.23	1.33
Spain	1.39	1.49	1.61	1.69	1.81	1.91
Sweden	1.63	1.64	1.75	1.81	na	na
UK	0.94	0.93	0.95	0.99	1.04	1.09
EU average	1.42	1.49	1.57	1.65	1.74	1.83

*includes drinks and spending in bars and restaurants   **Source:** Economist Intelligence Unit

Activity 8.3

1 Calculate the total market for food by multiplying the per capita spending figures
   (see Table 8.3) by the population of each country.
2 Combine the figures obtained with consumption statistics in Table 8.4 (overleaf) to
   identify Member States offering the best prospects in different sectors of the food
   market. Be careful in your interpretation of the consumption figures since many
   variations will reflect cultural differences (e.g. high pasta and low potato consumption in Italy).

Table 8.4   Consumption per capita (kilograms) of food, 1986–87

	Beef	Pork	Mutton	Poultry	Fresh fish	Pasta	Vegetables	Potatoes	Fruit	Eggs[1]	Milk[2]	Bread
Austria	21.5	52.2	1.3	13.7	2.1	2.7	137.5	61.5	83.3	228.8	99.4	19.2
Belgium	20.2	43.1	1.7	18.0	4.0	3.2	179.1	99.4	78.6	98.5	66.7	46.5
Denmark	21.1	66.3	1.0	11.6	38.8	2.9	151.4	65.9	53.2	175.3	99.6	29.3
Finland	20.9	32.3	0.2	8.2	6.6	2.2	114.3	63.7	49.3	152.9	85.9	31.5
France	30.3	36.5	5.7	22.6	5.9	6.5	97.7	34.7	79.5	228.7	53.8	68.3
Germany	22.5	43.7	1.1	13.1	5.7	4.5	114.5	54.4	70.4	205.2	47.7	55.6
Greece	22.1	21.2	14.2	17.1	4.1	4.0	286.8	84.5	90.2	274.7	55.9	29.4
Ireland	16.6	35.4	8.9	22.9	12.9	0.9	240.9	142.9	42.9	174.3	142.9	63.3
Italy	26.7	31.5	1.8	19.2	6.9	25.9	152.7	34.6	108.1	215.7	53.1	67.0
Luxembourg	21.1	50.0	1.9	15.8	4.4	3.4	176.3	94.7	76.3	105.5	110.5	47.4
Netherlands	17.6	44.5	1.4	18.1	7.5	2.0	144.0	44.6	66.1	166.6	60.6	60.0
Portugal	14.2	25.1	3.9	18.7	19.8	5.4	143.1	63.3	35.7	155.3	63.0	12.4
Spain	12.6	49.4	6.4	23.1	11.7	4.2	124.0	57.3	105.9	218.4	97.0	56.8
Sweden	18.2	32.0	0.8	6.6	6.1	3.6	108.6	60.0	57.8	105.7	106.9	33.0
United Kingdom	21.1	21.1	7.0	18.1	1.0	4.9	81.7	47.6	30.0	156.3	102.5	47.1

Source: Euromonitor

All values represent consumption in kilograms per person, except:

1   eggs counted in units
2   milk measured in litres

High-growth segments include fish and seafood, animal and poultry, prepared meat, and processed fruit and vegetables. Food is a 'mature' product area with a growth rate of 2.5–4.0 per cent per annum up until the early 1990s.

Nevertheless, the industry is not very concentrated compared to the USA, for example. Only ten of the top 45 EU food companies are present in all of the five largest Member States with most EU food companies focused on their home country markets, Unilever being one of the few exceptions to this general rule. The Single Market is likely, therefore, to lead to a spate of mergers and takeovers in this sector.

The Four Ps and the food market

You will recall that the so-called *Four Ps* are product, promotion, place and price.

Product

It is important to consider the different segments of the food market. As consumers become more affluent, there is an increased demand for luxury and convenience foods, for high-quality, unusual and exotic products, and for prepared or semi-prepared foods, including frozen and microwavable products as well as fresh and vacuum-packed items. These trends are reinforced by increasing numbers of women going out to work.

Environmental concerns also impact on food, possibly increasing prices as environmental standards become more stringent. The demand for purer foods as well as more organic methods of production should also be taken into account.

Table 8.5 shows where the UK food industry is currently strong and weak.

Table 8.5   The UK food industry, 1992

Major exports	£ billion	Major imports	£ billion
Whisky	1.9	Fresh fruit	1.4
Meat	0.8	Fresh meat	1.0
Confectionery	0.4	Wine and champagne	0.9
Wheat	0.4	Fresh vegetables	0.8
Milk	0.3	Cheese	0.6
Fresh fish	0.3	Sugar	0.6
Shellfish	0.2	Fresh fish	0.5
Biscuits	0.2	Bacon	0.5
Pet food	0.2	Confectionery	0.4
Barley	0.2	Butter	0.3

Source: The British Food Export Council

The British Food Export Council (BFEC) has analysed UK food imports to identify opportunities for UK business to supply what is currently imported. This was done by identifying what proportion of UK imports are unavoidable because:

- the UK climate prevents the production of certain foods (e.g. bananas);
- the UK season for many fruit and vegetables is limited (e.g. fresh strawberries in December);
- quotas in the production of some products necessitates imports;
- there is a demand for imported products considered 'authentic' (e.g. port, sherry, French cheese and wine).

This gives the opportunities shown in Table 8.6 (overleaf). It shows that in 1992, there was an estimated £5.9 billion of business potential for UK companies to supply the UK market.

Table 8.6   Opportunities in the food market for UK business, 1992

Category	Current imports (£ billion)	Unavoidable (£ billion)	UK opportunity (imports-unavoidable)
Indigenous ex-farm	3.5	1.6	1.9
Processed food	5.3	1.6	3.7
Drink	1.6	1.3	0.3
Total	10.4	4.5	5.9

Source: The British Food Export Council

But what about the rest of Europe? Here statistics show increases in UK exports of meat, dairy, cereals and sugar particularly to France, Ireland, Holland and Germany. Hence, the world-wide ban on imports of British beef by the EU in 1996 because of fears regarding infection with BSE was a severe blow in what is a growing export market for the UK.

Promotion

The British Food Export Council (BFEC) has existed since 1971 to promote the UK's food industry. It acts as the agent for the Government-sponsored 'Food From Britain' campaign which has overseas offices in Belgium, France, Germany, Italy, the Netherlands and Spain.

BFCE members are entitled to:

- a free half day's consultation with each of the overseas offices advising on market entry, distribution, promotions and research as well as introductions to overseas buyers;
- participate at reduced rates at key overseas trade fairs, and obtain help with pre-show planning, stand design, PR and on-site back-up;
- overseas introductions to buyers, distributors, wholesalers and agents through BFEC inward and outward trade missions;
- overseas in-store promotions of their products (in the past these have included cheese, salmon, meat, whisky, confectionery and fresh foods);
- a monthly magazine containing market information.

Case study

Barilla

With a 22.5 per cent market share this Italian company is the European market leader in pasta products and pre-eminent in Italy with a 35 per cent domestic market share. Its biggest competitor is Buitoni, owned by the Swiss firm, Nestle.

Barilla's 30 subsidiaries make products in two categories – first pasta (including pasta sauces) where it competes in the medium- and top-price pasta ranges, and secondly oven baked products including fresh bread, crackers, biscuits and cakes. Expansion has been targeted towards Greece, Spain and Poland, and the American (north and south) continent.

The company advertising has taken into account changing consumer perceptions. A 1970s campaign for the White Mill brand focusing on a family living close to nature in a white mill and eating wholesome products has been replaced by a more realistic image featuring city life in Venice and Rome, whilst in Spain, France and Germany, Barilla uses personalities such as Placido Domingo, Gérard Depardieu and Steffi Graf to advertise its products.

It is relevant that the pasta market in Italy lies amongst traditional, conservative consumers whereas elsewhere it is the better off, forward looking, younger consumer that is relevant.

Activity 8.4

1 Identify the advantages and disadvantages of a two track promotion campaign for Barilla's products; one for Italy and one for its other EU export markets?
2 Can you identify food products from other Member States which might have this type of dual image?

Place

Understanding retailing trends is vital to the successful marketing of food in the EU. Although some specialist foods are sold by mail order, retail outlets continue to be the main method of distribution for the foreseeable future. Concentration and out-of-town superstores are both increasing throughout Europe, as well as the UK, as a result of higher car ownership and consumer demand for wider choice under one roof. However, France and the UK are experiencing planning restrictions on out-of-town retailers as the resulting decline of town centres has become obvious.

Most food products are sold through supermarkets but increasingly niche market foods are sold through specialist retailers, such as wine merchants and health and wholefood shops, especially in Germany and Luxembourg.

Price

The UK food distribution system is highly organised by big supermarket chains dominated by Sainsbury and Tesco but this may change with the arrival of discount retailers from other Member States, notably Aldi from Germany and Netto from Denmark. These are discount retailers in the Kwik Save mould offering a restricted 600 brands at very low prices in a no-frills environment, from cheaper town sites. They work on 1 per cent margins in contrast to the lavishly equipped out-of-town superstores which work on 6.5 per cent margins and carry 20,000 lines.

In 1993, Netto had 46 stores in Northern England and was expanding into the Midlands and Scotland. There were also 12 other discount chains compared to only one in 1989. These developments have forced UK companies to adopt the same format. One such example is Shoprite in Scotland with about 70 stores in 1994 and a projected 200 stores by 1996. The established supermarkets have responded by expansion into the rest of Europe by various means including acquisition and joint ventures to give them greater purchasing power as well as share expertise.

PEST analysis of the food market

Below are examples of some issues to be considered in the external environment of the food market. They come under the PEST headings – political, economic, social and technological.

Political

● The EU's Common Agricultural Policy (CAP) raises the prices consumers pay for some basic foodstuffs. CAP reform has been forced on the EU by some Member States (mainly the UK), the international trade agreement, the General Agreement on Tariffs and Trade (GATT), changing production patterns and costs.

- The EU has stopped trying to define food products, the so-called 'recipe' directives, which defined items such as jam. This should give manufacturers more freedom to develop food products.

Economic

- Where different value added tax (VAT) rates apply food tends to be low or zero-rated since it is a basic product rather than a 'luxury' item.
- Food demand varies with economic conditions: consumers purchase luxury, exotic and convenience foods more during good times, reverting to more basic and less pre-pared foods when they need to save money.

Social

- Microwavable snacks and meals are rare in Italy compared to the UK, Germany and France, due to the Italian preference for daily shopping as well as the safety fears Italians have about the use of microwaves.
- Although many food products have been launched by multinational companies, recipes tend to be tuned to national tastes with relatively few multi-cultural variants, such as Chili Con Carne, which sells across all markets.
- Lifestyle differences also affect the food market. More convenience meals are sold where a high proportion of women work and where it is acceptable to eat 'on the run' or in relays within the family home.

Activity 8.5

Use your EU contacts to carry out a survey of eating habits and compare them with UK eating habits by carrying out a similar survey in your college. Areas covered should include:
- whether the family eats together at the table, or on their laps in front of the television, or at staggered intervals;
- who cooks and shops;
- arrangements for mid-day meals at work or school;
- eating out frequency;
- what is eaten as everyday food and as a special treat;
- meal times, duration and what is considered the main meal.

Draw conclusions about likely differences in the two food markets.

- Biotechnological advances have been restricted by environmental and animal rights pressure groups. In the Netherlands, where such techniques are amongst the most advanced in the world, food companies would invest an estimated two to three times more in this research if they did not fear retaliation. Genetically engineered potatoes have been dug up and a complete boycott of all Nutricia products was threatened when the company considered a joint venture with a US company producing powdered baby milk from genetically engineered cows. Nutricia withdrew from the agreement.

Technological

- Heat processed products for microwave oven re-heating emerged during the late 1980s. Packaging developments enabled presentation at room temperature of food with a long shelf life, which could be cooked within its storage container.

- The irradiation of food to prolong its shelf-life is another technological advance affecting the food market. The EU will allow this as long as such foods are clearly marked.
- Genetically modified food plants may also prolong the shelf life of fresh fruit and vegetables; the first genetically engineered tomatoes are already in US shops.

Consumer durables

The consumer durables market includes;
- white goods (mainly kitchen appliances);
- brown goods (mainly audio-visual electronics);
- furniture and furnishings.

Consumer durables are fairly similar across the EU, although differences do exist. For example, Danish toasters to toast rolls are as common as those to toast slices of bread while the French still prefer top-loading washing machines.

The pattern of demand for consumer durables

Generally, the consumer durables market is very cyclical and dependent on the economic climate since spending on these items can be delayed when finances are tight. Like food, the percentage spending in this market has decreased since 1979 (see Table 8.7) but this still represents modest growth in the market as incomes have grown.

Since these items are commonly bought on credit, high interest rates can also depress demand.

Table 8.7 Percentage consumer spending on consumer durables in the EU

Year	%	ECU billion (current prices)
1979	7.2	82
1984	6.2	116
1989	6.2	163
1994	6.3 (estimated)	229 (estimated)

Source: Economist Intelligence Unit

Activity 8.6

Use your EU contacts to find out what credit controls (usually minimum deposit and/or maximum repayment period), if any, apply to the purchase of consumer durables in a selection of EU Member States. Discuss the implications for the market in those countries.

White goods

Some sectors of the white goods market (e.g. washing machines and refrigerators) have reached saturation point all over Europe (see Table 8.8 overleaf). However, tumble dryers, washer-dryers, dishwashers and freezers still offer opportunities for growth. The microwave oven market is mature in the UK but there remains scope for much growth in Italy and Spain if health worries in those countries can be overcome. Growth in demand has been about 3 per cent a year in the late 1980s and early 1990s but lower during the recent recession.

Table 8.8   Ownership levels (%) of the major consumer durables across Europe, 1990

	1	2	3	4	5	6	7	8	9
Austria	96	24	61	35	31	1	97	39	86
Belgium	95	26	86	26	21	1	90	45	88
Denmark	98	20	94	26	13	3	98	39	80
Finland	94	19	72	31	–	4	98	46	76
France	93	23	77	33	25	–	97	43	88
Germany	98	24	73	34	36	3	95	42	92
Greece	94	5	26	10	2	0	93	37	74
Ireland	94	14	58	15	20	3	96	43	81
Italy	94	16	89	20	10	3	91	24	96
Luxembourg	98	30	92	54	15	1	96	39	94
Netherlands	97	43	82	12	19	6	98	47	91
Portugal	92	9	91	–	4	–	87	24	66
Spain	98	11	55	11	9	1	98	44	87
Sweden	97	17	70	31	37	6	96	48	74
UK	98	20	80	12	49	4	95	58	78

Key

1 Televisions	4 Dishwasher	7 Refrigerators
2 CD player	5 Microwave oven	8 Video recorder
3 Freezer	6 Mobile phone	9 Washing machine

Source: Euromonitor and *Reader's Digest*

Electrolux (from Sweden) is the biggest European manufacturer with the US Whirlpool company being the world's largest. High transportation costs ensure the European market is largely supplied by regionally located production facilities (which may be foreign subsidiaries). The sector is highly concentrated with 810 EU producers in 1980 down to 430 in 1989.

Case study

Washing machines, tumble dryers and dishwashers in Italy

Italy is the largest producer and exporter of white goods in Europe with exports eight times greater than imports. Imports tend to be high-quality, high-price brands, mainly from Germany. The market for dishwashers is saturated and tumble dryers are not widely used in Italy; the sales for these two products and for washing machines declining slightly in 1993. Sales were expected to increase by 1995 in all three markets by 5–8 per cent.

Five companies – Electrolux (including Zanussi and AEG), Whirlpool, Merloni (Ariston and Indesit), Candy and Ocean – account for 79 per cent of washing machine sales and 64 per cent of dishwasher sales. The German companies Siemens/Bosch and Miele are strong in the dishwasher market. The UK is the major source for tumble dryers and France for top-loading washing machines. Most of these companies are also involved in the market for industrial laundry machinery.

Built-in dishwashers are becoming increasingly popular. In 1992, 55 per cent were installed in fitted kitchens; this has implications for their distribution. Washing machines are less commonly fitted since they are often placed in the bathroom.

Activity 8.7

What opportunities can you identify in the Italian market for a UK manufacturer of washing machines, tumble dryers and dishwashers?

Brown goods

The brown goods market is more promising. Increased demand for televisions comes from additional portables for kitchen and children's rooms but higher growth is expected from video recorders, camcorders, satellite dishes and home computers which are all still relatively new products.

Furniture

All over Europe spending on furniture and furnishings has been low. Although consumers have spent more on housing they have been extremely price conscious when furnishing them. The biggest market is for dining and living room furniture and about two-thirds of demand is for replacement. Germany specialises in kitchen furniture and Italy, Belgium and Denmark tend to be net exporters of furniture.

Case study

IKEA

Out of the three sectors making up consumer durables, furniture and furnishings are thought to be the most liable to cultural differences. Yet the Swedish company IKEA has had unique success in becoming a pan-European furniture retailer carrying identical stock in all countries including Germany, its biggest market, Denmark and the UK which will eventually have ten stores. It may be that the Scandinavian style travels the best across national boundaries. IKEA's major selling point is its low prices in relation to quality, i.e. good value for money.

The Four Ps and the consumer durables market

Product

The brown goods sector offers the best opportunities for increased demand through new products such as:

- digital compact cassette (DCC) from Philips in 1992 and the mini-disc from Sony in 1993 to replace audio cassettes and compact discs (CDs);
- compact disc interactive (CD-I) an interactive multi-media system merging CDs and video;
- widescreen television;
- high-definition television;
- digital audio broadcasting (DAB);
- traffic guidance systems;
- continued innovation of computer/video games.

The successful introduction of these products relies on the support of 'software' industries such as the music companies to put albums on DCC and the film companies to put films on CD-I.

Case study

Compact disc interactive (CD-I)

Philips launched this new product at the Cannes film festival in 1993. It offers digital quality films and rock videos with surround sound as well as extremely realistic digital video games, educational programs, fitness videos, video magazines and karaoke. Philips' research found that interest in the product was high with 31 per cent very interested and 48 per cent quite interested in CD-I.

Learning from previous difficulties when introducing CD players at a time when little was available on CD, Philips ensured that there was a great deal of CD-I program material ready to hit the market at the same time as the launch of their equipment in the UK in October 1993, the Benelux countries in November 1993 and the rest of Europe during 1994.

Activity 8.8

The case study above describes the CD-I market as it was in 1994. Assess how the market has developed since then. Has the product taken off or been overtaken by new developments or the standards set by a competitor?

In the furniture market, innovation comes from the use of stronger and cheaper materials but mainly through the design of flat-pack items which can be sold and transported more cheaply.

Promotion

In the consumer durables sector it is more usual to advertise the brand rather than the individual product. The following case study illustrates one approach to the difficulty of breaking into a mature market.

Case study

Philips-Whirlpool

The US company Whirlpool is the largest domestic appliance manufacturer in the world but by the late 1980s was unknown in Europe. The company decided that Europe was too large to ignore and decided to sell there through a joint venture with the well-established Dutch firm Philips. This led to the eventual takeover of the Philips domestic appliance division by the US company.

As a result of the takeover the US company was able to use the familiar (to Europeans) Philips name whilst introducing their Whirlpool brand name. This was done through dual marketing of the name Philips/Whirlpool with the aim to phase out the Philips name by 1998. However, the Whirlpool brand has established itself sufficiently strongly in four of the EU markets, including the UK, to allow the Philips name to be dropped ahead of schedule.

Place

For consumer electronics, multiple chain stores dominate through their strong bulk buying ability, efficient distribution and national advertising. There is little difference between chains and great over-capacity in the UK as shown by the closure of the Rumbelows chain in 1995. The lower mass market niches are seeing the introduction of large out-of-town discount stores whilst the up-market niches are usually catered for by specialist retailers such as Bang and Olufsen.

Much the same applies to the domestic appliance and furniture markets except in furniture where the retailers have the market power since there are very few large furniture companies.

Price

Many Member States have abolished the higher luxury rates of VAT into which consumer durables often fall. However, the recession affecting all Member States in the early 1990s has forced down prices in these markets (partly financed by a reduction in advertising) to overcome the resulting lack of consumer confidence.

PEST analysis of the consumer durables market

Below are examples of some issues to be considered in the external environment of the consumer durables market.

Political
- The EU is likely to require higher environmental standards for products in the consumer durables market. For example, CFCs (chlorofluorocarbons) in refrigerators must be eliminated by 1995; the forthcoming Packaging Directive will have implications.
- The EU recognises that consumer electronics companies with a technological edge will be the successes of the 21st century and therefore supports research work on high-definition television and large flat screens through the Eureka, Race and Esprit programmes. The EU also plans to offer financial support to broadcasters to convert to the new technology. A further advantage is that it is the successful companies which set world standards so if European companies can set the standards they will avoid the cost of adapting to, say, Japanese standards later on.
- Companies in the consumer durables sector will have to comply with the 1994 EU Regulation limiting electrical interference of equipment using mains supply; this may require the redesigning of some models.

Economic
- To reduce government deficits, taxation (direct and indirect) is increasing all over Europe, reducing disposable income, and so forecasts for growth in this sector until 1996 are low.
- Many EU governments use high interest rates to reduce inflation, reducing demand in the consumer durables sector where credit is often used to finance purchases.

Social
- The trend towards more, smaller households due to increased divorce, single parenthood and affluence, increases demand in the consumer durables sector especially for small capacity appliances such as table-top ovens.
- Environmental concerns will also increase demand for energy- and water-efficient appliances. In furniture, concern is growing about the use of unsustainable tropical hardwoods.
- Manufacturers of washing machines and dishwashers can apply to win the eco-label that tells consumers which are the most environmentally friendly choices in those product groups (see Chapter 3). Companies must pay a fee to be considered for the award of the label which entails a thorough examination of all aspects of the production process. Even if they are judged to be among the most environmentally friendly,

the label is only valid for three years, after which time the company must re-apply to see if it is still among the most environmentally friendly within its product group. Other consumer durables are likely to be brought within the scheme at a later date if it proves useful to consumers.

Technological

- In white goods, consumers may be stimulated to replace existing equipment by the inclusion of electronic components which increase efficiency and ease of use.
- In consumer electronics there is a trend towards convergence with telecommunications, computer and media technologies. Thus companies in these three sectors must now be seen as competitors or possible partners.

Summary

- Pan-European brands are more common in the consumer durable market than the food market.
- Growth sectors within the food market include exotic, prepared and convenience food.
- Opportunities exist for UK businesses to replace existing food imports.
- The role of the British Food Export Council is described.
- Growth sectors in the consumer durable market are mainly in brown goods with the white goods market being largely mature.
- A PEST analysis is outlined for both food and consumer durables.

Information sources

- *Panorama of EC Industry 1994*, European Commission.
- *Food and Drink Trade Review*, published annually by Food from Britain.
- Euromonitor publications.
- Economist Intelligence Unit (EIU) publications.

Assignment 8.1
Daloon

This assignment fulfils the following criteria:
RSA   13.2.1 to 13.2.6

Daloon was started in 1960 by a Chinese immigrant to Denmark making pancake rolls. It now has two production sites in Denmark and one in Newark, England. Daloon's product portfolio includes a range of filled spring rolls as well as samosas, savoury souffles and ice cream pancakes. The range includes low-calorie and vegetarian products and company policy is to use no colourings, flavourings or preservatives.

Sales of deep fried rolls are declining so the company concentrates on products for oven or frying pan and is working on microwaveable rolls where the main problem is to crisp the rolls. The 'roll' (the pancake) is virtually the same for all products but the filling can easily be varied, enabling the company to take advantage of economies of scale even when producing small runs of specialised fillings. The pancake machinery developed by the company is protected by patents.

By 1992 the company employed 250, producing almost 150 million rolls sold in 25 countries. Since 1988, the German market has grown by 500 per cent, mainly through the Aldi supermarket chain which accounts for almost 30 per cent of sales, as do Denmark and the UK respectively. Daloon's customer base keeps expanding through industrial concentration which presents opportunities for rapid growth but is also very risky (i.e. Daloon's customers take over other companies, thereby increasing the size of orders abruptly by a large amount).

In the past, Daloon found it easier to enter foreign markets through catering establishments such as works canteens, higher education establishments, hospitals and the military, rather than the retail sector. Daloon's success in the German catering sector is because Germans expect hot food for their mid-day meal, unlike the traditional Danish cold table. Daloon entered all new markets both under their own brand name and using their customers' label. Although not European, there are variations in what different EU markets think of as pancake rolls. In Holland, customers expect the drier Indonesian style with more chicken and bean sprouts while in France they are used to the thinner Vietnamese rolls.

In 1992, Daloon successfully persuaded McDonald's (Germany) to take their products for a two-week China campaign. McDonald's requested major product changes, insisting on a 20 gram roll (compared to the normal 100 gram version) requiring extensive adjustments to production machinery. This was so successful that McDonald's (Germany) wants to re-run the campaign. McDonald's (UK) ran an identical China campaign in February 1993 and McDonald's (Sweden and the Netherlands) both expressed great interest. The two-week German campaign required the production of an additional 26 million small rolls.

Your tasks

1 Use the information above to produce a brief SWOT and PEST analysis of the company on a European scale. What is the effect on your analysis of the fact that the products are non-European ethnic foods? (Are cultural differences to be expected?)
2 Advise Daloon whether or not it should expand its links with McDonald's in the rest of Europe. What are the implications for production capacity, for example, if the Daloon roll became a permanent feature of the McDonald's German menu?

Part of your background research could include a visit to a large supermarket to check Daloon's current product portfolio available in the UK (e.g. through Kwik Save, Waitrose, some Co-ops, and Tesco's own label).

9 Distribution

Use this chapter to help plan how to get goods to the rest of the European Union (EU) by:

- choosing the best transport method;
- weighing up costs against level of service.

This chapter covers the following performance criteria:
BTEC   16.1.4
RSA   13.2.1, 13.3.1 to 13.3.6

Introduction

Having established a demand for your product elsewhere in the EU, part of your marketing strategy must include consideration of how best to get the product to your customer. Many choices are open to a prospective exporter but the right choice is vital since distribution method affects not only the final price to the client but also the level of service which forms part of your product package. In product areas with little product differentiation, distribution speed and efficiency are the key to success. Distribution will also be a factor in choosing suppliers for raw materials and components.

Chain of distribution

The chain of distribution describes the way in which goods reach the final customer from the manufacturer. Figure 9.1 shows the available choices.

Generally, the fewer links in the chain, the lower the price to the final customer and the more control you have over the way your product is promoted. Route 2 is efficient when dealing with a widely distributed multiple or chain store but is very inefficient when dealing with small, independently-owned retailers. Route 3 may pass through more than one wholesaler with consequent effects on your profit margin. Route 4 could also involve more than one agent, an export agent in the UK and an import agent in each final EU market, for example.

It may be necessary to use different routes in the distribution chain in different Member States. Recall the importance of the independent retailer in southern Europe; possibly requiring heavier reliance on wholesalers than in France or Germany (see Figure 7.8).

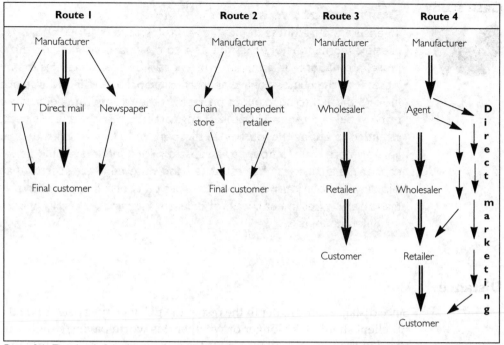

Figure 9.1   The chain of distribution: four optional routes

Activity 9.1

Using examples of local exporting companies with whom you have had previous contacts, find out which routes in the chain of distribution they use and why. Is there a difference between their UK and overseas distribution?

Practicalities

Increased complexity

Owing to the cultural and legal differences, and the greater distances involved, it is likely that your chain of distribution for supplying the rest of the EU will be more complex than for your domestic customers.

Export requirements

Although the EU has made great progress in removing obstacles to the movement of goods within its frontiers, there still remain specific requirements which must be met in the different countries. Specific licences may be required for certain goods, such as military equipment, computers and antiques, while the trade in others may be banned completely, such as narcotic drugs, or restricted, as in the case of firearms. For goods subject to tariffs or quotas, Certificates of Origin may be needed to verify where they were made. The DTI can advise on requirements. One issue of recent concern was the movement of live animals.

Case study

Transport of live animals

To ensure the freshness of meat it seems logical to slaughter animals at the last possible moment before they are sold to the final consumer. As this trade becomes more international, in common with most other products, this has meant an increase in the number of live animals transported and in the distance they travel. In 1994 this led to huge public protests in the UK and the demand was that such trade should be banned or at least regulated so that the animals' welfare was attended to during the journey. In this case, UK rules which state that when travelling for more than 15 hours to an abattoir, lorry drivers should break their journey so that the animals can be rested, fed and watered, were stricter than EU laws allowing 24-hour journeys. The Commission adopted amendments introducing mandatory refreshment breaks at different intervals (generally every eight hours) for different animals.

Distance

Since distances are greater to the rest of the EU, you must decide whether delivery to an EU client should take longer or whether it is worth paying a higher transport cost for speed in order to offer all EU clients the same level of service. Partly this will depend on who you see as your competitors; if they are located in the target EU market then you need to match their delivery times.

Deregulation and the Single Market

The Single Market programme included measures to ease the servicing of clients in other Member States. One was the abolition of customs controls to shorten frontier delays which on a 1200 kilometre journey could add six hours in addition to the 48 hours travelling time; another was deregulation to allow transport operators to run more efficiently. This simplified the rules allowing the carriage of loads on the return journey and the extension of the *right of cabotage*, whereby goods can be transported on routes wholly outside the home country of the operator. One distribution company advertised that its rates were up to 30 per cent lower with the advent of the Single Market.

Trans-European networks

Transport networks have tended to grow to meet national rather than international needs with many networks converging on capital cities or being incompatible with neighbouring states, such as different power systems in the case of rail. The EU has, therefore, examined the network across the whole territory and identified gaps which it will be prepared to help finance (through the new Cohesion Fund) and support in other ways. Its objective is to meet business needs and extend the network to the peripheral EU areas to bring the economic benefits of the Single Market to these areas too. Figure 9.2 shows the European rail network with the gaps identified by the EU. These it sees as essential to plug in order to have an efficient Europe-wide network.

On the roads, proposed electronic charging and traffic management systems should use compatible technologies. Other problems include pollution and congestion, the latter estimated to cost 2 per cent of total EU gross domestic product (GDP). One aim is therefore to reduce the amount of freight which goes by road by promoting intermodal

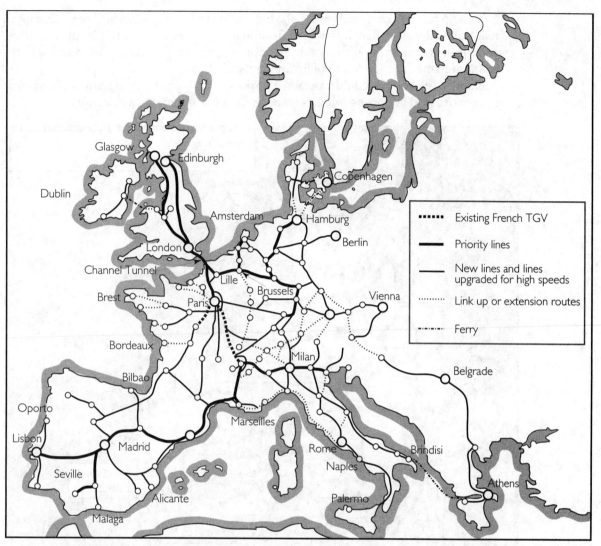

Source: *The Geography of the European Community*, J Cole and F Cole, Routledge, 1993

Figure 9.2 The European high-speed rail network

Legend:
- **••••••** Existing French TGV
- **——** Priority lines
- —— New lines and lines upgraded for high speeds
- ·········· Link up or extension routes
- —·—·— Ferry

transport. This would mean long distances are covered by rail or ship, transferring onto lorry for the final local leg.

The EU will co-ordinate and stimulate the creation of Trans-European Networks (TENs) of road, rail, sea and air links over the next 15 years at a cost of ECU300 bn. These plans extend beyond the present EU boundaries because several more countries may join the EU over the next decade and because East Europe is likely to constitute an important market in the future, whether inside or outside the EU. TENs consists of 14 infrastructure schemes which include high speed rail links between France and Madrid, motorways between Greece and Bulgaria and Malpensa airport in Milan. Other developments include the Channel Tunnel linking the UK and France, the Øresund bridge (to be completed by 2000) linking Sweden and Denmark, the alpine tunnel through the Brenner Pass, Austria (10 to 20 years away) and the completion of the Rhine–Danube canal linking the Benelux ports with the Black Sea in Romania. Europe-wide co-operation will create fewer air traffic control areas, joint time-tabling and through ticketing, all of which will improve transport efficiency.

To help plan international routes, the EU has identified high-standard cross-European roads and allocated them a standard E-numbering system. For example, the E15 starts at Inverness with the A9, goes on to London via the M1, and then goes onto Paris, the South of France and the South of Spain via the East coast.

Knowledge of planned European networks will help predict likely shifts in commercial centres so that Europe-wide operations can be planned more efficiently.

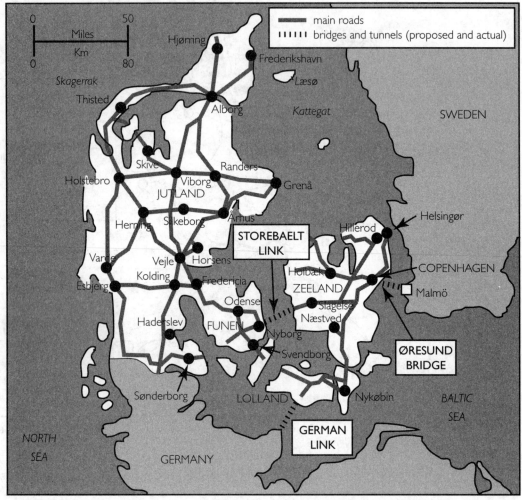

Source: *Financial Times*, 29 November 1993

Figure 9.3 The fixed link between Denmark and Sweden

Activity 9.2

Use Figure 9.3 to decide the likeliest routes currently taken by Swedish exporters and how these might change once the bridge between Denmark and Sweden is complete. Which areas of Denmark are likely to be affected and in what way? (Hint: is Denmark the most likely destination of Swedish exports?)

The balance of power

The balance of power between supplier, wholesaler and retailer will differ across Europe. In France and Germany, the retailer is likely to be dominant whereas the wholesaler is more important in Spain and Italy.

Terms of delivery

Pricing may need to be reviewed to take into account additional transport costs. When crossing international borders options exist to quote for delivery to different points in the chain, for example, to the quayside (known as free alongside ship (FAS)), delivered duty unpaid (DDU), etc. However, to compete effectively with local suppliers in the target market door-to-door delivery (delivery duty paid – DDP) should be the norm although in 1985 only 18 per cent of UK exporters to Europe used this as a basis for pricing.

Payment

Two factors are important here:
● the fluctuations in exchange rates and charges involved in exchanging currencies;
● method and security of payment.
A UK exporter will wish to quote prices in sterling, passing the possibility of variations in the exchange rate onto the customer but in Europe it is more usual for the UK exporter to accept the currency risk and quote in the customer's currency. Prices are increasingly quoted in ECUs.

There are two approaches to getting paid. For most EU trade, goods are sold on *open credit*, meaning that you trust the buyer to pay within the stipulated period, say, 30 days. Many British banks have branches overseas and if you anticipate regular remittances of money from another Member State it may be worth opening an account there so that your organisation gains title to the money as soon as possible and it also means that payees can use their usual payment methods. The transfer of many small amounts of money should be avoided since the transaction costs will soon mount up. Alternatively, your customer could have an external account in the UK with its bank and could send your organisation a cheque drawn on this account. This would only be a good idea if you were happy with your customer's creditworthiness.

Some banking systems, such as in Spain, are very slow and bureaucratic in their international transfers. A common payment method for bills under £3000 are international money transfers which come by mail while higher bills can be paid by telegraphic transfer which are sent by telex or other telecommunication means. Another safe method of payment is a banker's draft drawn on a UK bank.

The second approach to payment, the safest method, is the *documentary letter of credit* whereby the bank in the buyer's country will only release essential documents transferring ownership of the goods on payment of the required amount. However, care needs to be taken with this method since in 1991, two-thirds of letters of credit were rejected on first presentation because they were incorrectly filled in.

Activity 9.3

Find out what payment services the major high street banks offer to exporters to the EU. How would you choose which offers the best service?

Security and insurance

With longer distances and handling by more intermediaries, the possibility of damage or theft is greater; therefore insurance is essential. The policy will depend on the terms of delivery and should cover the goods until their ownership transfers to the buyer whether this is ex-works, at the destination port or at the buyer's site. If your buyer presents a financial risk, it may be worth obtaining credit insurance against the possibility of non-payment. Practical measures also need to be taken to ensure the safe delivery of the goods including appropriate packaging and environment for products with special needs such as specific temperatures or humidity. For large deliveries, sealed containers reduce the risk of theft whereas small deliveries could be safeguarded by using the tracking systems offered by express delivery firms such as DHL.

Transport methods

Whichever distribution option is chosen, the exporter will have to ensure transportation of goods to the first link in the chain.

Table 9.1 shows that as the scale of operation changes so does the preferred method of transport. Domestic trade is largely serviced by road transport, whereas trade between the Member States makes much more use of sea and inland waterways, with road still predominant. Sea transport is the most commonly used method for trade between the EU and the rest of the world.

Table 9.1 Most commonly used transport methods for different EU trading situations (percentage)

	Road	Sea	Rail	Inland water	Air
Total EU domestic and between Member States	87	–	7	6	–
Between Member States	40	30	8	21	0.1
Between EU and rest of the world	11	78	5	5	1

Source: Eurostat

Road

The proportion of goods carried by road continues to increase despite environmental worries about noise, pollution and the destruction of the countryside. Its main advantage lies in the convenience of door-to-door delivery while other transport methods must invariably transfer the goods to road for the last leg of the journey from the node (port, railway station or aerodrome) nearest the destination.

Road is most often used to transport manufactured articles, foodstuffs and agricultural products. Speed limits of 80 kph, restrictions on weekend driving and drivers' hours regulations must all be taken into account when projecting the estimated time for a road delivery. In February 1994, the Swiss voted to ban transit freight traffic through their country within ten years to avoid the increasing environmental damage created by the growing volume of traffic. This illustrates the dilemma faced by the EU if it improves road infrastructure, as this invariably causes environmental problems. Not only do people complain, but care for the environment is now also one of the EU's major policies.

Activity 9.4

1 Compare the distances and routes taken by an Italian exporter from Turin to Frankfurt before and after the Swiss ban.
2 Estimate what difference this will make to delivery times.

Activity 9.5

1 Consider the case of a company based in Bristol making 20 full lorry deliveries a week each to Manchester and London. Use Figure 9.4 (overleaf), which gives average road delivery times between major centres in Europe, to calculate the total number of hours you can expect your fleet to be on the road per week, to carry out these deliveries. (Add up the figures between any two destinations to obtain the total journey time, for example, Paris to Bordeaux is 7 plus 2 which is 9 hours.)
2 Now consider the effect on this company if it obtains more business in Glasgow, Hamburg and Lyons – each destination requiring an additional three deliveries a week.
   a How many extra hours does this add to the existing commitment?
   b It is likely that these three new customers will increase their orders in the near future so would it be worth relocating from Bristol to, say, Rotterdam?
   c At what point does it become worthwhile to relocate and would Rotterdam be the best destination?

A full load is one of 15 to 16 tonnes in weight and/or 45 to 50 cubic metres in capacity for which you can expect quick and personalised handling. For smaller loads, the carrier takes the cargo to a depot where it is consolidated or grouped together with other deliveries. This may slow down the service waiting for deliveries to the same destination and requires intermediate handling to separate the deliveries at the destination depot.

Rail

Transport by rail is on the decrease, partly due to the fact that rail is commonly used to transport goods in the declining primary and heavy secondary sectors (e.g. metal products, ores and solid mineral fuels). Rail is also widely used to transport manufactured articles. It is best for large and regular deliveries although the grouping of small loads, as for road, is possible.

The EU is supporting the establishment of an efficient Europe-wide, high-speed rail network as part of its Trans-European Network programme, partly because railway transport is seen as environmentally more acceptable than road. However, there are technical compatibility problems as Spain has a different railway gauge (although this is being changed), France and Germany use different power voltages, and height limits for tunnels differ in the UK. These factors all add to journey times as the rolling stock is adjusted or swapped at national frontiers.

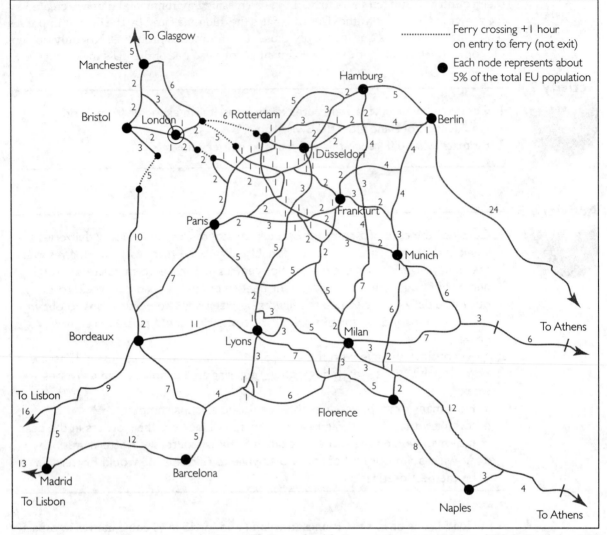

Figure 9.4 within the map:

To Glasgow

Manchester

Bristol

London

Rotterdam

Hamburg

Berlin

Düsseldorf

Frankfurt

Paris

Munich

Bordeaux

Lyons

Milan

To Lisbon

Florence

Barcelona

Madrid

To Lisbon

Naples

To Athens

To Athens

.... Ferry crossing +1 hour on entry to ferry (not exit)

● Each node represents about 5% of the total EU population

Source: *The Geography of the European Community*, J Cole and F Cole, Routledge, 1993

Figure 9.4 Average road delivery times within Europe

Rail becomes economic only at distances over 250 kilometres, competing with road over shorter distances and air or water over longer distances. British Rail expects that the opening of the Channel Tunnel will treble UK rail freight within two years.

Inland waterways

This is the cheapest transportation method and has increased in popularity although the UK network is little used at present. The network of rivers and canals is especially good between France, Germany and Benelux. Speed is low and this method is best for large, regular deliveries of bulky products such as coal, steel, chemicals, hazardous substances and containerised goods.

A major improvement in the network was the opening of the Rhine–Danube canal. Joining the two rivers creates a 3500 kilometre waterway from the North Sea to the Black Sea, through the Netherlands, Germany, Austria, Hungary, the former Yugoslavia, Bulgaria and Romania (see Figure 9.5).

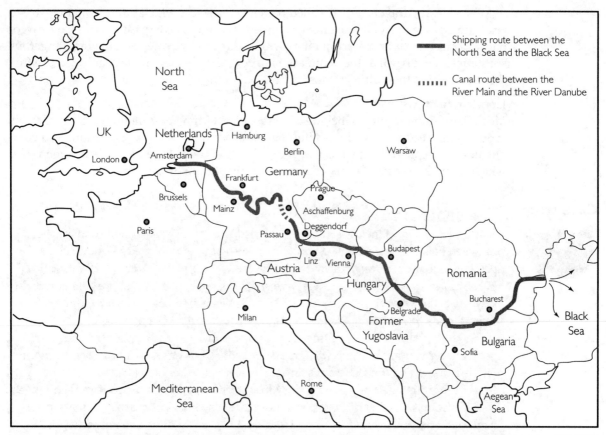

Source: *Transport and Distribution in the Single Market*, the European Business Guides series, CBI, 1992

Figure 9.5 The Rhine-Danube Canal

Sea

Sea transport is another cheap but slow method of transportation, recommended for deliveries between the peripheries of the EU such as between Portugal and Denmark or Ireland and Greece.

Deliveries from outside the EU are increasingly likely to involve one stop only at Antwerp or Rotterdam for onward delivery throughout the EU. Much sea cargo is now carried by container.

In the UK, Hull (and the Humber estuary ports generally) are becoming increasingly important as routes for freight from Scotland, Ireland, northern England and the Midlands to Rotterdam for onward distribution across most of Europe within 24 hours. The other east coast ports of Ipswich, Felixstowe and Harwich also benefit from the Single Market.

The EU is considering the creation of a common European flag and register (called Euros) to ensure EU shipping operates to common safety standards and has cabotage rights.

Air

Air freight is an expensive option suitable for high-value or perishable goods where speed of delivery is crucial. Commonly transported items include high-value electronics, urgent spare parts, perishable fruit and vegetables, flowers, fresh and frozen meat and fish, live animals such as day-old chicks or unhatched eggs, and frozen livestock semen.

Most air cargo travels on scheduled passenger services which limits container size to 60 centimetres high and it must not be dangerous cargo. The biggest airlines have cargo-only aircraft which can take containers with less restrictive rules on carrying dangerous substances. On arrival at the destination airport, the goods will inevitably require further transport to their ultimate destination.

Combined transport

Most distribution solutions include a combination of transport methods. In the UK this is due to the need to cross the sea but there are also other reasons. For example, a combination of sea and inland waterway may allow the goods to remain on the same vessel which reduces the cost of transfer from one transport method to another.

Case study

The Channel Tunnel

The Channel Tunnel includes shuttle services for people, vehicles and road freight between Folkestone and Calais; through-trains from London to Paris and Brussels for passengers only; and freight services from nine UK terminals to about 20 mainland European terminals (see Figure 9.6). Freight will largely be in containers and in future may travel 'piggyback', whereby the lorry trailer is loaded complete onto the rail wagon, once the necessary raising of tunnels and bridges has been made.

The tunnel should be less susceptible to delays due to bad weather than sea transport and often prior booking will not be needed. However, the major selling point for distributors will be the fast transit times. For example, the tunnel has reduced the Rover car group's delivery times to Italy from eight days down to two days. The tunnel should also make rail freight economic now that longer journeys are possible and may help food companies gain a valuable 12 to 48 hours extra on the supermarket shelf.

As south-east England suffers increasingly from traffic congestion, some companies may base distribution centres for this area in northern France. At a European level, some companies could serve the whole of northern Europe from northern France, using the tunnel to reach the UK and Ireland.

Containerisation

Most goods have to be transferred to road for the last leg of the journey regardless of how the bulk of the travel was made. Efficiency requires that these transfers are kept to a minimum and that, if necessary, they are made as easily as possible.

A development which has eased swapping from one form of transport to another is the increasing use of containers (see Figure 9.7). These metal boxes of varying sizes can be carried by lorry, rail, air and water, and are easily transferred between all four transport modes. An added advantage is that they can be securely sealed after customs inspection. This increases security of the goods and reduces the need for further customs inspection as long as the seal remains unbroken.

The exporter needs to decide whether the quantities to be carried will fill a container or whether to share a container. Special needs can also be catered for with, for example, ventilated or refrigerated containers. Typical dimensions for a container are:

- 12.19 metres (or 6.15 metres) long
- 2.59 metres high
- 2.44 metres wide,

giving a usable capacity of almost 67 cubic metres or 26,600 kilograms.

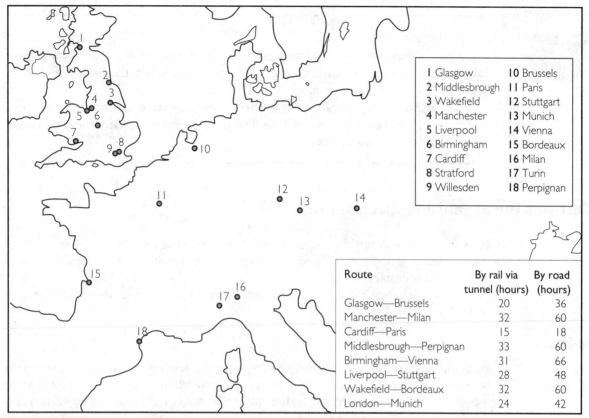

1 Glasgow	10 Brussels	
2 Middlesbrough	11 Paris	
3 Wakefield	12 Stuttgart	
4 Manchester	13 Munich	
5 Liverpool	14 Vienna	
6 Birmingham	15 Bordeaux	
7 Cardiff	16 Milan	
8 Stratford	17 Turin	
9 Willesden	18 Perpignan	

Route	By rail via tunnel (hours)	By road (hours)
Glasgow—Brussels	20	36
Manchester—Milan	32	60
Cardiff—Paris	15	18
Middlesbrough—Perpignan	33	60
Birmingham—Vienna	31	66
Liverpool—Stuttgart	28	48
Wakefield—Bordeaux	32	60
London—Munich	24	42

Figure 9.6 Channel Tunnel terminals

Figure 9.7 Containers on board ship

Source: Sea Containers Services Ltd

Activity 9.6

Arrange a visit to either:

a a rail or sea container terminal for a guided tour to find out more about the types of goods carried by container, the terminal's main customers, the most popular destinations, the equipment used, etc., or

b a local company using containers as part of its distribution operations to find out the frequency of container use, the destinations, the goods carried, the time taken, and any other relevant information.

Options for organising distribution

Choice of option will partly depend on the objectives of the distribution plan:

- Will faster (and hence more costly) delivery result in greater cost savings by reduced stockholding costs?
- Will faster delivery increase sales to more than compensate for the extra transport cost?

In-house

This involves the exporter taking responsibility for the delivery of the goods direct to the customer using the exporter's own fleet (most commonly road transport). This may be the best option for large, regular orders although in fact most companies still tend to carry out their own distribution. The work of scheduling will include choosing the best transport method, ensuring all export requirements are met, estimating costs and time, and deciding on the details of collection and delivery. A first-time exporter will usually lack the confidence for this and contract-out delivery to a specialist company especially if exporting is an irregular occurrence. However, many experienced exporting companies now concentrate on their core businesses and contract-out distribution so this is a declining option.

Freight forwarder

Transport organisation can be delegated to a freight forwarder experienced in export procedures including customs and insurance (although one result of the Single Market is to reduce the paperwork). Freight forwarders can also negotiate the best transport deals with transport operators for their exporting clients.

Transport operator

Instead of going through a freight forwarder, exporters could deal directly with transport operators, booking containers, ships, lorries or space on a freight train. This requires good in-house expertise to put together the best combination of transport routes and methods but still leaves the exporter with responsibility for all documentation, finance and insurance.

Integrated distribution

Integrated distribution companies meet distribution needs by providing 'one-stop shopping'. Their services include logistics planning, transport, warehousing and freight forwarding. They usually expect long-term contracts of five to ten years with client companies and as businesses become more cost-conscious this option is increasingly popular.

Case study

> **Laura Ashley**
>
> The UK clothing and furnishing retailer Laura Ashley decided to stop arranging its own distribution and in 1992 gave a ten-year contract to Business Logistics (part of Federal Express) to cover its worldwide distribution needs. Laura Ashley has 540 shops in 28 countries, obtains goods from suppliers located all over the world and offers a home delivery service. Appointment of a specialist company was expected to save 10 per cent of the company's annual distribution costs (saving £1.5 million in 1992), as well as enabling 48-hour delivery anywhere in the world from 1993.

Express services

These are the most visible companies and include names such as DHL, Federal Express, TNT and UPS. You may have seen their advertisements on television and in glossy business magazines. Generally, express services are the most expensive option, suitable only for urgent parcels under 30 kilograms in weight rather than bulk freight. However, they have a role in sending samples or one-off urgently needed parts and the largest express service companies also offer integrated distribution services.

Case study

> **ICL Data**
>
> This UK-Norwegian company sells, installs and maintains personal computers (PCs) and PC networks, and offers training courses and services for data processing and data communication to seven European countries. The company decided to locate in the Netherlands because its advisers felt that Dutch customs facilities were well geared to the Single Market, infrastructure is good, the location is central and there are many suitable distribution companies to choose from in the Netherlands.
>
> ICL Data provides its own transport for deliveries within the Netherlands because distances are so short but has contracted a distribution company to carry out the remaining distribution functions. It expects its distribution costs to fall from 5.5 per cent of the purchase value of the goods to half that figure as a result. In addition, the service should improve with deliveries to Spain taking only 24 hours compared to a week and a half in the past.

Costs

The way in which costs vary are the same both in the UK and the EU as a whole. In general:

- large, regular deliveries are cheaper per unit kilometre than small irregular or one-off deliveries;
- loads requiring special care conditions, such as refrigerated transport, are more expensive;

- long-distance deliveries are cheaper per kilometre than short distances;
- door-to-door, fully tracked and traced deliveries are more expensive;
- sea transport is usually quoted on the basis of a full container load (FCL) in US dollars on a port-to-port basis although it is also possible to get quotes for door-to-door delivery and for less than full container load (LFC) which are quoted per freight tonne;
- road transport rates from the UK to mainland Europe include the sea or Channel Tunnel crossing in the price;
- rates are lower when the vehicle can pick up a return load to avoid returning empty.

Table 9.2 shows how non-UK firms price outward deliveries from the UK lower than onward deliveries thus reducing the number of empty return journeys.

Table 9.2 Pricing to avoid empty return journeys

Route	Full load price (£) outwards from UK	Full load price (£) inwards to UK
London–Milan	800	1400
London–Paris	350	700
London–Frankfurt	500	800
London–Amsterdam	400	700
London–Antwerp	250	400

Source: *European Logistics*, Cooper, Browne & Peters

You will find it difficult to obtain prices from transport operators as this highly competitive market likes to deal with each customer on an individual basis rather than offering set prices.

A study in 1989 showed that the cost of transporting a load by road over 500 kilometres was 510 ECU regardless almost of company or route. The exceptions were Spanish and Greek companies which quoted prices 15 per cent lower, mainly due to their lower labour costs.

Case study

From Denmark to the UK by United Parcels Service (UPS)

UPS is one of the world's leading express companies, carrying deliveries of up to 1500 kg. Below is an example of its charges as at August 1995, assuming that a delivery of four 15 kg packages, each measuring 75 × 40 × 40 cm, from Copenhagen to Manchester is required.

Gross weight of the delivery is 4 × 15 kg which is 60 kg. However, transport operators also use the concept of volumetric weight which in this case would be calculated as follows:

$$\frac{75 \times 40 \times 40 \text{ cm}}{6000} = 20 \text{ kg per package}$$

Since there are four packages, total volumetric weight comes to 80 kg in all.

Different companies may use slightly different formulas to calculate the volumetric weight but in all cases, it is the highest value which is used in calculating the cost of delivery. In this case volumetric weight is more than gross weight so the tariff for 80 kg is charged.

UPS then gives customers a choice between an express (next working day) delivery or what they call an expedited delivery, which travels overland rather than by air, and may take one or two days longer. For 80 kg its express service costs £442 and its expedited service costs £123.

Industrial distribution

Just-in-time (JIT) distribution and inventory systems are increasingly adopted in industry and require frequent and reliable deliveries of raw materials and components just before they are required in the manufacturing process. This reduces storage and stock-holding costs and enables manufacturers to produce small batches profitably. However, JIT places a great responsibility on the supplier to deliver often and at specified times.

JIT is a complicated process made possible through the faster and more efficient computer software and hardware now available, especially when the manufacturer has direct links with its suppliers.

Case study

Avesta Sheffield

This Swedish steel company has replaced its network of small-scale local warehouses with a co-ordinated distribution system divided into three European regions (see Figure 9.8). The Nordic area is serviced from Eskilstuna, Sweden; the UK and Ireland area from Birmingham; and the Central European area from just outside Düsseldorf, Germany for flat products whilst pipe and tube fittings are co-ordinated from the Netherlands. This distribution system reflects the fact that 47 per cent of Avesta's sales come from the UK, Germany and the Nordic area.

The result is that standard products available from stocks can be delivered to most customers within 24 hours which is necessary with the increasing application of just-in-time systems.

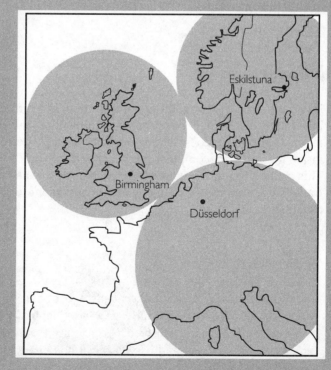

Source: Avesta Sheffield *Annual Report 1993*

Figure 9.8 Avesta Sheffield distribution system

Since JIT implies long-term relationships between supplier and manufacturer this means that manufacturers will reduce the number of suppliers with whom they deal. The supplier who is able to offer JIT delivery, which may involve locating a facility close to the manufacturer, will secure contracts.

Retail distribution

Trends show that hypermarkets are increasing and that there is a rise in franchising and a proliferation of forms of distance selling. Apart from a different retail structure, there may also be cultural differences, such as the fact that French retailers like to hold six weeks of stock whereas UK retailers hold much less. Retailers operate through wholesalers much more in Ireland and the southern European states of Spain, Italy, Portugal and Greece where the small independent shop is much more common; elsewhere the remaining wholesalers are expanding in size and reducing in number.

The trend in Europe has been for vertical integration of the chain of distribution with much more co-operation (mainly through the exchange of information on consumer purchasing patterns) along the chain to reduce stock levels and delivery times. In food, the retailer is dominant, often requiring suppliers to deliver to central distribution depots rather than to individual stores. In product areas such as clothing and electrical goods, manufacturers have taken the lead. Some retailers have grouped together to form pan-European purchasing groups such as the agreement between Sainsbury, Esselunga of Italy, Delhaize of Belgium and Docks of France, whose combined size should secure further bulk discounts.

Threats and opportunities

Integration is more common in northern than in southern Europe and means that suppliers must increasingly be prepared to fulfil large-scale orders. This may prove difficult for small suppliers. To facilitate information exchange, regular suppliers are required to install the necessary computer hardware and software to communicate with their clients. This could also represent an expensive barrier to small suppliers. However, more centralised decision-making may be more convenient for a supplier to secure large-scale orders.

Case study

Marks & Spencer

Marks & Spencer have eight stores in France and two in Belgium which it services from one centralised distribution centre just north of Paris. Goods are routed into that centre from three UK contractor depots. Each of the UK depots serving the European mainland receives merchandise from suppliers, collates the product and produces customs and other official documentation before dispatching forward, using its European fleet. Some companies may feel that single site servicing along these lines leaves them vulnerable, should a problem, such as fire, arise at the site.

Information technology (IT)

Improvements in distribution efficiency result as much from more sophisticated information systems as from, say, increased average speed of transport vehicles.

The internationally standardised barcoding system enables goods to be tracked and traced through the distribution chain and allows more sophisticated applications to be based on the barcodes.

Retailers and manufacturers increasingly require suppliers to be electronically linked so that orders are instantly relayed as stocks run down (see Figure 9.9).

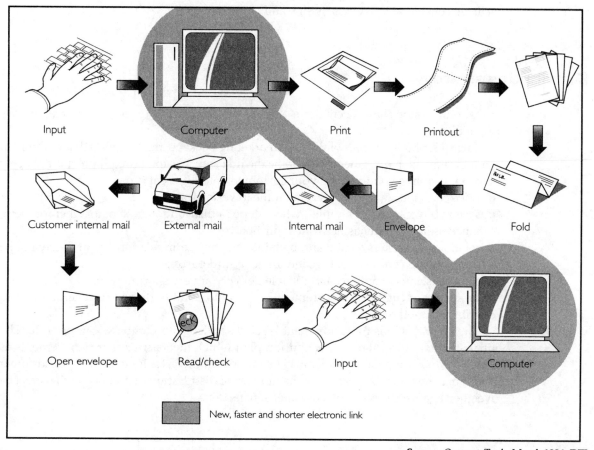

Source: *Overseas Trade*, March 1994, DTI

Figure 9.9 EDI and paper systems compared

Standardisation of electronic data interchange (EDI) systems has enabled their use across national boundaries. European-scale just-in-time systems rely on the use of EDI to work effectively. The whole paper cycle of order, advice note, invoice and statement can be transmitted and acted on through the EDI system.

The stages in the purchase cycle have been reduced to standard formats, easily read by any computer and its users. This is similar to the standardisation of international trade documents so that it is not necessary to know the language in which information is written because the same piece of information always appears in the same place on the form.

The customs and excise authorities are also encouraging the installation of EDI equipment to ease processing of VAT payments and statistics which all exporters are now responsible for.

Scheduling

EDI can also help with scheduling and routing of delivery vehicles which in the past has been done manually by a delivery planner allocating consignments to particular vehicles. Details of consignments that must be delivered on a given day are allocated to vehicles in the fleet according to the carrying capacity of individual vehicles and the features of the product (e.g. weight, size, volume and special requirements such as temperature or security). The delivery planner will then decide a routing for the vehicle depending on customer location and any constraint on delivery such as times when deliveries would not be accepted. Computer software can now be used to take over this work and achieve considerable savings in time and costs.

Distribution strategy

So far only options have been discussed. The next stage is to develop a practical distribution plan.

Since distribution is part of the total marketing package, this suggests that finding out your customers' requirements should be the first step. Customer requirements are likely to differ enabling you to group your customers into different types such as:

- price conscious (a no-frills service at the lowest price);
- system buyers (want a supplier who will put a distribution system together for them, if necessary by purchasing from a third party);
- relationship seekers (will want to maintain a long-term relationship and may not be happy if you contract out distribution to a third party);
- time conscious (want fast and reliable delivery at very short notice).

Your survey of customer requirements is likely to point to the use of several different distribution methods.

The second step is to decide what level of service your company can provide. The final step is to formulate a distribution plan which meets customer requirements as much as your company is able. It may be uneconomic to cater for every type of customer and it may be necessary to reduce the number of distribution methods, but this must be weighed against the effect on customer satisfaction.

Conclusion

Figure 9.10 summarises what is involved in distribution.

Systems of national distribution are increasingly inappropriate and exporters should be planning on a European scale. Large companies now tend to locate production at a few key locations from which they supply all of Europe. For example, Rank Xerox in the UK has five equipment supply centres in Europe and one centre in the Netherlands distributing spares.

Distribution should be geared to customer needs which points to the need for a close working relationship with those in the distribution system. As barriers have come down, it becomes easier and more efficient to deliver direct to the retailer or end-user rather than going through various middle-men.

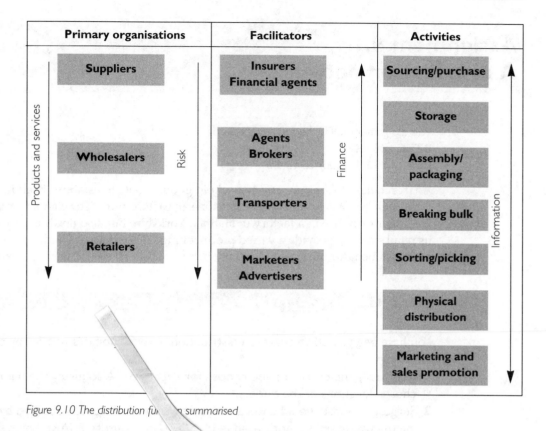

Figure 9.10 The distribution fu... ...n summarised

Summary

- Practicalities of distributing to th... ...st of the EU are considered.
- The main transport methods are de... ...ibed; road being the most important.
- There are five different ways of orga... ...ing distribution.
- Containerisation has now become sta... ...rd.
- Transport costs vary according to differe... ...circumstances.
- Industrial clients will increasingly require... ...rvicing through just-in-time methods.
- Retail structure differs between Europe's n... ...h and south.
- Information technology will lead to major di... ...bution improvements.

Information sources

- *The Geography of the European Community*, by J Cole and F Cole, Routledge, 1993.
- *Transport and Distribution in the Single Market*, in the European Business Guides series published by the CBI, 1992.
- The Simplification of Trade Procedures Board (SITPRO).
- Port and airport freight departments.
- Express parcel companies such as UPS, DHL or Federal Express for rates.
- DTI Export Control Enquiry Unit (Tel: 0171 215 8070).

Assignment 9.1
A distribution network

This assignment fulfils the following criteria:

BTEC 16.1.4

RSA 13.2.1, 13.3.1 to 13.3.6

A UK retailer of furniture and household goods wants to establish itself in two to four other Member States, with up to four stores in each country. The company manufactures the larger furniture in a factory in Halifax, Yorkshire but also needs to buy in stock for its retail stores to provide a varied product range. The company finds that weekly stock replenishment for the stores is usually between 25 to 60 cubic metres per store.

Your tasks

You have been asked to suggest a distribution network for this retailer by doing the following:

1 Justify fully the countries you choose for expansion. Also justify the number and chosen locations of the outlets.

2 Suggest how you would ensure all stores are kept adequately stocked by considering the transport methods used (and, if relevant, routes). RSA students should also explain:

● by which method and how quickly stock levels should be communicated;

● whether the bought-in stock should be delivered separately from the company's manufactured items;

● how you would schedule the deliveries to arrive when needed including transport method, export requirements, estimated costs, estimated timescales and details of collection and delivery.

10 Cultural influences

In this chapter you will discover:

- why it is important for businesses and job seekers to be aware of cultural and lifestyle differences;
- how businesses have had to take account of cultural differences;
- the boundaries of the main cultural areas in Europe;
- specific aspects of culture in the market for food;
- how cultural differences affect working life.

This chapter covers the following performance criteria:

BTEC	16.2.1, 16.3.1, 16.3.2, 16.3.3, 16.3.4
RSA	13.2.4 (culture)

Introduction

Differences between countries can provide opportunities for business and employment. These differences are usually due to cultural variations. What does the word 'culture' mean to you? Shakespeare plays, operas and Constable paintings may come to mind in relation to the UK and you may wonder how these relate to the EU. However, culture includes many other aspects of life and it will become obvious in this chapter that to ignore cultural differences could have dire results for business and an individual's job prospects. Remember the CBI survey (Chapter 1) in which large experienced companies put cultural differences third on their list of remaining barriers to European trade.

Culture and lifestyle

Culture refers to the rules, habits, traditions and beliefs which determine the way in which we live. We learn many of these things, first from our parents when we are young, then from school and finally from our peers and other people whom we respect or admire. Recently the mass media, in particular television, has become a very strong cultural influence. What do we learn from these sources? Suggestions include:

Source	What learned
Parents	Table manners, how much to spend on presents, how much to help in the house, acceptable and unacceptable behaviour.
School	How to interact with other people, qualities needed to be a good employee (e.g. punctuality).

Peers	How many times a week we should be taking a bath or shower, at what age you can start going to parties and having boyfriends/girlfriends.
Mass media	What music we should be listening to, what we should be wearing, what the latest slang is, what we should think of the political parties.

You may disagree with the above and can probably add to the list, but already we can say that culture consists of a code of behaviour. 'Lifestyle' has the narrower meaning of behaviour, covering eating, entertainment, work and all our bad habits, such as drinking and smoking, and is therefore of great interest to market researchers. There are many aspects to culture and Figure 10.1 lists some which may be worth considering.

Childcare	Cooking	Courtship
Criminality	Death, funerals	Decoration: home
Decoration: personal	and mourning	Division of labour
Eating	Education	Ethics
Etiquette	Family groups	Games
Gender and sex	Gifts	Greetings
Hairstyles	Hospitality	Humour
Hygiene	Language	Law
Marriage	Modesty	Music
Names	Politics	Property rights
Religion	Science and technology	Sports
Status	Superstition and luck	Surgery/medicine
Taboos	Trade	Visiting
Weather	Working together	

Source: adapted from *European Business*, R Welford and K Prescott, Pitman, 1992

Figure 10.1 Different aspects of culture

Activity 10.1

1 Try to make some statements about the UK attitude (i.e. culture) to as many of the items as possible in the list shown in Figure 10.1.
2 If possible, ask your EU contacts to compile a similar list for their own countries. It is highly unlikely that your EU contacts will make suggestions for every aspect listed in Figure 10.1 but, for those listed – which may include childcare, personal decoration, hygiene habits, gift traditions and visiting – identify any differences from the UK. What are the marketing implications of these differences?

Stereotypes

It is likely that in considering other countries some stock images readily come to mind; these may include the formality of Germans and the excitability of Italians. These stereotypes are often based on a grain of truth but can be dangerously out-of-date and you should try to find out the true situation rather than acting on these stock images.

A stereotypical image of the UK is that men wear bowler hats and carry rolled umbrellas. This may have been an accurate picture of town life in the nineteenth century but is hardly true now except possibly in the City of London. So a Spanish company thinking it could export bowler hats to the UK would not make much of a profit.

Similarly, if you planned to apply for a job in Barcelona thinking that you would not have to work as hard as you do in a similar post in the UK, then you might be well advised to talk to someone already employed there to discover if your image of working in Spain is valid.

Some stereotypical images are true but are a negative way of explaining a feature which also has a positive side. Excitable Italians would see themselves as merely human, with the British, by contrast as cold and unfeeling.

A warning!

Different does not necessarily mean worse. People usually feel most comfortable within the culture that they have been brought up in. Faced with a different way of doing things often makes us feel uncomfortable mainly because we are no longer sure what is expected of us. However you should guard against condemning other practices as wrong or stupid.

For example, carpets of any kind are very rare in homes in southern Spain but when you have experienced the heat in that area, it is easy to understand that heat retaining fabrics like carpets would only raise the inside temperature still further. In other cases there will be no reason for the differences and cheese for breakfast would just have to be accepted as a fact of life in Belgium, the Netherlands and Scandinavia.

Why do we need to know about culture?

In the context of the EU it is essential to be aware of cultural differences and similarities in the following circumstances:

As a prospective employee in another EU country

- applying for a job;
- assessing promotion prospects;
- day-to-day work.

As a business

- arranging business meetings;
- the product itself may need to be adjusted;
- planning advertising and promotion;
- deciding whether to change the product name;
- considering packaging;
- deciding whether or not to emphasise the country of origin;
- deciding on best distribution methods;
- when setting up a foreign production facility and employing local people.

Business etiquette

This is important in dealing with buyers when exporting, and with employees if you are opening an additional business facility in a new country when you would need to be aware of:

- the attitude to time keeping;
- the level of formality including expected dress, use of first names, relationships with subordinates, and the extent to which you need to confirm arrangements in writing;

- attitude to business entertaining, such as which meal it is usual to use for meetings, whether it will be in a private home or a restaurant, who should pay the bill, acceptable topics of conversation, etc;
- whether gifts are expected or would be regarded as a bribe and what type of gift would be suitable.

As an employee you should pay attention to:

- whether to wordprocess or hand write a job application;
- what to include in your CV;
- how to relate to your peers and superiors.

Aspects of working life which may have to be taken into account include the following.

Timekeeping

For Ireland, old stereotypes would not be useful since the famed relaxed Irish way of life no longer extends to business where punctuality is expected. In Portugal, however, punctuality is not as important.

Decision-making

In Germany and the Netherlands, where decisions are taken by consensus, managers spend a great deal of time in discussion and seeking the opinions of their employees. A German manager cannot be expected to make an on-the-spot decision but once taken, the decision is unlikely to be reversed. In France, however, the boss will consult employees for information but will then make decisions independently.

Formality

In Germany and Portugal, relationships at work are very formal by comparison with the Dutch and the Danes where dress is more relaxed and colleagues are likely to address each other by their first names.

Personal space

We tend to feel uncomfortable when people, especially strangers, get too close when they are talking to us. But 'too close' varies across Europe. The Danes, Greeks and Spaniards are comfortable with distances of as little as 20–30 centimetres whereas Norwegians can feel threatened even when you are 2 metres away and the Portuguese also like to keep their distance.

Activity 10.2

1 Devise a way of discovering the average distance with which Britons feel comfortable in their dealings with work colleagues.
2 Discuss the implications of different personal space requirements when attending job interviews or conducting sales negotiations elsewhere in the EU.

Geographical variations

There are strong geographical differences in Europe. Although there seems to be a common European culture which could be contrasted to that of Japan, China or the Middle East, there are nevertheless some important differences within Europe itself which you should know about when looking for work or doing business. It can be useful to look at four different aspects of people's attitudes. These have been called inequality, individuality, masculinity, and uncertainty avoidance.

Activity 10.3

When you have finished reading the following section, you should look at Table 10.1 (overleaf) with the figures for the UK, and any other EU country with which you are familiar, hidden from view (for which you may need an accomplice) and try to guess the values for each column. If you are close then you know those countries well.

Inequality

Table 10.1 shows that the more a country is tolerant of large differences between people, the higher the score. So Austria with a score of 11 has few class distinctions and there is little distance between senior management and employees, whereas France scores highest and senior management is very remote from employees. With the exception of Austria and Ireland (which has been very much influenced by Protestant Britain), this score also mirrors the religious background of each European country with high scorers being Catholic and low scorers being Protestant, creating a north–south European division.

Application

Table 10.1 helps you to predict, for example, the role of the secretary in the company, who in Denmark may have great power and discretion compared to France, where decisions would have to be referred back to the manager.

As an employee, this factor would also help you predict how formal you can expect your relationship with your superiors to be.

Individuality

A high score in Table 10.1 means that people feel responsibility only to themselves and their immediate family, whereas low scores indicate countries where the extended family and the local community are more important than individual ambitions. Increased affluence may promote individuality because a higher income enables you do things more for your own benefit. Only Greece and Portugal score low on this aspect.

Application

Where individuality is high, children tend to leave home sooner and performance-related pay may be a common way of rewarding employees.

Masculinity

A high score here indicates a country where masculine attitudes, such as achievement and success, are paramount. A low score indicates a society where quality of life matters more than material success and where there is concern for the welfare of people in general (rather than just for your local community as measured by the individuality column). Low scorers here tend not to divide the roles between men and women very strictly which means you will find many women working and more in senior positions while men are willing to participate in childcare and domestic chores.

Application

It would be inappropriate in advertising to show a man doing domestic chores in countries with high scores on this trait. Women may find they have better career progression opportunities in low-scoring countries.

Uncertainty avoidance

Countries with a high score are those where people cannot tolerate uncertainty and have many systems and rules to cover what should be done in the event of almost every conceivable possibility. Low uncertainty avoidance means that this is a country where conflict and competition are seen as natural and people feel secure; secure enough to take risks.

Application

In high-scoring countries you may find little scope for exercising your initiative in work since there will be a rule to cover most eventualities.

Brand loyalty may be strong making it difficult for you to introduce a new product. It probably also means that there is a wariness of foreign products in general.

Table 10.1   Cultural differences between countries

	Inequality	Individuality	Masculinity	Uncertainty avoidance
Austria	11	55	79	70
Belgium	65	75	64	94
Denmark	18	74	16	23
France	68	71	43	86
Germany	35	67	66	65
Greece	60	35	57	112
Ireland	28	70	68	35
Italy	50	76	70	75
Netherlands	38	80	14	53
Portugal	63	27	31	104
Spain	57	51	42	86
Sweden	31	71	5	29
UK	35	89	66	25
Japan	54	46	95	92
Malaysia	104	26	50	36
Singapore	74	20	48	8

Source: G Hofstede, 'National Cultures in Four Dimensions', *International Studies of Management and Organisation*, Vol XII, Nos 1–2

In Table 10.1, the last three non-European countries are shown for comparison. Although this work was done many years ago (in 1970), basic attitudes do not change that quickly and so the results are still useful today.

Cultural regions

So far, we have concentrated on the differences between countries. But some countries are more similar than others and within countries there can exist wide cultural differences. This is especially true of the larger European countries. You may already have met examples of cultural differences within the UK by consulting *Social Trends*, *Regional Trends* or market reports from such organisations as Mintel. For example, the highest consumption of potatoes is in Wales and of whisky is in Scotland.

Case study

How Europe can be divided into regions for food marketing

Food is sometimes cited as one of the areas where cultural differences are greatest and most persistent, and certainly it should be easy for you to list some of the foods associated with Italy, Germany, Spain and Greece. However, for marketing purposes, it is not only what people eat which is important but also how they eat it. For example, cheese is widely eaten at the end of a meal in France and the UK but in Belgium, the Netherlands and Denmark cheese is a breakfast food. This would have important implications for advertising as you would have to ensure that you show the cheese at the appropriate meal in the different countries.

Research which looked at people's eating habits, as against what was eaten, in the different regions of Europe enabled a comparison to be made as to which region's eating habits were most similar. (Each country was divided into regions.) The investigation looked at factors such as:

- whether people liked to nibble;
- whether they were often on a diet or tried to adopt healthy eating habits;
- to what extent they relied on convenience food;
- how often they liked to eat out.

Not surprisingly, most of the regions proved to be most similar to the other regions in their own country first, showing that there are indeed strong differences between countries. From a European marketing point of view, however, what was more interesting was the next stage of the investigation which showed which countries' eating habits were the most similar. This can indicate where common advertising and promotion will be successful.

Using sophisticated statistical techniques, the survey found that Denmark and Sweden were most similar in their eating habits. Then the UK and Ireland proved to be the next most similar to Denmark and Sweden, forming a four-country group. You can see how this group developed in Figure 10.2.

Surprisingly, Norway proved different enough to join the group several stages further on. This means that Norwegian eating habits are very different from the other two Scandinavian countries so that a UK food exporter would be wrong to treat the Scandinavian countries as a culturally similar group. Figure 10.2 also shows that a UK food exporter may have to make the fewest adjustments when selling to northern (Flemish) Belgium, Denmark, the Netherlands, Sweden and Ireland, whereas the temptation may be to target the largest market first which would be Germany.

The Euro-consumer

Companies wishing to target the whole of Europe are asking whether it is possible to divide Europeans into different types. This means that geography becomes less important than lifestyle. One attempt to define the Euro-consumer was made by the French advertising agency CCA which identified 16 different types of Euro-consumer based on

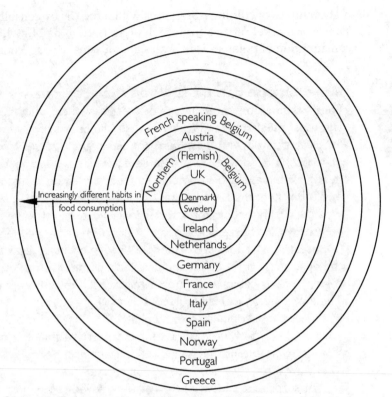

Figure 10.2 Diagram to illustrate countries with the greatest similarities in eating habits

their attitudes to change and materialism (Figure 10.3). CCA also estimated the percentages of Europeans falling into each category as well as the percentages for individual countries. (The latter, however, is commercially sensitive information.)

Activity 10.4

Use the illustrations and their position against the two axes to draw up a description of all 16 European types shown in Figure 10.3. The description should include attitudes, activities and lifestyle.

Those groups in the upper right-hand corner are likely to be those most difficult to target as a whole in Europe since they are very traditional which probably means they prefer their own local brands and habits. Those in the upper left-hand corner are well-off and open to new ideas so are easy to sell to at first, but they may quickly abandon your brand as new ones come along.

Application

This type of information could be used by the food industry. Those in the lower right-hand corner of Figure 10.3 cover 26 per cent of Europeans and could be summarised as the middle classes who, in food terms, go for quality and safety and are sceptical of novelties. They like natural ingredients with a classic taste and look and go for well-known brands. They will pay a high price for good quality. The packaging would have to be of old-fashioned materials, such as glass and wood rather than plastic, and should be easy to transport and store. In advertising this group would be convinced by reason.

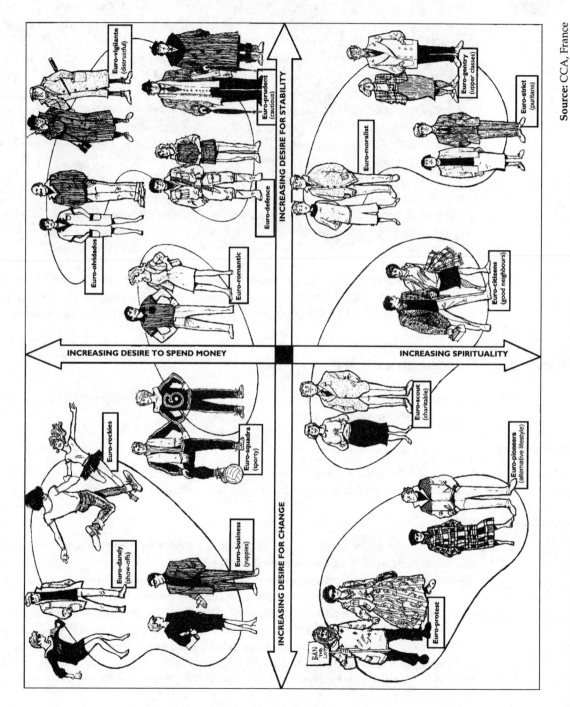

Source: CCA, France

Figure 10.3 CCA's 16 Euro lifestyles

Case study

> ### Impulse
>
> The body spray *Impulse* was, until recently, promoted with the slogan 'Men just can't help acting on impulse' and featured good-looking young men who did crazy things such as buying a complete stranger a bunch of flowers just because she was wearing the body spray. The new advert was designed to run across Europe, and possibly beyond, with as few alterations as possible.
>
> Market research identified a stereotype of an independent young woman, attractive but not too sexy, which the advertising agency called the 'free spirit' and which they thought appealed right across Europe. The advert was set on an exotic beach, which also proved to be appealing to women across the whole continent and was run to the tune of 'Fever' by Peggy Lee. It was launched almost simultaneously in the UK, Italy and Germany, and the company have been very pleased with the increase in sales.
>
> So does this prove that there is such a thing as the Euro-consumer? On the surface yes, but the advertisers also prepared some changes which could be included in the advert to cope with different countries. Most notably, where in the UK the model sprays her naked back, in Spain, she sprays her arm, which is more modest.

The evidence suggests that overall, food, drink, advertising, printing and publishing are sectors where cultural differences are very important whereas high-tech consumer and industrial products can be sold on a more European basis with few cultural barriers.

Aspects of European culture

Chapter 12 gives information on culture in individual EU Member States and below are some general comments relating to the headings used.

Resources

Countries with poor economic resources tend to be more outward looking since they will have a history of needing to trade with other countries going back many centuries.

Land and climate

This does exert an influence on the character of a country's inhabitants encouraging much interaction with other people where the weather is often warm, and isolation in the home where the weather can be harshly cold. Mountainous areas such as Austria and watery areas such as Finland have also reduced mobility in the past. The environment affects people's behaviour on a practical level too. It may therefore be true that in Spain only 'mad dogs and English men go out in the midday sun' while the Spaniards themselves sensibly wait until temperatures have moderated somewhat, to resume work in summer at 5 p.m. until about 8 p.m. This, together with the hour difference in time from the UK, can make business communications with Spain difficult.

Language

Many European languages have a formal and informal form of 'you' and care needs to be taken in knowing when to use either. This occurs in French, German, Danish and

Italian. In Danish the formal 'you' has all but disappeared; in French the formal 'you' is used less and less; whereas in German and Italian great offence can be caused by inappropriate use of the informal 'you'.

Language is also important in the area of marketing, although note that EU law requires that product labels should be in a language that the consumer can reasonably be expected to understand. Table 10.2 shows language proficiency across selected EU Member States.

Table 10.2   Language proficiency across Europe

Language	Percentage of adults in EU countries speaking European languages								
	B	D	F	G	Ir	It	N	S	UK
English	26	51	26	43	99	13	68	13	100
French	71	5	100	18	12	27	31	15	15
German	22	48	11	100	2	6	67	3	6
Italian	4	1	8	3	1	100	2	4	1
Spanish	3	1	13	1	1	5	4	100	2
Dutch	68	1	1	3	–	–	100	–	1

Key: B – Belgium, D – Denmark, F – France, G – Germany, Ir – Ireland, It – Italy, N – Netherlands, S – Spain, UK – United Kingdom   **Source:** *Doing Business in the European Community*, Paul Gibbs, Kogan Page, 1990

Those countries speaking the less well-known tongues, such as Dutch and Danish, will tend to have English as their second language and certainly, since the fall of Communism in East Europe there has been an explosion in the demand for English. However, UK companies cannot assume that everybody will understand and welcome advertising in English. In 1994, there were moves once again in France to try and limit the use of English by law. Even more sensitive will be the business negotiations which take place before a product can be sold in a new market. Here the rule is most definitely to sell in the buyer's language.

Only UK importers should expect to be able to negotiate in English. Where the local language is to be used the translation of marketing material presents many problems.

Activity 10.5

1 To demonstrate the problems of translating advertising copy, slogans and brand names, you should obtain a sample of adverts from different parts of the EU. You could use your foreign contacts or copies of appropriate newspapers and magazines which may be available in your college or local library. Video tapes of the commercial breaks on foreign satellite channels could also be used.

   Use the various language skills available in your group to have these translated into English.

2 In small groups, discuss whether these adverts, slogans and brand names are effective in English and if not, why not? Has a double meaning been lost? Is the setting inappropriate for the UK? Would it offend the average Briton?

3 What lessons can be learned from this exercise? Draw up a list of guidelines for UK companies needing to advertise in other Member States.

Education

Education, recruitment, responsible authorities and working methods vary greatly across the EU. Care is needed in understanding familiar words such as 'college', 'grade' and 'faculty' which can have different meanings. Even within countries, there can be different systems in each region (e.g. Germany and Belgium) much as the set-up in Scotland differs to that in England and Wales. Private schools are more common than in the UK, have less of an exclusive air and are often church-run.

There are great differences in teaching styles with the formal lecture style favoured in Germany and a more active style close to the UK practice in Denmark. Exams range from open book to the prevalence of oral exams in Italy. The competence based type of course which combines experience with a qualification, such as the Advanced GNVQ which you may be working for, is a new development, not widespread in the rest of the EU although Ireland has a similar system for apprentices.

Education differences affect your employment prospects; in Belgium where the school leaving age is 18, you would have difficulty in finding a job there if you are younger. Figure 10.4 summarises the main features of secondary schooling across the EU.

In many countries, such as Belgium, France, Spain and Italy, unsatisfactory performance at school means that the year must be repeated which leads to weaker pupils reaching school leaving age without having obtained their certificate of satisfactory completion of studies.

Some attempt is being made in higher education to agree on equivalencies of modules especially in institutions whose students take part in European exchange programmes such as SOCRATES.

In spite of the recent expansion of higher education in the UK, many other EU Member States have a higher proportion of young people entering higher education. Therefore you may be competing with graduates for jobs. Even if you become a graduate yourself, you will find that other European graduates are in their mid- to late-twenties when they join the job market because degree courses are longer and many EU Member States still require males to complete some military service. Many countries are introducing the shorter four year bachelor's degree, for example in Denmark, Spain and Portugal.

Training

EU Member States vary in the amount of training offered to employees; very little is offered in Portugal and Greece (funding from the European Social Fund helps however) where training needs to begin at a very basic level since there is high illiteracy. Northern European countries place a great deal of emphasis on training, often stimulated by government incentives such as the French tax credits when employers spend more than 1.5 per cent of the wage bill on training.

All EU Member States offer the option of beginning vocational training whilst still in full-time education, such as the GNVQ, followed by day or block release arrangements whilst with an employer, such as Youth Training (YT). In Belgium, Denmark, France, Germany and Luxembourg employees are entitled to educational leave from their jobs. In France companies must compile a training plan and training provision has been part of some collective agreement settlements, for example in the insurance industry in 1992 when it was agreed that certain workers should be given 400 hours of training credits. In Belgium the provision of work placements is compulsory for most companies who will then have their employer contributions reduced.

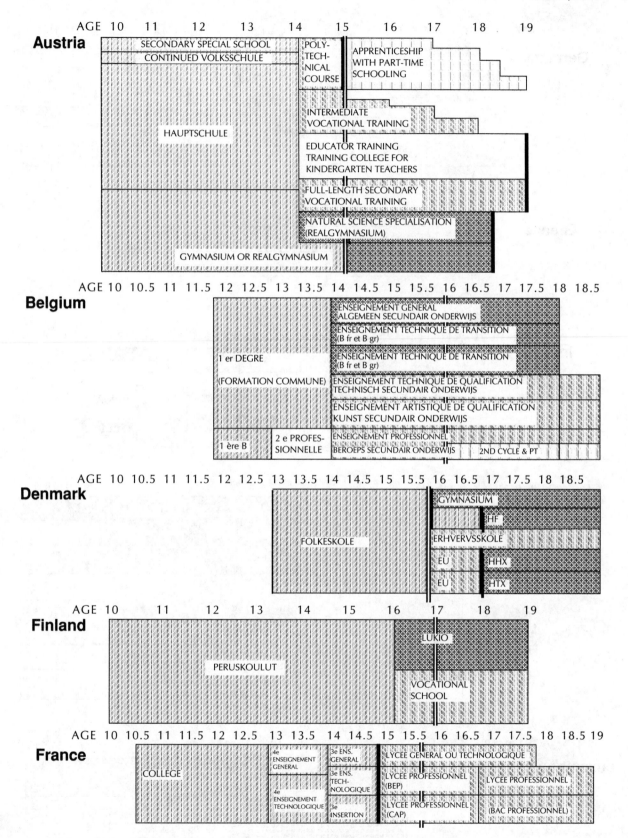

AGE 10 10.5 11 11.5 12 12.5 13 13.5 14 14.5 15 15.5 16 16.5 17 17.5 18 18.5 19

Germany

ORIENTIERUNGS-STUFE	HAUPTSCHULE		BERUFSGRUND-BILDUNGSJAHR	DUALES SYSTEM
			BERUFSFACHSCHULE
	REALSCHULE			BERUFSAUFBAUSCHULE
				GYMNASIALE OBERSTUFE
	GYMNASIUM			FACHOBERSCHULE
	GESAMTSCHULE			GYMNASIALE OBERSTUFE

AGE 10 10.5 11 11.5 12 12.5 13 13.5 14 14.5 15 15.5 16 16.5 17 17.5 18 18.5 19

Greece

GYMNASIO		LYKEIO
		PT
PT		TES
		PT

AGE 10 10.5 11 11.5 12 12.5 13 13.5 14 14.5 15 15.5 16 16.5 17 17.5 18 18.5 19

Ireland

SECONDARY SCHOOL	TRANSITIONAL YEAR	SS
		SS
VOCATIONAL SCHOOL	TRANSITIONAL YEAR	VS
		VS PT
COMPREHENSIVE SCHOOL	TRANSITIONAL YEAR	CS
		CS
COMMUNITY SCHOOL	TRANSITIONAL YEAR	CS
		CS

AGE 10 10.5 11 11.5 12 12.5 13 13.5 14 14.5 15 15.5 16 16.5 17 17.5 18 18.5 19

Italy

SCUOLA MEDIA	LICEO CLASSICO
	LICEO SCIENTIFICO
	LICEO ARTISTICO
	SCUOLA MAGISTRALE
	ISTITUTO MAGISTRALE
	ISTITUTO D'ARTE
	ISTITUTO TECNICO
	ISTITUTO PROFESSIONALE

AGE 10 10.5 11 11.5 12 12.5 13 13.5 14 14.5 15 15.5 16 16.5 17 17.5 18 18.5 19

Luxembourg

	LYCEE GENERAL
LYCEE TECHNIQUE	REGIME TECHNIQUE
	REGIME DE FORMATION DE TECHNICIEN
	REGIME PROFESSIONNEL PT

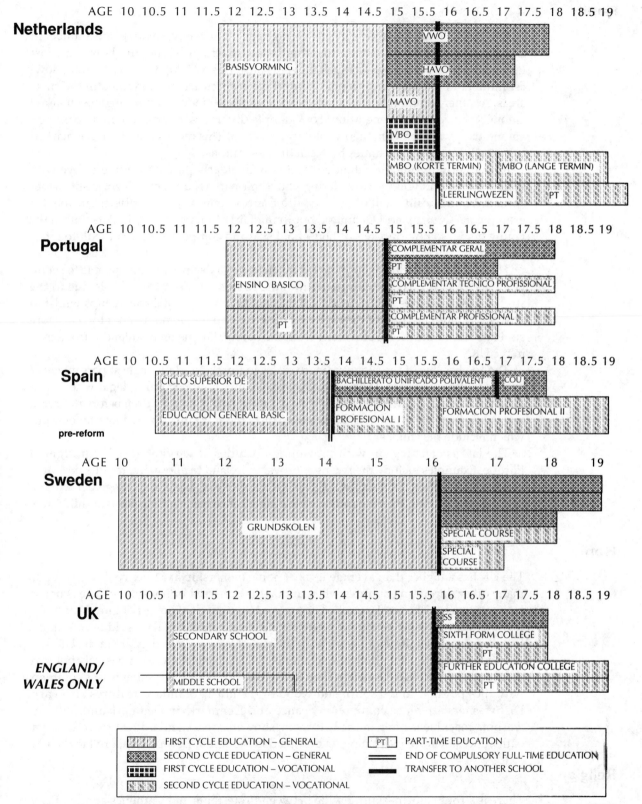

Source: *Key Data on Education in the European Union 94*, European Commission, 1995 and the *Education Yearbook*, OECD

Figure 10.4 *EU secondary schooling*

Family

Across the EU there are differences in average age on marriage, divorce rate, number of children and attitudes to living together before marriage. Generally however most European urban areas display much the same attitudes with highest divorce rates, lowest number of children and so on. Cultural differences are most marked in the rural areas. Another common European feature is that these modern trends are most marked amongst the youngest generation. For example divorce is everywhere more common among the young than among the older generation. This means that there are marked cultural differences in attitudes between the generations.

In southern Europe the extended family, with elderly parents tending to live with their children and young adults living with their parents until marriage, is still widespread. Young adults will often live with their parents also in northern Europe, for example in Germany and Denmark, but living fairly independently in flats within the family home, so raw statistics of household size and composition are difficult to interpret.

There is generally throughout the EU much less of a desire by young people to set up home as soon as possible compared to the UK. In some countries this is due to the strength of family ties and reduced willingness to rely on casual friendships whilst in others it is more because of the high cost of setting up home independently. Far more students attend their local university from the parental home on mainland Europe than in the UK.

The UK has one of the highest divorce rates in Europe and the highest percentage of one person households. In Ireland, divorce is only now becoming legal whereas in Denmark couples often wait until they have one or two young children before marrying and this is perfectly acceptable; local newspapers there are full of wedding photographs which include the children.

The law is catching up with prevailing attitudes at varying speeds throughout Europe. Examples include the recent approval in Ireland to allow divorce, the introduction of co-habitation contracts in Belgium for couples who want to live together without getting married, and the recognition of the inheritance rights of illegitimate children in France.

Home

The UK has a higher than average level of home ownership at 61 per cent compared to many other European countries where renting is preferred or housing finance is not so easy to come by. The semi-detached house is not common in the rest of Europe and neither are large housing estates of ready built houses which are then sold individually. Flats are also generally more popular in the rest of Europe than they are in the UK.

Inside the home, other European countries tend to furnish more expensively but may redecorate and replace less often than in the UK. For floors, carpeting is less common, with tiles popular in the south and wood in the north. Standard features also vary. Dishwashers are more common in France and Denmark; in Denmark and Italy the washing machine is often in the bathroom; showers are a standard feature rather than baths; and bidets are much more widespread in the rest of Europe compared to the UK.

Religion

There is a rough north–south divide between Protestants and Catholics and the EU is predominantly Catholic. Church attendance is fairly low everywhere in Europe but particularly so in the UK. However Church based festivals still form an important part of mainstream life such as Christmas and Easter rituals and the preference for marriages and funerals to be held in church.

Many European countries also have sizeable minorities practising other religions, in particular Islam. These groups tend to be more devout in adherence to their faith and may also require special consideration in work conditions, for example the provision of a trouser version of uniforms for Muslim women.

Diet

As discussed earlier, food is an area where cultural differences are still very marked, not only what is eaten but when and how. Italy is rightly famous for its high consumption of pasta, Spain for its late lunches which can begin at three or four in the afternoon and France for its use of food for all manner of social occasions. Where eating is important as a social activity in its own right, you will find less fast or takeaway food available.

Leisure

Leisure activities will differ according to income; poorer countries will be less inclined to go in for expensive leisure pursuits. However other cultural aspects will also affect how leisure time is spent and in countries where the family unit is extended or lives close together, socialising within the family will take precedence with activities based on hobby clubs and societies seen as less attractive.

Arts

Each European country has its own distinctive history of literature, architecture, theatre, cinema and other activities which can be used to good effect in advertising and promotion for example. Attitudes towards the arts also differ; in the UK it can be seen as rather snobbish to be interested in high culture whereas elsewhere all types of people may read the 'serious' newspapers or be interested in opera.

Working conditions

Many UK companies will take advantage of the Single Market by setting up production, distribution or sales facilities in other Member States. Individuals may decide to take advantage of their EU rights and seek work in other Member States. So in employment too it is very important to be aware of cultural differences. Chapter 12 contains information of specific differences.

Understanding and allowing for the effect of cultural differences could affect significantly the success of a relocation to another part of the EU.

Activity 10.6

Consider the case of a UK bank which has just acquired a Danish subsidiary.
1 Danish employees dress noticeably more casually, especially in the service sector such as shops and banks. Would it be a good idea to introduce a company uniform for staff, assuming that the UK parent company bank already has one?
2 Rather than staying on until the job is done, Danish employees will expect to go home punctually at 4 p.m., having started at 8 a.m., as they often need to collect

their children from daycare promptly. How would you ensure that urgent work is completed?

3 There is a very high level of trade union membership in Denmark across all types of job. Trade unions are regarded partly as professional organisations and also have a major role in administering unemployment benefits. The unions also work closely with management to set working conditions. In the UK parent company bank there is a staff association approved by the company but no recognised trade union. What should the policy be in the new Danish subsidiary?

4 Will you need to make any adjustments to your recruiting procedure? For example, it is rare to see a salary quoted in a Danish job advert. Also the spread of pay between the highest and the lowest is narrower in Denmark, while gross salaries are much higher than in the UK since most Danes lose about 50 per cent (as compared to about 25 per cent in the UK) in taxes.

Structure of the working day

The UK and Ireland and Portugal remain one hour behind the rest of Europe and this can severely restrict the amount of potential contact time between businesses since many Europeans start work earlier anyway. This means that important phone calls must effectively be made before 3 p.m. if there is to be a reasonable chance of action. Lunch times are also extremely variable ranging from the 15 minute break at 10.30 a.m. for the Greeks to the two to three hour break beginning at two in southern Spain.

Actual total working hours vary widely as Table 10.3 shows, with the Portuguese working 14 per cent more hours than the Danes, and the Spanish having 45 per cent more paid holiday than the British or Portuguese.

Table 10.3   Working hours across the EU

City		Working hours per year	Holiday per year*
Amsterdam	(NL)	1792	27.5
Athens	(GR)	1775	24.5
Brussels	(B)	1725	24.5
Copenhagen	(DK)	1669	25.0
Dublin	(IRE)	1727	23.4
Frankfurt	(D)	1725	31.2
Helsinki	(SU)	1726	28.1
Lisbon	(P)	1908	22.0
London	(GB)	1880	22.1
Luxembourg	(L)	1780	30.6
Madrid	(E)	1721	32.1
Milan	(I)	1785	24.8
Paris	(F)	1790	27.9
Stockholm	(S)	1803	25.7
Vienna	(A)	1744	26.8

* Paid working days

Source: *Prices and Earnings around the Globe,* 1994 edition, Union Bank of Switzerland

Part-time/full-time

There is great variation in the amount of part-time work across the EU (see Table 10.4). This is partly to do with female participation rates since when women work, they tend to favour part-time but it is also very dependent upon whether employment law favours part-time work.

Table 10.4 Part-time work in the EU, 1994

	Percentage of working population
Austria	9
Belgium	13
Denmark	21
Finland	8
France	15
Germany	16
Greece	5
Ireland	11
Italy	6
Luxembourg	8
Netherlands	36
Portugal	8
Spain	7
Sweden	25
UK	23

Source: *Eurostat*

Seasonal variations

The practice of taking a major break during the summer months is widespread across the EU and you should expect some difficulty in scheduling business meetings during these times. Other European countries are less willing than the UK to stagger the timing of their summer holiday even when they are not tied by school holidays. For the French, August is the holiday month and many small shops and businesses will be closed during this time. In other countries the holiday season is at a different time with June and July being the peak time for Scandinavia. The Germans, by contrast, do stagger the school summer break between June and September across the different Länder.

The other bottleneck is Christmas and New Year. In some countries Christmas is little more than a day's interruption to work whereas in others, like the UK, there is a virtual shutdown for a week or more between Christmas and New Year. For the French, this is a peak time for taking a skiing holiday. Remember also that some northern European countries have a different date altogether for Christmas – in the Netherlands it is December 6.

You should also be aware of the public holiday calendar in other European countries so that you do not schedule meetings when the country is shut down for the day.

Case study

The friendly takeover

In 1986, the German car company Volkswagen took over the ailing Spanish company SEAT. Spanish middle managers were upset to be demoted as German managers were brought in, temporarily, to replace them. The German and Spanish employees seemed not to mix, partly due to the difficulty the Germans had in learning Spanish. German attempts to improve efficiency at the car plant, such as the proposal to ban smoking on the shop floor and to carry out a work study to find ways of improving output per worker, were resented by the Spanish workforce.

Another clash occurred due to the importance Spaniards place on family and community activities and hence their wish to have time off simultaneously. Car plant workers had every weekend off and the factory closed down completely for the month of August. Volkswagen wanted to extend the working week and avoid the annual closure but after three years had only managed to gain an extra eight working days per year.

Use of information technology (IT)

Information technology is being rapidly adopted all over the EU to improve business efficiency. Some countries, such as France and its Minitel system, developed their systems with strong government backing. Others, such as Ireland, are using their IT facilities as a major attraction to foreign businesses. Countries, like Portugal, whose infrastructure has lagged behind in the past, have invested heavily in IT so that its international companies at least, lack little in this area.

Another possible effect of increasingly connected information systems – the so-called *information superhighway* – is that it may enable people to obtain work in remote and rural areas, an option of great relevance to two of the newest EU Member States, Sweden and Finland, since they include large areas of remote country on the periphery of Europe. Companies are not tied to employing workers in their own country with reports of UK companies using people in Ireland and the Far East for work which can be delivered electronically.

Mobility

Where the family is an important social support, labour mobility will tend to be restricted geographically although it may be high across job sectors – people willing to try different types of jobs in order to remain close to the family. Another factor restricting mobility is where there is high female participation as it becomes more difficult to find a job for the second spouse if the first is moved.

In the poorest parts of Europe there has been a pattern of single members of the family migrating and sending money home to support the family, particularly the Spanish and Portuguese. However as these countries have become richer, this type of labour mobility has greatly reduced.

Mobility is also affected by the housing market. In Belgium, where people tend to make a house purchase only once in their lives, they say that Belgians have a 'brick in their stomach' meaning that once they have secured the house of their dreams they are unlikely to move.

Hence all over Europe there is a reluctance to move and this may make unemployment worse than it need be. Conversely, this immobility means that mass migration has not happened across Europe even though the restrictions on the movement of workers have been greatly reduced. In fact statistics show that it is Britons who are leaving their home country in the greatest numbers compared to other EU Member States.

Employment law

Most EU Member States have minimum wages. Many also classify employees, commonly as blue or white collar workers, which can make a difference to working conditions, generally to the benefit of white collar workers.

Many EU Member States pay social security benefits in relation to previous salary rather than the flat rate given by the UK benefit system.

Trade unions

The level of trade union membership varies greatly within Europe (see Table 10.5). The role of the unions also differs, varying from approximating to a professional organisation in Denmark, to being an active partner in shaping government policy in Belgium, to having relatively little influence in Spain.

Table 10.5 Level of trade union membership, 1988

Country	Level of trade union membership (%)
Austria	67
Belgium	65
Denmark	80–5
Finland	65–90
France	10
Germany	39
Greece	25
Ireland	50
Italy	40
Luxembourg	50
Netherlands	30
Portugal	30–40
Spain	13
Sweden	82
UK	46

Sources: *Pay and Benefits*, European Management Guides IDS/IPM 1992, Price Waterhouse

Case study

Toys 'R' Us in Sweden
This American company caused a great deal of anger when it set up in Sweden and refused to include its workforce in a collective agreement in a country where 85 per cent of the workforce belongs to a union. In addition, the company was allegedly requiring its workforce to agree to be routinely searched for stolen items and that they should not socialise with one another after work or talk to the media. This caused such offence in a country where workers are used to being

> trusted and consulted by management that it resulted in widespread strikes and boycotts by their suppliers such as the bank, advertising agency and transporters.
>
> By contrast, the chief executive of the American division of Swedish furniture company IKEA, Goran Carstedt says 'I feel that I am failing if my presence in the store or in the cafeteria makes some employees nervous.'
>
> **Source:** The *European*, 21 July 1995

Equal opportunities

Military service is compulsory in many EU Member States and therefore equal opportunities legislation usually also ensures that those called up are entitled to their jobs back once their military service is over.

Many countries have a written constitution in which certain rights are accorded to workers, such as equal opportunities, but these constitutional rights are not always reflected in legislation which means that they are difficult to enforce since application to a constitutional court is usually a lengthy and expensive business. There are different degrees to which equal opportunities are safeguarded, the narrowest protection being that against dismissal which assumes that the person was able to get a job in the first place.

Work roles

The use of formal person specifications varies greatly. In the 'high context' Latin countries of France, Italy, Spain and Portugal, there exist extensive information networks among family, friends, colleagues and clients and so, much is implied or understood. Here a formal written specification would be deemed unnecessary whereas in the so-called 'low context' Germanic and Nordic countries where such networks do not exist you are more likely to have your work role explicitly explained to you.

Tasks and responsibilities

A job title may imply very different levels of responsibility in different countries. The required tasks may also differ considerably. For example, 'secretary' can mean anything from typist (low level tasks, very little responsibility) to personal assistant (wide variety of complex tasks with great responsibility). According to the *European*, 'senior secretaries face a north–south divide when it comes to bosses' attitudes towards them. In Scandinavia, executives see their secretaries as key management people, while in southern countries the image still persists that they are 'just pretty girls taking a few notes and brightening up the office.' Another example is that in many European countries, such as Belgium, France and Germany, teachers do not have the pastoral and administrative work which UK teachers assume as part of their jobs.

Skills

Skills required for a specific job should be the same wherever it is performed assuming that the employee also has the appropriate language skills. To highlight this the EU has enacted several directives requiring employers to recognise qualifications for professional and other jobs wherever they were obtained in the EU, although in practice a great deal of discrimination against non-national qualifications still occurs (see Chapter 3 for more detail).

The main source of differences in skills required will derive from the level of computerisation. European organisations everywhere are rapidly introducing IT where appropriate. Hence IT skills will soon be a basic skill, along with numeracy and literacy, required of every employee. Another major source of difference is in foreign language skills which are essential in multi-language countries such as Belgium and Luxembourg or in the smaller export oriented countries such as the Netherlands and Denmark. For example, in the Netherlands most secretaries need to be able to wordprocess and produce business correspondence in three languages including Dutch.

Employment and career progression

Qualifications are generally much more important in securing a job in north European countries and for professional and skilled jobs in southern Europe than in the UK. Relevant previous experience is often not regarded as an adequate substitute for the specified qualification. Learning 'on the job' is also much less common in the rest of the EU compared to the UK. For managers, the required qualification is likely to be technical or engineering contrasted to the acceptance of arts graduates for management in the UK. The EU's directives on mutual acceptance of qualifications is not yet uniformly applied across Europe.

People tend to stay with an employer for much longer periods in continental Europe – there is less of a career mentality, more one of breadwinning, especially in the southern states. You may find that there are therefore penalties attached to 'job hopping' such as loss of pension rights since the system will not be geared towards this pattern of employment. For example, Belgian teachers moving to another school automatically start at the bottom of the salary scale again. Promotion is often on the basis of reaching the required age or having had the relevant number of years in service.

The process of obtaining a job differs greatly. For example, speculative letters to prospective employers is the main method of graduate recruitment in France suggesting that it would be unwise to rely solely on press adverts there. French employers and an increasing number in other EU Member States are also very likely to analyse your handwriting in the belief that this will say something useful about you as an employee. You therefore need to follow job application instructions carefully as it is not compulsory to warn you of this graphology analysis in every EU Member State. You could try to find out in advance how your handwriting would be interpreted.

Pay is rarely included in job adverts in Belgium and Denmark and many other EU Member States. In many countries pay is determined by age and job grade rather than competence and performance. In Belgium you can be recruited on the basis of whether you will be of a similar age group to your colleagues and younger than your supervisor. One pleasant surprise is the prevalence of thirteenth, fourteenth and sometimes, even fifteenth month bonuses. This refers to the practice of paying employees an extra month's salary, often in December, for Christmas, or June to help finance holidays or both (e.g. in Belgium, Netherlands, Ireland, Greece, Portugal, Spain and Germany). Bonuses are also given on marriage and maternity (Spain) or regularly as long as you have dependent children (Germany).

Cultural change

Attitudes may change only slowly but lifestyles do alter mainly for two reasons – rising incomes and improved communications. Rising incomes change the pattern of demand for products and also enable changes in lifestyle such as being able to commute long distances into work if one has a car or being able to afford to leave home at a younger age. Improved communications started with cinema and radio and continued with national television. Satellite television and electronic telecommunications now mean that ideas, fashions and trends can sweep across the world at low cost and high speed. On the work front this is expected to lead to much greater telecottaging or distance working with employees working from home or local telecommunications centres linked to their office electronically.

Conclusion

There is probably such a thing as a European culture which can be used to sell strongly branded products across the continent. However there remain very marked differences between EU Member States and there are even wide lifestyle differences within countries especially the larger ones. As communications improve, more isolated areas, such as southern Spain or the Highlands and Islands of Scotland, may lose some aspects of their distinctive way of life. These differences must be taken into account by businesses and EU citizens wishing to settle in other EU Member States. When running a foreign enterprise, you need to be aware of the differences, and decide whether you are going to fit in with expectations or whether it is worth trying to introduce what you may see as the more efficient UK operating method.

Summary

- Cultural differences will be evident in business practices, employment, advertising, packaging and distribution.
- Differences in culture can be mapped geographically when a strong north-south divide is apparent.
- Another way of classifying culture in Europe is by identifying consumer types.
- Within Europe there are differences of attitude and in habits which companies and employees must be aware of.

Information sources

- *Foreign Bodies – A Guide to European Mannerisms*, Peter Collett, Simon & Schuster, 1993.
- *EuroManagers and Martians*, Richard Hill, Europublications, 1994.
- *Doing Business in the European Community*, Paul Gibbs, third edition, Kogan Page, 1994.
- *Mind Your Manners*, John Mole, Brealy Publishing, 1993.
- European Management Guides published by the Institute of Personnel Management and Incomes Data Services cover legal and cultural aspects of employing people all over the EU. A useful one in the series is *Terms and Conditions of Employment*, published in 1991.
- *Royal Mail International Business Travel Guide*, third edition, 1992/93.
- Foreign contacts.

Assignment 10.1
Settling in

This assignment fulfils the following criteria:
BTEC 16.2.1, 16.3.1 to 16.3.4, 16.4.1 to 16.4.3

Helena Thyskos is a 20-year-old Greek woman who has just found a job working in the export sales department of a company located close to your college. You have been assigned to help her settle successfully in the UK. This will require you to know the differences between life in the UK and Greece. For example, if there is no requirement for a television licence in Greece, it probably will not occur to Helena to obtain one until it is too late.

Use the sources of information listed in this chapter as well as the appropriate country file in Chapter 12. It would also help to interview a Greek recently arrived to work in the UK.

Your tasks

1 Compile a list of what Helena needs to do within the first three months of her arrival in Britain. You will need to cover finances, transport, insurance, health, social security provision and accommodation, amongst other things.
2 Select from the list the items which will be the most different from her native Greece and carefully explain the differences.
3 Prepare some advice on how to succeed at work in the UK contrasting your advice carefully with the way things are done in the Greek workplace. This may be written or presented orally or on a tape.
4 How would your advice differ when helping Jon Svensson, a 25-year-old Swede coming to the UK with his partner and two young (one and three years old) children? (You need to repeat tasks 1 to 3 for Sweden.)

11 Trends

This chapter will help you to:

- compare the main social and economic indicators across Europe;
- use the indicators to identify business and work opportunities;
- predict trends in the indicators for the near future;
- apply the knowledge gained to some actual companies.

This chapter covers the following performance criteria:

BTEC   16.1.1 to 16.1.3
RSA   13.2.1, 13.2.4, 13.2.6

Introduction

The sources identified in previous chapters can be used to extract information about the economic and social situation in other EU Member States. This chapter will indicate what use can be made of the information gained both when setting up in business and seeking employment in the rest of Europe. Unavoidably some of the data relates only to the pre-1995 EU of 12 Member States. Included are illustrative extracts from selected EU companies' annual reports.

Where the indicators show an opportunity or a threat for employment or business you will find the following signs:

☺ Opportunity

☹ Threat.

Social indicators

Here we concentrate on the more measurable aspects of behaviour whilst Chapter 10, on culture, considers the more descriptive aspects, such as attitudes and habits. The issues examined below are only a selection and for more ideas you could look at the table headings in *Social Trends*.

Population

At a basic level, the number of people determines the potential demand for a product so figures for standard of living set out in Table 11.8 ought to be examined in conjunction with population size.

☺ Germany may present the best opportunities for a product, with the biggest population and high per capita income, whilst countries like Greece and Portugal may be too small, as well as too poor, for all but specialist products in niche markets.

Is the population increasing?

Figure 11.1 shows that the European population is expected to increase but at a modest rate in comparison to other parts of the world. Thus, for the purposes of mass marketing, opportunities may be increasing faster elsewhere. Note needs to be taken of where the highest population densities occur (see Figure 11.2 overleaf). This is particularly important in planning the location of retail and other service outlets such as theme parks.

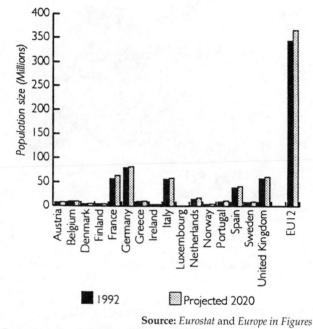

■ 1992   ▨ Projected 2020

Source: *Eurostat* and *Europe in Figures*

Figure 11.1 Population size (1992 and 2020)

Golden triangles and hot bananas

Within the previous 12 Member States, a 'Golden Triangle' has been identified (see Figure 11.3 later). This contains 60 per cent of the EU's population and spending power. This is the most densely populated area with the highest per capita consumer spending and highest productivity levels per worker. Depending on how the area is defined it sometimes looks more banana-shaped, so you may find references to Europe's 'Hot Banana' to describe this area.

Many companies target the affluent Golden Triangle area first in their pan-European sales efforts, minimising their distribution costs since most customers live in it. This may make the Triangle even more 'golden' with areas outside offering fewer attractions as trade barriers disappear under the Single Market and business gravitates towards the Triangle.

Activity 11.1

Discuss whether the Golden Triangle will continue with the admission of new members to the EU or whether its shape will change. What evidence would you seek to support your views?

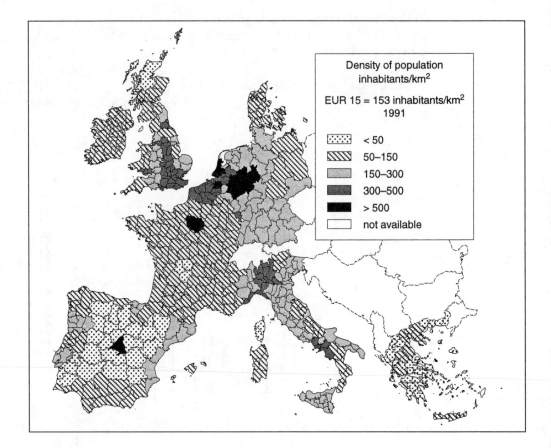

Source: *Eurostat*

Figure 11.2 Population distribution across the EU

Migration

The right to work in any part of the EU might be expected to lead to widespread migration within the EU but in practice cultural and language differences appear to dampen EU citizens' enthusiasm to cross borders. When there is a single European currency making it less risky and costly to move, Europe may then experience a 'Florida effect' with retired and mobile workers migrating to the more pleasant Mediterranean climate in the southern European states. This has major implications for the infrastructure needs in this area and poses a further danger of increased decline in both rural and urban northern communities.

Of greater significance is migration into the EU from the formerly Communist East European countries and the prospect of mass migrations from the African continent if climatic conditions continue to worsen. At present, migration from East Europe, especially into Germany which has received 500,000 people from the former Yugoslavia, pro-

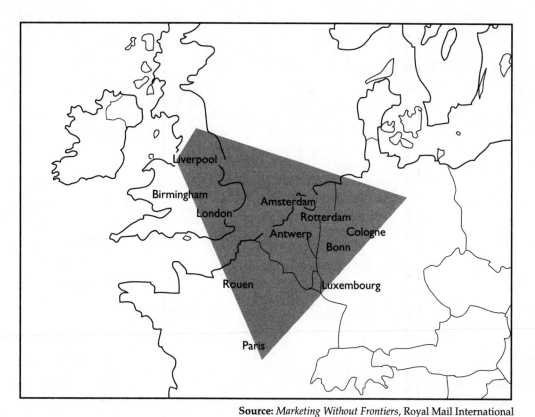

Source: *Marketing Without Frontiers*, Royal Mail International

Figure 11.3 The Golden Triangle

vides the main source of immigrants into the EU. In 1989, 2.5 per cent of the population in the EU was from non-EU countries and 1.5 per cent of the population were EU residents who had crossed borders (see Table 11.1 overleaf). Finally, people are still migrating towards the urban centres of Europe with depopulation occurring within the rural areas.

Ethnic groups

One aspect which will differ markedly across the EU is the ethnic structure of the population. You may be familiar with the marketing opportunities and cultural differences presented by the Afro-Caribbean and Asian populations in the UK; in Germany there is a significant Turkish minority and in France the ethnic minorities are largely north African.

Population structure

Breaking population down into age groups shows that, compared to other nations or to their own historical structures, it is clear that a larger proportion of the EU population is falling into the retired age group. This presents both threats and opportunities for business (see Table 11.2).

Table 11.1 Migration in the EU

To From	Belgium	Denmark	France	Germany	Greece	Ireland	Italy	Luxembourg	Netherlands	Portugal	Spain	United Kingdom
Belgium	–	460	6,605	4,521	360	156	1,654	1,176	5,402	412	689	4,000
Denmark	305	–	1,324	3,534	202	167	269	220	469	132	106	1,000
France	7,473	1,260	–	17,701	n/a	n/a	4,206	n/a	2,835	n/a	2,472	15,000
Germany	3,343	2,425	16,944	–	16,258	5,084	10,733	1,071	11,003	4,901	2,671	29,000
Greece	649	248	n/a	29,332	–	n/a	642	n/a	966	n/a	24	5,000
Ireland	314	185	n/a	5,837	n/a	–	189	n/a	851	n/a	30	n/a
Italy	2,557	547	4,654	38,372	483	24	–	219	1,521	115	324	6,000
Luxembourg	1,017	118	n/a	1,111	n/a	n/a	165	–	182	n/a	28	1,000
Netherlands	6,120	497	474	9,949	1,919	1,167	714	254	–	532	488	6,000
Portugal	1,726	126	n/a	11,489	n/a	n/a	378	n/a	1,033	–	404	1,000
Spain	1,488	948	1,613	8,523	n/a	n/a	1,277	n/a	1,953	40	–	4,000
United Kingdom	2,761	3,672	20,000	20,174	3,000	n/a	3,162	n/a	7,699	1,000	1,496	–

Source: *Eurobusiness*, July/August 1994

Table 11.2 Population structure (1993) in Europe

| | 1993 by age group (%) | | | |
	0–19	20–39	40–59	>60
Austria (1991)	23.8	32.1	24.0	20.1
Belgium	24.3	30.5	24.2	21.1
Denmark	23.8	29.9	26.2	20.1
Finland (1992)	25.4	29.7	26.3	18.7
France	26.8	30.0	23.6	19.7
Germany	21.5	31.6	26.5	20.4
Greece	24.6	29.6	25.0	20.8
Ireland	34.9	28.9	21.0	15.3
Italy	22.6	30.9	25.3	21.3
Luxembourg	23.3	32.4	25.2	19.2
Netherlands	24.6	32.9	24.9	17.6
Portugal	27.4	29.4	23.7	19.5
Spain	26.5	31.3	22.7	19.6
Sweden (1989)	25.4	28.0	24.6	23.0
United Kingdom (1990)	25.9	29.9	23.5	20.7

Source: *Eurostat*

Case study

Saga

Saga was set up 40 years ago by a hotelier who saw an opportunity to fill his rooms outside of the high season by offering cut-price rates to pensioners. Today the company offers holidays, financial services and magazines to the over-sixties.

Saga recognised what the retired wanted which included people to carry their luggage and no steep stairs to climb but also realised that older people are sophisticated travellers so the range includes £100 UK seaside holidays right up to a £30,000 round the world trip, with whale-watching and trekking holidays in between.

The company already operates in the USA and sees good opportunities in northern Europe.

Activity 11.2

What evidence is there in this chapter or elsewhere to support the last sentence of the Saga case study?

Examples

'The health and beauty care markets are growing at about 4 per cent per annum. As the population of the Western world ages, the need for beauty and skin-care products appears to be rising.'

Source: Carnaud-Metalbox (French packaging company), 1992

'The group plans to accelerate expansion over the medium term, with an emphasis on Europe.'

Source: OGF PFG Group (French funeral services company), 1993

The burden of paying state pensions to this growing elderly population, especially with large numbers out of work and unable to contribute to the social fund, means that the tax burden is growing. Most European governments realise that state pension schemes will run out of money within the next few years and are taking steps to remedy the situation by:

● reducing eligibility (e.g. increasing the retirement age);
● reducing the value of the state pension;
● encouraging people now in work to make their own provisions.

At the other extreme, the number of young people is declining, so employers will have to make recruitment attractive to the long-term unemployed and mature women, and be prepared to offer the retraining needed for new jobs.

Example

'We have a consistently high number of applications – in spite of unfavourable demographic developments. The bank improved its equal opportunity arrangements and measures to ensure the compatibility of career and family. This includes parental leave and ongoing support of female employees during the family phase. We also provide our employees with child-care support.'

Source: Bayerische Hypotheken-und Wechsel Bank (German Bank), 1992

Assuming competent language skills, you may find good employment opportunities in other EU Member States where there is a shortage of young people.

Increased affluence and divorce rates in the EU have reduced the average size of household from 2.9 persons in 1977 to 2.6 in 1990 which increased the number of households. (The average number of people in a household for the Member States is shown in Table 11.3.) So a stable population presents different opportunities depending on age distribution and household size.

Table 11.3 Average household size across the EU, 1990

Country	Persons in a household (average)
Austria	2.5
Belgium	2.5
Denmark	2.2
Finland	2.4
France	2.6
Germany	2.5
Greece	3.0
Ireland	3.3
Italy	2.8
Luxembourg	2.6
Netherlands	2.4
Portugal	3.1
Spain	3.3
Sweden	2.1
UK	2.5

Source: *Eurostat*

The sex ratio is also changing as more men survive to old age with consequent effects on the demand for products related to elderly men.

Economic indicators

Market research by a new exporter should start with looking at the economic indicators in the target market. You met the major economic indicators in Mandatory Unit 1. The significance of each indicator comes with experience but at the very least you can compare those of your target market with their UK equivalents. For example, if you know that you can live with 2.7 per cent inflation in the UK then you can sell in Italy where inflation is 4.5 per cent but may have difficulty in matching prices in the Netherlands where inflation is only 0.4 per cent. It also helps to take a wider view by comparing economic indicators in non-EU countries, such as the USA and Japan, or the emerging economies of Singapore and South Korea.

Another reason for examining economic indicators is when considering overseas location, either a complete move away from the UK to another Member State or simply to add to existing production facilities. Unemployment rates will help to show whether the labour you require would be available and per head gross domestic product (GDP) will give you an indication of the level of wages you may have to pay.

The main economic indicators to examine are:

- industrial structure;
- gross domestic product (GDP);
- economic growth;
- unemployment;
- inflation;
- exchange rates.

Industrial structure

Business analysts have found it useful to divide the economy into three sectors as follows:

- primary sector – agriculture, mining and extractive industries of raw materials such as coal and petroleum;
- secondary sector – manufacturing (i.e. the combining and processing of primary sector products);
- tertiary sector – services to support the primary and secondary sectors, including accountancy, banking and other financial services, transport and distribution, wholesaling and retailing.

You should have examined these for the UK in Mandatory Unit 1.

As a country's economy develops, most people are employed in the primary sector, then the secondary sector gradually becomes more important and, finally, the primary and secondary sectors shrink as jobs in the tertiary sector increase.

At which stage is Europe now?

Some analysts predicted that the old industrialised countries, including most of Europe, would increasingly obtain their income from the tertiary sector where higher levels of education and sophisticated information systems, the so-called 'information society', give these countries an advantage. However, Europe cannot abandon manufacturing altogether because most manufactured goods would then have to be imported, with adverse effects on the balance of payments. Furthermore, know-how (trained people and information) is increasingly mobile and is easily transferred to lower labour cost countries so European advantage in this area need not necessarily remain in Europe.

Maybe we are looking to a future in which, like agriculture, only a small proportion of the population will work in a highly efficient secondary sector. The problem for Europe at the moment is that although industry is shedding labour as people are replaced by more efficient methods and machinery, the service sector is not demanding an equivalent number of new workers. The result is the present massive unemployment in Europe. Business success in the future may well lie in localised services which can never be provided at a distance.

How helpful is it to identify the three sectors?

Examining the different European economies using the three defined sectors may help businesses predict which sectors should increase and which decrease. This may identify the future pattern of a European company's operations and may help it to decide where to locate and concentrate its sales efforts.

Primary sector

Figures 11.4 and 11.5 show that agriculture employs a tiny proportion of the workforce in Europe (typically less than 10 per cent) and contributes about the same percentage to GDP. Therefore, the fact that most of the EU budget goes on agriculture is rather puzzling but is because in the fifties, when the European Community was created, agriculture employed far more people than it does now. Efforts are now being made to reduce agricultural support and many argue that the EU should now be targeting most effort into improving the efficiency of the secondary sector instead (see the example below).

☺ If you are planning to work in the primary sector, such as farming, you may find better opportunities elsewhere in Europe where that sector is larger.

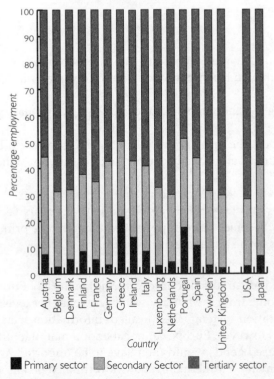

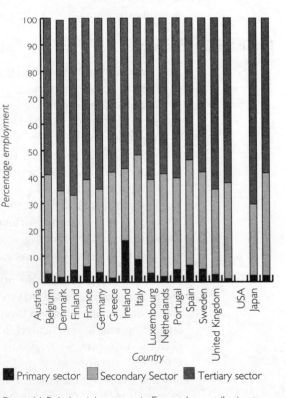

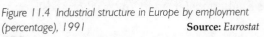

Figure 11.4 Industrial structure in Europe by employment (percentage), 1991 **Source:** *Eurostat*

Figure 11.5 Industrial structure in Europe by contribution to GDP (percentage), 1991 **Source:** *Eurostat*

Example

'The improvement in Modo Skog's result is due to improved efficiency in harvesting. The very dramatic reduction (in employees) has primarily been made possible by further mechanisation of what used to be manual work in the forest.'

Source: Modo Skog (Swedish paper and forestry products company), 1992

Secondary sector

Europe seems to do best in low-tech manufacturing industries, such as textiles, leather tanning and wood processing, whereas the most profitable opportunities occur in industries such as computers, office equipment, medical equipment and motor components. This does not bode well for the future.

Pharmaceuticals is a strong European industry but this is moving away from chemical based drugs to biotechnologically engineered products, and here again Europe is not at the forefront. Job losses in manufacturing would be more acceptable if European manufacturing was gearing itself up for a profitable future in the next century, but the signs are that current strengths will soon be outdated (see the example below).

Example

'The steel crisis which has long been affecting other Western countries also hit the German steel market. Cheap imports from eastern European countries and large excess capacities led to ruinous prices.'

Source: VIAG (German company involved in aluminium, steel, chemicals, energy, glass, metal packaging and transport), 1992

Tertiary sector

In the service sector, European companies remain very much national rather than international. In industries such as air transport and retailing many restrictions remain, for example, national state monopolies or strict shop opening laws, which limit the growth of service companies. Cultural differences are also much more important in the sale of services as the example below demonstrates.

Example

Credit Local de France (CLF) has for many years been one of the largest financial institutions lending money to French local government authorities to carry out large projects such as the building of town halls, hospitals, conference centres and tourist facilities. It is only since 1992 that it expanded rapidly abroad by, for example, acquiring a controlling interest in the Municipal Mutual Bank in the UK. In the UK it was the first time that local authority financing had been put in private hands and hence for CLF the opportunity to expand into the UK had not previously existed.

Another critical factor is size of enterprise which is shown below in Table 11.4. We saw, for example in Chapter 7, that there are many more small shops and wholesalers in the southern Mediterranean countries and this had an impact on the best way of reaching these outlets.

Table 11.4 Size of enterprises

	Micro (0–9)		Small (10–99)		Medium (100–499)		Large (500+)	
	% establishments	% employment	% establishments	% employment	% establishments	% employment	% establishments	% employment
Austria	n/a	n/a	n/a	n/a	n/a	n/a	n/a	30
Belgium	94	31	5	26	<0.5	14	<0.2	29
Denmark	72	17	26	42	2	23	<0.5	18
Finland	n/a	19	n/a	44**	n/a	n/a	n/a	n/a
France	94	22	6	26	<0.5	15	<0.1	36
Germany	86	18	13	27	1	19	<0.2	36
Greece	93	19	7	19	<0.5	63	*	*
Ireland	37	4	54	37	8	36	<1	23
Italy	91	40	9	33	<0.5	9	<0.1	17
Luxembourg	88	26	11	30	<1	19	<0.2	24
Netherlands	92	19	7	26	1	16	<0.2	39
Portugal	95	36	4	28	<0.5	17	<0.1	19
Spain	95	41	5	37	<0.3	14	<0.1	8
Sweden	n/a	n/a	n/a	n/a	n/a	n/a	n/a	n/a
United Kingdom	91	23	9	24	1	23	<0.2	30

Source: *Eurostat*

Notes:

* Figures for large companies are included together with those for medium.

** Figure is for small and medium sized companies.

Where is industry located in Europe?

The present distribution of economic activity (see Figure 11.6) is partly explained by factors which were important locating influences in the past such as proximity to fuel (coal) and raw materials (iron ore). Some of these influences lead to the clustering of industry whilst others lead to its dispersal.

Activity 11.3

1 List ten business activities to benefit from locating close to the most densely populated areas of Europe and explain in each why the activities benefit.
2 List some businesses which do not require this proximity.
3 How could you test the accuracy of your answers (i.e. which sources would you use)?

Figure 11.6 shows noticeable areas of decline and growth. Declining industries tend to be in heavy manufacturing, overtaken by competitors elsewhere, such as steel and ships which are more cheaply produced in East Europe and South-East Asia. Newer industries tend to be more footloose and locate in areas people find pleasant to live in. Since the new industries require scarce, highly-trained personnel, a pleasant location is another way of attracting skilled employees. Presently, the factors concentrating industry in a few areas seem stronger than those causing its dispersal.

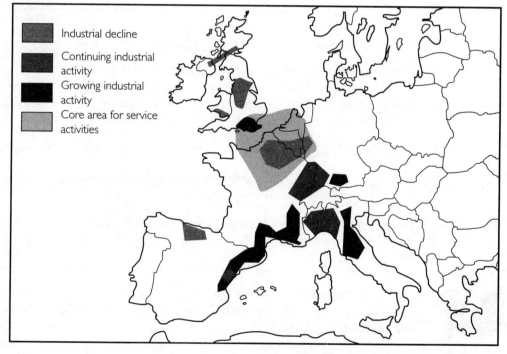

Industrial decline

Continuing industrial activity

Growing industrial activity

Core area for service activities

Source: The European Round Table of Industrialists

Figure 11.6 An industrial map of Europe

Standard of living

Gross Domestic Product (GDP), covered in Mandatory Unit 1, measures the value of all goods and services traded in any one year and is used as a major indicator of economic well-being. The GDP figures for European countries in 1991 are shown in Table 11.5 with the USA and Japan included for comparison.

Table 11.5 GDP in Europe, 1991

	Actual 1000m ECU
Austria	132.9
Belgium	159.2
Denmark	105.3
Finland	100.6
France	970.3
Germany	1274.0
Greece	57.1
Ireland	35.1
Italy	930.9
Luxembourg	7.6
Netherlands	235.2
Portugal	55.5
Spain	426.5
Sweden	191.7
United Kingdom	816.5
USA	4527.9
Japan	2720.4

Source: *Eurostat*, 1993

There are three methods of using the GDP figures shown in Table 11.5.

Method 1: direct comparison of per head GDP with the UK
Dividing the actual GDP by the number of people in a country gives you a rough idea of the standard of living in that country. Figure 11.7 shows that only Greece, Ireland, Portugal and Spain are poorer per head than the UK.

☺ Countries with higher GDP per head are likely to offer you higher wages.

☺ As long as the product you are selling is not a basic commodity, potential demand could be stronger in most other European countries than it is in the UK.

Direct comparison shows that Europe lags behind the income of the USA and Japan, and that there is a great potential for increasing GDP in Europe.

Example

'While our results in Europe as a whole were under pressure, those in South America and Asia were good to very good. Our expansion policy in South America and Asia will continue unabated.'

Source: SHV Makro (a Dutch wholesaling company), 1993

Method 2: comparison over time as measured by economic growth
Look at Figure 11.8. You will note that, with the exception of Greece, it is the poorest countries which seem to have been growing the fastest over the period 1986–91.

Source: *Eurostat*

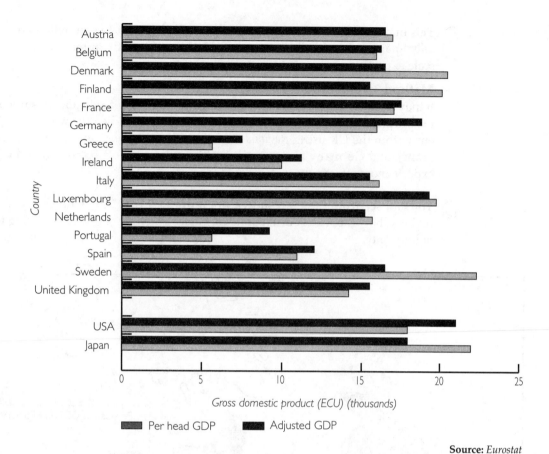

Source: *Eurostat*

Figure 11.7 GDP per head and GDP per head adjusted for purchasing power, 1991

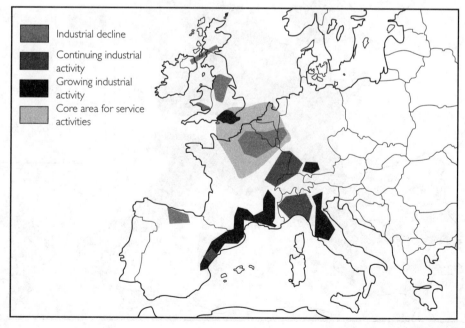

Source: *Eurostat*

Figure 11.8 Economic growth across Europe, average annual rate 1986–91

😊 This may be a reason for targeting Ireland, Portugal and Spain with exports although only Spain, out of the three, has a population sufficiently numerous to consider large-scale exporting.

Method 3: regional breakdown

It may be helpful to break down the larger, more populated countries into regions for the purposes of GDP analysis. You will already have studied the wide disparities apparent within the UK using *Regional Trends* or *Social Trends*. Similar gaps occur in Italy, France and Germany and identifying the most well-off regions may help to target exports more effectively.

😊 You can see from the map shown in Figure 11.9 that Italy's northern and southern regions show the widest discrepancies. Hence you may consider exporting to the north of Italy only.

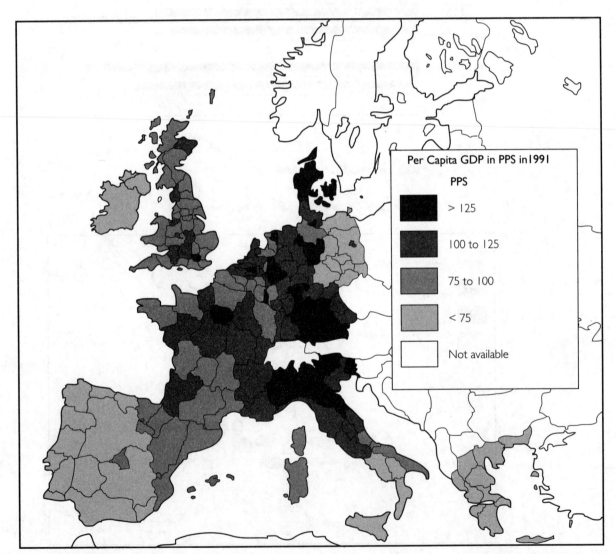

Source: *Europe in Figures*

Figure 11.9 Regional GDP in the EU

Standard of living can be indicated by disposable income which is indicated in Table 11.6. This table indicates the amount of income over which individuals have discretion in the way in which it is spent. In a country with high taxes and high social provision, for example subsidised child care and comprehensive health service, there may be lower disposable income. However what is left over may be available to spend on luxury items whereas in a country with low social provision, much disposable income may have to be spent on education, health and pension provision with less available for luxuries.

Table 11.6   Disposable income across the EU

Country	$ per capita 1994
Austria	13,463
Belgium	13,953
Denmark	14,826
Finland	10,084
France	13,792
Germany	14,425
Greece	5,611
Ireland	7,860
Italy	11,172
Luxembourg	14,850
Netherlands	12,981
Portugal	4,950
Spain	7,782
Sweden	11,781
UK	10,964

Source: *European Marketing Data and Statistics 1996*, Euromonitor

The distribution of income, shown in Table 11.7 (overleaf), indicates how a country's income is spread within the population. Two countries may have identical overall levels of income but in one it may be fairly evenly distributed throughout the population whilst in the other there may be a few very well off people with the majority very badly off. This has implications for the size of market for specific goods. For example, an exporter of luxury yachts may do well in the second country whilst an exporter of more mundane household items might do well in the first country where income is more evenly spread. The distribution of wealth includes income and other assets such as land and company shares. Figures for this are not easily available and where wealth is taxed, the figures tend to underestimate the true situation as people try to minimise their tax bill. Hence distribution of income figures will have to act as substitutes for distribution of wealth information.

Cost of living

Simply dividing a country's GDP by its population is not the best way of discovering the standard of living as this gives no idea about living costs. Where costs are low, such as in Portugal, money goes much further. Statistical sources such as Eurostat adjust these per head figures to reflect average costs such as for rent, fuel, food, and so on (as in Figure 11.7). This makes countries like Portugal appear better off and reduces the apparent income of high-cost countries such as France, giving a more realistic impression of how well off people really are. Table 11.8 (overleaf) gives an indication of prices in the EU.

Table 11.7   Distribution of income in the EU, 1995

| | Percentage of household incomes going to | |
	the lowest 20%	the highest 20%
Austria	na	na
Belgium	7.9	36.0
Denmark	5.4	38.6
Finland	6.3	37.6
France	5.6	41.9
Germany	7.0	40.3
Greece	na	na
Ireland	7.2	39.4
Italy	6.8	41.0
Luxembourg	7.9	36.0
Netherlands	8.2	36.9
Portugal	5.2	49.1
Spain	8.3	36.6
Sweden	8.0	36.9
UK	4.6	44.3

Note: The closer both figures are to 20%, the more evenly income is distributed.

Source: *The World Competitiveness Report 1995,* The World Economic Forum

Table 11.8   Prices across the EU, 1994 (in US $)

	Female clothes[1]	Male clothes[2]	Cheap monthly rent	Household appliances[3]	Bus ride	Car purchase	Car service (labour)	Eating out[4]	Services[5]
Austria	480	760	410	2090	1.69	16,900	228	33	340
Belgium	390	890	630	2830	1.44	18,900	26	28	320
Denmark	730	1020	620	3000	3.04	26,200	156	28	450
Finland	400	610	470	2460	1.65	20,200	80	22	350
France	550	1020	750	2660	1.13	18,400	35	22	320
Germany	350	570	590	1990	1.48	21,700	178	25	350
Greece	370	900	440	2310	0.30	23,700	61	20	220
Ireland	230	570	430	1660	1.37	23,600	72	29	270
Italy	390	750	670	1890	0.74	15,200	92	31	270
Luxembourg	330	570	1080	2520	1.01	14,900	104	31	320
Netherlands	410	710	520	1880	1.56	17,200	62	26	330
Portugal	240	420	690	2020	0.55	20,500	32	19	200
Spain	290	590	470	2500	0.91	12,700	109	22	250
Sweden	450	580	600	2320	2.21	20,300	205	25	390
UK	340	570	810	2040	1.94	20,100	119	23	300

[1] Dress, skirt, tights and shoes
[2] Suit, jacket, jeans, shirt, shoes and socks
[3] Fridge, pan, sewing machine, TV, camera, iron, vacuum cleaner and hair dryer
[4] Steak + 2 veg, desert, no drinks
[5] 19 items including haircut, dry cleaning, phone, cinema ticket, etc.

Source: Union Bank of Switzerland

Activity 11.4

Compare the costs of your own expenditure with two other EU countries using Table 11.8 and other sources such as your EU contacts. What differences are there? Would you change your purchasing habits if you lived in the other two countries?

Unemployment and the labour force

The number of people available for work varies according to the school leaving and retirement age (Table 11.9), how usual it is for women to work (Figure 11.10 overleaf) and the level of immigration and emigration (Table 11.1 earlier).

Table 11.9 School leaving and retirement ages across the EU

Country	Men	Women	Earliest school leaving age
Austria	65	60	15
Belgium	60–65	60–65	18[1]
Denmark	67	67	16
Finland	65	65	17
France	60	60	16
Germany	65	65*	18[2]
Greece	65	60	$14\frac{1}{2}$
Ireland	65	65	15
Italy	60	55	14
Luxembourg	65	65	15
Netherlands	65	65	18[1]
Portugal**	65	62	15
Spain	65–69	65–69	16
Sweden	65	65	16
United Kingdom	65	60***	16

*   from 2006
**   no compulsory retirement; ages stated are usual retirement ages
*** 65 is to be phased in gradually by 2020
1. Last two years can be part time.
2. Last three years can be part time.

There is a Europe-wide trend for both the school leaving age and retirement age to increase, the latter due to the need to generate funds for pension payments. Throughout Europe the percentage of women working is increasing (see Figure 11.10 overleaf), creating demand for convenience foods and servicing such as cleaning and childcare. However, the careful exporter will note the wide differences and target those countries where female participation is highest or growing the most rapidly.

Activity 11.5

1 Compile a market report on the effects of increased female participation on demand in the following product areas:
   ● cars
   ● insurance (all types)
   ● cleaning and maintenance services.

2 What changes will have to be made to the product portfolio of typical companies in these sectors?

3 What new products should they be developing in response to this trend?

4 Which Member States present the best opportunities and why?

It may help to consult reports of both UK and other EU companies in the designated product areas.

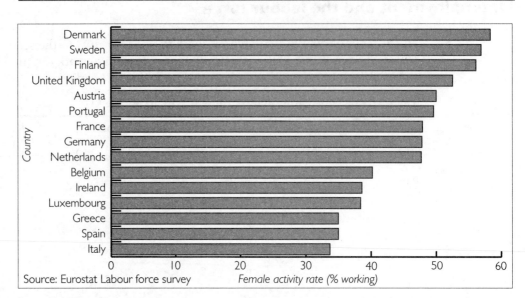

Source: Eurostat Labour force survey — *Female activity rate (% working)*

Figure 11.10 Female participation rate

The resulting supply of labour is shown in Table 11.10.

Table 11.10   Supply of labour and unemployment across the EU

	Labour supply (as % of population) 1991	Unemployment (as % of working population) 1991	1995
Austria	46	3.3	4.6
Belgium	41	7.5	14.7
Denmark	56	8.9	9.8
Finland	50	7.5	16.2
France	43	9.5	11.5
Germany	47	4.2	9.2
Greece	39	7.7	4.7
Ireland	38	16.2	14.5
Italy	42	10.0	11.7
Luxembourg	44	1.6	2.6
Netherlands	46	7.0	7.0
Portugal	49	4.1	7.2
Spain	39	16.3	15.4
Sweden	53	2.7	7.6
UK	49	9.1	8.1

Source: *Eurostat* and the *European* newspaper 23 November 1995

Naturally, not all those available for work are in work and the levels of unemployment across the EU are also shown in Table 11.10.

Although jobs are being lost in the primary sector (coal mining is a recent UK example) most are lost from the secondary sector as productivity increases through better machinery and methods such as 'just in time'. These tend to be male jobs, using specialist skills which are not transferable.

New jobs tend to be either part-time, paying insufficient wages for a head of household or require highly specialised skills which the newly unemployed from manufacturing tend not to have. Insufficient new jobs are being created to make up for these losses and so for the past 10 to 15 years the general trend is for unemployment to increase in most European countries.

Table 11.10 shows that wide variation exists, from Finland with 16.2 per cent to Luxembourg with 2.6 per cent. Governments would probably be happy with 5 per cent unemployment.

☺ As an exporter you could assume that in a country with less than 5 per cent unemployment, wages (and hence disposable income to spend on your products) are likely to be rising as employers try to bid employees away from current jobs to work in their companies.

☹ A country with high unemployment is likely to prove difficult to find work in unless you have a skill which is in short supply.

☹ A country with high unemployment is likely to have reduced spending power so reducing the potential demand for your products.

If you are scouring Europe for a new production location, you may be attracted to a country with higher unemployment where you may find the labour you need. Unfortunately, unemployment is becoming a permanent feature with a large proportion of the jobless being classified as long-term unemployed. If you need specialist skills, then a large pool of unemployed is unlikely to yield the workers you need unless you are prepared to invest heavily in training.

Another consideration is the cost of labour including the level of employer social security contributions which may be high, adding considerably to your labour costs (see Table 11.11 overleaf).

Example

'The possibilities of obtaining supplies from low-wage countries will be included in discussions with suppliers.'

Source: DAF (Dutch truck maker), 1993

It is not just the cost of labour which is important but also its quality which can be measured by the highest educational level of workers. Table 11.12 overleaf shows that Italy has the highest percentage of the workforce qualified to higher education level but that Germany and the Netherlands have the highest percentage educated to upper secondary level which is probably industry's greatest need.

Table 11.11 Hourly labour costs including employer contribution to social protection, 1994

	Gross income in $	Net income in $	Taxes & social security as % of gross income	Employer contribution as % of total hourly labour cost, 1991
Austria	13.5	9.9	26.4	na
Belgium	13.4	8.6	36.1	29.8
Denmark	19.1	11.7	38.5	3.7
Finland	11.5	7.8	32.0	22.5
France	11.3	8.5	24.6	31.5
Germany	17.0	11.3	33.6	23.4
Greece	6.0	4.9	18.9	20.0
Ireland	9.4	7.1	25.0	17.8
Italy	10.6	7.3	31.1	29.4
Luxembourg	17.1	13.8	19.4	16.7
Netherlands	13.4	9.2	31.5	27.2
Portugal	5.0	4.0	20.5	25.7
Spain	9.2	7.5	18.1	24.9
Sweden	12.1	8.6	29.0	30.9
UK	10.4	7.1	31.3	12.8

Source: Union Bank of Switzerland and *Eurostat*

Table 11.12 Highest educational level across the EU, 1992

	Percentage*		
	Third level	Upper secondary level	< upper secondary level
Belgium	16.0	28.4	55.6
Denmark	13.2	44.9	33.5
France	11.4	19.0	69.3
Germany	15.0	50.2	25.0
Greece	9.2	24.6	66.2
Ireland	13.4	25.3	61.0
Italy	22.5	10.7	66.8
Luxembourg	9.7	22.1	68.1
Netherlands	15.7	53.1	30.9
Portugal	7.6	10.1	82.2
Spain	9.4	13.9	76.6
UK	12.9	24.6	41.8

* Percentages do not always add up to 100.

Source: Eurostat

☺ In recent years, much effort has been put into modernising machinery and manufacturing methods. The next step is the modernising and restructuring of the workforce which will need a huge retraining effort.

It is probably safest to assume that mass unemployment will remain a feature of Europe for the foreseeable future.

Inflation

For an exporter, the significance of inflation rates (annual average rates of price increases) is not so much the actual inflation rates but the rate in the target market compared to that in the exporter's domestic market. Generally, it is easier to sell in countries with higher inflation rates as the exporter's prices appear progressively cheaper as domestic competitors in the target market are forced to raise their prices to meet increasing costs. Conversely, importers should buy from countries with lower inflation than that in the UK to maintain attractive prices for UK customers.

☺ The 1995 data (see Table 11.13) show that for a UK company, Italy would be a good country to export to, and that Finland would be a good country to import from.

Table 11.13 Inflation rates across Europe, 1995/96

	Percentage rate
Austria	1.8
Belgium	2.0
Denmark	1.8
Finland	0.5
France	2.4
Germany	1.7
Greece	8.4
Ireland	2.0
Italy	4.5
Luxembourg	1.1
Netherlands	0.4
Portugal	2.4
Spain	3.4
Sweden	1.7
UK	2.7

Source: *The European*, 18 April 1996

Activity 11.6

1 Use the inflation data in Table 11.13 to identify other Member States which a UK company could best export to and those which would be recommended as sources for imports into the UK on the basis of inflation rates.
2 Draw up a similar list for a business based in Germany and one based in Italy.

☹ Inflation is often controlled by increasing interest rates. Countries selling investment products will have limited sales in Member States where interest rates are high, as this increases the cost of borrowing to finance major investment.

Exchange rates

The Exchange Rate Mechanism (ERM) proved very unstable in 1992 and so the target of achieving a single currency by 1997 or 1999 looks increasingly unlikely. Since the UK,

Italy and Greece are not even in the ERM this means that fluctuations in exchange rates are still very relevant for exporters and likely to remain so for the medium term. The difficulties this may cause for exporters and importers were discussed in Chapter 2.

Examples

'There was a decline in the competitiveness of German industry as a consequence of the changed exchange rate parities in the EMS.'

Source: VIAG (German aluminium and steel company explaining poor results), 1992

'The strengthening of the Finnish mark reduced exports.'

Source: Partek (Finnish industrial group), 1994

Clearly, even when a single European currency is achieved its value will still vary against non-EU currencies. This will, therefore affect purchases of raw materials and components, and the sales of the finished product to the rest of the world.

Example

'Purchasing of raw tobacco cost 20 per cent less than in the previous year partly due to the favourable trend of the peseta against the dollar.'

Source: Tabacalera (Spanish state tobacco company which buys some of its tobacco from the USA), 1992

☹ If the pound continues to decline then British savings will be worth less and less if you live elsewhere in the EU.

Conclusion

Unemployment is the big economic problem in Europe at the moment now that inflation is largely under control. As well as reducing GDP and the demand for goods and services, it also places enormous strains on the public sector. The ageing population adds to these strains which are expected to worsen in the foreseeable future. Otherwise economic indicators seem to be converging across Europe although there are still wide differences which a small-scale exporter ought to be aware of in order to target the most profitable markets first.

Summary

- The population is almost static but its structure is changing with an increase in the retired population, leading to changed patterns of demand.
- Economic indicators are useful to analyse when considering relocation as well as exporting.
- The primary and secondary sectors are shrinking and the tertiary sector increasing, but manufacturing needs to be more geared to high-tech sectors if it is to remain strong in the long term.
- It is a good idea to examine potential European markets regionally as there are considerable disparities within some countries.
- The poorer Member States are growing the fastest.

- Unemployment is likely to remain a long-term feature of European economies.
- Restructuring of the labour force (i.e. training) is necessary and likely to present large-scale business opportunities.
- Countries with high inflation will find it difficult to export.

Information sources

- *Basic Statistics of the Community*, published annually by Eurostat.
- 'Country data' section in the Business and Economics supplement of the *European*.
- *Europe in Figures*, fourth edition 1995, Eurostat (presents the facts in a visually appealing format).
- *The National Economies of Europe*, edited by David Dyker, Longman, 1992.

Assignment 11.1
Career move

This assignment fulfils the following criteria:
BTEC 16.1.1 to 16.1.4

Pick an area of commercial work in which you might be interested in working. For example:
- farming and horticulture
- hotels, leisure and tourism
- manufacturing
- financial services
- retailing

Assume that you either want to find a job or set up a business in your chosen sector elsewhere in the EU. Your objective is to choose a suitable EU region in which to work.

Your tasks

Stage 1: Pick two EU Member States
To make the task more manageable you should use the information provided in this chapter to pick the two most suitable EU Member States for further research. Which of the factors are relevant to your chosen industry and in which Member States are the factors most favourable? For instance, you may need to choose only Member States with a high per capita GDP and low inflation if your intention is to sell luxury goods. (Use marketing information from Euromonitor and statistics from Eurostat.)

Stage 2: Target the region
Do some more detailed research into your two chosen EU Member States to pinpoint the best area for a job search or a new business. This could include:
- location, accessibility and size of relevant companies;

- availability of relevant training;
- regional age structure;
- regional variations in average wage in your chosen industry;
- regional unemployment rate;
- local taxes.

(Use business directories, European contacts, copies of local newspapers in the target area and relevant embassies to help you.)

Job seekers

Scan the trade and business press for news of a relevant company with interests in your chosen EU region and write a speculative letter of application which makes it clear that you have done your 'homework'.

Starting a business

Your new venture may need some financial support. Write a brief summary of your findings and why you think the venture will succeed to be sent to potential investors in your business as part of a more detailed business plan.

Final assignment outcome

For assessment purposes you should have available a portfolio of your research efforts.

12 The country profiles

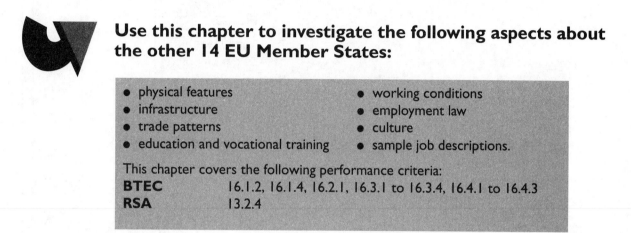

Use this chapter to investigate the following aspects about the other 14 EU Member States:

- physical features
- infrastructure
- trade patterns
- education and vocational training
- working conditions
- employment law
- culture
- sample job descriptions.

This chapter covers the following performance criteria:

BTEC   16.1.2, 16.1.4, 16.2.1, 16.3.1 to 16.3.4, 16.4.1 to 16.4.3
RSA   13.2.4

Introduction

Figures 12.1, 12.2 and 12.3 will give you some idea of the transport links between the Member States. You may need to refer to these figures as you read the data on various countries.

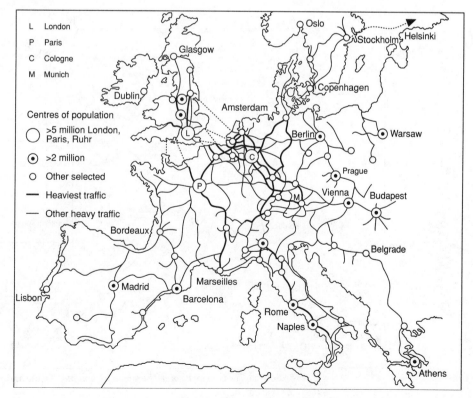

Source: *The Geography of the European Community*, J Cole and F Cole, Routledge, 1993

Figure 12.1 The major road routes of the EU

209

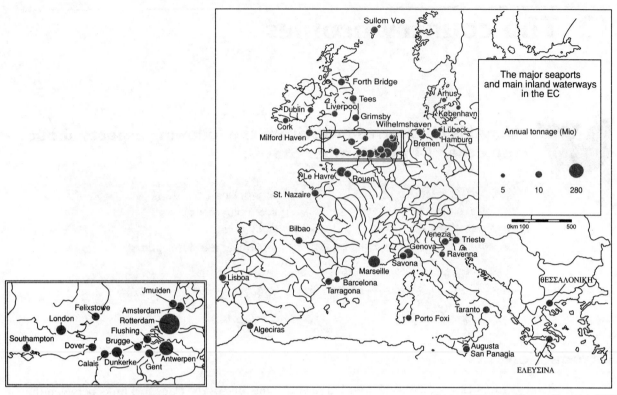

Source: *Europe in Figures*, Eurostat, 1992

Figure 12.2 The major freight waterways of the EU

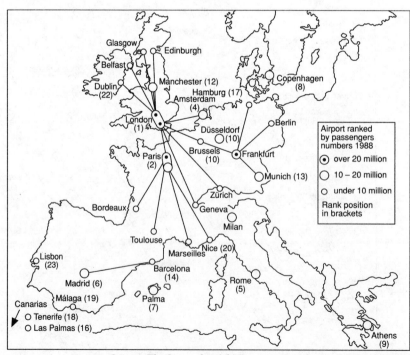

Source: *The Geography of the European Community*, J Cole and F Cole, Routledge, 1993

Figure 12.3 The major air hubs of the EU

Austria

Main features

- Suffers from a large amount of through freight traffic
- Trade link between the EU and the emerging market economies of eastern Europe
- High emigration from eastern Europe

Resources

Austria mines the ores of magnesium, copper, lead and zinc as well as salt. Timber and hydropower are other natural resources and it also benefits from a very highly skilled workforce. It is a strong economy with close links with German industrial companies. Austria is almost self-sufficient in food and its other strengths lie in niche markets like tourism and banking. Due to its strategic location it should benefit as eastern European markets continue to open up and thereby it should become less dependent on Germany as its major trading partner.

Land

The Austrian Alps cover two-thirds of the country. This very mountainous terrain limits transport, the spread of population and agriculture. The populated flat area is in the east.

Climate

This is a moderate continental climate with warm and pleasant summers and cool nights, and sunny winters with sufficient snow for extensive winter sports.

Language

German is spoken all over Austria although there are strong regional dialects. There are small pockets speaking Italian in the south, Romansh in the south-east and also Hungarian, Slovene and Croatian.

Telecoms

Highly developed and efficient with 4 million phones although not as advanced in many aspects such as investment, cost and lines per person as the UK system.

Other links

Austria is a landlocked country with a strategic location at the crossroads of central Europe with many easily traversable Alpine passes and valleys. Recent moves by Switzerland to limit through road traffic may have a knock-on effect and increase traffic in Austria. There is already conflict about the increased traffic through the Brenner Pass used by vehicles between Germany and Italy. An electronic motorway toll system is planned for 1997 to raise money for further improvements. The River Danube which flows through the country is a major carrier of cargo between north and central Europe, a route of increasing importance with the emergence of market economies in eastern Europe. Austria's rail routes are also of strategic importance for through freight.

Trade flows

Main trading partners are Germany (60 per cent), Italy, Japan, Switzerland and France.

Major exports: machinery and equipment (especially construction and optical equipment), iron and steel, timber, textiles, paper products and chemicals. On the invisible side tourism is a major earner.

Major imports: petroleum, foodstuffs, machinery and equipment, vehicles, chemicals, textiles and clothing, pharmaceuticals.

The DTI has identified the following as good opportunities for UK exporters to Austria:

- quality adults' clothing
- computer software and services
- food and drink
- security equipment.

Education

Compulsory school

For the 6–15 year age group. The independent sector is negligible. On completion of primary school at ten most children go on to the hauptschules. After four years of secondary schooling, most then go on to a pre-vocational year before going into apprenticeship.

Alternatively, students can take five-year, full-time courses leading to qualifications equivalent to apprenticeship in the fields of teaching, skilled industrial, commercial, business and agricultural occupations. The other available secondary option is to attend a gymnasium for an academic education culminating in the Reifeprufung exam after eight years. Entry to the academic option is determined by primary school results, satisfactory performance in an entry exam or outstanding performance in the hauptschule leading to a transfer.

Qualification at 19

Reifeprufung/Matura. University and polytechnic entrance is open to all who obtain the Reifeprufung and is very competitive. Those with vocational qualifications may gain entry to the polytechnics only by taking an entrance exam. There are post-secondary high schools for vocational non-advanced further education.

Training and skills

Austria has a high literacy rate and its education system is rated very highly as a good preparation for working life. Unqualified adults may catch up on their secondary education by attending evening classes at schools and colleges and upgrading of skills is also available for qualified apprentices.

Employer involvement

The apprenticeship scheme lasts for up to four years after the end of compulsory schooling and consists of day or block release and training at work given by qualified instructors acting on national syllabi. The apprentice gains a Journeyman's Certificate on successful completion of an exam at the end. Apprentice training contracts are monitored by the relevant chamber of commerce.

Employment conditions

Contract of employment

May be written, oral or implicit.

Public holidays

13 days – January 1, January 6 (Epiphany), Easter Monday, May 1, Ascension, Whit Monday, Corpus Christi (early June), August 15 (Assumption), October 26 (National Day), November 1 (All Saints'), December 8 (Immaculate Conception), December 25, 26. Members of certain religious faiths get 14 public holidays as Good Friday is included.

Paid holiday

30 (36 after 25 years' experience) working days plus public holidays. There is also provision for the payment of a 13th month's salary by no later than June 16 and a Christmas 14th month's salary payable no later than December 14.

Working hours

Between 36 and 40 hours a week.

Minimum wages

A uniquely Austrian phenomenon is the Parity Commission comprising representatives from employers, unions and government, which, amongst other things, recommends minimum wages. These recommendations have no legal status but are usually incorporated into the collective agreements negotiated between individual employers and unions. These agreements are then usually extended to non-union members. In this way minimum wages emerge for the different industries in an amicable way.

Working practices

Normal office hours are 8 a.m.–12.30 p.m. and 1.30 p.m.–5.30 p.m. with an hour for lunch.

Use of information technology

Austria's technological infrastructure is rated as somewhat better than the UK's.

Mobility

Geographical mobility is low as people tend to want to stay close to their families and in rural areas, where a property is more likely to be owned than rented, selling would be a problem. Austrian students show little interest in studying abroad. With low unemployment there is little need for geographical mobility.

Tax

Taxable income over ATS8840 (£580) is charged at 10 per cent with income bands being charged progressively more up to ATS700,000 (about £45,850) which is charged at 50 per cent. Local taxes are charged on the value of land at 0.8 per cent per annum. Total social security deductions are 17.7 per cent of pay for blue collar workers and 16.35 per cent of pay for white collar workers.

VAT is 20 per cent, 25–34 per cent on cars and 10 per cent on basics such as food, books, newspapers, magazines, transport and hospital services. There are various other taxes such as a 1 per cent tax on personal assets.

Social security

The system is comprehensive and provides a high level of benefits in the event of sickness, disability, retirement or unemployment.

Trade unions

Austria is highly unionised since two-thirds of the workforce are members. Industrial relations are based on a co-operative attitude towards management. There is one central trade union with many divisions. In all companies with over four employees there is an elected workers' council.

Equal opportunities

An equal treatment commission deals with gender discrimination and sexual harassment cases. The constitution also prohibits discrimination on the grounds of race, nationality and religion. However the burden of proof lies with the complainant to satisfy the constitutional court that he or she was discriminated against. Also, since pursuing a case to the constitutional court is such an overwhelming undertaking few individuals would be prepared to take this route. The public sector is generally better at actively promoting equal opportunity.

Health and safety

There are a range of health and safety regulations which companies in Austria must abide by and this is monitored by visits from labour inspectors. No capital equipment can be introduced for use on premises until it has received a safety inspection. Enterprises whose activities include dangerous procedures or the use of hazardous materials can expect their premises to be inspected fairly regularly once every year or two.

Medical care

Treatment is mostly free at the point of use. Entitlement to facilities derives from employment and in some cases dependents are liable for fees, such as 10 per cent of costs after four weeks in hospital, which the directly insured worker does not incur. Dental treatment is free for everyone. The quality of treatment is highly rated but many Austrians still prefer to use private health services.

Culture

Austrians have a reputation for being conservative in their attitudes but hospitable hence perhaps their success in the tourist industry. It is also a very regional country with strong regional loyalties. As with the Germans, Austrians have a reputation for working together towards a common goal rather than fatalism or outright competitiveness. Austria is the birthplace of psychology with Sigmund Freud and Jung.

Family

Austrians tend to live in larger than European average size households. Marriage rates have not fallen as steeply as elsewhere in Europe but Austrians tend to marry late. Divorce rates are low especially in the rural areas, partly due to the strong catholic influence. Birth rates are stable. Children are pampered especially the boys and particularly the oldest son. Children tend to leave home relatively late in life unless they go on to higher education when they live in student accommodation. Women have a traditional role. It was only recently, for example that the law was changed to end the designation of superior and subordinate in a marriage, to allow wives to work without their husband's permission and to end the requirement that the wife should go to live at her husband's house. The family is all-important followed closely by lifelong friends.

Home

Housing is expensive and purchase costs are high too mainly because Austrian houses are built to a very high specification. This does not necessarily imply luxury fittings or the use of the most modern materials but refers more to the certainty Austrians want that the house will last over several generations. Austrians expect that their descendants will continue to occupy the house after them. Inside, the house will be furnished with traditional furniture made out of solid wood such as oak although mid-price multiples such as IKEA are now popular. The lounge will be the best furnished room in the house.

There is a shortage of accommodation all over the country and the owner occupation rate is 50 per cent; higher in rural areas and lower in the cities.

Religion

Austria is 78 per cent Roman Catholic and 6 per cent Protestant. The church is a respected institution.

Diet

Austrians like to live well and this is reflected in their diet, which whilst using ingredients common in British food, is cooked in a particularly Austrian way. The diet is rich and sweet dishes are very common. Coffee houses are a particularly Austrian institution where coffee is drunk in many different ways accompanied by rich Austrian cakes such as apple strudel. The main meal of the day is lunch at about 12.30 with an early dinner often of cold meats and salad. Austria is a significant wine producer mainly of white wine. Typical Austrian dishes include Wiener Schnitzel (breaded veal escalopes), a large variety of sweet (such as damson) and savoury (such as bacon) dumplings and soups which start lunch. There are also many regional dishes.

Leisure

As in many other Member States eating out with friends or family is a popular pastime. Snow sports, especially skiing, are widely practised whilst ice hockey and dog sledging are major spectator sports. In the summer soccer, walking and climbing attract large numbers.

Arts

Austria has large numbers of castles and stately homes, a legacy of its former status as an empire from the 14th to the 20th centuries. Ancient monasteries are also very common. There are a large number of museums housing art treasures acquired during Austria's imperial past. Much of what is termed classical music originated with Austrians such as Mozart, Brahms, Hayden, Schubert and the Strausses. There are therefore many music festivals during the summer – another major attraction for tourists. Vienna and Salzburg in particular are renowned cultural centres including the Vienna Boys choir. Religion has given rise to the elaborate spectacle of the Miracle Plays.

Further information

- Internet address: The following address will lead you to many different aspects of Austria. http://austria-info.at/
- *Austria, Facts and Figures, 1994*, free from Austrian embassies

Belgium

Main features

- Densely populated with 325 people per square kilometre
- Strong divide between the French and Dutch speaking areas
- A heavily regulated labour market

Resources

Belgium has a strategic location at the cross roads of Europe and hence is often chosen as European headquarters for many non-European companies. It is also closely linked with Luxembourg economically, sharing, for example, a common currency. The traditional industries of textiles, coal and steel in the French speaking area have declined greatly and Belgium now has few natural resources. Growth is presently concentrated in the north, the Dutch speaking part of Belgium, which includes Antwerp port, the second largest in Europe after Rotterdam (its traditional rival) and an important gateway for goods into Europe. Antwerp is the world's centre for the trading, cutting and polishing of diamonds. Flanders has also become a focal point for burgeoning high-tech industries and its agriculture is also very productive.

Land

Belgium is relatively small and could be crossed by car in about three hours. It is intensively agricultural with 47 per cent of its land given over to farming. The wooded and hilly region of the Ardennes in the south is a popular recreational area used for skiing in the winter and other outdoor pursuits in the summer. 20 per cent of Belgium is wooded. The sandy beaches on the North coast attract many tourists during the summer. Antwerp port lies in the upper reaches of the river Scheldt.

Climate

Similar to southern Britain, Belgium has a temperate maritime climate with abundant rainfall.

Language

Dutch is spoken in Flanders and French in Wallonia with twice as many Dutch speakers as French. There is also a small German speaking area of Belgium. It is important to communicate in the right language. Trying to speak French in a Flemish area may be counterproductive and English may, in fact, be more tactful if a visitor does not speak Dutch. Although Belgians learn the two main official languages at school, they tend to be more proficient in English as a second language and this causes problems for employers wanting to recruit people who will be able to operate effectively throughout the whole of Belgium.

Telecoms

Belgacom came into being in 1992 as the privatised telecommunications company needing to make many improvements to a poor service. One objective was to take no more than five days to instal a new phone line by 1996, whereas not so long ago it could take one to six months. The service is of a high quality using the latest technology. Belgium is the most cabled Member State which at present means a multiplicity of foreign TV stations, including the BBC, are available. However this could be exploited in the future for other uses such as electronic banking, home shopping and Internet links.

Other links

Belgium has a good transport system both for people and goods. The waterway network is much denser and more heavily used than in the UK with good links to Antwerp port. The road network is good and toll free. The rail network is one of the densest in Europe and by the year 2000 a large investment in high-speed lines will significantly reduce journey times between Brussels, Paris, Cologne and Amsterdam in an extension of trans-European networks. Belgium is also well served by ferries to the UK. Its international airport at Brussels is not such a hub as nearby Schipol in the Netherlands.

Trade flows

Belgium trades principally with France, Germany, the Netherlands and the UK.

Major exports: Manufactured goods and machinery, tractors, diamonds, petroleum products. Belgium is very heavily dependent on exports with 70 per cent of its GDP sold abroad.

Major imports: Manufactured goods and machinery, mineral fuel, gem diamonds, grains, chemicals, foodstuffs.

The DTI has identified the following as good opportunities for UK exporters to Belgium:

- environmental protection goods and services
- soil decontamination
- telecoms.

Education

Compulsory school

For the 6–18 year age group. Since 1989 education policy has been devolved to the regions so it is likely that differences in education will emerge between the French, German and Dutch speaking parts of Belgium.

Note that the language of instruction will vary according to which part of Belgium the school is in. In Brussels there is a choice between Dutch and French medium schools. Dutch medium schools tend to be the choice of middle class parents.

Between 50 and 70 per cent of students attend independent schools, called free schools, which tend to be Catholic although the number of practising Catholics is much smaller at 15 per cent. Many pupils repeat a year or more due to unsatisfactory progress. A certificate is awarded for successful completion of primary school at 12. Recent educational reforms have sought to make secondary education more comprehensive whilst still preserving the choice between an academic or vocational education but also giving increased opportunities to move between the streams.

Education divides at 14 into general (academic preparation for university), technical (preparation for technical higher education), vocational (preparation for work) and artistic. Although school is compulsory until 18 (the highest leaving age in the EU), from the age of 14 students have the option of making this part-time if they have a work training contract. Successful completion of secondary school in any stream entitles the school leaver to a place in higher education.

Qualification at 18

Diploma or Certificate of Secondary Education.

Training and skills

There is an increasing demand for, and shortage of, people who are bi- or tri-lingual. Vocational training can be provided by the employer or the state employment service. Basic skills teaching such as literacy, maths and job search, was introduced in 1991.

Apprenticeship contracts are for those aged 16–18 only and comprise a mix of work and college attendance according to a training programme. These are an alternative to school during which time the apprentices receive a portion of the minium wage appropriate to their industry.

As a way of obtaining practical experience, never-employed people under 30 are able to apply for up to six months' work experience whilst still on benefit and companies are obliged to supply a certain number of such placements.

Employer involvement

Employers pay 0.04 per cent of gross salary towards educational leave and employees can take up to 240 hours leave a year for professional training or 180 hours for general education. Employers must also contribute 0.25 per cent of their wage bill into a fund which provides vocational training, subsidies for hiring hard-to-place apprentices (such as those with few qualifications) and training subsidies to new companies in the development areas of Wallonia. Employers together with the unions are on the joint industry boards which design the apprenticeship training programmes and organise the exams. Incentives such as reduced social security contributions are offered to employers who hire permanently any of the work placement trainees they are obliged to take.

Employment conditions

Differences in labour law apply to different categories of worker in Belgium, broadly defined as white and blue collar.

Contracts of employment

The law has specific contracts for different classifications of workers such as inland boatmen, professional sports people and domestic workers. Types of contract include temporary, fixed-term, specified task and open-ended. Written contracts of employment are compulsory for temporary and part-time work or where a job includes a probationary period.

Public holidays

11 days – January 1, Easter Monday, May 1 (Labour Day), Ascension, Whit Monday, July 21 (National Day), August 15 (Assumption), November 1 (All Saints' Day), November 11 (Armistice Day), December 25. There is also a Dutch holiday, July 11, and a French holiday, September 27, both celebrating a past victory of the holidaying community over the other.

Paid holiday

20 working days per year plus an allowance of 85 per cent of one month's gross salary.

Working hours

Standard working hours are eight hours a day or 38.5 hours a week. Special permission is needed for a maximum of up to 12 hours in any one day which must be compensated by the overtime equivalent in paid time off within three months.

Minimum wages

These are mainly negotiated by the unions, other workers are covered by a statutory minimum.

Working practices

Normal office hours are 8.30 a.m.–5 p.m. with 30 minutes for lunch. The main holiday period is July and August.

Use of information technology

This is not as extensive as in the UK in general although Belgium is a world leader in electronic financial transfers.

Mobility

This is restricted by the linguistic divisions although Flemish speakers are better linguists and hence more able to operate across the whole of Belgium than the French speakers. Once Belgians have bought a property, which may be late in life, they are unlikely to move again.

Tax

Tax free allowances: Single person BF176,000 (£3790), married couple BF139,000 (£2995) for each partner, BF37,000 (£780) for the first child, BF59,000 (£1270) for a second child plus deductions allowed for insurance premiums, pension payments, mortgage repayments and so on. Taxable income is charged at 25 per cent up to BF245,000 (£5280) and rises progressively up to 55 per cent for income in excess of BF2,347,000 (£50,550).

Local taxes vary between 6 and 10 per cent of income tax.

VAT is 6 per cent on basic food, publications, medicines, coffins, hotels and transport; 12 per cent on cigarettes, tobacco, coal and margarine; and 19.5 per cent on most other goods.

Social security

Social security contributions are 12.07 per cent of income. This is administered by local councils. Minimex (minimum needs of existence) is the system of paying subsistence allowances to those over 18 who have no other means of support and who have not met the contribution conditions. Additional social welfare support, such as help in obtaining a job or counselling to overcome other problems, is also available. Sickness and unemployment benefit are 60 per cent of your salary for a year. The benefits, including pensions, are some of the highest in the EU and may shortly be reduced in an effort to reduce Belgium's large public sector deficit.

Trade unions

There are three trade union federations in Belgium organised on political, religious and linguistic lines. Belgium is relatively heavily unionised with over 70 per cent of the workforce being union members.

Equal opportunities

Equal opportunities legislation to promote parity between the sexes has been in force since 1975. This is deemed to be comprehensive enough to prevent sexual harassment as well. There is also legislation to prohibit discrimination on the grounds of race, colour, ethnicity or nationality. Whilst there are incentives for employers to take on disabled workers, there are no statutory requirements to do so.

Health and safety

Every employer must have accident insurance covering employees. Every business with over 50 workers must have a health and safety committee which is entitled to relevant information in order to give informed advice. Employers are under an obligation to pursue a policy of active prevention and although under no obligation to follow the committee's advice, they must state why the advice is not being followed if this is the case. In businesses with over 20 employees, the employer must designate a separate safety officer. Every employee is required to contribute to a health care insurance scheme.

Medical care

Sickness/disability insurance is compulsory for all in Belgium. Everyone must join a 'mutuelle' (co-operative insurance company) to ensure at least partial refund (70–80 per cent) of medical costs since payment must be made, for example to the general practitioner, at the time of the visit. The quality of care is very high.

Culture

The most noticeable aspect about Belgium is its division between French-speaking Wallonia in the south and Dutch speaking Flanders in the north. The two areas are almost as distinct as if they were two separate countries. Since 1988 Belgium has been run as a Federation so that both areas have their own budgets and ministers and there is the possibility that the country may eventually be further divided since there is great rivalry between them. Brussels is officially a third area of Belgium which is both French and Dutch speaking although French seems to be the dominant language there probably because of the large contingent of foreigners serving the EU who live in the city.

At present, Flanders is the strongest region economically and Wallonia is lagging behind since this was where the once pre-eminent coal and steel industries were located. Despite the rivalry noted above, Belgians tend not to be very nationalistic but it is irritating, however, for Belgians to be mistaken for French or Dutch people.

Family
Family ties and long-term friendships are more important to Belgians than striking up casual acquaintanceships. Although it is unlikely that more than two generations live in the same house, the rest of the family are likely to live close by in the same town. Children tend to remain at home until their mid-twenties.

Home
Rented accommodation only tends to be available unfurnished and long-term (in three-year blocks). Belgians find it odd that anyone should want to use someone else's furniture hence furnished rented accommodation is rare. They spend a great deal of money on high-quality but old-fashioned furnishings including oak furniture, tapestry, stained glass and many rugs, carpets, curtains and table runners. The home will either be rented or a house especially built and from which they are therefore unlikely to move within their lifetime. Owner-occupation is 61 per cent, the same as in the UK.

Religion
15 per cent of the population are practising Catholics although nominally 75 per cent of the population are Catholic which is reflected in the large number of Catholic schools and universities in Belgium.

Diet
Belgians like to eat well which translates as a liking of rich food. Think for example of Belgian chocolates which enjoy a world reputation for high quality. Belgian restaurants offer food of a very high quality which is often deemed to be better than the more renowned French restaurants. Belgium is also famous for its huge variety of beers which include fruit flavoured ones and some of the more famous ones are brewed by monks. Chips with mayonnaise can be bought on many street corners. The main meal of the day is in the evening.

Leisure
The Belgians are very sociable and most events have their social side. In February there are many Lenten carnivals which are particularly spectacular in the Flanders region and from April to August a large proportion attend the many festivals which occur all over the country. The Belgian fondness for good food means that eating out is a popular activity. There are many facilities for swimming and other sports in every small town. The landscape lends itself to cycling and this is very popular both as a cross-country activity and as a spectator sport. Soccer, pigeon-racing and billiards are other popular

pastimes. Many of these activities are undertaken through clubs which Belgians are keen to join. A favourite destination for outdoor activities is the Ardennes for walking and cross-country skiing. Having spent a great deal on the home, Belgians spend much of their leisure time there with family or close friends.

Arts

The Flemish style of art gave rise to many internationally renowned artists beginning with Jan van Eyck in the 15th century and continuing with Bruegel in the 16th century, Rubens in the 17th century and Magritte in the 20th century. There is a close connection in artistic tradition with the Netherlands reflecting the proximity and former close political ties between the two countries. This legacy of great art can be found in museums all over Belgium especially in Brussels, Antwerp and Ghent. There is also a great deal of medieval architecture (such as in Bruges) throughout Belgium together with many impressive chateaux. Towns and villages retain many ancient carnivals and festivals which the locals enjoy. Today, as in so many other aspects of Belgian life, there are two cultural ministries, one Flemish and one French.

Further information

- *Live and Work in Belgium, the Netherlands and Luxembourg*, A de Vries and G Adams, 1992, Vacation Work
- *Newcomer*, an introduction to life in Belgium, twice yearly free magazine (available from the Belgian embassy)
- Belgian embassy in USA internet address giving information to travellers and business is http://www.belgium-emb.org/usa/

Denmark

Main features

- Low employer social security contributions but high pay and high income taxes
- Few large companies
- Population concentrated around Copenhagen

Resources

Denmark has never had large-scale heavy industry, lacking natural resources until recently discovered reserves of North Sea gas. So Danish industry developed largely from its agriculture with grain, potatoes and beet supporting the development of beer, liquor and sugar industries. Danish bacon is well known but its livestock tradition has also made Denmark a world leader, for example, in the production of insulin for diabetics, which, although now an industrial process, was formerly derived from animal intestines.

Land

Denmark is largely based on sand, boulder clay and bog and therefore has no highlands or prominent rocky features. It is extensively cultivated with 67 per cent of the land used for agriculture and 12 per cent is wooded. The major part of the country consists of mainland and two large islands but there are hundreds of smaller islands, many of them inhabited. So the Danes have a long tradition in shipping (Mærsk is one of the world's leading shipping companies) and have become world class experts in building long bridges.

Climate

Winters can be cold with a great deal of snow whilst summers are mild and can be very sunny. Generally warmer in summer than Scotland which is on the same latitude. Every few years the winter weather freezes the coastal waters, known in Denmark as an ice winter.

Language

Danish helps you to understand Swedes and Norwegians and is therefore a gateway to the Nordic region. Most Danes, especially those under the age of 40, also speak English very well and many speak German, especially along the West Jutland coast where there are many German tourists.

Telecoms

Denmark has a high standard of telecommunications. As part of project 'InfoSociety 2000' Denmark aims to complete the privatisation of its TeleDanmark telecoms company and become the world's cheapest and most efficient telecommunications service provider by the turn of the century. (It is currently 13th most expensive in the EU.) Denmark has the cheapest mobile phone system in Europe and the high usage rate of 7 per cent. It is the first country to have a national information superhighway of optical fibre network using ATM technology and with links to Stockholm and Oslo.

Other links

There is an extensive and efficient ferry and air transport system to link the islands. As more bridges and tunnels are built this linkage is becoming equally efficient by rail and road. Two huge projects linking Zealand (the island on which Copenhagen lies) with Sweden in one direction, and Funen, the next largest Danish island, in the other, will provide a link of international significance between Sweden and the rest of southern Europe. These will be a mix of bridges and tunnels, for both road and rail. The Swedish link is due for completion in 2000. The next big project is a bridge between southern Denmark and Germany to improve communications between Copenhagen and the rest of continental Europe.

Trade flows

Exports most to Germany, then Sweden and the UK.

Major exports: components such as thermostats, refrigerator compressors, high-tech pumps, cement-making machines and high tension cables, comprise 70 per cent of exports. The rest include meat (7 per cent), furniture (4 per cent), fresh and frozen fish (3 per cent) and medicinal products (3 per cent).

Major imports: machinery and equipment (31.6 per cent), food, beverages and tobacco (11.7 per cent) and iron, steel, paper and chemicals.

The DTI has identified the following as good opportunities for UK exporters to Denmark:
- electrical components
- food and drink

- clothing
- computer hardware and software
- textiles
- car components.

Education

Compulsory school

For the 7–16 year age group. Private schools are state subsidised so that the 10 per cent of pupils who attend them pay only 15 per cent of the cost in fees. Compulsory education takes place in one school, the folkeskole. The leaving examination qualifies 33 per cent of pupils to go onto the academic gymnasium. A further 50 per cent go on to vocational training courses in one of three areas – technical, commercial or health (personal services, care and therapies). The latter is usually oversubscribed. Training is a mix of college and on-the-job and lasts two to four and a half years. Agricultural training is also available. All these courses are regularly updated to reflect labour market demands and their capacity is planned to double shortly. Advanced vocational courses lasting one to three years are available once the basic vocational training has been completed.

Qualification at 19
Studentereksamen (three years) or HF certificate (two years).

Training and skills
There are several different types of institutions offering vocational training for adults including adult education centres, folk high schools and day high schools which offer courses of varying lengths from two weeks to a full academic year. The HF certificate is usually taken by those with some experience of work and can be studied one subject at a time at various places including county adult education centres. It is therefore a method of continuous education. Adults are encouraged to undergo full-time training or education through the special scheme of study leave which means that an unemployed person can have experience of doing your job while you are paid 80 per cent of your former salary to study for up to a year.

The government is particularly keen to encourage workers to update skills in important export industries and those required by the new technologies. Publicly run training (about 50 per cent of available training) is 80 per cent funded by the state as long as it is part-time and available out of working hours. The state employment service also runs full-time training centres for the unemployed and those with special needs to prepare them for the work environment.

Danes are naturally inclined to pursue education as a pastime and this contributes to them being considered the most receptive in the EU to training and retraining.

Employer involvement
Most Danish vocational education includes some work element with an employer. The qualifications gained after three to five years are recognised throughout the country and industry helps to devise the requirements for each occupational area. During the first year trainees are financed as students but later they become apprentices paid relevant rates by the employer. Any training agreement not endorsed by the local job centre is invalid.

Employment conditions

Contract of employment
This need not be written. One of the Danish employers' associations and one of the

unions have both devised a standard employment contract and these are widely used where no special conditions apply. Blue collar workers tend to be hired on an oral basis with their conditions regulated by union negotiated collective agreements.

Public holidays
9.5 days – January 1, Easter Thursday (Maundy), Friday and Monday, General Prayer Day (April/May), Ascension Day (mid-May), Whit (late May/June), June 5 (Constitution Day – half a day), December 25 and 26.

Paid holiday
Most workers are entitled to a minimum of five weeks' paid leave excluding public holidays. The FerieGiro system requires employers to set aside an additional 12.5 per cent of salary to be paid to employees when they take their holiday.

Working hours
No legal restrictions but most jobs specify 37 hours as the normal working week with additional work paid at overtime rates.

Minimum wages
No statutory minimum but most workers are covered by collective agreements which usually include a minimum wage. Once a collective agreement has been made, it is binding. Many collective agreements are extended to cover non-union members with the agreement of the employers.

Working practices
Normal office hours are 8 a.m.–4 p.m. with half an hour for lunch. The main holiday period is late June and July since school starts again in early August. This together with the many public holidays in May means that May to July is the most difficult time of the year to reach mutually agreeable meeting dates since this period coincides with the longest day length, of which the Danes, in common with the other Nordic countries, like to take full advantage for leisure time.

Use of information technology
Office work is highly computerised with 85 per cent of Danish office workers using a computer compared to 57 per cent in the UK.

Mobility
Danish workers are reasonably occupationally mobile but not so geographically mobile. One restricting factor is the prevalence of dual-career families as this makes it difficult to find two appropriate jobs in the new location rather than just one. Unemployment benefit is also generous enough to reduce the incentive to look elsewhere for work.

Tax
Local, state and social contribution taxes are all deducted at source from income. Since local taxes vary – the average is 29.5 per cent – total deductions depend on where you live.

Income is taxable after the first £1400. As well as deducting travel to work expenses in excess of 24 kilometres, trade union subscriptions, unemployment insurance and pension contributions and interest payments such as on a house mortgage or car loan are all tax deductible.

State tax is then a further 14.5 per cent plus 4.5 per cent on the first £14,000 and 12.5 per cent on anything above £25,000, giving a top rate of 61 per cent.

VAT is 25 per cent and there are various other taxes such as a carbon tax on motor and heating fuel. Danes also pay a church tax.

Social security

High taxation pays for a high level of welfare provision including the following:

- childcare from the age of six months; available almost on demand at a subsidised price
- unemployment benefit is relatively high, up to a maximum of £265 per week, and is available for three years after which time income support is available
- maternity leave and pay
- special leave to study or look after children at £200 a week (80 per cent of maximum unemployment benefit)
- retirement pension
- residential care of the elderly.

Trade unions

Trade union membership is high at over 80 per cent of all workers with the unions not only helping to negotiate pay and conditions but also administering unemployment benefits.

Equal opportunities

Equal pay for men and women is required under a 1989 Equal Pay Act which covers equal terms for like work or work of equal value at the same workplace.

Offenders run the risk of a six-month prison term if discrimination is on the grounds of race, colour, nationality, ethnic origin, belief or sexual orientation.

Health and safety

The Danish Health and Safety Act of 1985 encourages the promotion of a safe and healthy working environment as far as current technology allows. Secondary legislation governs:

- the introduction of safety measures at work
- the rights and duties of employers and employees
- the use of equipment, substances and materials
- rest periods.

Medical care

This is operated on a similar basis to that in the UK with medical care mostly free at the point of use, with contributions required for eye and dental care as well as for prescriptions. There are many alternative therapies available on a purely private basis including osteopaths, aromatherapists, reflexologists and so on. There is also a great emphasis on preventative health measures, for example every council has a dedicated child dentist providing free treatment up to the age of 18. The standard of care is high. It is possible to opt for private medicine, the main effect of this being to cut the waiting time for treatment.

Culture

British people tend to find that Denmark is not too different from the UK. The main difference lies in the more relaxed Danish pace of life, including a more open attitude to issues such as nudity and sexual conduct which would cause embarrassment in the UK, and work not being allowed to lower the quality of family life. Danes tend to be very proud of their country especially concerning the welfare state. This is in contrast to the Belgians, for example, for whom their country is little more than the place where they live. Otherwise it is not the done thing to stand out or appear eccentric in Denmark.

Family

Although the outward signs, such as a high level of divorce (two out of three marriages fail) and the social acceptance of living together and having children without being married (46 per cent of children are born outside marriage), make it seem that the family is less important, this is not so. Single parenthood is very low by European standards. Danes tend to want to remain close to their family which restricts labour mobility and they are also happy to socialise with the family on holiday and at weekends so that leisure activities are very much home based.

Home

Away from the city centres houses are detached and spacious with a garden and are usually owned, whereas flats tend to be rented. Fitted carpets are not common, with wooden floors popular as are tongue-in-groove ceilings. Most Danish homes are very well equipped with electrical appliances such as dishwashers as standard.

Religion

The Church of Denmark is Lutheran Protestant and 91 per cent of Danes are affiliated. Although they are not great church goers, some of the major events in the calendar are church based – in particular, most children want to be confirmed in their early teens, if only to take part in the parties and attract the traditional gifts of money.

Diet

The stock of the average Danish supermarket would enable you to make most traditional British meals however there are some specifically Danish dishes. One is the Smørrebrød or open sandwich which most Danes have for lunch whether at home, school or work. A favourite Smørrebrød topping is soused herring which is obtainable in many different flavours such as curry or marinated in sherry. Another topping is leverpostej, a kind of liver paté. Danes eat more meat than the British, mostly beef and pork, very little lamb, and consequently the choice and quality in vegetables tends to be less than in the UK.

Beer is often drunk with the meal and is almost always Danish. Wine is also popular. Very strong real coffee is another feature of the Danish diet with very little instant coffee consumed.

Leisure

An important Danish tradition is that of taking holidays in summer houses which are either rented or, more often than not, owned. Many attractive areas in Denmark are designated summer house areas where permanent residence is not allowed. The EU permission to restrict ownership of summer houses to Danes was withdrawn in 1996. The Danes participate in many sports especially handball. Cycling and jogging are also very popular. In common with the other Scandinavian countries, Danes are very keen on education as a leisure activity and are keen evening class attenders as well as finding time to attend residential courses for up to a year at a Folkehøjskole. Football is very popular both as an activity and as a spectator sport – the English league is followed during the winter since the Danish football season is during the summer. Danes spend a large proportion of their income on leisure especially on brown goods and outdoor pursuits. Foreign holidays to the rest of Scandinavia and the Mediterranean are popular.

Arts

As a small country Denmark does not have many internationally renowned artistic strengths with the exception perhaps of the Royal Danish Ballet. Danish design has a good international reputation particularly in home furnishings and appliances, for example Bang and Olufsen. Copenhagen was the designated European city of culture for 1996. During the summer months there are dozens of music festivals all over Denmark covering different styles including jazz, country, rock and world music. One of the biggest is the Roskilde festival in July which attracts international performers such as Björk, Peter Gabriel and the Cranberries.

Further information

- *Live and Work in Scandinavia* by V Pybus, 1994, Vacation Work
- Ministry of Foreign Affairs, Asiatisk Plads 2, DK 1448 Copenhagen K
- Federation of Danish Industries, HC Andersens Boulevard 18, 1790 Copenhagen V 2

Finland

Main features

- Highest unemployment in the EU
- Wealth and population concentrated in the south west
- Best telecommunications in the EU

Resources

The main industries are agriculture, forestry, metal and engineering manufacturing. Wood is the chief natural resource but Finland is also a leading European producer of copper and nickel. Infrastructure is of a high quality, for example, there is a highly integrated public transport system. Although Finland has undergone a very deep economic recession since 1990 with the loss of its major Soviet trading partner, it is still one of the EU's most prosperous members.

Land

Finland extends from a latitude level with Shetland to well above the Arctic circle. There is little highland and most of its vast area is still under natural vegetation cover with little cultivated or cleared land; only 8 per cent of Finland is cultivated. 60 per cent of Finland is forested giving way eventually to open tundra in the far north. There are also thousands of lakes.

Climate

Although cold, the climate is dry so it feels warmer than you would expect. The snow generally starts falling in November and stays until April, later in the north. For two months the sun never rises in the winter above the Arctic circle and in summer never sets. Summers can be hot and sunny with temperatures up to 30°C. It is a continental type climate. Average temperatures in the north are 3°C lower than in the south.

Language

There are two official languages, Finnish and Swedish. 94 per cent are Finnish speakers and 6 per cent Swedish but most people can also speak English. The Finnish language is quite unlike any other EU tongue and is therefore difficult to learn. In the north the Sami people speak their own language moving freely between Sweden and Finland.

Telecoms

With an advanced and streamlined system, linked with the UK's BT company, Nokia is the world's second largest telecommunications company. Finland also has the third highest penetration of mobile phones in the world at 10 per cent. Half the population of the Helsinki metropolitan area works with information technology linked to the telephone system. Finland was rated as having the best telecommunications infrastructure in the EU in the 1995 World Competitiveness Report which also noted that it had the cheapest international call rates (the UK came second).

Other links

There is an extensive, frequent and efficient road, railway and air network with a bias towards north–south routes. The road system tends to be better in the south than in the north. There are rarely delays during the winter despite the severity of the weather. There are also a great many natural coastal harbours, the commercial ones are kept open by icebreakers during the winter. Work is in hand to improve freight rail links with Russia from St Petersburg to Turku via Helsinki with support from the EU as this is one of the 'missing links' to be supported by the trans-European networks programme.

Trade flows

These are with Germany, Sweden and the UK; some important trade links with the former USSR remain.

Major exports: forestry products (40 per cent), machinery and transport equipment.

Major imports: machinery and transport equipment, basic manufactures, mineral fuels.

The DTI has identified the following as good opportunities for UK exporters to Finland:

- vehicle components and accessories
- food and drink
- design services
- financial services
- telecoms
- public sector utilities.

Education

Compulsory school

For the 7–17 year age group. Although compulsory school starts at seven most Finns send their children to pre-school at six. Books, lunch and transport over 5 kilometres are free. Finns attend the same school from seven until 16. A further three years is possible in a lukio school to compete for university entry via the matriculation exam, an option taken by 55 per cent of 17-year-olds. A further 25 per cent continue their education in a vocational school for two to five years depending on which of 160 career options were chosen. The longest courses entitle their graduates to go on to university. Apprenticeship training is an option taken by only 1 per cent of school leavers.

Some of the senior secondary and vocational courses are taught in a language other than Finnish or Swedish and this is often English.

Qualification at 18/19
Matriculation.

Training and skills

Adult education includes much vocational training either to upgrade skills or to retrain into completely new areas. These are run by different types of organisations most of which are partly funded by the government such as the workers' institutes equivalent to the Workers' Educational Association in the UK (where courses are more cultural than vocational). There are also residential folkschools similar to Denmark. In response to the recent high rates of unemployment, the government has set up a wide range of skills training courses at technical colleges as well as updating courses for people still in jobs who are given time off to complete this training. This gives unemployed people a chance to obtain work experience by covering for permanent employees on educational leave. This training is tightly targeted especially towards new technology.

Employer involvement

Apprenticeships are much less common in Finland than in other Member States. The usual conditions apply with on the job training provided by the employer and time allocated for off the job training at a relevant institution. Whilst at work the apprentice receives wages and whilst at college, other allowances.

Employment conditions

Contract of employment

Parental permission is required to enter into a contract of employment between the ages of 15 and 18. Contracts may be oral but are usually written.

Public holidays

10.5 days – January 1, January 6 (Epiphany), Good Friday, Easter Monday, April 30 (half day), May 1, May (Ascension), Whit (May/June), Midsummer Eve and Day (June), November 1 (All Saints'), December 6 (Independence/National Day), December 24, 25 and 26. January 6, Ascension, Whit and November 1 are adjusted to fall on Saturdays.

Paid holiday

The usual allowance is five weeks in addition to public holidays, one week of which must be taken during the winter. Employees are entitled to an additional half month's pay during their summer break.

Working hours

The legal working week is 40 hours, with an eight hour working day but more flexible arrangements are being introduced because of the recession, including job sharing and educational leave.

Minimum wages

There are no statutory minimum wages but union agreements will usually state a minimum for the category of workers covered by the agreement which apply to all even if they are not union members.

Working practices

Normal office hours are 8.00 a.m.–4 p.m. with an hour for lunch. The main holiday period is a month during early July to mid-August but other slack periods include two weeks around Christmas, the spring half term at the end of February when many people go skiing and Easter for a week.

Use of information technology

In 1995 Finland had the highest computer power per head and fastest developing technological infrastructure in the EU.

Mobility

Finns tend to change jobs frequently in order to develop their career although this may well be internally with the same employer.

Tax

Income tax is charged on taxable income after deduction of allowances on a progressive scale from 7 per cent to 39 per cent (from 40,000 FIM to 275,000 FIM which is approximately from £6150 to £42,300). In addition there is a local tax charged at a flat rate which varies according to location from 14.5 per cent to 20 per cent of income. Social security deductions are a further 8.4 per cent.

VAT is 22 per cent and there are various other taxes such as very high excise duties on alcohol and a church tax of between 1 and 2 per cent.

Social security

Finland has a very comprehensive social security system including pre- and post-natal care, childhood services, unemployment and subsistence benefits, occupational disability benefits and care for the elderly though benefit levels are not as high as in Sweden and Denmark. Nevertheless sickness benefit is 80 per cent of previous salary for a maximum of 300 days. The money to finance these schemes comes from employer (75 per cent) and employee (25 per cent) contributions from salaries which further entitle employees to sickness, accident and unemployment benefit.

Trade unions

Unions run unemployment benefit schemes paying unemployed members 60 per cent of previous income for up to two years. There is a high rate of union membership ranging from 65 per cent in the service sector to 95 per cent in the metal and paper industries. In 1995 there were three times as many days lost through industrial disputes in Finland as in the UK. Any organisation employing over 30 workers must provide an opportunity for worker consultation even if they are not union members.

Equal opportunities

Equality between the sexes and the races is required by the constitution and reflected in employment law. The comprehensive equal opportunities legislation is backed up by good childcare facilities and maternity provision which means that Finnish women are able to make good career progress. The law also prohibits discrimination on the grounds of religion, age, political views or trade union activity.

Health and safety

The law requires employers to provide occupational health care free of charge to employees including regular health checks. The employer must appoint an occupational health and safety chief while employees elect an occupational health and safety delegate. Where there are more than 20 employees, these two officials participate in a health and safety committee which makes proposals, carries out inspections and plans relevant training.

Medical care

Private and public systems are available all of a very high standard. There is a health service especially for students. Most hospitals are in the public system whereas there is a choice between private and public GPs. Certain hospital expenses have to be paid for but will be refunded above a certain minimum. Dental treatment is free until the age of 17. As in the UK, prescriptions must be paid for except for the chronically sick for whom medication is free. Medical care is organised by local centres where a full range of GP, dental, nursing and physiotherapy services are available. The centres cater for in and out patients with referral to a hospital only for complicated treatments.

Culture

The older generation have a reputation for being reserved perhaps because they did not have much contact with foreigners when Finland was linked with the Soviet Union (although it was never a Communist state). With the demise of the USSR, Finland is currently extending links with neighbouring Baltic states especially Estonia. The young are very European in outlook but Finns are more used to emigrating than to welcoming foreigners to their country. The pace of life is more relaxed than in the UK. As in Sweden, the sale and consumption of alcohol is highly regulated. In business and other aspects of life, the Finnish approach is to make decisions by consensus.

Family

Many couples choose to live together rather than get married. In 1992 Finland had the highest EU divorce rate after the UK. Generally, however, Finland is family and especially children oriented which is backed up by good government facilities for childcare and parental leave. Proportionally more Finns live alone than in any other Member State.

Home

More than half the housing in use in Finland has been built within the last 25 years. Around 75 per cent of Finnish households are in privately owned accommodation, higher than the UK figure. About 40 per cent of homes in Finland have a sauna. Even blocks of flats would include sauna facilities as an integral part of the block. Building regulations require a high standard of insulation and other energy saving features such as triple glazing. Finnish furniture, textiles and household equipment enjoys a world-wide reputation for good design and perhaps as a consequence there is a distinctive Finnish look which is apparent in most homes which tend to be large by European standards.

Religion

89 per cent are Lutheran Protestant and 1 per cent Orthodox christian. Church attendance is very low.

Diet

Finnish food is a mix of West and East European styles. As in other Scandinavian countries, pickled fish is very popular, whereas the pastries and stews are of Russian origin. Fruit and vegetables play a minor role since they are not easily grown in Finland and hence are very expensive. Breakfasts are substantial and may include porridge, rye bread, herring, cereals, salami, eggs and ham. Lunch is the biggest meal of the day with soups and stews and is eaten relatively early at 11 a.m. The traditional Finnish huffer is a spread of fish, meat, soups and salads. July and August is the fresh crayfish season and this is an occasion for big celebratory meals. Coffee is widely drunk especially on social occasions with cakes. Milk or beer are popular accompaniments to a meal. In the north many dishes are based on reindeer meat, and forest fruits such as cloudberries, blueberries, lingonberries and cranberries feature in typically Finnish recipes.

Leisure

A very high percentage of families own a holiday home or hut in the country to which they can go to take part in the favourite Finnish pastimes of cross-country ski-ing, boating and fishing. Otherwise there is a high level of active sports participation in, for example, jogging, swimming, cycling and ice hockey. Finland produces a disproportionately large number of Olympic champions. Popular spectator sports are ski-jumping, regatta sailing and hockey. As with the other Nordic countries, the most intensely social period is during the summer when the weather is warm and the days are long. Alcohol plays an important role in many social activities and this is why its purchase is strictly controlled through high prices and restricted accessibility. Finns are not very interested in going abroad for their holidays.

Arts

Finland is renowned for its present day skills in design and architecture which is evident in abundance in the buildings of the capital city, Helsinki. Its history of domination by the Swedes and then the Russians means that there is little recorded Finnish art from the past and therefore Finnish artistic reputation is based very much on modern art and living artists. In the 19th century there was the National Romantic movement which included the Golden Age style in painting and Finnish language literature celebrating the attractions of the Finnish rural way of life whilst under Russian rule. This mood was also reflected in the music of Sibelius. With a small population concentrated in the southeast near Helsinki, it is the capital which is the hub of all cultural activities. In relation to its population Finland has many venues for musical performances and supports music generously through almost 130 institutes and direct funding for musicians and music festivals.

Further information

- Internet addresses:
  http://www.csc.fi/tiko/finland.html
  http://www.mofile.fi/fennia/um/-engl.htm

France

Main features

- High employer and social security costs
- Extensive high-speed rail network
- Fourth strongest world economy after USA, Japan and Germany

Resources

The French economy is based on a wide diversity of industry and commerce. Old industry established on its natural source of coal and iron ore has been run down and replaced by newer activities such as computers and telecommunications. The service sector has lagged behind that of the UK but the newer technologies and privatisation of banks, insurance companies and other financial bodies means that great improvements are being made. Lacking any of its own fuel resources France has expanded its nuclear power industry so that it now generates over 60 per cent of the country's power. France also has the largest tourist industry in the EU.

Land

France consists of mostly flat plains or gently rolling hills in the north and west with the remainder mountainous especially the Pyrenees in the south and Alps in the east. Its terrain and climate mean that France is suited to the cultivation of many agricultural crops including widespread vineyards, cereals and many fruits and vegetables as well as livestock. Agricultural use covers 55 per cent of the land with wheat occupying the greatest area and 27 per cent is wooded.

Climate

Since it covers a large area, France experiences substantial differences in climate from the temperate areas of the northern coast to the Mediterranean climate in the south and including the cold mountainous areas of the Alps and the Pyrenees.

Language

French is the first language for the vast majority with some areas also having their own local language, such as Breton in Brittany which is closely related to Welsh, whilst other areas are bilingual such as on the German border. Other languages spoken in France include Alsatian, Basque, Catalan, Corsican and Provencal French.

Telecoms

The service is fully electronic and provided by the state-owned France Telecom which is about to be privatised in line with EU requirements for telecommunications deregulation. The company is well prepared to enter the private sector with its many foreign interests including subsidiaries and joint ventures. It is very strong in the development of multi-media products.

The Minitel system was introduced by France Telecom in the early eighties which placed computer terminals free of charge into most homes and many other organisations such as post offices. It is a database system whose primary use was as a replacement to the telephone directory but can now be used for over 26,000 other information services including home shopping.

Overall the French telecom service is rated as slightly better than the UK's.

Other links

France's main transport links are strongly centred on Paris to the detriment of links in other directions. France has an extensive road network of high quality, including a modern motorway system on which tolls are payable. Equally, a great deal of investment has been put into the French railway system with the developments of the TGVs (Trains à Grande Vitesse) which pose serious competition to internal air travel and are integrated into the European railway network with connections to all neighbouring countries and beyond. The French also ensured that their side of the Channel Tunnel is serviced by the fastest available rolling stock.

Trade flows

France trades mainly with Germany, Italy, Spain and Belgium.

Major exports: machinery and equipment (43 per cent), food, beverages and tobacco (14 per cent), armaments and chemicals.

Major imports: machinery and equipment (39 per cent), food, beverages and tobacco (9 per cent), mineral fuels.

The DTI has identified the following as good opportunities for UK exporters to France:

- building materials and supplies
- career and workwear clothing
- electronic components
- high-energy research facilities
- public sector security equipment.

Education

Compulsory school

For the 6–16 year age group. Schools are comprehensive and follow a common curriculum both in the primary and secondary phases up to the age of 15 when pupils take the brevet de colleges exam which marks the end of compulsory schooling. Students may then go on to an academic lycee, professional lycee or apprentice training centre. This choice does not depend on the brevet result but is a free choice. At the lycees, students take the baccalaureat in one of three streams – general, technical or vocational. There is no school on Wednesdays.

In 1992, 65 per cent of 18/19-year-olds obtained a bac. The bac entitles its holder to a university place as of right hence French university courses are extremely overcrowded especially in the first year before a large proportion drop out. About 20 per cent are in private education. Students wanting to go on to the elite grandes ecoles, from which the top grades of civil servants and politicians emerge, must take a highly competitive entrance exam in addition to obtaining the bac. This usually adds another two years to their secondary education. As elsewhere in the EU, unsatisfactory progress in any school year may result in a student being required to repeat the year.

Qualification at 18/19

Baccalaureat.

Training and skills

Most French workers have had some form of apprenticeship or specialist training. Vocational training is under regional rather than national control. The apprenticeship option, whereby apprentices work under an apprentice work contract learning a trade both on the job, under the supervision of an apprenticeship trainer, and off the job at apprentice training centres, is taken by 10 per cent of 16 year olds. Over three-quarters of the centres are run by Chambers of Commerce, training companies or joint bodies. The successful apprentice is awarded a vocational bac. Training credits are available for young people without a school qualification to enable them to pursue a tailored training programme whilst receiving unemployment benefit.

Employer involvement

Business must allocate 1.5 per cent of wage costs to adult training resulting in one-fifth of employees receiving training annually. Companies are also required to draw up a training plan for their workforce. Most employees have a right to claim educational leave for a year's full-time study and 1200 hours of part-time training. Apprentices spend up to 75 per cent of their one to three years with the employer. However the apprenticeship system has been criticised as being just a means of cheap labour for employers who then fail to offer a permanent job when the training ends. Apprenticeships have therefore not been as popular as they are in Germany and account for only 15 per cent of those in vocational training.

Employment conditions

Contract of employment

An employee may have an indefinite length contract (the most usual), temporary, fixed term or on-call contract. The last three should be in writing but the first one need not be. In an attempt to prevent employers turning to the temporary or fixed term contract these may only be for a maximum of 18 months and may only be renewed once after which the intention is that the employee should be hired on a permanent basis.

Public holidays

11 days – January 1, Easter Monday, May 1, Ascension Day, May 8 (Victory Day), Whit Monday, July 14 (Bastille Day), August 15 (Assumption), November 1 (All Saints' Day), November 11 (Armistice Day) and December 25.

Paid holiday

30 working days per year.

Working hours

Should not exceed ten hours per day; the standard working week is defined as 39 hours for the purposes of identifying overtime and part-time work.

Minimum wages

For those over 18 in private sector work in 1994 these were 34.83 FF an hour (about £4.52).

Working practices

Normal working hours are 8.30 a.m.–6.30 p.m. with a long lunch period. The main holiday period is July/August and school starts again in September. Strenuous efforts have been made to encourage the French to stagger their holidays over a longer period but most still concentrate their annual break in July/August. Small businesses tend to shut down completely during this period and many small shops in towns and villages also close.

Use of information technology

This is somewhat lower than in the UK according to several factors surveyed by the World Competitiveness Report of 1995.

Mobility

There is a relatively low level of employee mobility although executive mobility is increasing rapidly. A 'good' job is still almost certainly located in the Paris area and once located there, there is little need for geographical mobility.

Tax

Income tax is not deducted on a 'pay-as-you-earn' basis and individuals must therefore calculate their own liability which is then paid as three lump sums during the year. There are many allowances available which can be deducted from one's gross income to arrive at the residual taxable income. These include alimony payments, dependent children up to 18 years old, disabled dependents etc. Rates vary from 5 per cent on incomes above £2225 up to 56.8 per cent on incomes over £30,260.

Local taxes – Taxe d'habitation is approximately equivalent to the old rating system in the UK where the property you live in is allocated an assumed rental income with the tax set at a percentage of this. Receipts pay for local services. In addition, the owner of a property pays a taxe fonciere.

VAT is 20.6 per cent.

Social security

Social security contributions from salary pay for unemployment benefit, sick pay, retirement pension, death grant, maternity benefit, housing benefit, family allowance and industrial accident insurance. Rates vary according to former salary with 50 per cent paid for sickness benefit and 40 per cent paid for if unemployed.

Trade unions

Employees have the right to join a trade union but membership in the private sector is low at about 10 per cent of the workforce. Works councils have traditionally been alternatives to trade unions and are legally required for all companies having 50 or more employees. Trade unions have negotiating rights and play a part in developing French labour law. The encouragement of settlement by negotiation has reduced the number of days lost by strikes and other industrial action in recent years.

Equal opportunities

The law ensures equality of treatment at work between the sexes but cases rarely come to court and then usually only deal explicitly with pay rather than with issues of indirect discrimination. Marital status and pregnancy are also not allowed to determine a recruitment decision. Once employed, the law prevents sexual harassment and the need for this may stem from the strong hierarchical nature of French society. Discrimination on the grounds of ill-health (including AIDS) is unlawful. All organisations employing over 20 people must fulfil a 6 per cent quota of disabled employees. There is also legislation to prevent discrimination against ethnic minorities on the grounds of origin, race or religion. Some union agreements include provisions against discrimination. In the chemical and metal working industries, for example, age must not be used as a selection criterion.

Health and safety

All companies employing 50 or more staff must set up a health and safety committee. Employers must keep the workplace clean and hygienic, sufficiently ventilated, heated and lit. Employers have a legal duty to protect employees against falls, collisions and suffocation and must guard potentially dangerous areas and machinery which must be properly installed and maintained. All employees have the right to stop work if they feel that their health or safety is threatened.

Medical care

This is paid for by social security contributions which can be up to 18–20 per cent of a managerial salary. Even so except in the case of serious illness, the system often only pays 75–90 per cent of the cost of treatment and 40–70 per cent of the cost of medicines so most French people take out additional private health insurance to cover these costs. When visiting a doctor or dentist the full cost must be paid and the percentage refund claimed later.

Culture

The French are very aware and proud of their contribution to high culture in the world. In the past, French was the language of international negotiation. They are also very keen to maintain a distinctly French character, as demonstrated by recent legislation which requires a minimum of 40 per cent of radio, TV and cinema output to be in French. In the workplace, other nationalities find the French very hierarchical with decisions made by one top person.

Family

The family unit, although no longer extended, is still very strong with social life being centred around family and close friends. The French do not tend to want to move very far away from their family and it is common for children to stay at home until well into their twenties.

Home

The French prefer homes built within the last 20 years to high specifications and within easy commuting distance rather than the quaint old country houses in isolated villages which are so popular with some Britons. Renovation and interior decoration is not such a popular pastime as in the UK and living in a flat is much more accepted with 46 per cent of French people living in this type of accommodation. The French move much less often than the British.

Religion

France is 90 per cent Catholic although the number of active church goers is decreasing rapidly and was recently estimated to be about 13 per cent of the population. France also has a sizeable minority of Muslims from its former North African colonies.

Diet

French cooking is famed world-wide and should be considered as a very important component of French culture. This ability in cooking could derive from the great diversity of ingredients available within France's own borders, not forgetting of course the accompanying wine. French food is characterised by its sauces often created with a great deal of cream or wine or both. There are distinct regional differences reflecting the differing availability of ingredients (e.g. many recipes use apples in Normandy) and the influence of neighbouring countries such as the Germanic influence in eastern France. With such a long and strong tradition in cooking, there is little outside influence such as Indian restaurants.

Leisure

Eating and drinking are the main social activities. The French are not as fond of joining clubs and societies as the British and socialising tends to be restricted to family and close friends. Relationships with work colleagues tend to be very formal and hence not a common source of friends. One in ten French people have a second home, which can be either a house, holiday flat or a caravan or motorhome, reflecting the strong ties which the French feel with the countryside.

Arts

France has been the source of many great writers, philosophers, film directors and artists who have found international fame. French fashion also sets the pace across the world for the well-off. The government supports the arts enthusiastically in the form of generous state financing but the current worry in France is the fear of being overwhelmed by American culture especially in cinema and television. This even led to disagreements during the free trade GATT talks over whether it would be permissable to restrict the amount of American TV sold in France. Attempts have also been made to restrict by law the amount of English being adopted into the French language with implications for advertisers.

Further information

- *Live and Work in France*, V Pybus, 1994 2nd edition, Vacation Work

- *How to Get a Job in France*, Mark Hempshell, 1993, How To Books
- *How to Live and Work in France*, Marie Prevost Logan, 1991, How To Books
- Internet address:
  Franceway at http://www.franceway.com/

Germany

Main features

- Strongest economy in Europe
- Largest population in the EU
- Highly regional in law, administration and media
- Great differences in lifestyle, salaries and work between former East Germany and West Germany

Resources

Germany has important mining and iron and steel industries based on its natural resources. From these, engineering, vehicle-building, chemical, textile paper and optical equipment industries have developed. The big issue for Germany is the success of the reunification between East and West which occurred in 1989. Economically, the Communist East lagged behind the West in quality of infrastructure and the attitude towards industry, production and work was wholly different. As industry in the East becomes more efficient so unemployment is much worse there than in the West.

Land

Germany is heavily wooded (29 per cent), the Black Forest being the most famous example and much area is given over to agriculture (54 per cent). Southern Germany borders on the Alps. Eastern Germany has many lakes amongst undulating lowlands. Northern Germany is also predominantly lowland whilst central Germany is upland.

Climate

Climatically, Germany divides into north and south, with the north having a wetter more maritime climate than the south where it is more continental with hot summers and cold winters especially in the Alpine areas.

Language

German is spoken throughout the country but with very different accents and dialects which can make it very difficult to understand especially in the south around Munich.

Telecoms

The German telecoms service is of a good standard but below that of the UK's in many aspects. For example, equipment is rented and international calls are much more expensive than in the UK although this may change after privatisation. The system will be completely digital by 1997. The East German system is experiencing rapid growth since it is in need of complete modernisation. Businesses there are given priority over private individuals in the installation of new lines.

Other links

The Rivers Rhine, Elbe and Danube and the Kiel canal are of major importance in cargo transport and Hamburg on the north coast is a major port of entry of sea-borne cargo. The German road system is renowned for its good quality and efficiency as is the rail network which is well integrated with international services linking Germany to neighbouring states. A new high speed (up to 500 m.p.h.) magnetic levitation (Maglev) railway service is being built between Hamburg and Berlin, Germany's restored capital. The country is also well served by its air network. Services in all these areas are much worse in eastern Germany but huge investments are being made by both Germany itself and the EU, and improvements are rapidly being made.

Trade flows

Germany trades mainly with France, Belgium, the Netherlands, Italy, the UK and USA.

Major exports: manufactured products, machinery, road and rail vehicles and chemicals.

Major imports: oil, natural gas, electrical products, motor vehicles, farms and forest products, mining products, food and raw materials.

The DTI has identified the following as good opportunities for UK exporters to Germany:

- marine equipment
- airport development
- building materials
- chemicals
- quality adult's clothing
- electronic components
- mechanical engineering
- soil decontamination
- food and drink
- gardening equipment
- instrumentation
- medical equipment
- power generation
- rail components
- port security.

Education

Compulsory school

For the 6–16 year age group. School is in the mornings only, concentrates on the imparting of knowledge and does not include the British emphasis on social responsibility, sports and the arts. Unsatisfactory progress may require the repeating of a year. The East German system has been changed to fit in with West Germany. After primary school, pupils are streamed into one of the three types of secondary schools, the only system in the EU to do so. The choice is between academic or vocational schools.

Qualification at 18

Abitur from gymnasium, Realschulabschluss from Realschule.

Training and skills

The German education system is highly rated as delivering a well skilled workforce. A

UK report in 1995 concluded that Germany's high skills levels led to better quality production partly due to the apprenticeship system which concentrates on linking theoretical knowledge with thorough practical experience in the workplace. Every employee has an entitlement to one week's training per year. German youth training is widely thought to be the best in Europe.

Employer involvement

The employer pays most of the training costs of the apprenticeship scheme. The trainee works and trains with the company and also attends vocational college which includes general and specialised education which is closely co-ordinated with the training received at work. Courses for jobs such as hairdressing, clerical work and car mechanics, last for two to three years during which time the trainee receives a low wage from the employer which rises significantly on completion of the training. The scheme's success is reflected in the lowest youth unemployment rate in Europe.

Employment conditions

Contract of employment

This need only contain the time and nature of the activity because everything else concerning the employment relationship is specified either by law, collective agreement between the unions and employers, or by negotiation at the workplace. It need not be in writing.

Public holidays

9 days – January 1, Good Friday, Easter Monday, May 1, Ascension Day, Whit Monday, October 3 (Unification Day), December 25 and 26. There are various other public holidays related to religious dates, or restricted to specific regions or towns.

Paid holiday

Most workers are entitled to 42 days a year although the statutory minimum is 18 days a year.

Working hours

These are amongst the lowest in Europe averaging 37.7 per week.

Minimum wages

There is no minimum wage but 90 per cent of employees are covered by collective agreements concluded by the unions. This is because agreements reached by the unions are often extended to all workers in the industry regardless of membership.

Working practices

Working conditions in East and West are very different although converging. Normal office hours are 8 a.m.–4 p.m. and often an early finish on Friday afternoon. The main holiday period is not as concentrated as elsewhere in the EU because school holidays are staggered by Länder from June to September.

Use of information technology

Deployment of IT is slightly below that of the UK.

Mobility

Labour mobility is restricted by many factors. Geographically, the shortage of housing is a problem and it is also administratively difficult to move between Länder in many jobs. There also tend to be fairly strict qualification requirements for many jobs making inter-job mobility difficult.

Tax

Income tax is much higher on a second income (regarding couples) and ranges from 19–53 per cent of income after deductions. Local taxes are levied on the rentable value of property owned.

VAT is 15 per cent (7 per cent on food) and there are various other taxes such as church tax which comes to about 3 per cent of income.

Social security

Contributions are high at 18 per cent of salary to cover unemployment, pension and health. Unemployment benefit is generous at about 65 per cent of salary in the first year and thereafter about 55 per cent. Pensions are paid at about £15,000 a year in 1995. State childcare is not widely available.

Trade unions

About 40 per cent of German workers belong to a trade union. Unions in Germany tend to be organised by industry rather than by job so most companies only need deal with one union which simplifies negotiations. The role of the unions has also been formalised in the compulsory works councils which employers must organise with the unions. These are a means of consulting and informing the workforce about important developments within the company such as investment plans but also include discussion about health and safety, catering arrangements and other working conditions. Annual wage increases agreed between employer organisations and unions are legally binding. Unions often subsidise professional training for their members.

Equal opportunities

There is a general legal presumption that all persons should be treated equally, regardless of gender, descent, race, language, homeland and origin, creed, religious and political beliefs, birth out of wedlock or trade union affiliation. The law is weak on preventing discrimination in recruitment and promotion although equal pay is required once a woman has been employed. Even then, there is difficulty in proving a case of discrimination since the onus of proof is on the aggrieved woman to prove that she does comparable work to a nominated man.

In organisations with over 16 employees, 6 per cent should be disabled or a regular monthly fine paid. In 1985, one-sixth of the quota was unfilled. Disabled employees also have special protection against dismissal and other privileges such as an extra week's holiday per year and the right to refuse overtime.

Health and safety

All employers must set up arrangements to ensure the health and safety of their employees. Establishments with more than 20 employees or in certain hazardous industries must appoint a works safety expert and a works doctor to monitor and advise on health and safety and to train safety officers. The works council is entitled to relevant information to help it make decisions in conjunction with management about appropriate health and safety measures. The Labour Inspectorate is the external agency charged with ensuring legal enforcement and it visits one in four employers every year. This results in a high level of compliance since the Inspectorate has wide powers of enforcement.

Medical care

Germany has an extremely high-quality health care system which is probably better than the UK's but it is very expensive and paid for by insurance schemes taken out by employees. Free treatment at the point of use is then guaranteed upon production of a valid insurance certificate when you visit the doctor. Patients are free to choose their doctor and hospital.

Culture

The German area has not been subject to invasions or widespread immigration in the recent past and so a distinctive German character and culture exists. The general perception of Germans as highly ordered and disciplined tends to be true in formal and public settings. This means that there is less tolerance of eccentricity or public misbehaviour such as littering. Germans do not rate sarcasm or self-deprecation highly as sources of humour whereas these are very important to British humour, hence the Germans' reputation for being humourless, whereas in fact their sense of humour is just different.

A major cultural phenomenon is the reunification of Germany. Over 45 years and working under two very different systems, different attitudes developed. Although referred to as re-unification, East Germans (or Ossies as they are sometimes known) feel that they have been taken over by the West and are a little resentful as a result.

Family

The small nuclear family is the norm with increasing numbers of couples choosing not to have children at all. Where couples do have children it is difficult for the wife to go out to work since childcare is not easily available and a second income is more heavily taxed; hence the participation rate for women in employment is low in Germany.

Home

West German houses tend to be relatively new and of high quality as 75 per cent of the housing stock was rebuilt in the aftermath of the Second World War. Most Germans (60 per cent in the West and 75 per cent in the East) are happy to rent houses as buying property in Germany is very expensive and lending institutions require a 30–40 per cent deposit. East German housing stock is older and of much poorer quality.

Germans like to be at home and so spend a great deal on furnishings. The typical German house is characterised by the three-piece suite, heavy coffee table in the living room and huge beds and combination wardrobes in the bedroom. Germans spend a great deal on plants and flowers to go into their homes. Home is also open mainly to family and very close friends.

Religion

Protestant (45 per cent) and Roman Catholic (37 per cent) make up the majority. The north is predominantly Protestant with 10 per cent regular church goers while the south is strongly Catholic with 33 per cent regular church goers. A church tax is payable in addition to income tax. Both churches administer kindergartens, schools, hospitals, old people's homes and other social institutions to such an extent that the church is a much more important part of German life than the church attendance figures suggest. This is probably why 90 per cent of Germans pay the church tax even though it is voluntary, although this proportion has been decreasing recently.

Diet

There are great regional variations in the preferred food of the Germans although some generalisations can be made. Germany is famous for the many types of sausages (or wurst), rye breads and dumplings and of course sauerkraut, fermented cabbage. Meats both cold and hot are the major part of a German meal and consequently vegetarians find it difficult to eat out. The main meal is usually lunch. Beer consumption is high and is almost invariably German with very little inroad from foreign brands whether from Denmark, Holland or Australia. Germany is also an important producer of wine especially in its western regions. The popular native spirit is schnapps.

Leisure

Much leisure time is spent at home but otherwise the Germans are very active in sports with over 20 per cent members of a sports club; football, athletics, gymnastics and tennis being the most popular sports. A great deal of central and local government money has gone into providing local sports facilities. One very popular activity which can be classed under both leisure and health is visiting spa facilities. Costs are often reimbursed under health insurance.

Arts

Germany has a world renowned cultural inheritance in music (Bach, Beethoven and Handel), literature (Schiller, Goethe and Brecht) and ideas (Nietzsche, Hegel and von Humboldt). The arts are popular and well supported by the state. For example, a small town of 50,000–60,000 people may well have its own subsidised theatre and opera house. Festivals and carnivals also play a prominent role in German life. There are the beer festivals, the best known of which is the Munich beer festival in September. Carnival season is January and February and most large towns have one which includes processions and balls.

Further information

- *Live and Work in Germany*, V Pybus, 1992, Vacation Work
- *How to Live and Work in Germany*, N Loewenthal, 1992, How To Books

Greece

Main features

- Huge EU financed infrastructure investments scheduled for completion by 1999
- Self-employment is very high at 40 per cent of the labour force
- Agriculture employs 25 per cent

Resources

Raw materials to be found in Greece include oil, lignite, bauxite and aluminium, all of which have potential for much greater exploitation whereas capital equipment has largely had to be imported. Greece still has a significant agricultural sector while other major industries include banking, commerce, shipping and tourism. There are very few large companies in Greece and economic growth is mainly delivered by small and very small enterprises. Energy is provided by imported oil, but also by indigenous hydro and geothermal electricity and lignite powered generating stations. Fishing is an important activity.

Land

Greece is the only Member State not to share a land border with another Member State. It has over 2500 islands and 15,000 kilometres of indented coastline, two factors which, together with the Mediterranean climate, make tourism a major earner. Only about a third of the land is cultivable. 40 per cent of the population live in the Athens and Salonika urban areas leaving large areas of Greece very sparsely populated. This is partly due to the mountainous and barren nature of much of the Greek interior.

Climate

Climate is continental temperate with the mountainous areas the coldest during the winter. In summer, May-October, it is dry and hot everywhere (28–40° C, a major attraction for the ten million or so tourists which come to Greece annually.

Language

Modern Greek is very different to the ancient Greek taught in academic schools throughout Europe. It does however retain a different alphabet. English is widely spoken especially by those likely to be involved in international business. There are four minority languages spoken (Arvanite, Aroumanian, Slav-Macedonian and Pomak) but these are not officially recognised or supported. The Greeks are very skilled linguists.

Telecoms

The Greek telephone system requires great improvement and lags behind all other EU systems. For example, there can be problems at peak times and there is a shortage of lines especially in Athens. An improvement programme is in progress.

Other links

Greece is a world centre for shipping. Although other transport networks, such as rail, are limited they tend to be efficient. The road system was considerably improved in the eighties and main roads are of good quality although local roads can be more of a problem. The undeveloped interior should benefit from an EU-supported trans-Greece motorway which will enable growth of microchip mass production for middle eastern and European markets. Distribution is slow and expensive to Greece's 150 inhabited islands. The wars in former Yugoslavia have also caused transport problems by shutting off the cheaper land route to the rest of Europe and forcing business to use the more expensive and slower option of taking a ferry across the Adriatic to Italy. EU funds have been allocated to finance a new airport and underground system in Athens and many other port, regional airport, bridge and road improvements throughout the country.

Trade flows

Greece both imports and exports mainly with Germany, Italy and France. The UK is in fourth place.

Major exports: clothing, fruit, vegetables and textiles.

Major imports: machinery, transport equipment, food, live animals, petrol and petroleum products.

The DTI has identified the following as good opportunities for UK exporters to Greece:

- meat
- vehicle components and accessories
- building materials
- clothing
- electronic components

- gas distribution equipment
- waste management
- food and drink
- equipment for the disabled
- medical supplies
- power generation
- rail components
- security equipment
- telecoms.

Education

Compulsory school

For the 6–15 year age group. The Greek school system is heavily academic and formal in approach. Pupils then go onto a gymnasium for three years after which there is a choice of continuing onto one of three types of lycea, general (chosen by 74 per cent) or technical and vocational (chosen by 20 per cent) for a three year course. An integrated option linking the two approaches is also available. Alternatively, students may attend a technical and vocational school, chosen by 4 per cent, for a two-year course, completion of which can then followed by a lycea course or entry into the labour market. Many students also attend private crammers after school to improve their performance. Lycea students not wanting to continue onto higher education can acquire professional and technical skills in training centres. Those wishing to go to university must take an entrance exam which is highly competitive.

Qualification at 18

General examination. 17 per cent of university students study abroad.

Training and skills

There is a shortage of people with specialist skills, especially in high-technologies, although basic skills are widely available as unemployment is relatively high. Vocational education is not chosen by many pupils and little practical experience is included. 15-year-old school leavers also have the option of completing a three-year apprenticeship which begins with full-time education and progresses in the third year to three days a week at work and the remainder at apprentice school.

Public and private professional training institutes were created in 1993 open to both adults and secondary school graduates. This is partly to offset a general lack of retraining and updating available for adults. These courses are relatively cheap to encourage employers to make use of them. For example only 0.04 per cent of GDP was spent on training in 1988 although by 1991 this had risen to 0.24 per cent – still very low compared to the EU average. The courses offered full-time to secondary students in the technical and vocational schools are also available on a part-time basis over three years.

Employer involvement

There is no entitlement to paid training leave except in certain cases for public sector employees. A large number of manufacturing employers provide training schemes for their staff. These are often subsidised by the government and the EU with particular emphasis on highly technical training. Employers pay 0.2 per cent of the payroll into the Greek manpower organisation (OAED) to finance vocational training programmes. Some unions have funded training for senior managers where this is becoming crucial. Small firms, which form the majority, are much less inclined to provide training preferring instead to hire pre-qualified staff.

Employment conditions

The informal economy contributes a large part of GDP (about 30 per cent) which means that Greek labour law is often not followed.

Contract of employment
Part-time and fixed-term contracts are allowed as alternatives to the indefinite contract but since the former must be for 20 hours weekly as a minimum, part-time working is not very common in Greece. Most contracts are unwritten even for professional jobs.

Public holidays
12 days – January 1, January 6 (Epiphany), first Monday of Lent, March 25 (Independence Day), Good Friday, Easter Monday, May 1, Whit Monday, August 15 (Assumption), October 28 (National Day), December 25 and 26.

Paid holiday
20 working days for a five-day week or 24 working days where a six-day week is the norm to be taken usually in one continuous block. Many employers also grant three to five days' paid leave on marriage. Unpaid leave of up to three months for each parent to care for a child under two and a half is available but this only applies to parents employed in large organisations (over 100 employees). All employees also get an extra month's pay at Christmas and half a month's extra pay at Easter. There is also a holiday bonus of 15 days' pay.

Working hours
Legal maximum of 48 hours per week (managerial employees are exempt from these restrictions). The average is 40 hours per week.

Minimum wages
These are set by negotiation between unions and employers and vary according to whether a worker is trained or not.

Working practices
Normal office hours are 8 a.m.–4 p.m. in summer (half an hour later in winter) with only a short break of about 15 minutes for lunch at about 10.30 a.m. or a late lunch after work at 3.30 p.m. since Greek employment legislation does not cover the right to a lunch break.

Use of information technology
Greece lags behind the rest of the EU in most aspects such as the prevalence of computers and pace of implementation. Banking is the most advanced sector for IT implementation.

Mobility
There is a long history of emigration to countries such as Germany and the USA and even now Greek graduates often spend some time abroad gaining work experience. There is a drift to Athens, and it is very difficult to entice Athenians to other parts of Greece despite recent attempts at decentralisation.

Tax
Taxable income over 1 million Dr (£2670) is charged at 5 per cent, the next 1.5 million Dr (£4010) is charged at 15 per cent, the next 3 million Dr (£8015) at 30 per cent and the remainder at 40 per cent.

VAT is 18 per cent standard rate, 8 per cent for basics including food, 4 per cent for printed material and 36 per cent for luxury goods.

Social security

Sickness, maternity and unemployment benefit and pensions are provided through contributions to the state institution of social insurance and topped up by compulsory contributions to many private insurance companies through different occupational schemes. There is therefore no universal level of contribution or level of benefit. Employers pay 23.75 per cent and employees 13.75 per cent of pay towards social security. There is also a deduction to pay for training. All benefits are related to previous salary.

Trade unions

These are mainly organised according to occupation and negotiate almost exclusively on pay in contrast to other Member States where general working conditions are also negotiated by the unions. Overall, 25 per cent of employees belong to a union but these are mainly public sector workers since private employees rarely belong to unions. Employees have a right to belong to a trade union and union officials are guaranteed protection and facilities within the workplace but they often lack training in their duties. Since 1988, workers have been able to discuss relevant issues with their employers through enterprise based works councils instead of, or as well as, through the unions although this has not become a widespread practice.

Equal opportunities

Legislation exists specifically to protect women, foreign workers and trade union members against discrimination in pay, access to education and training, employment and career progression. Otherwise there is a general legal presumption that everyone is entitled to equality of treatment. There is a high female participation rate.

Health and safety

Enterprises employing 20 to 50 workers must have a safety representative. In larger businesses, a health and safety committee (including a safety officer) must be set up of elected employees with advisory powers and rights to information such as the proposed introduction of new processes. The committee also informs management about hazards and proposes solutions to overcome them. For enterprises of more than 50 people a works doctor must be appointed to oversee their well-being. Unfortunately, there is a shortage of people qualified to take on the roles of works doctor and safety officer.

Medical care

14 per cent of Greeks are covered by private insurance; otherwise employees are covered by the state institution of social insurance. Within the Greek health service consultation of your doctor and hospital treatment is free whilst prescriptions are charged at 25 per cent of full cost. In remote areas, treatment costs are only partially reimbursed by the system.

Culture

Greece is best known world-wide for its ancient civilisation and the ideas of this era, such as the philosophy and mathematics of Aristotle and Socrates, as well as the monuments that culture left behind such as the Acropolis of Athens. Greece is very much at the crossroads between east and west which is reflected in its culture. Religion is an east European variant of Christianity, whereas food and culture is middle eastern. With recent developments in eastern Europe, Greece is looking to build more links there especially with the Balkan states of Bulgaria and Albania where it is investing heavily. The Greeks have a reputation of generosity and hospitality with a strong attachment to family and church.

Family

Family is extremely important in Greece and closely linked with place and work since many businesses are family run with family members as employees either officially or unofficially. There is a strong sense of obligation to one's family which extends to giving them employment. Family ties are being loosened by the migration from agriculture to employment in the urban areas but there is often a longing to return to one's home village expressed through frequent visits. Women play a more traditional role especially in rural areas, where, for example, the cafes are male preserves.

Home

The cost of housing is high and rising, especially rents. 70 per cent of Greeks are home owners and over half of all housing has been built within the last 25 years. In the tourist areas, many Greeks take in visitors on a bed and breakfast basis. The focus of the home is the living room cum kitchen where most activities take place. Parents often buy their children a house on marriage. Greek women take great pride in keeping the house scrupulously clean and in decorating it with handmade furnishings.

Religion

Greece is home to the Greek Orthodox church to which 98 per cent of Greeks belong. There are plans to increase tourism from the former East European Communist states, especially Russia, which share the faith by highlighting the large number of religious sites, such as monasteries, to be visited.

Diet

Greece's entry into the EU made foreign food products cheaper so that there has been a shift in purchasing patterns towards Irish butter, British biscuits and French cheeses, for example. The traditional Greek emphasis on extra virgin olive oil (Greeks have the world's highest per capita consumption of olive oil and cheese), greens (horta), pulses and dairy products made from sheep's and goats' milk is still very evident in the popularity of moussaka (aubergine and minced lamb), stivado, dolmados (vine leaves stuffed with rice and meat), shell fish, various sea fish, salads, feta and other cheeses. Yogurt has always been popular and is becoming more so with young people. Greece also produces many different varieties of wine, the best known of which is retsina. Ouzo is a common aniseed aperitif. The Greek method of making coffee is also very distinctive. Cakes and other sweetmeats are extremely popular and sold in specialised shops. The main meal is a late dinner at 9 p.m. or later.

Leisure

The Greek language does not have a word for leisure, and it is not until recently that Greeks have had sufficient disposable income for such activities. Greek social life revolves around food and the favourite form of entertainment is going out for a meal to a taverna. Greeks spend over 40 per cent of their income on food, far more than Italy or Spain with comparable standards of living, so that this statistic is an indication of preferred lifestyle rather than an indication of poverty. Until recently, young Greeks particularly liked to stay out at bars, pubs, cafes and discos until very late in the evening although there is now legislation forcing these venues to close earlier. Although men and women are nominally equal, girls are unlikely to go out alone. Greeks frequently spend their weekends visiting the coast where they swim, fish and sail. Tennis is becoming more popular and football and basketball are the favourite spectator sports. Skiing is available in the winter in the mountains of north and central Greece. The good weather means that outdoor activities are very popular. Easter is traditionally a time to return to one's home village for a week or two when amongst other things, Greeks can stock up on home produced food such as olive oil and cheese.

Arts

In 1997 Salonika, Greece's northern city port, will be European City of Culture which should give a boost to cultural activities there and throughout Greece. Otherwise the cultural centre of Greece is Athens in terms of available venues, audiences and performers. Outdoor performances are common during the summer including classical Greek plays performed in ancient amphitheatres and drive-in cinemas. There are many local festivals throughout the country during which bouzouki and other Greek folk music is performed using traditional instruments such as the lute. There is also a popular tradition of oral poetry recitals. The Ministry of Culture devotes 50 per cent of its budget to sport, providing facilities and subsidising events; another substantial part of the budget is devoted to financing archaeological activities. It also finances opera, theatre companies, orchestras, all museums and art exhibitions, and adult education.

Further information

- Internet address:
  Aegean Web Server at http://agn.hol.gr/
  Also of interest may be:
  http://www.ensmp.fr/~scherer/adminet/world/gr/

Ireland

Main features

- High international labour mobility in response to high Irish unemployment
- Large pool of well-educated, computer literate, young employees
- The greatest proportion of young people in the EU

Resources

Ireland's major economic resource is a climate and landscape which produces grass, since this supports its export-oriented cattle agriculture and foreign tourism where a major attraction is the green scenery, golf and fishing. Ireland has few physical resources although there is zinc, lead and copper mining. In particular it lacks energy supplies. Attempts to overcome this have included building peat-fired power stations which use a plentiful resource but which mar the landscape leaving black deserts from areas where peat has been stripped.

Ireland has traditionally been an agricultural country and although employment in this sector is much reduced, its efficiency has greatly increased and Ireland is using its relative lack of heavy industry as a marketing strength in promoting the purity of its agricultural products. The unspoilt environment also has great tourist potential and this sector is very important in the Irish economy and expected to continue to expand significantly especially if peace in Northern Ireland continues. Ireland has projected its young, well-educated workforce as a major resource in attracting a great deal of foreign investment especially from American and UK companies in high-technology and finance sectors.

Land

Approximately half Ireland's area is lowlands with many lakes and rivers while the remainder is hill or mountain concentrated in the coastal counties. It is a very rural landscape with only Dublin on the east coast as a sizeable urban area. Only 14 per cent of the land is used to grow crops while 71 per cent is meadow and pasture for livestock, mainly cattle. Tree cover is low at 5 per cent.

Climate

Ireland has a fairly wet climate compared to most of the rest of Europe catching westerly rain showers direct from the Atlantic. Winters are mild averaging 4°C with snow extremely rare. Summer temperatures average 15–20°C.

Language

The first official language is Irish, an ancient Celtic language with links to Scottish Gaelic and Welsh. It is taught in schools but few people use it as their everyday tongue, except on the west coast. English is the second and most used official language.

Telecoms

Ireland has been very successful in promoting itself as an ideal location for electronics manufacturers and activities heavily reliant on good computer and telecommunications links such as the new financial services centre in Dublin and tele-sales companies. Ireland claims that these facilities are state of the art and world class and more than offset the additional transport costs entailed in locating to an island on the periphery of the EU. However Ireland is placed about number seven within the EU for its telecoms facilities, according to the latest *World Competitiveness Report* which suggests that its huge investment programme of the eighties is already being overtaken by other Member States. The forthcoming privatisation of its monopoly supplier in partnership with one of the world's larger telecoms companies may provide the opportunity for further improvements.

Other links

The sparse population outside of Dublin means that Ireland has a good road network although it is most often only two lanes since the volume of traffic does not justify wider roads. The rail network is sparse linking only the main centres of population including a Dublin to Belfast (in Northern Ireland) line. A great deal of EU money has gone into improving the Irish transport infrastructure. There are ferry links to Wales from the west coast and Cork as well as to France. Shannon airport, on the west coast near Limerick, has been designated a free port area in a bid to attract more freight and manufacturing business. Overall Ireland has had to make special efforts to overcome its isolation on the periphery of the EU.

Trade flows

With a small domestic market Ireland needs to export to generate income. About 60 per cent of manufacturing output is exported. The value of Irish exports amounts to two-thirds of GDP. Tourism generated 7 per cent of GDP in 1990. 80 per cent of visible exports are manufactured items with most of the remainder agricultural products. Main trading partners are the UK, USA and Germany.

Major exports: computers, chemicals, electrical goods, milk, butter and beef.

Major imports: machinery, transport equipment, food, live animals and chemicals.

The DTI has identified the following as good opportunities for UK exporters to Ireland:

- building materials
- quality adults' clothing
- waste management
- rail components
- telecoms.

Education

Compulsory school

For the 6–15 year age group. Irish pupils can attend a secondary school, comprehensive, vocational or community school. Most schools are state aided independent church schools.

Qualification at 18

Leaving Certificate which is a nationally administered exam giving entry to employment and higher education. At 15, pupils can take the Junior Certificate and at 16/17, the Senior Certificate or a Vocational Preparation and Training (VPT 1) programme (funded by the European Social Fund).

Training and skills

Irish education is regarded as the best preparation for working life in the EU but thereafter Irish employers give very little training to their employees in spite of having to pay a training levy of 1 per cent of pay, 90 per cent of which is refunded in the event of an approved training programme being in operation.

In the past, four-year apprenticeships combining on and off the job training (at Regional Technical Colleges), could begin at the end of compulsory schooling at 15 but increasingly Irish apprentices have first completed their Leaving Certificate. If successful, the apprentice will be awarded a National Craft Certificate which is a standards based qualification similar to the UK's NVQs.

The government training agency, FÁS, provides a great many courses resulting in vocational qualifications (many are UK City and Guilds certificates) targeted at the young and women returners. Programmes for the unemployed are provided by FÁS. Both the Alternance programme for unemployed adults and the Community Youth Training Programme for young people, provide basic skills training and work experience. Since tourism is very important to the Irish economy there is also a state training agency for hotels, catering and tourism (CERT) which runs relevant VPT 2 courses.

Employer involvement

Vocational schools, specialist colleges and continuing adult education are organised by Vocational Education Committees which are local organisations including local authority and local business representatives.

Employment conditions

Contracts of employment

These are usually in writing and may often include a clause that the employee accepts collective agreements negotiated by the unions.

Public holidays
Eight days – January 1, March 17 (St Patrick's Day), Easter Monday, first Monday in June, first Monday in August, last Monday in October, December 25 and 26. There is provision for employees to substitute some of these dates with church holidays such as August 15 (Assumption).

Paid holiday
The legal minimum is three weeks' paid leave per year but most employers offer 20 days as a minimum.

Working hours
Maximum working week at basic pay is 48 hours after which overtime rates must be paid. Average working week tends to be 40 hours with many unions negotiating for a reduction to 39 hours a week.

Minimum wages
In industries where union membership is low (e.g. catering, hairdressing and textiles), the government has often formed a Joint Labour Committee to decide on minimum wage levels. Otherwise there are no statutory minimum wages.

Working practices
Normal office hours are 9 a.m.–5.30 p.m. with an hour for lunch, usually 12.30–1.30 p.m. For shop workers this one hour interval is a legal requirement. The main holiday period is June/July and school starts again in August.

Use of information technology
On most aspects of IT use Ireland is slightly behind the UK. Ireland promotes itself as an electronics centre and has attracted many high-tech American companies to base their European operations there. However, these until recently have been mainly assembly work and have little effect on increasing the use of IT in Irish industry in general.

Mobility
Ireland has a long history of emigration of its young people especially to the UK, USA and other English speaking countries. This trend is continuing, especially for graduates in electronics and software engineering, in spite of Ireland's recent economic improvement generated in part by the high-tech field.

Tax
In the 1995/96 tax year taxable income over I£2500 is charged at 27 per cent low rate (first I£8900) and 48 per cent high rate. In addition 5.5 per cent of taxable income is paid into the social security fund; 1.5 per cent for health care and 1 per cent for training.

Local taxes – most local authorities levy a water and land tax, the latter based on the value of the property. Some also charge for individual services such as refuse collection.

VAT is levied at six rates ranging from zero to 21 per cent for luxury goods. The standard rates for most consumer goods are 12.5 and 16 per cent.

Social security
Employee contributions of 5.5 per cent of income secure access to a range of benefits including unemployment, disability and maternity benefit and retirement pensions.

Trade unions
As in many other European countries, pay agreements increasingly tend to be made at a company level rather than for the industry as a whole. There are over 50 unions, mainly organised by job role. There is no legal requirement for employers to deal with

the unions but since membership is relatively high and the unions generally accept working together to present a united voice, most employers find it convenient to negotiate through them.

As elsewhere in Europe, union membership is in decline but not to the same extent as in the UK. The decline is due to increased unemployment, when union membership tends to lapse, and also because new jobs tend to be in new technology companies, small service firms or as self-employed, or non-unionised foreign (especially American) companies. The unions are consulted regularly by government on relevant matters.

Equal opportunities

It is illegal for an employer to discriminate on the grounds of gender, marital and parental status. Indirectly this means that it is also sometimes illegal to discriminate on the grounds of age. In addition, dismissal because of trade union activity, disability, race (including Irish gypsies), religion or sexual orientation is also illegal. Women are guaranteed equal pay and have rights to maternity pay and job reinstatement after maternity leave. Female participation is low especially for women over 30.

Health and safety

Irish law requires a pro-active approach, for example, safety statements are required which set out the employer's health and safety programme for the workplace, identifying all hazards, necessary safeguards and responsible persons. The law provides for employee consultation on health and safety matters and the appointment of a safety representative who has legal rights to relevant information.

Medical care

Medical care and prescriptions are only free to those on very low income who are given a Blue Card. Those with low incomes are entitled to hospital treatment paying a maximum daily charge of I£20 (or I£200 in any one year), I£6 per visit to out patient departments, I£12 per visit to a doctor and for medication. Otherwise hospital charges vary from I£23–I£50 a day with consultant's fees in addition. Private health insurance is therefore popular and often offered as part of a remuneration package for employees.

Culture

Ireland is known especially for its folk and literary culture with names such as George Bernard Shaw, James Joyce and Oscar Wilde world famous. The Irish have a reputation for being hospitable and friendly which may have helped to make Ireland into a successful tourist destination. The stereotypical slow pace of life can be found in rural areas but not in urban areas where 60 per cent of the Irish live.

Family

The long history of emigration means that most Irish families have relatives abroad especially in the UK, Canada and the USA. Nevertheless, the family unit is very strong and families tend to be larger than the European norm because of stricter adherence to Catholic rules on contraception and abortion. Almost 50 per cent of the population is under 25 as a result and in spite of high emigration levels, especially of the young. Divorce is only now becoming legal although separation has always been possible where a marriage breaks down. The role of women in Ireland is more traditional than is found elsewhere in northern Europe hence, for example, the low participation rate in paid employment.

Home

Home ownership is high at 80 per cent. This is a cultural phenomenon resulting from the insecurities felt by the Irish when they were frequently dispossessed by their land-lords. Consequently, most Irish people feel a great need for a piece of land which is indisputably theirs. It also means there is a large amount of new housing built singly on individual plots of land which is relatively cheap. Irish houses are large by EU standards but household size is larger too.

Religion

Ireland is 93 per cent Catholic and in many ways the most strongly Catholic country in Europe with 86 per cent church attendance and a long tradition of the church providing everyday services such as schools and hospitals. Divorce was narrowly approved in a recent referendum, contraception is available only in very limited quantities and abortion practically illegal. However the strong influence of the Catholic church is declining.

Diet

This is very similar to the British diet but there are a few Irish specialities. Potatoes are associated with Ireland and are still eaten in abundance, Irish stew is also well known and Irish expatriates often long for soda bread which is made without yeast. Ireland's rivers and coast yield many fish especially salmon and oysters. Beer is dominated by the milk stouts, including Guinness and Murphys, and Ireland has an important whiskey industry. Overall, food in Ireland is in the country cooking tradition rather than haute cuisine. Meal times are similar to the UK.

Leisure

A great deal of socialising goes on in pubs and bars where the whole family, including children, gather. Folk music and dance are very popular both at organised events and simply as a spontaneous performance in bars. Foreign tourists come to Ireland to play golf and fish but the Irish also enjoy horse and greyhound racing as well as gaelic football and hurling. Many Irish also like to own a horse, many of which are kept in the urban areas, causing problems. Holidays are most likely to be spent at home.

Arts

Ireland encourages the arts in several ways, one of which is to exempt from tax all earnings from work of creative or artistic merit. This is designed to encourage the retention or return of Irish artists. There is also the Aosdana organisation with a restricted membership of 150 which entitles its members to receive £6300 a year to give them time to produce artistic works. This is meant to add to the limited corporate sponsorship available in such a small economy. In addition, the government subsidises the arts in the traditional ways which concentrate on expanding public access to the arts. In recent years the government has set up financial incentives to make film making in the Republic an attractive proposition. This seems to have worked, with Irish films such as 'The Commitments' and 'My Left Foot' enjoying great success, as well as others without a specifically Irish setting.

Further information

- Industrial Development Agency, Wilton Park House, Wilton Place, Dublin 2, Tel: +353 1 668 6633, Fax: +353 1 660 3703
- Internet addresses: The best of Ireland is at:
  http://www.internet-eireann.ie/tasc/thebest.htm
  Doing business in Ireland is at:
  http://www.itw.ie/ltw/binirl

Italy

Main features

- Lowest birth rate in the EU
- Strong regional differences especially between north and south
- Industrial centres are in Milan, Turin, Genoa and Rome whilst areas favoured for retirement by Britons, Germans and the Dutch are in Tuscany and Umbria
- Cost of living is high in Italy especially for food, petrol and accommodation

Resources

Italy has few basic resources having to import 80 per cent of its oil and having recently voted in a referendum to phase out its nuclear energy programme. Italy is world renowned for design especially in the fashion industry. Industry is dominated by motor vehicles (Fiat, Ford, Renault) and electrical appliances (Merloni, Zanussi and Electrolux). It also has highly skilled labour for its high-tech industries. A very large section of industry is in the public sector. The south is generally much poorer and more barren than the north and infrastructure is much worse although there are substantial government and EU financial incentives for industry to locate there. One resource particularly lacking is water which can have serious consequences both for business and ordinary life. The landscape and abundant cultural remains attract a great deal of foreign tourism.

Land

In the north lies the Italian section of the Alps where winter sports are popular. The rivers draining from the mountains have given rise to the Italian Lake District with, for example, Lake Garda and Lake Como. Central Italy has a varied landscape of high mountains, fertile plains, long sandy beaches and pine and olive groves. The south is wilder than the north with flat coastal plains. There, land is lower but still hilly and thickly forested, and home to bears and wolves. This area is also volcanic which makes the landscape extremely rugged and gives rise to periodic eruptions and earthquakes. Italy also includes Sicily and Sardinia and several other small islands such as Capri.

Climate

The Italian climate varies from the Alps in the north to the Mediterranean climate in much of the rest of the country. Average temperatures range from 2°C in January in Milan to 26°C in July in Bologna.

Language

Italian is the national language although there are many different regional variations, some of which are difficult to understand. In some areas a different language is spoken altogether including French and German in border areas, Greek and Albanian in Sicily and Spanish in Sardinia. Although English is now taught in schools, it is not widely spoken and the Italians are, like the British, not good linguists.

Telecoms

The telephone system has had a poor reputation but is being modernised. It can take up to two years for a new line to be installed. International phone calls were the second most expensive in the EU after Spain until charges were reduced early in 1996. International post is efficient but internally it is very unreliable despite the privatisation of postal services in 1995.

Other links

The road system, both the motorways, on which tolls are payable, and the regional roads, are generally of a high quality. There is also a good rail network. Both these networks are well connected with France and the rest of Europe. However there are new restrictions on road freight on the direct route to Germany through Switzerland which road hauliers must consider. The alternative Austrian route to Germany is also likely to be restricted by the Austrians if it becomes overused. Transport networks in the south are not as dense or efficient.

Trade flows

Principal trading partners are Germany, France, the USA and UK.

Major exports: metals, textiles, production machinery, motor vehicles, transport equipment, clothing, footwear and chemicals.

Major imports: industrial machinery, chemicals, transport equipment, petroleum, metals and foods.

The DTI has identified the following as good opportunities for UK exporters to Italy:

- cereals, livestock and seed potatoes
- vehicle components and accessories
- knitwear and menswear
- waste management
- food and drink
- instrumentation and scientific equipment
- medical supplies and veterinary products
- power generation
- rail components
- telecoms.

Education

Compulsory school

For the 6–14 year age group. Schooling and training are quite separate. School is still largely in the morning only. Schooling is common to all pupils until they begin secondary school at the age of 14 when they may opt for an academic or vocational institution. Vocational training is available both in state upper secondary schools and regional training centres. The two systems are not co-ordinated, with the regional centres generally considered to be for those who fail, while the vocational upper secondary schools are more theoretical and less practical. Pupils can be required to retake a year if unsatisfactory progress is made and in fact this discourages many of the 85 per cent of primary pupils who enrol onto secondary education since half do not complete it.

Qualification at 18

Maturita. Those who gain their maturita are entitled to enrol onto the university course of their choice, which leads to great overcrowding in the universities. Only 30 per cent of those who register at university go on to obtain degrees. There are few other institutes of higher education in Italy.

Training and skills

The Italian workforce is generally lacking in the necessary skills for a modern economy hence Italy receives a great deal of financial support from the European Social Fund to upgrade skill levels. The regional training centres deliver job specific training and are closely linked to the needs of industry. It is through these centres that European supported (such as ESF) training courses are mostly delivered.

Employer involvement

The oral vocational exams are assessed by a board including industry representatives as well as teachers. No legal obligation exists for employers to provide employee training. However there are incentives to employ those under 30 years old on a two year training contract in return for a reduction in employer social security contributions. Employers also participate in the apprenticeship system whereby 14–21 year olds alternate on the job training with college work. Many unions have negotiated study leave (commonly 150 hours) for their members but these are often only basic skills courses. Employers are legally required to facilitate this right to study by not requiring overtime to make up for the hours lost in study and by giving paid time off to take exams.

Employment conditions

Contract of employment

This need not be written unless there are special conditions such as a probation period or restraint of trade clause.

Public holidays

10 days – January 1, January 6 (Epiphany), Easter Monday, April 25 (Liberation day), May 1, August 15 (Assumption), November 1 (All Saints' Day), December 8 (Immaculate Conception), December 25 and 26; plus various local public holidays which add an average of three days to the annual total. On public holidays offices, shops, banks, post offices and schools are all closed.

Paid holiday

Between five and six weeks per year depending on length of service in addition to the annual ten public holidays.

Working hours

40 hours per week is the average and 48 hours the legal maximum.

Minimum wages

There are no statutory minimum wages in Italy but rates negotiated in collective agreements tend to be extended to non-union employees.

Working practices

Normal office hours are 9 a.m.–1 p.m. and 3 p.m.–7 p.m. with two hours for lunch. Due to legal obstacles part-time work is very uncommon accounting for only 5 per cent of jobs. Public officials are not usually available for meetings in the afternoon.

The main holiday period is August when businesses shut down for the whole month. School starts again in mid-September continuing until mid-June. The Italian way of doing business is very sociable and it is unacceptable to stick to business during negotiations. Business is often done over a good meal and weekend meetings are common.

Use of information technology
On several different measures of the use of IT, Italy tends to score third worst in the EU, beating the UK only in terms of the amount of investment being made in telecommunications. However it does have by far the highest use of robots in industry per employee.

Mobility
There has been a long-standing migration from the poor agricultural south to the industrial north. Mobility is also increasing as a method of career progression. However for those interested only in a job, rather than a career, mobility is low because of strong local ties.

Tax
Income tax deductions vary from 12 per cent to 62 per cent of taxable income. Social security payments take an additional 8 per cent of gross income. Local tax is 17 per cent of the rental value of the property in which you live. Rates are also payable for rubbish disposal and water, based on the floor area of the property. VAT is 19 per cent and 38 per cent for luxury goods.

Social security
The Italian system provides old age and disability pensions, sickness and unemployment benefit and health care. All, apart from pensions, are pretty low sums whereas pensions are renowned for their generosity. For 1 per cent of gross earnings contributions, a person could receive 60 per cent of their average last five working years' income as pension after working 30 years. Future Italian governments will have to restrict them in order to save state money especially as retirement ages are so low in Italy (55 for women and 60 for men). Amenities such as free or subsidised sports facilities, public libraries, meals on wheels or employment retraining are lacking.

Trade unions
Unions tend to be grouped according to political sympathies as well as according to industry or type of job. Industrial relations tend to be bad every two or three years when the two- or three-year pay agreements need to be renegotiated. Italy had over three times as many days lost in industrial disputes as the UK in 1991–93. 60 per cent of the workforce was unionised in 1988. Anti-union behaviour by the employer is illegal.

Equal opportunities
Italian law prohibits discrimination on the grounds of race, language, sex, religion, age, political conviction or trade union sympathy. Italian women tend to earn 84 per cent of the equivalent male wage compared to 69 per cent in the UK.
Employers can take positive action to promote opportunities for discriminated groups such as women, for example, by providing targeted training courses.

The Italian system of recruitment requires that in most cases this is done on behalf of the employer by the state placement service after the employer has specified the numbers and skill levels of the personnel required. Only in rare cases have employers been able to request a named person to be taken on. Although this system is being deregulated so that only 50 per cent of employees are hired in this way, it has probably helped to reduce the amount of discrimination.

The Italian public sector is legally required in most cases to recruit by open public examination, those obtaining the highest marks being awarded the available jobs, and this could be another way to minimise discrimination.

Any enterprise (including the public sector) employing more than 35 persons must ensure that 15 per cent of its employees is made up of widows, orphans, disabled, refugees or otherwise socially disadvantaged persons.

Health and safety

Employers must adopt all necessary measures to protect the physical, mental and moral well-being of their staff. Employees are entitled to check that health and safety regulations are being met at their place of work. Accident prevention committees are made up of company and union representatives to identify risk factors and propose appropriate safety measures.

Medical care

The Italian state health service is not of a very high standard and is available free to those who have paid their social security contributions, the unemployed, pensioners or those under 18. Visits to the doctor and dentist must be paid for however. Many Italians take out private insurance which gives access to a very high level of care.

Culture

Italy is a country with very marked regional differences and indeed one political party has as its central aim independence of a northern region from Italy. The differences are particularly marked as between the wealthy industrial north and the poor agricultural south. The extreme south and Sicily undoubtedly suffer from the effects of the Mafia and organised crime despite recent efforts to clamp down on this by the Italian authorities.

Italians are very style conscious in their personal lives which means looking good both in terms of clothes, figure and personal cleanliness, and ensuring that gifts are of a high quality. This sense of style generates significant income for Italy in the fashion and household item industries. There is little public drunkenness since it gives no status even in youth culture.

Family

Family loyalties are very strong and Italians will never feel the same level of obligation to friends as they do to their family. They keep very close ties with their family, and children are likely to choose to live close to their parents. By UK standards Italian children, especially the boys, appear to be very spoiled. However from the Italian point of view, the British do not care about their children enough. Italy has the lowest divorce rate in the EU (apart from Ireland where divorce is only just becoming legal). This is partly due to the Catholic background and partly because divorce only recently became legal in Italy. Most of these comments apply to the rural and southern areas in particular since the urban areas are closer to the north European countries in their attitudes and habits.

Home

About 60 per cent of Italians own their own homes. Before they set up home Italians tend to live in large family apartments and so accommodation for single people is difficult to find. Italians are also quite happy to stay in the parental home and a survey in 1995 found that in the 25–34 age group 41 per cent of men and 26 per cent of women still lived with their parents. Lack of work and difficulties in finding accommodation also play a role in this finding. Italian homes are kept very clean and household appliances are regularly replaced on average every seven years. For those who can afford it furnishings will be of very high quality, otherwise homes are furnished very cheaply and it is only recently that the mid-market niche has been filled by companies such as IKEA.

Religion

Italy is the world's centre for Roman Catholicism with the Pope based in the Vatican City State in Rome. However the Italians themselves have been declining in religious adherence. Divorce was made legal relatively recently as was abortion, both strongly disapproved of by the Catholic Church.

Diet

Italy conforms to its stereotype in that pasta is indeed the staple diet accompanied by the usual meats of beef, pork and lamb. Italian cheese is an important ingredient; you may already know mozarella and parmesan. Another typically Mediterranean ingredient is the abundant use of olive oil both for cooking, dressings and as an alternative to butter on bread. Meals often start with antipasta, cold meats and salad. Italian ice cream is world renowned and Italy is the home of the pizza. The southern regions spice their food more. Italy is a major wine producing country although wine consumption is declining in favour of mineral water. Breakfast is not a substantial meal and traditionally lunch has been the main meal of the day with dinner being late, between 8 and 10 p.m.

Leisure

Individual pursuits are not common, with Italians favouring enjoying themselves in groups especially in bars, cafes and restaurants. Italians are avid sports spectators especially of football and motor racing but not keen sports participants except for cycling. They have a reputation for spending a great deal of time (and relative to other Europeans on similar incomes, money) shopping, particularly for clothes and accessories which should preferably be designer labels such as Georgio Armani, Gucci, Louis Vuitton and Rayban. They also spend more on live arts than other Europeans.

Arts

Italy has one of Europe's richest cultural heritages including architecture, art and opera which are all widely enjoyed but the state does not have the resources to conserve the vast number of buildings and art works found in Italy. Hence, for example, Venice, which is in danger of being overwhelmed by the sea, obtains a great deal of renovation support from abroad but other areas are neglected. Florence is the great art centre. Italian museums have recently been reformed to open seven days a week, introduce entry fees and provide additional services such as restaurants and souvenir shops. Italian films also have a very high standing world-wide and the Venice film festival in September is one of the big three, the other two being Cannes and Berlin.

Further information

- *Live and Work in Italy* by V Pybus and R Robinson, 1992, Vacation Work, Oxford
- Italian State Tourist Board, 1 Princes Street, London, W1R 8AY
- Internet addresses:
  Made in Italy about Italian design is at:
  http://www.flashnet.it/made.htm
  Trade-net Italy is at:
  http://www.tradenet.it/

Luxembourg

Main features

- One of the highest per capita incomes and lowest unemployment in the EU
- Highest proportion of immigrants in the EU
- 25 per cent of the workforce commutes in from outside its borders

Resources

Luxembourg's wealth was originally based on iron and steel using indigenous iron ore. This is still an important industry but it has been modernised and the country now derives its wealth from a variety of sources in addition to this, including agriculture, light manufacturing and, best known perhaps, banking and insurance. It is also one of the bases for the European Parliament and European Commission, institutions which attract a great many foreigners as workers.

Land

Luxembourg has no coast and is wedged between Belgium, France and Germany. Tourists visit the north and Ardennes region which are hilly and wooded. The remainder is wooded farmland and the Moselle valley in the south-east is a vineyard area. Forest covers 20 per cent of the land area and 44 per cent is used for agriculture.

Climate

Cold and wet in the winter, warm summers, generally similar to southern Britain.

Language

Lëtzebuergesch is the official language since 1984 but it is mainly an oral language, little used for writing, when French and German are used instead. Most natives are therefore trilingual. German is the language of instruction at school. French predominates in bars, restaurants, commerce, parliament and the courts; German in newspapers, magazines and television. Another consideration is that a third of the inhabitants of Luxembourg are immigrants, largely from Latin language countries, especially Italy and Portugal, so they find it easier to communicate in French rather than German.

Telecoms

The sophisticated phone system is highly developed and efficient but business suffers from a lack of international lines. Mobile phone coverage is national. Overall the telecommunications system comes not far behind that of the UK's.

Other links

Luxembourg is on the route of the express train between Belgium and Switzerland. Rail and bus services are fully integrated although the rail network is not very extensive. Travel in the capital is slow due to the narrow cobbled streets and lack of parking space. It has one small international airport.

Trade flows

Luxembourg's main trading partners are Germany, Belgium and France.
Major exports: finished steel products, chemicals, glass, plastics and rubber.
Major imports: minerals, metals, foodstuffs and quality consumer goods.
The DTI has identified the following as good opportunities for UK exporters to Luxembourg:

- environment
- soil decontamination
- telecoms.

Education

Compulsory school

For the 4–15 year age group. Most schools are in the state sector. Most of the private schools are Roman Catholic and all are state-subsidised. Entry to the two types of secondary school at 12 years old is determined according to exam results at the end of primary school. High performers go to the lycee whilst most of the rest go to the lycee technique. For those unable to get the required grade there is a three-year post primary option during which pupils can improve their performance to get into the lycee technique or leave at 15 to go to work. The lycee technique prepares its students for a variety of jobs but its strengths lie in preparation for banking, agriculture and engineering, three important economic activities in Luxembourg.

The lycee technique also runs two apprentice systems during which a student's time is divided between school study and on the job training. One system is for the completion of an apprenticeship within a certain period whereas the other is open-ended with students completing modules as they become ready.

Qualification at 18

Examen de fin d'etudes secondaires (lycee); bac technique, diplome de fin d'etudes secondaires technique, diplome de technicien (from the lycee technique) or certificate of professional aptitude (apprentices).

There is no university in Luxembourg as its population is too small to support even one, although a foundation year is available at Centre Universitaire de Luxembourg. The only other higher education possibilities are in teaching and engineering.

Training and skills

There is a skill shortage in Luxembourg. The small economy is vulnerable to economic change if it becomes too dependent on one sector. Previously, success was built on the iron and steel industry which then declined. Currently the Duchy has an international reputation in financial services which may be under threat if EU directives on reducing secrecy in banking are agreed. The government therefore decided that it ought to promote high-tech and knowledge-based activities in a systematic way and has identified the skills needed for this. This has necessitated close collaboration with foreign universities to which Luxembourg students must go.

20 days training leave in any two-year period is available to those under 25 to complete vocational courses. There are government schemes to retrain workers faced with redundancy. Apprenticeships are organised in different ways: either a one- or two-year full-time course followed by in-company experience, or three years of on the job experience with eight hours of college work a week. For unemployed young people under 30, work experience contracts are available.

Employer involvement

Employee training is lacking in small and medium-sized firms. A professional institute of continuing education has been set up to address this problem. Employers taking on young people under the work experience scheme must pay them 85 per cent of the minimum wage for unskilled persons.

Employment conditions

Contract of employment

This should include working hours, duration of the contract and any trial period which applies, initial salary, periodic salary increases and overtime.

Public holidays

10 days – January 1, Easter Monday, May 1, Ascension Day, Whit Monday, June 23 (National Day), August 15 (Assumption), November 1 (All Saints Day), December 25 and 26. Dates falling on a Sunday are moved to the following Monday. There are additional dates in February, March and November when shops and businesses often close although these are not official public holidays.

Paid holiday

25 days plus special leave in the case of marriage, birth or death of a close relative.

Working hours

40 hours a week and an employer must obtain official permission before requiring overtime.

Minimum wages

These are statutory and dependent on age, marital status and whether you have had training.

Working practices

Normal office hours are 8.30 a.m. – 6 p.m. with two hours for lunch starting at noon. The main holiday period is July/August.

Use of information technology

Luxembourg is slightly less computerised than the UK.

Mobility

The problem in Luxembourg tends to be that of labour shortages rather than mobility especially since the longest distance between any two places in the country is less than 40 miles. There is therefore a high percentage of cross border commuting from France, Belgium and Germany as well as a large (about 30 per cent) resident immigrant community of other EU nationals.

Tax

Income tax varies from 15 per cent on low incomes to a top rate of 50 per cent. Local government charges a tax based on the value of property to pay for local services. VAT is 15 per cent but taxation generally in the Grand Duchy is low.

Social security

Unemployment benefit is funded through supplementary income tax and a special unemployment tax which entitles contributors (up to a limit) to draw 80 per cent of their former salary for up to 12 months. There is a state run old age pension scheme from which no-one can opt out although they are free to top it up with private schemes. Family allowances and some health charges are also paid such as prescriptions, doctors' and dentists' fees.

Trade unions

Luxembourg is heavily unionised with around 50 per cent membership. There is a good record of co-operation between the trade unions and employers. Companies with more than 15 employees must have employee representatives and those with over 150 employees must have a works council which considers working conditions, job stability and grading, can give advice to management and can summon an external inspector if a problem cannot be overcome.

Equal opportunities

Men and women are guaranteed equal access to education, employment and vocational training. Women have protection when pregnant with entitlement to resume their former employment up to a year after the end of maternity leave. There is a 3 per cent quota of jobs which must be reserved for workers who have become disabled (defined as a 30 per cent or more reduction in their working capacity).

Health and safety

Luxembourg has the usual range of health and safety regulations. The Work and Mines Inspectorate has the power to enter any premises unannounced and may require the elimination of dangerous practices even if this means closure and evacuation of the works.

Medical care

Although hospital facilities are state-run, financing of the health service is private through insurance schemes. The standard of care is high.

Culture

Luxembourg is such a small country that there is little which is typical of the Grand Duchy. On the other hand this does mean that the Luxemburgers are receptive to foreign influences. Luxembourg is closely linked with Belgium economically in that they share a common currency. Belgium has its own Luxembourg region and the Belgian Ardennes continues into Luxembourg. Luxemburgers are often mistaken for Germans which they find irritating.

Family

Luxemburgers tend to live in nuclear family units rather than the extended family more common further south in Europe. The very large proportion of career immigrants in banking and EU administration tend to be young with few, if any, children and no other family ties. Marriage rates have increased in the Grand Duchy.

Home

The option of buying a plot of land on which to build is very popular but only 33 per cent are home owners because there is a serious housing shortage. The homes, whether owned or rented, are furnished to a very high standard and ownership of household appliances is among the highest in Europe.

Religion

Luxembourg is 97 per cent Catholic although a low number attend church regularly. The remainder are mainly Protestant.

Diet

Luxembourg cooking could be described as German quantities with French quality. There are a few Luxembourg specialities. Pork is a favoured meat rather than being regarded as a poor substitute for beef or lamb as it is in many other European countries. The white wines from the Moselle valley are highly regarded and often served with pike fish caught in the river. Luxembourg also produces a strong lager type beer.

Leisure

National Day, June 23, is an occasion for fireworks and festivities but otherwise Luxemburgers go in for private and quiet entertainment. Various games and sports are popular and the most common way of enjoying them is to join a relevant club.

Luxemburgers also derive satisfaction from the responsibilities which go with club administration. Football and skittles clubs are the most numerous followed by table tennis and fishing. Most Luxemburgers take their holiday abroad.

Arts

There is little that is indigenous but active support for the arts results in many museums, exhibitions, galleries and performances. Luxemburgers like classical music in all its forms and towns will often have their own choir or band. Foreign tourists are attracted by the many fine medieval castles and other buildings dotted around the countryside. Luxembourg was European City of Culture in 1995. The old city of Luxembourg has been added to UNESCO's list of heritage sites of world importance.

Further information

- *Live and Work in Belgium, The Netherlands and Luxembourg*, A de Vries and G Adams, 1992, Vacation Work
- *Living in Luxembourg*, twice yearly magazine available from the embassy
- *Doing Business in Luxembourg*, Price Waterhouse, 1990 (with 1993 update supplement)
- Internet address giving access to a variety of Luxembourg pages is: http://www.restena.lu/other/luxservers.html

Netherlands

Main features

- An attractive European distribution centre, based around Rotterdam, the world's biggest port
- Highest population density in the world
- World's largest exporter of dairy and horticultural products especially potted plants and cut flowers

Resources

The Netherlands has few natural resources with the exception of Rotterdam which has become Europe's largest port. The Dutch have therefore become strong in trading and related services such as distribution. The Dutch have sought to extend what few resources they had by land reclamation and protection against the sea which has been going on for hundreds of years and in which the Dutch have unrivalled expertise. This skill they export to the rest of the world and it may be of critical relevance in other areas now that global warming is expected to raise sea levels so that other countries will be seeking protection from the encroaching sea. The Netherlands does have large gas reserves from the North Sea. Otherwise its major resource is its agricultural land.

Land

The Netherlands is famously flat, although there is a hilly area in the south close to the German and Belgian borders. Much of it is below sea-level which causes problems with salt encroachment and the potential for flooding. The densest canal network in Europe is as much to control the water level as it is to provide a means of transport. Freight is also carried on the Maas, Scheldt and Rhine, all major rivers. There is very little wooded area (8 per cent) and most is agricultural (54 per cent) used for food crops, livestock and horticultural products (especially cut flowers such as roses and tulips). The land area of the Netherlands has been increased by a quarter through large-scale land reclamation projects in the sixties which created the new area of Flevoland. A notable geographical feature is the Randstad, the name given to the ring of towns formed by The Hague, Amsterdam and Rotterdam, to emphasise that this is virtually one continuous urban area rather than a series of discrete towns and cities.

Climate

The climate is temperate, maritime and very changeable. It is often wet and windy.

Language

Dutch is the official language. Frisian is spoken by a small and declining number of people in the northern province of Friesland. English is very widely spoken followed by German and French.

Telecoms

Overall, Dutch phone tariffs are the lowest in Europe. The telecoms system has recently been converted to a fibre optics network. ISDN is available as well as many other high-tech services including satellite link-up giving the telecoms service a huge potential far in excess of what is needed today which should enable it to cope with all the upcoming telecoms services such as electronic data and money exchange. As a leading distribution centre, the Netherlands offers some advanced integrated telecoms services exchanging information between shippers and hauliers, shippers and customs and excise, and matching supply and demand for air cargo. All these reduce transport costs. In addition, most households are linked up to cable TV.

Other links

There is a well maintained road system with good facilities for bicycles in towns. The Netherlands also has a highly efficient and reasonably priced rail network. A cargo-only line is to be built running from Rotterdam to the German border to encourage freight off the roads and to maintain Rotterdam's pre-eminence as the main port of entry for mainland Europe. This should be complete by 2005. Schipol airport near Amsterdam is an important European hub and is requesting a fifth runway to cope with traffic. The Netherlands has the densest canal and waterway network in Europe which is extensively used in trade especially in conjunction with the port at Rotterdam (Europoort).

Trade flows

The Netherlands trades mainly with Germany, Belgium, Luxembourg, the UK, France, the USA and Italy.

Major exports: machinery, transport equipment, chemicals, live animals, raw materials, manufactured articles, mineral fuels and food.

Major imports: machinery, transport equipment, basic manufactures, manufactured articles, mineral fuels, food, live animals and raw materials.

The DTI has identified the following as good opportunities for UK exporters to the Netherlands:

- building materials
- biotechnology

- career and workwear, quality adult clothing
- computer software and services
- furniture
- packaging
- telecoms.

Education

Compulsory school

For the 5–16 year age group and part-time education until 18. Approximately 75 per cent of Dutch secondary schools are private but state subsidised hence there is a great choice from the academic schools (gymnasium, athenaeum and VWO) leading to university on completion at 18, to the junior general or vocational secondary schools which in four years prepare their students for senior vocational secondary school leading in turn to higher vocational education. The type of secondary school chosen at 13 or 14 years old depends on the results of a transition year at 12.

Qualification at 18

VWO certificate for entry to university; MBO vocational certificate leading to middle management jobs.

Training and skills

In the early 1990s the Labour Ministry identified ten growth sectors including telecommunications, medical technology, environment technology, transport, information technology, agriculture and the service sector. Emphasis was put on these sectors in vocational education by increasing the number of apprenticeships and training places and by investment in appropriate technology to deliver training in these areas. The apprenticeship-training option can be started at 16 on successful completion of the junior secondary course (either general or vocational). It lasts three to five years, alternating school with on the job experience.

In anticipation of increased student mobility in the Single Market, the Dutch government made sure that there was appropriate information available on higher education in the Netherlands and the rest of the EU as well as making sure that there would be enough accommodation and health care for the foreign students in addition to places in the educational establishments themselves.

The Dutch government has recently started a Dutch open university which gives adults a second chance since no qualification is required to start a degree course in contrast to the other Dutch universities which require a satisfactory secondary education record.

Employer involvement

Dutch companies invest a great deal in training with, for example, one in four employees having received some form of training during the preceding year (from a study carried out in the mid-eighties). State financial aid is available to employers covering wages, travelling and course costs for approved training. Subsidies are available for groups of companies providing joint training programmes. In its recent overhaul of school-based vocational education employers participated in decisions on changes to course content and teaching methods. Employers co-ordinate the educational and on the job training sections of apprenticeships through 31 industry bodies which also set and mark apprentice exams and monitor apprentice contracts.

Employment conditions

Contract of employment

Those under 18 need parental approval before entering into a contract of employment which can be oral or in writing. However, an employee must receive details of notice periods, any restrictions after termination of employment and disciplinary regulations in writing.

Public holidays

Nine days – January 1, Good Friday and Easter Monday, April 30 (Queen's birthday), May 5 (Liberation Day), Ascension Day, Whit Monday, December 25 and 26.

Paid holiday

20 days a year.

Working hours

39 hours a week average with 48 hours a week the legal maximum. A shorter, part-time day is available as unpaid parental leave to look after young children under the age of six.

Minimum wages

Statutory minima apply to workers over 23 years old. Dutch minimum wages are high in comparison to other Member States.

Working practices

Normal office hours are 8.30 a.m.–5 p.m. with a short break for lunch. The main holiday period is mid-July to August.

Use of information technology

The Netherlands rates slightly below the UK in this aspect. A large effort has been made to upgrade the equipment and expertise of teachers and trainers in IT as it was felt that this was a bottleneck to high-tech development.

Mobility

Job mobility has increased and it was estimated that 15 per cent of people changed jobs in 1993. Preference is usually given to internal promotion rather than external recruitment. Dutch vocational qualifications give employees a broad enough introduction to their chosen industrial sector for employees to be mobile within their companies.

Tax

Taxable income is charged at 38.55 per cent (13 per cent tax and 25.55 per cent social security premiums) on approximately the first £13,500 of income. The rate increases to 50 per cent and 60 per cent for higher incomes.

Local taxes are payable on the value of property owned.

VAT is 18.5 per cent standard rate and 6 per cent on necessities such as food, medicine, newspapers and public transport. There is also an annual wealth tax of 0.8 per cent payable on the value of most of what you own.

Social security

Contributions are high but so is the level of benefit. The system provides for support in the event of sickness (70 per cent of salary), disability and unemployment (70 per cent of salary) as well as providing an old age pension.

Trade unions

Trade union membership is relatively low at 30 per cent of the workforce. Unions tend to divide on political and religious lines. There is a good working relationship between unions, employers and government. Employers with over 35 employees must set up a works council to discuss matters such as a merger, closure, relocation or major restructuring.

Equal opportunities

There is legislation to prevent discrimination on the basis of gender, marital status and ethnic origin. In addition there is a requirement to employ a quota of between 3 and 7 per cent of staff from those registered disabled but in practice most employers do not meet this requirement.

Female participation rate has been lower in the Netherlands than in many other Member States although the figure is rising now. There is therefore no real history of women in the workplace and they have not risen to senior positions in any great numbers yet.

An attempt to help the employment of certain racial minorities was enacted in 1995 but looked unlikely to succeed. According to the new law, employers of over 35 employees were meant to take on Turks, Moroccans and Ethiopians amongst others, in proportion to their numbers in the local community. Employers resented the amount of paperwork that it created whilst representatives for the minorities objected that it did not cover Dutch born minorities or very small minorities such as Palestinians.

Health and safety

Employers have a legal duty to promote and ensure the health, safety and welfare of their employees by ensuring that relevant information is available, that duties are assigned according to ability and capacity, and to avoid monotonous work where possible.

Employees unhappy that an employer is not meeting his legal duties may call on the labour inspectorate, health and safety committee, works council or union to intervene. Additionally, workers have the right to stop work without loss of pay if they deem the situation poses a serious and immediate danger to their physical well-being.

Companies with over 500 employees must set up a safety department and those with over 750 employees must offer medical services.

Medical care

The health care system is divided into two. The state provides preventative care such as education, research, immunisation and screening for cervical cancers and heart problems for example. Medication and treatment are provided through a system of private health insurance schemes which are compulsory above a certain income.

Culture

The Dutch pride themselves on their tolerance and independence of spirit which is the reason why the Netherlands had some of the most relaxed drug laws in Europe although this is changing now that the problems of such an approach have become apparent. The Dutch tend to divide on religious rather than class lines, with those of the same religion having their own sports clubs, schools, hospitals, unions, political parties and TV stations.

Family

The family is very important and although you are unlikely to find more than two generations living in one house, the rest of the family are likely to live nearby. Otherwise Dutch society mirrors closely the situation in the UK with fewer children, increasing divorce rates and a willingness to set up home together without getting married.

Home

The Dutch like to spend a great deal of their leisure time at home and these therefore tend to be maintained to a high standard. 54 per cent of Dutch adults own their own home. Houses are filled with plants and flowers to a much greater extent than in other Member States.

Religion

The Dutch are made up of 35 per cent Catholics, 19 per cent Dutch Protestant church and 7 per cent of other Protestant groups. Although attendance is low many people define themselves through their religion by attending church run institutions in education, health and politics.

Diet

The Dutch diet is similar to ordinary British food of the meat and two veg variety. Bread and potatoes are staples. Breakfast is bread with cheese, cold meats and jam. Beer is the preferred drink and strong coffee is also widely drunk. The main meal of the day is a relatively early dinner between 6 and 7 p.m. As a result of immigration from Indonesia, the Netherlands' former colony, Indonesian restaurants are widespread.

Leisure

The Dutch are amongst the highest spenders in the EU, along with the Danes and Germans, on leisure. Some of this is spent on frequent holidays abroad (often camping or in a caravan), in contrast, say, to the French and Spanish who are happy to holiday within their own country. The rest is spent at home entertaining family or friends, reading, watching TV or using multi-media products rather than going for a night on the town, an option which is really only available in Amsterdam and Rotterdam. Otherwise the Dutch are great sports enthusiasts both as spectators and participants. Football is popular as are tennis, cycling and angling. In a cold winter, ice-skating on the many canals is a favourite pastime whereas in summer all kinds of water sports involving the use of boats are preferred.

Arts

The Dutch have an illustrious artistic history with paintings by Hieronymus Bosch, Rembrandt and van Gogh commanding some of the highest prices in the world. In modern times Escher's optical illusions achieved world-wide fame and are featured on endless products such as cards, jigsaws and T-shirts. The Netherlands is also famous for Delft pottery. The Dutch government offers wide ranging support for the arts, for example, in the widespread number of galleries and museums to be found all over the country and in the project grants given to present day artists. If public support for a government sponsored project is low then the subsidy is withdrawn. The public has increasingly had to pay for artistic events with those on low incomes subsidised where needed. Many cultural festivals are held annually, usually during the summer and often featuring jazz music which is especially popular in the Netherlands.

Further information

- *Live and Work in Belgium, the Netherlands and Luxembourg*, A de Vries and G Adams, 1992, Vacation Work
- Internet address:
  The Dutch Yellow Pages:
  http://www.markt.nl/dyp/index-en.html

Portugal

Main features

- Portugal includes the islands of Madeira and the Azores
- A high proportion employed in agriculture (12 per cent in 1994)
- Receives massive funding from the EU for infrastructure projects

Resources

Fishing off the Atlantic is an important resource. Portugal also has extensive cork forests and tungsten, iron ore, uranium and marble. The climate attracts many foreign tourists.

Land

Portugal is mountainous north of the River Tagus, with rolling plains in the south. 44 per cent of the land is used for agriculture and 40 per cent is woodland.

Climate

Cooler and wetter than Spain due to the influence of the Atlantic ocean but very pleasant. There is a north–south divide climatically as it is warmer and drier in the south.

Language

Portuguese with no minority languages. Compared with their near neighbours, the Spaniards, the urban Portuguese are much better linguists. Spanish is easy to understand for all Portuguese and many also speak either French or English.

Telecoms

Portugal Telecom is the state monopoly, already 25 per cent privately owned and due to be privatised in line with EU requirements. The system has been extensively modernised and all lines are capable of high-speed data transmission but there are still rural areas without services. In 1995 Portugal was making the greatest investment in its telephone system proportionate to GDP than any other EU country. Access to private telephones is relatively low so telemarketing, for example, would be difficult. Virtually the whole of Portugal is accessible by mobile telephone, which can also be used to communicate with all other Member States (except Austria), the EEA and Turkey, Hungary, Latvia and Estonia.

Other links

Great improvements have been made to the road system with the help of EU funds but there are still many rural areas badly served by roads, still less by railways. Ox carts are a common form of transport still in many parts of Portugal. Links between Portugal and Spain have been especially poor in the past as relations between the two countries were never that warm and Portugal looked to the sea as its main route to the outside world. The pace of development of basic infrastructure continues to be very rapid as Portugal has secured a further large amount of EU funding until 1999 under the ESF, ERDF and Cohesion Funds.

Trade flows

Main trading partners are Germany, France and the UK.

Major exports: clothing, textiles, footwear, pulp, waste paper and chemicals.
Major imports: motor vehicles, textile yarn, mineral fuels and foodstuffs.

The DTI has identified the following as good opportunities for UK exporters to Portugal:

- vehicle components and accessories
- building materials
- roads/bridges
- gas distribution equipment
- pollution control equipment and waste management
- rail components
- telecoms
- Expo '98 (a trade fair in 1998 to showcase European products).

Education

Compulsory school

For the 6–15 year age group. Schooling is common up to the age of 16 when a choice can be made between an academic route, which includes some basic vocational training, or a more vocational course, successful completion of which entitles the student to continue onto higher education. Efforts have been made to make the teaching style more active. The content of secondary education is also available as an evening course although the certificate gained is slightly different. A more intensive vocational education can be gained by leaving school at 16 and attending a specialist vocational college. After one college year and six months' work experience, a vocational certificate is achieved. Alternatively students can take the three-year option which gives them a technical certificate as well as the chance to go on to higher education. However, in the academic year beginning September 1995, 60 per cent of qualified applicants were rejected from the state universities through lack of places.

Qualification at 18

Certificado de fim de Estudo Secundarios.

Training and skills

Portugal has a poor literacy rate with 20 per cent illiteracy. These are mainly elderly females but it indicates the need to upgrade the skills of the adult population. After extensive reforms to the education system the young should now have access to an effective preparation for working life having been rated the worst in the EU by business in 1995 (with the UK second worst). The European Social Fund has disbursed large sums to help upgrade Portugal's education and training system both for children and adults. Distance learning, secondary education through evening classes and adult education are all available but concentrate on those under 45 years of age. An open university was created in 1988 although so far it concentrates on training for teachers. Employees have a legal right to educational leave of five to six hours a week. Special training schemes have been developed to help the disabled and women returners to work.

Employer involvement

Apprenticeships are available where the pay is a fraction of the minimum wage and the apprentice combines on the job training with attendance at a vocational training centre. Those between 14 and 24 are eligible to train as apprentices and the course lasts between one and four years. In 1990 only 1 per cent of 15/16 year olds were in such apprenticeship schemes. There is also a scheme of work experience for the young unemployed where the government pays 75 per cent of the minimum wage and the employer contributes the remaining 25 per cent. If the employer then decides to offer the trainee a job at the end of the nine-month scheme, the company will be paid a sum equivalent to 12 times the national wage in reward.

Foreign investors are used to help the training effort. For example, the new Ford-Volkswagen plant at Setubal south of Lisbon is one of the largest foreign investments ever in the country. Not only has it provided employment and business for suppliers but it has also provided much needed training for the suppliers.

Employment conditions

Contract of employment
These have made employees almost impossible to sack, which is further compounded by the lack of a statutory retirement age in Portugal. Increasing use is therefore being made of temporary contracts and early redundancy. Ordinary indefinite term contracts need not be in writing.

Public holidays
13 days – January 1, Shrove Tuesday (can be February or March), Good Friday, April 25 (Day of Liberty), May 1 (Labour Day), Whit (May/June), June 10 (Portugal National Day), August 15 (Assumption), October 5 (Republic Day), November 1 (All Saints' Day), December 1 (Restoration Day), December 8 (Immaculate Conception), December 25. There are also various local holidays.

Paid holiday
21 working days in addition to which an extra month's pay must be paid (the 13th month).

Working hours
40 hours a week.

Minimum wages
These are set but are very low.

Working practices
Normal office hours are 9 a.m.–1 p.m. and 3 p.m.–7 p.m. with two hours for lunch. The main holiday period is August.

Use of information technology
Portugal has a long way to go to catch up with the leading Member States in this respect.

Mobility
Training is acknowledged by Portuguese companies to increase job mobility. There has always been a degree of geographical mobility in that the male head of household has often left the family home to find work elsewhere in Portugal or abroad. Otherwise there is relatively low inter-regional mobility.

Tax
Income tax is payable at 25 per cent of the first £7000–£18,000 (after deduction of personal allowances) and thereafter at 40 per cent.

Local taxes: there is a property tax of 0.8–1.3 per cent based on the rentable value of the property.

VAT is 17 per cent standard rate, 30 per cent for luxury goods and 8 per cent for basic items such as food, wine, beer and educational materials.

Social security

Portugal has a social security system similar to other Member States with contributions payable both by the employer (14.5 per cent) and employee (11 per cent). This covers health care, pensions, sickness, unemployment, invalidity and maternity/paternity benefits. Sickness benefit amounts to 65 per cent of average earnings, whilst pensions are paid at £80 per month. Health insurance deductions are automatically made from salary.

Trade unions

Under the Salazar regime there was no right to strike but this has been restored and greatly used by public sector employees since Portuguese workers have a great deal to complain about including low wages and, in the past, non-payment of wages. The unions are included in consultations with employers and the government on training needs and in some cases set up courses themselves. In addition to trade union representation in the workplace, any employee may ask to establish a workers' committee. Union density is estimated at around 30 per cent.

Equal opportunities

The Portuguese constitution forbids discrimination on the grounds of sex, race, country of origin, ideology or religious belief. An employer may not arbitrarily discriminate between employees as regards their terms and conditions of employment, nor treat employees more or less favourably on the grounds of sex, religion, political affiliation or union membership. There is specific labour legislation to prohibit sexual discrimination which covers much the same circumstances as UK law.

Women have made great progress in Portugal since the end of the Salazar government in 1974 which restricted their job opportunities. It is the quality of job which is improving rather than the female participation rate which has always been high in Portugal but with women mainly working in agriculture. Now over half of university graduates are women. Legislation exists to ensure equal treatment of men and women in employment but the position of women remains poor especially in the rural areas. Women are still 75 per cent less likely to receive training than men.

Health and safety

A recent law has improved the way in which hazards are monitored including the identification of hazardous substances and procedures, accident reporting procedures and better safety training.

Medical care

Treatment, including dentistry, and medicines are free but service could be much improved and waiting lists are significantly longer than in the UK NHS. However there is now a commitment by the state service to pay for treatment in private facilities if public facilities cannot admit the patient within three months. Many Portuguese take out private health insurance.

Culture

The Portuguese are generally reckoned to be very hospitable, polite and friendly. They cannot, as a rule, be considered with the Spanish and are offended when Spain and Portugal are considered together. Many aspects of Portuguese life derive from its sea-going history such as diet and music. The Portuguese share, with the Spanish, traces of Islamic rule which ended 500 years ago.

Family

Family links have long been very important in Portugal but were even more so during the period of rule by the Salazar political regime which ended in 1974. The repression experienced by the Portuguese then meant that only family and close friends could be relied on for support. This does not mean that strangers and foreigners are unwelcome since Portugal has a long seafaring history and many Portuguese in more recent times have had to go abroad to earn a living so the Portuguese are quite outward looking, being enthusiastic supporters of the EU. As in Spain, children are greatly indulged and often looked after by their grandparents while the parents work. Women tend to play a traditional role in Portuguese society. The Portuguese get married at an earlier age than in any other Member State.

Home

There is a housing shortage in Portugal and only 40 per cent of Portuguese own their own homes. Since rents are high in comparison to earnings this means that children tend to live with their parents until they get married and often also for the first few years of marriage. There are still a significant number of Portuguese homes without electricity or mains water in rural areas. Homes also tend to be small by European standards. The Portuguese would rather spend their money on household appliances than holidays.

Religion

Mainly Roman Catholic (97 per cent). A large number of fiestas are part of Portuguese life and these usually have some religious connection.

Diet

Fish plays an important part and dishes are based on fresh fish, shellfish and spiced meats. Poultry is the favoured meat. Portugal is also a major wine producer hence wine is an accompaniment to many meals. Port also originates from Portugal. Meals are early compared to their Spanish neighbours, lunch beginning at 11.30 a.m. or noon and dinner at about 7 p.m. There are many regular markets from which to buy fresh food and there is much less branded food in Portugal than in northern Europe.

Leisure

Many tourists visit Portugal to play golf and tennis but for the Portuguese their social life revolves around meals taken with family and close friends rather than organised clubs or participation sports. Only 18 per cent take foreign holidays with Spain the most popular destination. The middle class may have a holiday home nearby. Football is followed as a spectator sport with great fervour. Cafes are popular but frequented almost exclusively by men.

Arts

Portugal is well known for its fado music, sad songs expressing the hope of returning home, derived initially from its strong sea-going tradition and still relevant today when many Portuguese work away from Portugal in northern Europe. It also has a very distinctive architectural style, the Manueline, which you can see in almost every small town. Very common is tile art which you can see on many houses and other buildings such as railway stations. Portuguese folk art and style is much in evidence in the goods found on sale in the many regular fairs and markets. These include patterned colourful ceramics, painted or glazed earthenware, osier and straw painting, blankets, bedspreads, cast iron objects, copper and brass work, wood carvings, objects made from cork, skins or leather and lace embroidery.

Further information

- *Live and Work in Spain and Portugal*, R Robinson and V Pybus, 1991, Vacation Work
- Internet address:
  http://www.lusodoc.pt/Portugal/portugal.html

Spain

Main features

- Economic success is concentrated in the north and east
- The regions of Spain have regained a great deal of legal and political power from central government
- High unemployment

Resources

Spain has coal and natural gas reserves and hydropower but these do not meet all its energy requirements. Other mineral deposits include uranium, zinc, lead and copper. The climate could be counted as a resource since it is the major attraction for the millions of tourists who generate almost 10 per cent of Spain's income per year.

Land

As well as mainland Spain the country includes the Balearic Islands (Majorca, Menorca and Ibiza) and the Canary Islands (Tenerife, Gran Canaria and Lanzarote) and four small strips on the North African coast (such as Ceuta). Spain is the highest and most mountainous EU country. The main physical feature of Spain is the central plateau divided by mountain ranges (sierras). Agriculture covers 62 per cent of the land and 31 per cent is wooded.

Climate

Spain experiences a diversity of climates because its terrain includes very high mountains such as the Pyrenees to sea level, and there is also a considerable distance separating north from south. The central plateau has the most extreme variation from 4°C in winter with snow and ice to the searing heat of summer which can reach 40°C. Rainfall is similarly variable with a wet north and a dry south where drought has been a problem for several years now both for farmers and individuals. The Canary Islands have a tropical climate while the rest of Spain is broadly Mediterranean.

Language

Castilian (i.e. Spanish) is the official language across the country but in the Basque country, Catalonia and Galicia, their three native languages are in common usage. The language of the region in addition to Spanish is a compulsory part of the school curriculum.

Telecoms

Spain has the lowest number of phones per capita in Europe and it can take several months to have a new line installed. Line installation and call charges are some of the most expensive in Europe. The mobile telephone system can reach 98 per cent of the population over 90 per cent of the Spanish land area but only 0.6 per cent of the population use it. ISDN coverage is patchy, concentrated on the major centres of population but improving.

Other links

Like the UK, but much more so, the Spanish road and rail system centres on its capital, Madrid. Madrid is in the middle of the country but this still makes links between other industrial cities and neighbouring countries, France and Portugal, less direct. A great deal has been spent by both the EU and the Spanish government in upgrading the road system, for example, to ensure that agricultural produce can be sold at peak freshness. Much still remains to be done especially in the south.

Trade flows

Main trading partners are the USA, Germany, France and the UK.

Major exports: motor cars, machinery, vegetable products, iron and steel goods, tourism.

Major imports: mineral fuels, petroleum products and iron and steel goods.

The DTI has identified the following as good opportunities for UK exporters to Spain:

- airport development
- pollution control equipment
- food and drink
- telecoms.

Education

Compulsory school

For the 6–16 year age group. Student centred learning and greater choice have been encouraged under recent educational reforms as progress previously depended on the grade obtained at the end of primary school at 14. Secondary school is either academic or vocational and there is free choice between the two types as long as a certain standard is reached in primary school. Those failing to obtain a place at secondary schools are offered youth training. Otherwise, three-quarters go on to the academic secondary schools and the rest on to vocational schools. Secondary education is complete after four years when students are assessed by internal examinations. Unsatisfactory progress may result in a year being repeated. Those wishing to go to university take the university entrance exam set by the university of their choice. There are virtually no national exams in Spain. The academic schools have been reformed to offer a balance between academic and vocational skills. Almost 20 per cent of schools are private, some of them receiving state support.

Completion of the first two years of vocational secondary school entitles pupils to the title of technician whilst those continuing on to the advanced level for two or three years earn the title of higher technician and are then entitled to go on to university. The European Social Fund helps to finance a work experience programme for those on the advanced vocational course. These programmes have become very popular and have replaced traditional apprenticeships.

Qualification at 17

Internal school assessment gives right to the title bachiller and the option to move to university preparation or advanced vocational courses. 35 per cent of 18 year olds go on to professional training (including university).

Training and skills

Educational reforms in 1990 introduced distance learning, adult education and basic skills education and also sought to improve and update the training available since this had been weak. During the 1980s the number of workers with intermediate qualifications increased by 100 per cent and the number with higher qualifications increased by 50 per cent. But these are spectacular increases from a low start and in 1991

only 30 per cent of Spain's workforce over 25 had some post-compulsory school training or education compared to 70 per cent in Denmark and Germany.

Employer involvement

60 per cent of training is delivered by employers helped financially by government subsidies and a reduction in employer social security contributions. A further 23 per cent of
training occurs through apprenticeships and the government promotes training through
specialised technical colleges. Spanish law makes provision for facilities, educational
leave and financial assistance for lifelong training and recognises the right to training
and career progression. Employers must now pay a training levy which helps to finance
the state support given to training. State support to training is distributed according to
an annual plan which sets out what training will be offered based on an assessment of
labour market needs made by the state, employers and trade unions together.

Employment conditions

Contract of employment

This is usually for an indefinite period which has contributed to the inflexibility of
labour in Spain. Written contracts of employment are not required but should cover
duties, length of contract, pay, hours, holidays and social security payments and often
includes a trial period. There are also special contracts for seasonal, trial period, training, part-time and temporary work.

Public holidays

14 days (12 national and two varying according to region) – January 1, January 6
(Epiphany), March 19 (St Joseph), Good Friday, May 1, Ascension, June 29 (St Peter),
July 25 (St James), August 15 (Assumption), October 12 (Colombus Day), November 1
(All Saints'), December 25.

Paid holiday

30 days including Saturdays and Sundays (equivalent to about 21 working days).

Working hours

40 per week which is also the legal maximum with a maximum of 80 hours overtime
per year which must be paid at a minimum rate of 175 per cent of the normal hourly
rate.

Minimum wages

These are legally set.

Working practices

Normal office hours are 9 a.m.–2 p.m. and 4.30 p.m.–8.30 p.m. with two hours plus for
lunch in order to accommodate the afternoon nap (siesta). This work pattern avoids the
worst heat of the day and in the south many organisations work what is known as the
intensive day starting early in the morning and working without a long break until 3
p.m. during the summer. Many large companies are going over to a more northern
European set of working hours. The main holiday period is July/August and school
starts again in mid-September for primary and the first week of October for secondary.
The school year lasts until the end of June.

Use of information technology

The application of electronic systems is rapidly increasing but is still a long way behind
the UK.

Mobility

Geographical mobility is low due to the importance of the family unit and mobility across job roles is high for unskilled jobs but low for professional jobs (i.e. a low incidence of accreditation of prior learning and experience).

Tax

Taxable income is anything above approximately £3500 after which income tax becomes payable at 10 per cent to 26 per cent. High incomes above about £45,000 are taxed at 56 per cent.

Social security contributions are compulsory and are a further 6 per cent of income.

Local taxes are based on the valuation of the property you live in (like the old UK rates system) but is fairly low.

VAT is 17 per cent standard rate, 33 per cent on cars, 6 per cent on basics such as fuel, books, medicines and food. There are various other taxes such as an additional 2 per cent income tax payable on the ratable value of your property.

Social security

The social security system provides high pensions (second only to Sweden), and also benefits for sickness, housing and unemployment, but not supplementary benefit once unemployment benefit (at 70 per cent of former salary) entitlement runs out after one or two years. Unemployment is the highest in the EU but since most of the unemployed are young people who have never had a job, they do not qualify for unemployment benefit so only approximately 50 per cent of the unemployed are in receipt of benefit. The remainder are meant to rely on their family for support.

Trade unions

All businesses with over 50 employees must have some form of worker representation whether by trade union or works council but they only have a consultative and advisory role. Trade unions were abolished by the authoritarian Franco regime, which ruled Spain between 1939 and 1975 and have only been legal again since 1977; hence membership is low at 16 per cent of the workforce. Pay and conditions negotiated by unions are the legal minimum for all workers in the relevant industry, trade or grade regardless of whether the workers are union members or not.

Equal opportunities

Since Spain became a democracy in the mid-seventies women's opportunities have advanced rapidly and there are now senior women in parliament, the police and universities.

The Workers' Statute of 1980 outlaws discrimination in employment on the grounds of sex, marital status, age, race, social status, religious belief, political opinion or trade union membership. Discrimination against the mentally or physically disabled is also illegal as long as the work would not be negatively affected by the disability. It is also illegal to discriminate against people who cannot speak the regional language in Catalonia, the Basque country and Galicia.

Positive action is taken in training and employment (by means of quotas or wage support) for women, the disabled, younger and older workers.

Health and safety

Employers and workers have various obligations under Spanish health and safety law including design and maintenance of work premises, use of machinery and tools, training in new methods and technologies, and medical examinations. Health and safety committees must be set up in organisations with over a 100 employees. The committee proposes measures to protect employees and has the authority to halt production if employees are in immediate serious danger.

Medical care

There is both a private and public health care system in Spain. The unemployed, young (under 18), pensioners or those on social security are entitled to free health care under the state system otherwise a contribution of 25 per cent of the costs must be met at the time of treatment. The state system now covers 97 per cent of the population where in 1982 it covered only 86 per cent. There are not enough state hospitals however so that waiting lists are long and it is for this reason that many people take out private health insurance in addition. Out patient and after care treatment are not highly rated.

Culture

Spain is a collection of very diverse regions but has a recent history of extreme centralisation in Madrid which is now beginning to reverse with the regions having more independence. There is a north–south divide with a more relaxed attitude in the south and a stronger entrepreneurial drive in the north. Spain had a period of Arab rule by Muslims ending 500 years ago and these effects are still apparent in aspects of Spain's culture such as its ancient monuments.

Family

Family is the paramount social unit in Spain and spans the generations to include the grandparents who may well be living with the next two generations. Children are greatly indulged by the whole family (which the British might see as 'spoiling'); this leads to confident adults although this confidence may not always be justified. Children do not tend to leave home until they get married. Divorce has only recently been allowed.

Home

Spaniards keep their homes scrupulously clean and spend a great deal on making the home attractive inside. 65 per cent own their own home. The focus of the home is the kitchen. Only family and close friends are invited into the home, other social contacts are made at bars. The Spaniards have until recently found modern, high-rise flats very attractive especially from a social point of view.

Religion

95 per cent of the population is Roman Catholic although church attendance whilst high, as elsewhere in Europe, is declining. However Catholicism forms the background to much of what goes on in Spain, for example the importance and frequency of fiestas. Spain has changed rapidly in the last 20 years from a strict, strongly religious and censored society to one where divorce, contraception and abortion are now legal, the status of women is rapidly rising and drug laws were relaxed for a time until the problems caused by this were recognised.

Diet

As in other matters, Spain shows a great diversity in eating habits mainly due to the different ingredients available throughout the country. The main meal of the day is a late dinner which can begin at 9 p.m. or later. Lunch could be tapas, several small samplers of Spanish dishes taken at about 2 p.m. Spanish food centres around dishes such as seafood, squid, paella (rice and seafood), gazpacho (cold tomato and pepper soup from Andalusia), and chorizo (smoked spicy sausage). Olive oil is the main fat used for cooking and salad dressings. Spanish wines are good quality and plentiful and the country is also known for its sherry.

Leisure

Social life centres around the bars where the whole family including the youngest children can be found eating out. The evening begins late to avoid the worst heat of the day. Bull fighting is very much part of Spanish life with fights being broadcast live on TV and the private lives of the star fighters featuring in the Spanish version of *Hello* magazine. Generally the Spanish spend much of their leisure time socialising informally rather than indulging in organised hobbies or sport.

Arts

There are many Spanish fiestas throughout the year and these serve as a focal point for activity for many weeks in advance of the event, to the exclusion of almost all other interests. Most have religious significance and the most spectacular are around Easter. Tourist interest in their fiestas is of secondary importance to the Spanish. Fiestas are more important in the south than in the north. Part of the fiesta tradition is flamenco dancing and music.

Spain has a world reputation in modern art such as Picasso and Salvador Dali. The Prado museum in Madrid is Spain's showcase for classical and modern art but does not have the space to display more than a small proportion of its store. Barcelona, Bilbao, Valencia and Seville are also great cultural centres in Spain with exhibitions and performances. There is currently great state support for the arts with ten new music auditoria being built throughout the country. Spain feared that the Single Market would result in the loss, through export, of many of its art treasures since it has a far greater store of valuable items than many other Member States, especially in its churches.

There are a great many impressive monuments to the Islamic period which can be visited such as the Alhambra in Granada.

Further information

- *Live and Work in Spain and Portugal*, R Robinson and V Pybus, 1991, Vacation Work
- Internet address:
  http://www.spaintour.com/

Sweden

Main features

- Taxation and welfare benefits are among the highest within the EU
- Relatively difficult access to markets
- Very diverse industrial production

Resources

Sweden's natural assets includes forestry which supplies a highly developed sawmill, pulp, paper and finished wood industry, 60 per cent of which is exported. Iron ore is mined in the far north and mainly exported. Hydro-electric power supplies 15 per cent of electricity.

Land

There is high land in Sweden but it is not as spectacular as in Norway. There are a great many lakes in Sweden and it has a very indented coastline. Most land is uncultivated and Swedish agriculture is concentrated in the south. Even so, Sweden is self-sufficient in basic foodstuffs with 6 per cent of Swedish land cultivated. Forestry covers 55 per cent of the land and is a major economic earner. Off the Swedish coast are hundreds of wooded islands. Northern Sweden is very sparsely populated, with mountain and forest. Inland central Sweden rises to mountains in the West where it borders Norway. The south and eastern area also has some hilly districts but is dominated by the fertile Skåne plains.

Climate

Sweden is very long on the north–south axis and therefore experiences a great difference in climate dependent on location. Average summer temperatures in the north are 13°C but 18°C in Stockholm in the south while in winter the north experiences average temperatures of −13°C and the south −3°C. There is a marked contrast in day length over the seasons with almost continuous daylight in the summer and vice versa during the winter. Winters are hard but continental so that floodlit winter sports are very popular.

Language

Swedish enables you to understand Norwegian and Danish and most Swedes speak English very well as their second language. In the north the Sami people speak their own language. Many other European languages are spoken since 15 per cent of the population are either immigrant or second generation immigrant.

Telecoms

Sweden is rated the second best telecoms system in the EU after Finland. It has the world's highest mobile phone ownership level at 10.9 per cent. A phone can be installed within five days.

Other links

Traffic is concentrated in the central and southern regions between Stockholm, Göteborg and Malmö. Seven trans-European roads cross Sweden including those linking Sweden with Norway and Finland. Sweden has a high railway mileage per person although the network is not dense in this vast area. Sweden will have a direct link through to mainland Europe when the Øresund bridge between Malmö and Copenhagen is completed in the year 2000.

Trade flows

Sweden is very dependent on income from exports. Its biggest markets are Germany, then the UK, the USA and the Nordic countries (Denmark, Norway and Finland). It imports mainly from the UK and Germany.

Major exports: cars, medical and pharmaceutical products, military equipment, industrial machinery, telecommunications equipment and forestry products.

Major imports: machinery and equipment for industry, office machinery, petroleum, iron and steel, foodstuffs and clothing.

The DTI has identified the following as good opportunities for UK exporters to Sweden:
- vehicle components and accessories
- food and drink

- design services
- telecoms
- public sector utilities.

Education

Compulsory school

For the 7–16 year age group. (This will be lowered to age 6 from 1997.) Education has recently been extensively reformed with the lowering of the school starting age, although most already attend a pre-school year anyway. Private schools have recently been permitted, the fees for which can be partly offset by vouchers equal to approximately 85 per cent of the cost of a state education. The awarding of grades will be started at 12 years old (currently grades are given only from the age of 15). Books and lunches are free. 90 per cent continue onto upper secondary, of which 35 per cent then continue onto higher education which usually lasts four years. Swedish pupils have a right to participate in the planning and evaluation of courses at school.

The curriculum is common to all pupils until the age of 12. It is not until 16 years of age when pupils transfer to upper secondary education in gymnasieskola that a major choice needs to be made between an academic or vocational line. Completion of these three year upper secondary courses is a pre-requisite for entry into higher education. As an alternative to upper secondary school apprenticeships are available.

Qualification at 18

There is no national exam in Sweden; pupils are given a certificate of completion of studies.

Training and skills

Adults are very keen participants of education generally and the Swedish labour force is highly skilled and very receptive to retraining. Residential folk high schools similar to the Danish and Finnish folk schools offer vocational courses as do government, employment agencies and 11 national adult education associations. Since 1974 there has been a legal entitlement to unpaid educational leave for an indefinite period. Vocational degrees are specifically geared towards the needs of the Swedish labour market.

Employer involvement

Employers are very keen to provide training for their employees whether for basic and advanced skills or new work and production techniques. Trade and industry associations are also very active in helping their members to organise training for their employees. Most of the training costs are borne by the employers themselves.

Employment conditions

Contract of employment

These need not be in writing and most tend to be oral except in the public sector where it is compulsory for employment contracts to be written.

Public holidays

12 days – January 1, January 6 (Epiphany), Good Friday, Easter Monday, May 1, Ascension, Whit Monday, Midsummer (June 21/22 approximately), November 1 (All Saints' Day), December 25 and 26.

Paid holiday

27 days a year is the minimum of which at least four continuous weeks should be available to take between June and August.

Working hours
The legal maximum is 40 hours per week but salaried employees often get reduced hours during the summer months. There is an annual limit on overtime of 200 hours to enable workers to fulfil their family duties as well as responsibilities to their employer. Employees with young children are entitled to work a six-hour day instead of the standard eight-hour day.

Minimum wages
No statutory minimum since most employees, with 80 per cent unionisation, are covered by collective agreements.

Working practices
Normal office hours are 9 a.m.–5 p.m. The main holiday period is June/July and school starts again in August.

Use of information technology
Swedish offices are equipped with computers to about the same degree as British offices. A survey in 1994 found that 12 per cent of workers telecommute and that a further 17 per cent would if they could.

Mobility
In the successful Swedish economy employees were very occupationally mobile, changing jobs every two to three years. However, in a period of recession, Swedes are less inclined to change their jobs.

Tax
The major taxes on income are charged by the local authorities at a flat rate which averages 31 per cent. State tax is payable only on high incomes of over SEK198,700 (about £19,000) at a further 20 per cent.

VAT is 25 per cent with a reduced 21 per cent rate for food, public transport and restaurant services. There are various other taxes such as on private pension savings and pollution emissions. Most Swedes voluntarily pay a church tax.

Social security
Includes sickness benefit of 75 per cent of normal pay for the second and third day and 90 per cent thereafter. The self-employed are also covered and receive slightly lower payments. Unemployment benefit contributions are 1 per cent of income and amount to 80 per cent of pay for 12 months when claimed. There is widespread support for childcare including widely available day nurseries, kindergartens and child minders and where these are unavailable, one parent may take leave on 80 per cent of pay for 11 months to look after their children. Parents can each take up to 60 days a year to look after their sick children on 80 per cent pay and there are tax free allowances for children up to the age of 16.

Trade unions
Membership is high and stood at 82 per cent of the workforce in 1990. As in other Scandinavian countries, the unions administer the unemployment benefit system. Employees have extensive rights to be consulted on major decisions, known as co-determination, and employers have a duty to make relevant information available and to consult the workforce prior to making decisions which affect employees. For example, unions have access to virtually all company documents. In companies employing 25 or more, two workers are entitled to be full members of the board of directors.

Equal opportunities

In 1986 an ombudsman against ethnic discrimination was appointed to counteract discrimination in the workplace and elsewhere. Legislation provides for equal opportunities with regard to race, religion and gender. However this is more successful in connection with promotions, dismissals and lay-offs than it is in ensuring that the initial hiring decision does not discriminate. The law also prohibits sexual harassment at work.

The law requires employers with ten or more employees to monitor pay differentials between the sexes which is to be used to draw up an annual equality plan of measures to be taken to improve equal opportunities.

In Sweden, equal opportunities is taken to include men's right to care for their children as well as women's right to work and this is reflected in parental leave entitlement and the maximum working week of 40 hours.

Health and safety

Working conditions are monitored by the National Board of Occupational Safety and Health. There is also a Labour Inspectorate to supervise the implementation of laws regarding working conditions. Safety representatives may halt dangerous work under certain circumstances. The tasks and responsibilities of safety committees are regulated.

Medical care

There is a single national health insurance system which entitles residents to medical care, medicine, hospitalisation and many dental services at low or no cost. Medical care is administered by the local authorities, comprising a choice of general practitioners attached to local health centres which also house district nurses. A small fee is payable for an appointment apart from the 5 per cent of doctors who are in private practice and to whom a full fee is payable. There are low prescription charges. Maternity, child health care and hospital stays are free.

Culture

There is a great difference between summer and winter. During the long dark winter Swedes work hard and socialise little. However summer is the time when Swedes want to make maximum use of the countryside and to socialise. This culminates in the national celebration of midsummer which usually falls in the third or fourth week of June. This is followed shortly after by the peak holiday time for Swedes.

One of the most noticeable differences between Sweden and the UK is the control of alcohol consumption. Alcohol purchase (apart from light beers) may only be made through the state owned shops, Systembolaget, which have restricted opening hours (e.g. not late at night and not at weekends or prior to major public holidays) and whose staff have a remit to notify the authorities of anyone they think has an alcohol problem. People are generally much less outgoing and demonstrative than southern Europeans.

Family

Life away from work is guaranteed by legislation, for example on the maximum working week and parental leave to look after young children. This helps to support the family unit although the parents may well not be officially married. There are few class distinctions, a relatively liberal attitude and a consensus approach to solving problems where the well-being of the group is more important than the individual. As a result, Sweden has gone a long way to promote equal opportunities between the sexes and races, and children's rights have recently been strengthened. It is illegal, for example, to hit children and children have their own ombudsman they can turn to as a last resort.

Home

Most Swedes rent their homes, whether flats or houses, although there are substantial government incentives to buy your own home. The standard of housing is very high as successive governments since the eighties have encouraged energy saving alterations partly to reduce oil imports and partly to ease unemployment. High standards extend outside the home with well-planned residential areas with safe areas for children to play in, childcare facilities and traffic calming measures. The traditional Swedish house is made of wood and painted yellow or rust red. Most homes come ready-equipped with fridge, freezer and cooker.

   Household size is small with elderly people encouraged to stay in their own homes by making relevant alterations such as the installation of stair lifts, plus plentiful provision of home helps, and at the other end of the age spectrum, young people tend to set up home fairly early.

Religion

Evangelical Lutherism is the protestant state religion to which 92 per cent of Swedes belong although only about 5 per cent attend church regularly. There are 140,000 Roman Catholics, 90,000 Eastern Orthodox Christians, 45,000 Muslims and 16,000 Jews.

Diet

Swedish food traditionally did not include many vegetables as these were difficult to grow and consequently expensive. The main meal is lunch which could be a Smörgåsbord, a cold table assortment of open sandwiches usually including many different fish dishes, accompanied by beer. Otherwise it will be a hot lunch of meat and potatoes. Fish is important in the Swedish diet and game delicacies include elk and reindeer. Breakfast is similar to the other Scandinavian countries including coffee, bread, cheese and cold meats.

Leisure

The Swedes are great outdoor lovers and like to ski, play football and go orienteering. The right to wander the countryside, swim, moor a boat, camp and pick fruits and mushrooms is traditional. Over 22 per cent own a holiday home in the country. Boating and sailing are also very popular and many Swedes own their own craft which are kept in one of the many marinas and harbours on the coast or on one of the many lakes in the interior. Two million Swedes belong to sports clubs – mainly soccer – and sport receives a great deal of government subsidy. Popular spectator sports are alpine skiing, soccer, ice hockey, track and field and motor racing.

   The most popular indoor pursuit is to take an evening class. 10 per cent of Swedes sing in a choir, the highest proportion in the world. There is little vibrant nightlife in Sweden away from the large cities. Local leisure centres are mostly geared towards the young and there are many youth clubs and organised after school activities, a legacy from the time when the Swedish authorities viewed young people with nothing to do as a threat to social order.

Arts

The sparse population has resulted in many cultural activities travelling around the country including theatre groups, exhibitions and musical performers. Public libraries are often cultural centres too which also helps to make cultural events accessible to those in the vast rural interior. There is a distinctive Swedish approach to film exemplified by Ingmar Bergman. Literary subsidies help to keep book prices down and finances the translation of books into Swedish from many other languages. Astrid Lindgren achieved world-wide fame with her Pippi Longstocking books for children, stories about an independent and resourceful little girl who could be taken to exemplify the respect Swedes accord to their children. Stockholm will be European City of Culture in 1998. Swedish design is a source of export revenue in furniture, interior decorating, glass, pottery, textiles and industrial equipment all characterised by simple, stark designs and light colours.

Further information

- *Sweden Today*, quarterly magazine about Nordic business free from Box 405, S-20124 Malmö, Sweden
- Internet address:
  http://www.westnet.se/sweden/

Selected work roles across the EU

Belgian work role

Trainee despatch clerk (chocolate manufacturer).

Tasks and responsibilities
- Checking mail and enclosing bills of exchange where necessary
- Filing orders and documents
- Logging invoices and filing according to country, customer and date
- No financial, training, health and safety or quality responsibilities.

Skills
- Satisfactory completion of secondary education
- Computer literate (training is available for working with specific packages) word-processing being most commonly used
- Telephone skills
- Dutch, French, German and English to be able to communicate with customers.

Employment and career progression
This is a one day a week work placement which was organised by the business college with which the student enrolled and which will continue for the full academic year of the course. There is therefore no career progression for this individual. However this student expects that his qualification in management of medium-sized companies, together with the work experience completed as part of the course, will enable him to get a good job in another company the following year when he qualifies. Many Belgians have little interest in being promoted and promotion when it does occur is often on the basis of age and/or the views of colleagues as to who should do the job.

Danish work role

Secretary to the Wetlands Group of the National Environment Research Institute (NERI) which is part of the Danish Environment Ministry. The post holder is therefore a civil servant. This is a half-time post. She has no subordinates and reports to the co-ordinator of the group – a task which rotates to a different scientist within the group every two years – and takes on work from all nine scientific staff in the group.

Tasks and responsibilities

- Translations
- Proofreading
- Typing and word-processing of letters and reports
- Layout of documents
- Photocopying
- Helping staff solve word-processing problems
- Taking minutes of meetings
- Catering arrangements for meetings.

Training

The employer expects the secretary to be able to function effectively from the start and little training is given except when a new word-processing package is introduced, when, for example, a day's training may be offered. Denmark has a system of paid educational leave which the secretary could take advantage of should she decide to take a course but in that case her employer would neither pay her salary (her allowance would come from the state) nor her course fees.

Quality assurance

The organisation does not implement quality systems.

Skills

- High level of spoken and written English and German although English is the most widely used foreign language
- Ability to use word-processing packages (Word Perfect and Word)
- Ability to use spreadsheets (Quattro Pro) and databases (Paradox)
- An eye for detail and accuracy in translations and other work for scientific publications
- An ability to prioritise and organise a variety of tasks.

Employment and career progression

Recruitment: This job was advertised in a national newspaper and applicants had to submit a written application and attend a selection interview. There were no tests (language or secretarial) during the interview. No secretarial qualifications were required but the post holder had to show evidence of fluent language skills by having studied to the level equivalent to an HND or ordinary degree. References are not often required and when required are often taken by telephone. Candidates may choose to include with their application the statement you always get from a Danish employer when you leave a job. This details what you did whilst with your employer and resembles the UK national record of achievement which is compiled as evidence of learning.

Career progression: Within NERI the possibilities for progression are limited since it is a small organisation. Occasionally the post of chief secretary arises but the post holder thinks that this job would not be so interesting as what she is doing currently. To apply for a similar job in another organisation the post holder would need to upgrade her qualification to a full bachelor's degree (an extra six months) and then to a master's degree in languages (a further two years).

French work role

Marketing assistant – manufacturing.

Tasks and responsibilities
- Review of European and trade press
- Collation of relevant marketing information
- Review of market research
- Preparation of small market studies
- Preparation of sales forecasts using standard administrative techniques
- Preparation of quantitative sales performance reports
- General administrative assistance.

Skills
- English, German and French (Italian useful)
- Basic understanding of marketing
- PC literate (spreadsheets and word processing)
- Numerate
- This French employer would probably require a bac plus two or three years of higher education for this role.

Employment and career progression
From marketing assistant progression could be expected as follows:
- European product manager
- European marketing manager
- Head of sales and marketing
- Commercial director
- Chief executive.

As you progress up the career ladder you would have increased responsibility for (in order of responsibility received):
- performance review
- sales forecasts (short term – three months)
- budget forecasts (annual)
- long term planning – three or five year plans relating to:
  - market forecasts;
  - technological trend forecasts;
  - competitor analysis;
- liaison with production, purchasing and sales departments.

German work role

Solicitor. A German solicitor can work as a high street lawyer, a public prosecutor, a notary public (notar) or a judge. This section will deal only with the high street lawyer known as a rechtsanwallt. All have the same preliminary training of a law degree which takes four to six years (can be up to eight or ten years) followed by two years' practical training (referendarzeit) followed by a second professional exam which is vocationally oriented.

Tasks and responsibilities
A rechtsanwallt gives advice to and represents clients in court. He does not draw up formal deeds or do conveyancing as a UK solicitor does. These are done by the notar who is more highly paid.

Skills
The rechtsanwallt must be a generalist with a knowledge of all aspects of law and is expected to advise on any aspect, whereas a UK solicitor would specialise (maybe in

commercial, patent or criminal law). In fact German lawyers are getting left behind because they are so general and are not able to compete in eastern Europe, for example, where UK and American lawyers have the specialist skills required. Advocacy and forensic skills are not so necessary as most of the court proceedings are conducted by the judge.

Employment and career progression

The rechtsanwallt works in a small partnership with two or three others and often on his own. Larger partnerships are uncommon (e.g. in the UK one can get up to 80 or over 100 partners in some of the largest London law firms). There is little career progression except in enhancing one's reputation, as the German local lawyer is only authorised to offer his services in the local area. Cases outside the local area must be passed on to a rechtsanwallt who has authorisation there. It is therefore difficult to get a good reputation nationwide. The profession is decentralised as against the UK where the high fliers must go to London for the best jobs.

Greek work role

Receptionist in a three or four star hotel of about 70 rooms.

Tasks and responsibilities

Responsible to the front office manager.

Tasks

- Contact and correspondence with guests before their arrival and other secretarial work
- Updating room availability, management of options and confirmations, processing of cancellations, 'no-shows' and over bookings
- Keeping records of bookings and compilation of statistics
- Reception and assistance outside the hotel for arriving guests and their luggage
- Guidance on guest decisions (upgrade/downgrade), room type, terms and price
- Recording and allocation of rooms to guests on arrival, instructions to other departments (such as room service orders) and handing over the keys
- Giving information to guests and helping with bookings such as taxis or theatre tickets
- Management of deposited valuables and strong boxes and luggage deposit
- Management of guest and hotel security
- Handling complaints
- Early morning call service
- Telephone switchboard, fax and telex operation
- Cash transactions and currency exchange
- Production and presentation of accounts to guests and collecting payment.

Training: No responsibility for training others.

Quality assurance: No explicit responsibility for quality control, first aid or safety and hygiene.

Skills

- Advanced language including written and oral fluency in one foreign language and oral fluency and acceptable written skills in a second foreign language (likely to be English and German)
- Intermediate business and accounting

- Good interpersonal skills
- Ability to operate standard word-processing and spreadsheet applications on computer.

Employment and career progression

Recruitment: Completion of the nine-year compulsory schooling followed by attendance at one of the state schools for tourist industry occupations specialising in hotel and catering is required. The latter lasts two years of which eight months is spent on work placement. Those already doing the job without a qualification now have the option of completing a five and a half month course to make them fully professional.

Career progression: This could be to front office manager. For this it would be necessary to have completed the three-year Lykeion Leaving Certificate after the end of compulsory schooling followed by a three-year higher education course at the Higher School of Tourist Industry Occupations in Rhodes after which a nine-month work placement is required.

Irish work role

Programmer, Bank of Ireland.

Tasks and responsibilities

The position is within the Bank's Information Technology and Operations Centre at Cabinteely south of Dublin. The centre employs over 500 people organised in teams including programmers, developers, testers, business analysts and team leaders. The business analysts bring the teams their tasks in the form of project definitions from the bank's branches and other departments. The team leader must then estimate the costs of the project and sets up a programming team. The number of programmers involved depends on the complexity of the project as well as how quickly it needs to be completed. A complex urgent project will warrant a large team of about 40.

The work involves finding a suitable 'off the shelf' software package to purchase, which will usually require a little tailoring for use in the bank. More commonly however, software must be developed from scratch, often because there are security or compatibility problems. Programmers therefore work intensively on one project, moving onto another when their project is complete.

Training: As a graduate entrant the programmer participates in the bank's graduate training programme. This includes training in relevant computer languages, such as C, and packages, as well as in quality procedures.

Quality assurance: As a major Irish company, the Bank of Ireland is conscious of the need to implement systematic quality assurance procedures partly because it deals with many other leading Irish businesses which themselves implement quality systems and partly because the bank does business abroad where again it is necessary to assure clients that quality procedures are effectively implemented. The bank's programmers follow quality procedures in their work.

Skills

- Computer programming
- Ability to work in a team
- Ability to work to tight deadlines
- Logical and precise.

Employment and career progression

Recruitment: The minimum qualification for this job is a second class honours degree. Interested applicants submit a CV with covering letter to the bank's graduate recruitment unit which will decide who to employ on the basis of an interview.

Career progression: As a graduate with a major Irish company there is a good opportunity of career progression within the company by becoming a Lead Applications Programmer, then a Team Leader and from there into management. The Bank of Ireland is looking towards a period of great change and innovation into the next century which means that opportunities for career development could be diverse within the company itself. However, since Ireland is pushing itself as a high technology, software localisation (i.e. tailoring software for different countries) and financial services centre for Europe then opportunities outside the Bank of Ireland could be even greater. For example, in January 1996 Stream International were looking to recruit a Localisation Project Manager for which it required a degree, two to three years relevant industry experience including at least one year in project management, exactly the experience which the Bank of Ireland's programmer would have.

The Irish IT industry in the eighties demanded low level production and data entry workers but now offers more opportunities as the numerous American companies based there begin to include R&D work within their Irish operations. Relevantly qualified Irish graduates have tended to go abroad for work as they feel that they will be more technically up to date if they do so. They also want to continue working within their specialist area and do not want to go into management whereas Irish-based high technology firms want technically qualified and experienced people to progress into management.

A shortage of employees with five to ten years experience, good people and project management skills is therefore forecast in Ireland towards the turn of the century which means that career opportunities should be good in this area.

Italian work role

Receptionist in a three or four star hotel of about 70 rooms.

Tasks and responsibilities

Responsible to the front office manager and supervises the uniformed porters' lodge staff.

Tasks: As for the Greek receptionist role plus the following:

- contacts with social recreation centres, travel agents and large clients
- management of overdue payments and associated reminders and recovery
- direct mailing of leaflets, booklets and special offers to guests
- PR and marketing with clientele, opinion formers and local authorities
- supervision of hall, lifts, porters' lodge and their associated uniformed staff.

Training: The receptionist has no training responsibilities.

Quality: There is no explicit responsibility for quality control, first aid or safety and hygiene.

Skills

- Advanced language
- Intermediate business and accounts
- Excellent level of inter-personal skills
- Basic ability with computers.

Employment and career progression

Recruitment: Italian receptionists need to have completed the eight years of compulsory schooling as well as the three year vocational diploma for 'reception services operators' in a state vocational institute for hotel and restaurant services. Students are 17 or older when they complete this qualification which includes some work experience.

Career progression: The obvious step is to progress to front office manager but in order to do this the applicant has to have completed a further two years at the state vocational institute specialising as a tourism and hotel industry technician to gain a vocational matriculation diploma. This can be completed by the age of 19.

Luxembourg work role

Vocational Guidance Counsellor (known in the UK as careers advisor) employed by the Ministry of Labour. Post holders are therefore civil servants.

Tasks and responsibilities

As Luxembourg is so small there are only six vocational guidance counsellors (VGCs) in the entire country, all reporting to the director of the vocational guidance service. The main purpose of VGCs is to help 14–18 year olds make career decisions by providing information and arranging work placements and apprenticeships.

Tasks: Routine tasks include:
- producing and disseminating information about different careers, training opportunities and required qualifications
- counselling individuals on their career choice including recommendation of psychometric tests where appropriate
- arranging the compulsory four to six work placements for students in year three of their upper secondary general or technical studies
- placing individuals into apprenticeships
- maintaining external contacts with employers, teachers and parents.

Occasional tasks include:
- keeping up-to-date with labour market trends
- guidance service planning and evaluation.

Training: Existing VGCs induct new VGCs into their jobs over a period of months. Becoming employed as a VGC means starting as a trainee and undergoing a minimum of three years' training mainly in civil service procedures. There is a lack of systematic training for VGCs especially in the counselling skills which eventually form a large part of the job as trainees usually start by concentrating on the apprentice placement tasks which dominate the work of VGCs especially from May to September.

Quality: All the VGCs meet every few weeks in a type of quality circle activity to find ways of improving the service and their work. This is not a systematically applied approach to quality however. Since Luxembourg is so small, all VGCs are heavily involved in international links especially for EU programmes such as the old PETRA scheme (now under SOCRATES). This generates very valuable exchange of information which the VGCs can then use to improve their work.

Skills
- Empathy with young people
- Ability to complete many different types of task; the staff is so small that there is no room for specialists
- Creativity to produce print and other material as careers information

- Ability to interact at all levels including company managers, parents and teachers, students and adult clients

Employment and career progression

Recruitment: The minimum qualification to become a VGC is successful completion of compulsory secondary education. Applicants must first pass a competitive civil service exam which is then followed by an extensive interview with the Director of the Vocational Guidance Service. A successful interview means employment as a trainee in the middle civil service which starts with a full-time six month course concentrating on civil service structures and procedures. This is then followed by two and a half years on the job training culminating in an exam on civil service structures and procedures. Counselling skills are learned on the job.

Career progression: A VGC can progress within the middle civil service grades by taking a promotion exam after three years experience as a fully trained VGC (i.e. six years after starting the job). After a further ten years of employment experience and additional civil service courses and exams, promotion to the higher civil service grade may be possible. There is of course only one director of the service in Luxembourg and this position requires a university qualification in psychology.

Portuguese work role

Senior secretary with an international intergovernmental organisation in Lisbon. The post holder is therefore in the international public sector.

Tasks and responsibilities

The secretary is part of a small team with no subordinates. Tasks involve:
- receptionist duties meeting senior diplomats, civil servants and politicians
- translating to and from both Portuguese and English
- operating office equipment
- mailing
- typing
- office housekeeping including filing
- banking of receipts
- helping staff arrange meetings and publications.

Skills
- Fluent English both spoken and written
- Good writing abilities both in Portuguese and English
- Able to work with computers especially word-processing and mail merge applications
- Good with people
- Ability to speak French and Spanish also useful.

Employment and career progression

Recruitment: The post was advertised in a national Portuguese business newspaper but written in English. Candidates had to be at least 35 years old and could be either male or female. The short period of 12 days between the closing date and notification of the successful candidate implied that the post would be filled on the basis of the applications alone.

Career progression: Since this is a small organisation little career progression can be expected within the organisation itself and there are few other similar organisations in

Lisbon for the employee to move to. However the experience gained here might be attractive to the increasing number of multi-national companies which are setting up in Lisbon. The salary is based on the United Nations salary scale, adjusted for Portugal and will increase as the employee gains experience.

Spanish work role

Administrative assistant in the Cota Donana Biological station (a state research institute). The post holder is therefore a civil servant.

Tasks and responsibilities

The administrative assistant has no subordinates and is responsible to 13 scientists including the station director. Tasks involve word-processing faxes, letters, reports and scientific papers, scanning article contents to pick out those of interest to the scientists, paying bills, sending cheques and making travel arrangements when the scientists need to travel to conferences and meetings, photocopying and generally acting as a point of contact between the scientists and everybody else.

Training: Very little is offered and most skills (such as the word-processing) are learned individually using manuals and asking for help when needed.

Quality assurance: There is no positive attempt to improve quality but a negative check on quality exists with regular visits by government inspectors to ensure that both work and workers are progressing well.

Skills

- Fluency in English since a great deal of the word-processing consists of English language texts
- Word processing using Word Perfect
- Good basic background knowledge of biology
- Ability to organise own work
- Ability to anticipate needs of the scientists.

Employment and career progression

Recruitment: Government jobs are advertised in the daily state newspaper. The recruitment process consists of sitting an examination, whose content relates to the job for which you are applying. The person obtaining the highest score is the one who will be offered the job. Interviews take place after the exam but are to discuss job details rather than acting as part of the recruitment process. For this work role it was necessary to have successfully completed secondary education in order to be allowed to sit the exam.

Career progression: There is no formal career progression path in this job and no incremental salary scale. The only way of getting a better job would be to sit an exam for another comparable job or for the post holder to get a degree. There are sometimes salary bonuses but these are divided equally between the workers and not awarded on merit. In Spain, workers' career paths tend to develop within the same organisation and are often based on seniority or length of service.

Swedish work role

PC co-ordinator for Save the Children Fund (Sweden) – the post holder therefore works for a charity.

Tasks and responsibilities

SCF (Sweden) is investing in extensive IT modernisation including a new accounting system, membership system and new means of communication including the Internet. The PC co-ordinator supports the 120 staff who use Windows and the SQL database package and are linked to the Internet through an OS/2 network (i.e. Mackintosh). The PC co-ordinator's day to day work is to make sure the staff's personal computers are functioning as well as installing, maintaining and administering the network as necessary. The job also entails ensuring the integration of the PC network with the other IT systems in use at SCF. Part of the job entails training up SCF staff in the use of their systems.

The co-ordinator is also expected to contribute to the continuing development of the network to ensure that it meets the requirements of management and the information processing needs of the organisation by taking advantage of relevant new technologies as they occur.

The PC co-ordinator works within an IT team of five, one of whom is designated overall IT manager. In practice Swedish management is consultative and not hierarchical which means that all workers exercise a great deal of discretion in their work.

Skills

In recruiting for this post SCF said they needed a 'technical humanist' meaning that they required technical competence together with a sympathy towards the aims of the charity. The post holder needs to be able to work well as part of the small IT team as well as to be able to help other SCF staff sort out their IT problems both informally on a day to day basis and formally in structured training events. Since the duties are so varied the PC co-ordinator needs to be able to work effectively on several projects simultaneously.

Employment and career progression

Recruitment: This job was advertised in a national Swedish newspaper and on the Swedish version of the charity's World Wide Web page. Candidates were given three weeks in which to send an application either by post or by e-mail. Prospective candidates were invited to speak to the existing manager or one of his staff for further information as well as to the two relevant union representatives. No specific educational requirements were set but a relevant PC background was specified.

Career progression: The only progression to anticipate in such a small team would be to become the IT manager in which case a relevant bachelor's degree would be required as well as demonstrable supervisory skills and a broad IT background. The only other alternative would be to seek a better job with another organisation. Since the job is based in Stockholm centre this would not be difficult.

Further information

Guide books

- The Insight series is the best covering all EU Member States except Luxembourg but further information is available from the Rough Guides, Time Out and Cadogans etc. Price Waterhouse guides 'Doing Business in ...' for each of the EU Member States, although addressed to business, give a great deal of background information on employment conditions. KPMG guides are similar to the Price Waterhouse ones mentioned above.
- *European Consumer Lifestyles*, Euromonitor, 1994

Internet sites

Pronet Enterprise's Europe page at:
http://pronett.com/europe/

Time Out city guides at:
http://www.timeout.co.uk/

Rough Guides at:
http://www.roughguides.com/RG_WWW/books/tbk_eur.html/rghome.html

Audio-visual

The Essential History of Europe, 12 programmes by the BBC, 1993. (Since these pro-grammes concentrate on cultural aspects, their content will be relevant for some years yet.)

Assignment 12.1
Careers exhibition

This assignment fulfils the following criteria:
BTEC 16.2.1, 16.3.1, 16.3.2, 16.3.2, 16.3.4

As a GNVQ advanced student your qualification will enable you to compete for entry into higher education. You may well consider an HND or degree course which entails an exchange with another European university under the EU's SOCRATES scheme. This assignment is designed to let you find out more about the differences between life as a student in the UK and the rest of the EU.

Situation

Your college/school is planning a careers exhibition. As a GNVQ student studying the European option you have been chosen to prepare a presentation about life as a student in other Member States. This can take the form of an illustrated talk or a display. Choose two Member States (preferably not neighbouring) which you might be interested in vis-iting as an exchange student and carry out the following tasks in preparation for your presentation. Throughout you should highlight the differences and similarities to the UK situation.

Note: Assume that language will not be a barrier, either because you have sufficient knowledge of the relevant language, as might be the case for French, German or Spanish or because the authorities run English medium courses as happens in Denmark, the Netherlands and Sweden.

Your tasks

1 What have students in your chosen country had to do to obtain their place in higher education? In other words: what exams or selection process have they gone

through? What subjects did they study for their exams? How do they compare in level to the GNVQ?

2 What methods of study can you expect in the chosen Member States? For example, is study principlally by large lecture or are there also small group tutorials and seminars? What type of exams can you expect? For example, one Spanish SOCRATES student was most surprised at the idea of an open book exam he was to take in Denmark. What, he wondered, could the lecturers be testing if you were allowed to take all your books and notes with you?

3 What would your daily life as a student be like? For example, where would you live? Is there a system of halls of residence as there are with many UK universities? Where, when and what would you eat? Is university social life as organised as it is in the UK? For example, are there special student clubs to join? Is there a student bar or just places in town where students tend to congregate? Do students socialise together or are they at home in the evenings?

Sources of information

People

This assignment will be better achieved through appropriate EU contacts and you probably need your tutor's help in setting these up well in advance. Perhaps there are SOCRATES exchange students either from your chosen Member States or British students who have already been on exchange in a local university. Alternatively, your institution may have done some exchanges with pre-university students and these contacts could be used. Another possibility is to ask for information in an appropriate newsgroup/forum on the Internet.

Publications

- Education/handbook for guidance counsellors, European Commission, 1994, free
- The European Choice – *A Guide to Opportunities for Higher Education in Europe 1995/96*, Department for Education and Employment, 1995, free
- *Key data on Education in the European Union 94*, European Commission, 1995, free
- Euro Challenge – *International Career Guide for Students and Graduates*, second edition 1995/96, N de Menezes & B Giesen, Staufenbiel (Institut fur Berufs und Aushildungsplanung, Postfach 10 35 43, D-50475 Köln, Germany)

Organizations

- The Euro adviser at Job centres will have access to the EURES database, which as well as holding job vacancy information also has a great deal of up-to-date background information on living conditions in the different Member States.
- University careers departments and SOCRATES exchange co-ordinators.
- Central Bureau for Educational Visits and Exchanges

Assignment 12.2
Career development

This assignment fulfils the following criteria:
BTEC 16.2.1, 16.3.3, 16.4.1 to 16.4.3

Situation

You work in the UK in one of the job roles described in this chapter and feel it would enhance your career to organise a year's work exchange with that country.

1 Compile a similar description for the equivalent job in the UK.
2 Supplement the foreign job description with additional information from appropriate contacts in the relevant country. What are the main differences between the job in the UK and the other Member State? Are these differences due to contrasts in culture, economic structure or legal system?
3 Use the information you have gathered to prepare the arguments you would use with your supervisor to try and convince her that she should grant you leave of absence for a year to work in the position described in this chapter. How will it enhance your experience and career prospects and therefore that of your organisation? For example, if the target country is less advanced in your career field you may be able to gain preliminary managerial and training experience. Conversely, if the other country is more advanced you may learn a great deal of transferable skills.

   The arguments can be given in written form or as a presentation to be given to your supervisor.

Sources of information

- Euro adviser at Job Centres
- The *European* Newspaper prints jobs wanted advertisements.
  It may be possible to find details of someone working in your chosen field in the relevant country whom you or the college could contact for further information.
- Foreign newspapers – translate the job adverts either using your existing language skills or with a relevant dictionary. Portuguese, Spanish and Italian are not too difficult to decipher if you already know some French for example.
- Careers Europe, Equity Chambers, 40 Piccadilly, Bradford, BD1 3NN, West Yorkshire Tel: 01274 757521 Fax: 01274 742332. This is an information service on careers in Europe with regular publications and other services. Your local Careers Office may hold some of their materials.
- Cedefop (European Centre for the Development of Vocational Training), Jean Monnet House, Bundesallee 22, D – 10717 Berlin, Germany. This organisation publishes a great deal of material some of which is job profiles for specific careers. These may be available in larger or specialist libraries and are published either for individual countries or as a comparison across several Member States. An example is given below: *Occupations in the tourist sector, a comparative analysis in nine Community states, 1994.*

Index

Bold entries indicate standard headings in the Country profiles (Chapter 12) which should also be consulted for the required country at the appropriate location in its file.